BUREAUCRACY

BUREAUCRACY

What Government Agencies Do and Why They Do It

JAMES Q. WILSON

A Member of The Perseus Books Group

Library of Congress Cataloging-in-Publication Data
Wilson, James Q
Bureaucracy : what government agencies do and why they do it / James Q. Wilson
p. cm.
Includes bibliographical references and index.
ISBN 0-465-00784-8 (cloth)
ISBN 0-465-00785-6 (paper)
1. Administrative agencies—United States. 2. Bureaucracy—United States. I. Title.
JK421.W52 1989
353'.01—dc20 89-42527
CIP

A Member of the Perseus Books Group
Printed in the United States of America
Designed by Vincent Torre

02 03 MV 29 28 27 26 25

To the Harvard Graduate Students

From Whom I Have Learned So Much

CONTENTS

PREFACE TO THE NEW EDITION

ONE OF THE CENTRAL THEMES of this book is that the management of government agencies is powerfully constrained by limitations on the ability of managers to buy and sell products or hire and fire people on the basis of what best serves the efficiency or productivity of the organization. Laws and regulations limit how people can be hired, greatly reduce the chances of firing anyone, and surround the buying and selling of buildings and equipment with countless rules about fairness and procedure.

There have been efforts over the last decade to alter these constraints. President Bill Clinton and Vice President Al Gore sought at the start of their first term to convert federal agencies into a government that "works better and costs less" by reducing red tape, inducing bureaus to put customers (that is, citizens dealing with the government) first, and empowering employees to get results. This effort was officially known as the National Performance Review (NPR) and popularly known as Reinventing Government, or REGO.[1]

The NPR effort marked a sharp departure from past reorganization plans. Of the seventeen presidents to take office between 1904 and 1992, eleven created reorganization task forces that were chiefly devoted to expanding accountability, increasing efficiency, and enlarging presidential authority.[2] (By *accountability* I mean increasing policy implementers' responsiveness to higher officials who must take responsibility for that policy.) This effort had some successes—for example, it equipped the president with more staff assistants and made more rational the way in which budgets were drawn up—but it did little about red tape.

The NPR began with very different assumptions. Where earlier reforms had stressed the accountability of officials to higher authority, the NPR emphasized agency responsiveness to the public. Where earlier reports relied on appeals to business efficiency, the NPR drew inspiration from the concept of entrepreneurial culture. And where preceding efforts urged an expansion of the power of the president, the NPR called for empowering government employees and restoring public confidence in government.

The dominant theme of the NPR was to solve the "root problem" of modern government—its excessive reliance on "large, top-down, centralized bureaucracies." This solution necessitated the creation of "entrepreneurial organizations" that have "constantly learned, innovated, and improved."[3] The NPR meant, in effect, marrying the youthful spirit of Silicon Valley to the old traditions of official Washington.

The main reason for this startling shift in federal reorganization efforts, however, was not admiration for clever young people who made computer chips or invented Internet sales programs but, rather, a desire to reverse the sharp drop in the public's confidence in the federal government. In 1964, three-quarters of the American people said they trusted Washington officials to do the right thing; today, fewer than one-quarter feel that way. Perhaps, the NPR staff thought, these citizens would like officials better if they "put people first" and "cut red tape." For that matter, government bureaucrats might like their *own* jobs better if they could put people first and cut red tape.

But putting people first is hard to do in a government that, ultimately, has the power to command people and even send them to prison. A business may put people first because businesses compete with each other in order to attract customers, but the government competes with nobody. And cutting red tape may be possible in a business firm that can tell whether it is doing a good job by looking at its sales and profits, but cutting it in a government agency is much harder because (ordinarily) government agencies deal with neither sales nor profits.

Changing government is difficult, but serious efforts have been made. Let me describe two important changes that should modify what you read in this book, which was written several years before the NPR had started.

Procurement

At several places in this book,[4] you will learn that it is hard for government to buy expensive items because it must follow an elaborate policy of describing in great, mind-numbing detail what it wants to purchase (often without any helpful contact with the firms that sell these items), and then it must advertise for bids. Usually it has to accept the lowest price it is offered, even if this bid comes from a firm that is less competent than one that charges more.

For example, when a public agency wants to buy a computer, it cannot do so in the same way that business firms do. The latter will discuss computers with their manufacturers and get help in finding or designing the right machine. Often they will buy what they need from a firm they know and trust without ever describing the computer they want, sometimes paying a higher price in order to get the right combination of product and service. But this is not an option for government agencies; indeed, even attempting to do so would invite legal action. In such circumstances, as discussed later in the book, an agency's purchasing agent may be accused of collusion, favoritism, unfairness, and sweetheart deals. Thus it has been next to impossible for the government purchaser to take into account its past experience with a supplier or that firm's intangible qualities. Instead, the agency must produce an elaborate report describing what it wants and then accept sealed bids, with the sale going to the lowest bidder. It is hardly surprising that the government often winds up with second-rate computers sold by unhelpful firms.

Buying things is not a minor problem for Washington. Each year (as of the late 1990s) it spends about $200 billion purchasing items from business firms. That amount is almost one-seventh of the whole federal budget.

During the 1990s, efforts were made to improve government's approach to purchasing. Steven Kelman, a scholar from whose research I took the computer story, was appointed by President Clinton to run the Office of Federal Procurement Policy (OFPP), part of the Office of Management and Budget. Kelman's attempt to improve purchasing was supported by the NPR staff. He helped persuade Congress to pass two important bills, the Federal Acquisition Streamlining Act of 1994 and the Federal Acquisition Reform Act of 1995.[5] Because of these laws and Kelman's bureaucratic nudging, several changes ensued. The law now permitted agencies to buy off the shelf, without elaborate contracting, things that cost less than $100,000. Many agency purchasing officers began using credit cards to buy routine supplies from businesses, just as households do, thereby avoiding the need to fill out complicated purchase orders. And several agencies agreed to take into consideration the past performance of business firms in deciding from whom to buy materials. (Of course, neglected firms could still complain, but an agency was able to defend itself by making a written record of its reasons for having passed them over.)

At the same time, officials in the Defense Department, on their own initiative, began to cut back on the amount of detail required in requests for new military hardware—emphasizing, instead, performance goals for the hardware. The Pentagon probably did the most to change its procurement policies, because it stood to gain the most. Its budget was being sharply cut at the time; so, if it was going to pay for the new equipment it wanted, it would have to stretch its procurement dollars. Buying things more simply and cheaply meant that it could buy more of what it needed. (Inasmuch as Defense officials began to change how it dealt with contractors, what appears on page 321 of this book is now a bit out of date.)

But the problems of procurement reform remain, whatever the laws may say or agencies may require. Kelman found that the key problem was implementation—that is, persuading officials to buy things in a more streamlined way. Some agencies continued to believe that buying things the new, improved way would only get them into trouble—a not unreasonable fear given the fact that generations of civil servants had gotten into trouble for appearing to favor certain suppliers or failing to draw up lengthy purchasing specifications. And in any case, many of the limits on procurement were still the law of the land. Legislation continues to require that agencies favor buying things from American firms, help out small businesses, and give special status to firms headed by women, handicapped persons, disabled veterans, and racial minorities.

What is remarkable is the fact that, despite these fears and laws, many government officials are trying to be more efficient about how they buy things. The legal system is part of the constraints on government officials, but so is the culture within which laws work. Only time will tell whether this culture will change over the long haul.

Personnel

The NPR also wanted to reform federal personnel policies. In 1993, the head of the Office of Personnel Management (OPM) said he was for "radical change,"[6] and the NPR has supported this view with ideas for letting agencies run their own personnel systems, making government employees accountable for achieving results rather than for following procedures, and encouraging entrepreneurial behavior. To signify the changes they wanted, President Clinton abolished the entire *Federal Personnel Manual*, the hopelessly long, intellectually arid legacy of all the rules that personnel specialists had accumulated over decades of effort.

But not much has happened in terms of how people are actually hired and managed. Indeed, little exists to take the place of the now-defunct personnel manual, leaving in place thousands of personnel experts who had grown up using the manual and its rules.[7] OPM was supposed to abandon its traditional role as a centralized enforcer of civil service rules and embrace instead a support role in which it helped agency heads recruit their own workers. The NPR also urged that the fifteen pay bands that cover most federal employees be changed into a smaller number of pay levels, with agencies given more freedom in passing out wages based on agency needs and employee abilities.

But legislation that embodies these new approaches or alters the mind-set of some personnel officers has, as yet, been impossible to pass. Several bills—the Civil Service Simplification Act, the Federal Personnel Systems Reinvention Act, and the Omnibus Civil Service Reform Act—all failed to become law. If enacted, these laws would have decentralized personnel matters to each government agency, sharply reducing the old powers of OPM.

Not only did the bills fail to become law, but the civil service itself has been getting smaller. Federal employment shrank by about 12 percent in the Clinton years (with the biggest loser being the Defense Department). Some of these reductions were obtained through the buy-out of federal employees not yet ready for retirement. But the effect of this buy-out was to make the federal work force older, depriving it of many of the younger people in line to become top executives.

Nonetheless, some changes were made. The Federal Aviation Administration (FAA) was exempted from many old civil service rules so that it would be better able to recruit qualified air traffic controllers. The great public criticism of the Internal Revenue Service (IRS) led to some steps that may help its personnel policies. And in some agencies, improvements have been made in the management of personnel.

But it is still hard to get able people to work for the federal government, even though nearly 70 percent of all new workers were hired without having to go through the old system of centrally administered tests and hiring. Federal pay scales are now often lower than private ones, competition is fierce for highly skilled talent, and the government must worry about how many ethnic and racial minorities it hires. The personnel culture itself has not changed, however; as Patricia W. Ingraham reports, federal agencies had become accustomed to the rules, so they have gone on following them.[8]

The pilot projects for improving federal management described in this book on pages 146 to 148, especially the effort to improve hiring and paying workers at the China Lake Naval Air Station, still have not been as influential as some people hoped. As the book originally suggested, Congress and other federal agencies have not been very sympathetic to what was tried at China Lake and a few other locations.

President Clinton attempted a new approach by creating a number of "reinvention laboratories" in several agencies. These were rather informal efforts to use employee suggestions to find ways of abandoning silly rules. (In one case, a laboratory figured out how to allow employees to charge on an agency credit card small amounts of money—say, $25 or $30—without getting an elaborate written approval.) These laboratories may yet turn out to be a source of important change, but it is too early to tell.

The central reason why it is so difficult to change the ways in which people are hired and managed can be found in the contradiction built into our view of civil service. As Ingraham points out, these laws have always had a split personality: "[I]t is their responsibility to protect the permanent career work force from undue political influence, while still providing political leaders with a responsive set of career employees."[9] Balancing political independence with political accountability is very difficult, whatever the NPR may say about employee "empowerment." The reality, as Paul Light puts it, is that rules will dominate: The government will "limit bureaucratic discretion through compliance with tightly drawn rules and regulations."[10]

Making the Bureaucracy Perform Better

In 1993 Congress passed and the president signed the Government Performance and Results Act, a law designed to make it easier to link individual performance, agency accomplishments, and social goals. One of its mechanisms is evaluation of employee performance.

But how can this evaluation be achieved? The great majority of employees are now given a very high rating because there are few objective ways to link what a worker does and what an agency accomplishes.[11] In a business firm, the pay an employee gets is set by management, not by a government pay scale, and (when there is an incentive compensation plan) it is often based on his or her performance coupled, in many cases, with the performance of the firm as a whole. If the firm does well (in profits, market share, or stock price), employees are eligible for pay awards; the exact size of the award will, in theory, be based on each employee's contribution to the firm's success. In a government agency, by contrast, pay is largely set by a legislative scale and there are few, if any, measures of how well the agency as a whole has done. As a result, government performance evaluations tend to be very high because the managers who make these evaluations know that there are few, if any, objective grounds for making them lower. And employees would surely complain if, without such grounds, they were given a low rating; it would be taken as a sign of favoritism toward some friend of the boss who got a higher rating.

There will continue to be pushes for better performance, given what has happened with respect to procurement and personnel, this book tells a story of bureaucracy that need not be changed in any fundamental way from the story it told when it was first published.

The NPR wishes to create a government that costs less; but real cost savings—savings of the sort that can be seen by a taxpayer—can be achieved not by making marginal improvements in government management but, rather, by cutting the programs that government manages. Yet voters, although they want the government in general to spend less, also want more money spent on a wide range of programs from crime fighting and drug abuse to education, civil rights, and the environment. In the 1950s, none of these programs made up a significant part of the federal budget; what the government did then was limited to rather simple things—delivering mail, building highways, acquiring parks, conducting research, providing subsidies to various interests, and defending the nation. Today, it would be fairly easy to measure agency performance by how well the mail is delivered, how costly the highways and parks are, and how quickly the subsidies are delivered. But it is next to impossible to measure how well any agency reduces drug abuse, enhances civil rights, or educates children.

The NPR also would like to cut red tape; but red tape, as Herbert Kaufman has pointed out, is usually produced by organized political groups seeking to protect their interests by constraining how the government is managed.[12] To many groups, less red tape means fewer benefits. For example, lots of groups want better highways, but by better they mean not only well constructed and inexpensive but built in ways that serve other interests. Consider the following example: In 1956 the Federal Aid Highway Act created the interstate highway system with a law that was only twenty-eight pages long. Thirty-five years later, that program was reauthorized by the Intermodal Surface Transportation Efficiency Act, but the new law was

293 pages long. The difference in length can be explained by the multiplication of constraints: By 1991 we not only wanted to build more highways, we wanted to build them in ways that would aid mass transit, reduce air pollution, encourage the use of seat belts and motorcycle helmets, preserve historic sites, control erosion and outdoor advertising, use recycled rubber in making asphalt, buy iron and steel from U.S. manufacturers, define women as disadvantaged individuals, and protect Native American reservations—among other things. You can look it up. But I doubt the 1991 highway bill has empowered employees or made managing them any easier.

Clearly, public confidence in government is much lower now than it was when government was doing fewer things. No doubt there are many reasons for this—the rise of an adversarial media, the impact of Vietnam and Watergate, and an increase in certain social problems. But one additional reason may be that we have less confidence in government precisely because it is trying to do many things that cannot be done, by anyone, very well.

And even when it does things that can be done well, government often suffers by comparison with competitive business firms—not because the firms hire better people but because they are competing for customers instead of serving (captive) citizens. The NPR would like to make the government customer-friendly, and no doubt it may succeed in getting some agencies to distribute better information, provide clearer guidance to government procedures, and answer the telephone after only three rings. It would be nice to be treated as well by a government agency as one is by minimum-wage employees at McDonald's or Burger King. But having visited both McDonald's and my local post office in the last few days, I am not optimistic that the NPR—or any government effort—will make a big difference.

After reading this long recitation of the constraints under which government works, you make think that I am pessimistic about our political regime. Not at all. Every democratic government has these problems, and our government does better than most others in attending to these defects and trying to fix a few of the worst ones. In fact, by the standards of most democratic governments, many agencies in this country are friendlier and more cooperative than their counterparts abroad. Our constitutional system so fragments authority and encourages intervention that it produces two opposing bureaucratic effects: citizen-serving agencies that are friendlier and more responsive, and citizen-regulating agencies that are more rigid and adversarial.

The book you are about to read is an effort to set forth what is generally true about bureaucracy. Although it was published ten years ago, none of its central themes needs to be revised. Of course, the finer points of bureaucracy's operations have changed, as evidenced by the ongoing struggles over procurement and personnel. And in time, the NPR may leave an important legacy of change. But for now we can say only that it is too early to determine the NPR's actual effect. In short, even if some details are altered by this and other efforts, the broad picture remains the same.

J.Q.W.

Notes

1. "Reinventing government" was the title of a popular book that analyzed government deficiencies and proposed new approaches—namely, David Osborne and Ted Gaebler, *Reinventing Government* (Reading, Mass.: Addison-Wesley, 1992). The authors of the book were involved in the National Performance Review.

2. What follows draws in part on my essay "Reinventing Public Administration," in *PS: Political Science and Politics* (December 1994), pp. 667–673.

3. *From Red Tape to Results: Creating a Government That Works Better and Costs Less*, Report of the National Performance Review, September 7, 1993 (Washington, D.C.: U.S. Government Printing Office), pp. 3, 5.

4. See pages 121–122, 240–241, and 321.

5. Here, I follow the account in Steven Kelman, "White House–Initiated Management Change: Implementing Federal Procurement Reform," in James B. Pfiffner, ed., *The Managerial Presidency*, 2nd ed. (College Station: Texas A&M University Press, 1999), pp. 239–264.

6. Quoted in Tom Shoop, "Managing Workers of America, Inc.," *Government Executive* (July 1993), p. 39.

7. Here and in the paragraphs that follow, I am indebted to Professor Patricia W. Ingraham. See, especially, her essay, "A Laggard's Tale: Civil Service and Administrative Reform in the United States," *Research in Public Administration*, vol. 5 (1999), pp. 173–187, as well as "Ingraham and James R. Thomson, "The Civil Service Reform Act of 1978 and Its Progeny: The Promise and the Dilemma," in Steven W. Hays and Richard Kearney, eds., *Issues in Contemporary Public Administration*, 3rd. ed. (Englewood Cliffs, N.J.: Prentice-Hall, 1994), pp. 54–56, 72.

8. Ingraham, "A Laggard's Tale," p. 179.

9. Ingraham, "A Laggard's Tale," p. 181.

10. Paul C. Light, *Monitoring Government: Inspectors General and the Search for Accountability* (Washington, D.C.: Brookings Institution, 1993), p. 12.

11. See the debate on this matter between Paul C. Light of the Brookings Institution and Janice Lachance, head of OPM, in *Government Executive* (October 1999 and December 1999).

12. Herbert Kaufman, *Red Tape* (Washington, D.C.: Brookings Institution, 1977).

PREFACE

THIS BOOK is an effort to explain why government agencies—bureaucracies—behave as they do. Though there may be lessons here for those interested in the behavior of government agencies abroad, the chief focus is on the United States. Toward the end of the book I offer a chapter's worth of speculation as to differences between American and foreign bureaucracies.

It is a book filled with details about police departments, school systems, the CIA, the military, the State Department, regulatory commissions, the Postal Service, the Social Security Administration, the Army Corps of Engineers, the Forest Service, and many others. The details are not there simply to make the book long, but rather to persuade the reader that bureaucracy is not the simple, uniform phenomenon it is sometimes made out to be. Reality often does not conform to scholarly theories or popular prejudices.

Historians and sociologists interested in the evolution of the modern state have had to come to grips with the bureaucratization of society. Max Weber was the founder of this tradition and, though many of his specific claims have been disproved, he still repays close reading. But such a reading will convey a view of bureaucracy as a monolith—a distinctive form of social organization which exists to increase the predictability of government action by applying general rules to specific cases. Its members possess the authority of office, enjoy lifelong careers and high social esteem, and operate the levers of power in a way that makes the bureaucracy an overtowering force against which citizens and politicians often struggle in vain.

This view is partly correct, but accepting it without substantial modification will leave the reader ill-equipped to understand some important features of American bureaucracies (and perhaps bureaucracies generally): Not only do many agencies fail to apply general rules to specific cases, they positively resist any effort to set forth their policies in the form of clear and general rules. In increasing numbers of agencies, members whose authority rests on the offices they hold are being eclipsed in power and significance by members whose authority derives from the professional training they received. The supposedly overtowering power of bureaucracies is hard to reconcile with the ease with which legislatures in this country challenge, rebuke, and otherwise influence these agencies. Bureaucratic action is sometimes regular and predictable, but just as often it is irregular and unpredictable. Some bureaucracies resist change, but others seem always to be engaged in reorganizing their structures and modifying their doctrines. Max Weber's insights are useful, but only up to a point. Beyond that point, distinctions are more important than generalizations.

Economists and political scientists have begun to apply to government agencies the same analytical methods that once were used to explain the behavior of business firms. Just as entrepreneurs are thought to be maximizing their "utility," bureaucrats are now thought to be maximizing theirs. The utility of a business person is assumed to be profits; that of a bureaucrat is assumed to be something akin to profits: salary, rank, or power. Since both bureaucrats and business executives are people, it makes sense to assume that they prefer more of whatever they like to less. Some interesting theories of bureaucratic behavior have been produced by making this reasonable assumption, but the theories so far have not explained very much. I suspect one of the reasons is that bureaucrats have a variety of preferences; only part of their behavior can be explained by assuming they are struggling to get bigger salaries or fancier offices or larger budgets. Besides, bureaucrats don't have as much control over their own salaries, offices, and budgets as do business people. For these reasons, or others yet to be discovered, it should not be surprising to find government agencies that actually refuse to take on new tasks or try to give up tasks they now perform.

Citizens and taxpayers have their own global view of bureaucracy. To them, bureaucrats are lethargic, incompetent hacks who spend their days spinning out reels of red tape and reams of paperwork, all the while going to great lengths to avoid doing the job they were hired to do. Their agencies chiefly produce waste, fraud, abuse, and mismanagement. That this view is an exaggeration is readily shown by public-opinion surveys in which people are asked about their personal experiences with government agencies. The great majority of the respondents say that these experiences were good, that the agency personnel were helpful, friendly, and competent.[1] This can only mean that those lazy, incompetent bureaucrats must work for some other agency—the one the citizen never sees. But it is not quite clear what that other agency is. No one can seem to identify it, but everybody is sure it must exist. Maybe it is the one that buys $435 hammers. But on close inspection, even that turns out to be a bit of an exaggeration—there *wasn't* a $435 hammer, though it is probably too late to convince anybody of that. (In chapter 17, I will try.)

Students of public administration have produced detailed studies of countless government agencies that, if one were to sit down and read them all, would put this into perspective. These books would show that some bureaucrats are hacks but most are not; that there is a lot of self-serving activity in agencies but also a lot that seems genuinely directed toward larger goals; and that some agencies work like Weberian bureaucracies, producing and applying rules, and some do not. But not many people are going to sit down and read them all. I have tried to. This book summarizes what I found.

It draws on over a quarter of a century of teaching and research on bureaucratic organizations, on the books and articles that others have written, and (especially) on the doctoral dissertations and seminar papers written by graduate students who have worked with me over the years. This academic knowledge has been supplemented by personal experience—as a naval officer for three years and as a part-time advisor to or member of various presidential commissions. Though I have learned a great deal from these encounters, nothing in this book consists of "inside dope" not already available in published sources. I dislike the kiss-and-tell memoirs that have recently become so popular—and so profitable. Many of them dishonor the public trust with which their authors were once endowed. From time to time, there will be unattributed statements about the workings of the FBI, the CIA, the State Department, and the Drug Enforcement Administration. These derive (unless otherwise noted) from my personal observations in an advisory capacity. Any scholar who studies these organizations will, I think, quickly learn the same thing without the benefit of privileged access.

I wish that this book could be set forth in a way that proved, or at least illustrated, a simple, elegant, comprehensive theory of bureaucratic behavior. When I was a young and giddy scholar, I had hopes that such a theory could be created (ideally, by me). I even tried my hand at a few versions. What resulted was not a theory of bureaucracy, but rather a few modest additions to the long list of theories about some aspect of bureaucracy. Over thirty years ago, James G. March and Herbert A. Simon wrote that "not a great deal [of theoretical interest] has been said about organizations, but it has been said over and over in a variety of languages."[2] That is still pretty much the case, as is evident from how often people still cite studies by March and Simon as support for one point or another. After all these decades of wrestling with the subject, I have come to have grave doubts that anything worth calling "organization theory" will ever exist. Theories will exist, but they will usually be so abstract or general as to explain rather little. Interesting explanations will exist, some even supported with facts, but these will be partial, place- and time-bound insights. Many scholars disagree with me. More power to them. Nothing would please me more than to have a comprehensive, systematic, and tested theory that really explains a lot of interesting things about a great variety of organizations. In the meantime, I think it might be helpful to public discourse and to college students if someone were to set forth what we now know about government agencies in all (or at least most) of their complexity, and to do so by sticking as close as possible to what actually happens in real bureaucracies.

Though what follows is not very theoretical, neither is it very practical. If you read this book, you will not learn very much—if anything—about how to run a government agency (though you might learn why it persists in running in a certain way despite your best efforts to change it). Why read it then? Only because you are interested, and might want to know a little bit more about why our government works the way it does. To me, that is justification enough. It has been for almost thirty years.

ACKNOWLEDGMENTS

MY CHIEF DEBT is to those students with whom I have had the privilege of working and from whose own research I have learned so much about bureaucracy and administration. Their theses, books, and articles are cited in the chapters that follow, but I learned far more from them than the conventions of scholarly citation can convey.

Much of the research of these people as well as most of my own was supported for many years by grants from the Alfred Sloan Foundation, first to Harvard and then to UCLA. Its vice president, Arthur Singer, early on took an interest in my efforts to learn more about public management and gave me steadfast encouragement and financial support. I am immensely grateful to Art, a man I regard as the perfect foundation executive: intelligent, interested, patient, and tolerant.

Several colleagues have read the entire book and given me their comments: Edward C. Banfield, Peter B. Clark, Martha Derthick, John J. DiIulio, Jr., Elisabeth Langby, Terry Moe, and John Tierney. Others have read selected chapters on which they are particularly knowledgeable: Joel Aberbach, Eliot Cohen, Morris Fiorina, Christopher Foreman, J. Ronald Fox, Bernard Frieden, Richard Helms, Norris Hogans, Robert Katzmann, Arthur Maass, Shep Melnick, Jeremy Rabkin, Susan Rainville, Stephen Rosen, Gary Schmitt, Kevin Sheehan, Curtis J. Smith, Nina Stewart, and Charles Wolf. Despite their advice, I have insisted on retaining the errors and omissions that no doubt pervade the pages that follow.

Three scholars undertook for me research into agencies and issues on which they are expert: Christopher Foreman, Robert Katzmann, and John Tierney. I am grateful for their willingness to take time from their busy schedules to enlighten me on matters about which a Californian cannot know much without moving back East to study them firsthand, and that is a price no real Californian would ever pay. I am also indebted to Martha Derthick and Steven Kelman for allowing me to read their (then) unpublished manuscripts on, respectively, the Social Security Administration and federal procurement policies.

I received valuable research assistance from Julia Watt Liebeskind and Carlos Juarez.

I am especially indebted to the John Anderson Graduate School of Management at UCLA and to its dean, Clay La Force. For reasons that still elude me, Clay and his colleagues have made it possible for me to pursue my own research interests even when they have had absolutely nothing to do with business administration.

J. Q. W.

PART I

ORGANIZATIONS

CHAPTER 1

Armies, Prisons, Schools

ON MAY 10, 1940, Army Group A of General Gerd von Rundstedt left its positions in Germany, moved through Luxembourg unopposed and through the southern part of Belgium with only slight opposition, and attacked France. By May 13, the 7th Panzer Division led by General Erwin Rommel had crossed the Meuse River near Dinant and elements of General Heinz Guderian's 19th Panzer Corps had crossed the Meuse near Sedan. On May 14, Guderian sent two armored divisions racing west; by May 19 they had crossed the Somme and later that day had reached Abbeville, a short distance from the English Channel. By the end of the month, the British had been evacuated from Dunkirk. On June 22, France capitulated. In six weeks, the German army had defeated the combined forces of Britain, France, and Belgium. It was, in the opinion of many, the greatest military victory of modern times.

The German success was an example of *blitzkrieg* (literally, lightning war). The word has become so familiar that we mistake it for an explanation. Military officers and historians know differently, but the public at large probably thinks that the key to the German victory can be found in some of the connotations *blitzkrieg* suggests to our minds: A fully mobilized German nation, striking suddenly and without warning, uses its numerical superiority and large supply of advanced tanks and aircraft to overpower a French army hiding in the forts and pillboxes of the Maginot line. The Germans, in this view, were superior to the French in strategy, in resources, and in the fanatical will to fight that had been achieved by ideological indoctrination and centralized command.

Virtually every element in this explanation is either wrong or seriously misleading. The Germans gave the French and British plenty of notice that war was imminent: In September 1939, Germany invaded Poland; France and Britain mobilized; and Allied troops moved into forward positions to defend against an expected German thrust. To be sure, the French and British armies were largely idle and increasingly demoralized during the eight-month-long "Phony War," but after the fall of Poland (and later of Norway) there was ample warning of German intentions. By March the French intelligence service had acquired a quite accurate understanding of the German military build-up opposite Sedan; the French military attaché in Switzerland had reported that the Germans had built eight military bridges across the Rhine and even predicted, quite correctly, that the Germans would attack toward Sedan between May 8 and 10.[1] Unfortunately, French aerial reconnaissance was almost entirely lacking; no one believed the report of a French bomber pilot that there was a sixty-mile-long column of German vehicles, all with their headlights on, moving toward the Ardennes. But the clues were there.

The German army was smaller than the French army[2] and did not have as many tanks as did the French. In 1939, the French army had over 2,342 tanks (compared to the German's 2,171), and the best French tanks were larger and more powerful than the best German ones.[3] (But French tanks, unlike German ones, lacked radios, and so it was hard to maneuver them in concert.) French aircraft were marginally inferior to those of the Germans, but if one adds to the French resources the air forces of Britain and Belgium, the strength of the Luftwaffe was probably no greater than—and may have been less than—that of its adversaries.[4] While the Panzer Corps that made the initial attack were heavily motorized, the German Army as a whole was not. In our vague recollections of lightning thrusts by tank formations, we forget that most of the Germany army in 1940 walked and most of its supplies were pulled along in horse-drawn wagons. (As late as 1943, the typical German infantry division had 942 motor vehicles and 1,133 horse-drawn vehicles and for its supply required twice as many tons of hay and oats as it did of oil and gasoline.[5])

Moreover, the key breakthroughs along the Meuse River front were not accomplished by tanks or aircraft. They were accomplished by foot soldiers who paddled rubber rafts across the water, after which they had to climb up steep banks or dodge across open fields under enemy fire. Supporting fire from artillery, aircraft, and tanks helped the crossing, but these crucial engagements were decided by the infantry.

Unlike the First World War, in the Second the French soldiers did not respond to their mobilization orders in a burst of patriotic enthusiasm. There was no crush outside the recruiting offices. "The memories of the Great War were still too recent," historian Alistair Horne was later to write. "The slogan of the moment . . . became 'Let's get it over with.' "[6]

But there is little reason to believe that Germans flocked to their recruiting offices, either; after all, both sides had suffered horribly in 1914–18. The German political leadership attempted to instill Nazi ideology in their rebuilt armies and may have succeeded with the officer corps; they certainly succeeded in the case of the SS divisions. At one time scholars were unanimous in their view that ideology played no role in German combat cohesion; now, newer studies are challenging that view. But however successful the Nazis were in motivating German soldiers, it is still not clear that this motivation took the form of Nazi zealotry among the rank and file.[7] The Germans fought hard in 1940 (and just as hard in 1944, when they were retreating in the face of vastly superior Allied forces), but there is no reason to think that political fanaticism had much to do with their combat cohesion. In Germany as in any nation, then as now, soldiers fight out of some mixture of fear and a desire not to let down (or appear to let down) one's buddies in the squad or platoon.

One might suppose that Germany's brilliant strategy was sufficient to overcome all these limitations in men and matériel. Because it worked, the German strategy was, indeed, brilliant, but it was also an extremely risky strategy that could well have failed. Moreover, it is not clear that the strategy itself was decisive.

Originally, Hitler had wanted to attack France by sending the German army through Holland and Belgium to the Channel coast. In October 1939, General Erich von Manstein acquired a copy of the plan and concluded that it would not work: It lacked any clear strategic objective and would not lead to an opportunity to destroy the French army, the bulk of which would presumably be stationed south of the German attack. Moreover, a German officer carrying top-secret documents fell into Belgian hands when his plane crashed; the papers pointed clearly to a German attack on Belgium, and accordingly elements of the French army moved north.

But if not through Belgium, then where? Manstein suggested the Ardennes Forest in the southernmost tip of Belgium and Luxembourg. This route had the advantage of putting the German army on a direct course toward Paris over a route that was flat and open—once it got through the Ardennes and across the Meuse River. But how could one get tanks, trucks, and tens of thousands of troops through that forest and over that river?

Consider the risks: To transport a single Panzer division by railway required no fewer than eighty trains of fifty-five cars each. And once the armored column left the train and started off down a decent road, it would stretch out in a line seventy miles long and move at a pace not much faster than that at which a man could walk.[8] One French reconnaissance airplane could spot this movement and know immediately the direction of the German attack days before it was launched. Now put that armored column on a narrow road that twisted and turned through rocky gorges and over hilly, forested terrain. If the lead tank breaks down, hundreds of tanks and trucks behind it are stalled and the invasion stops.

But suppose that there are no air attacks, no unmanageable breakdowns. The converging tank columns must avoid becoming entangled with one another as they emerge from the forest and then cross a river that is one or two hundred yards wide with a steep bank on the other side—a bank that is hard for attackers to climb but easy for defenders to hold. And then suppose that somehow these barriers are surmounted. At last you are in open country, rolling toward Paris and the English Channel. But by turning from south to west, you expose the entire southern flank of your column to the French army. German Field Marshall Fedor von Bock argued that it was "transcending the frontiers of reason" to suppose that such a plan could succeed. "You will be creeping by ten miles from the Maginot line with the flank of your breakthrough and hope the French will watch inertly! . . . And you then hope to be able to lead an operation as far as the coast with an open southern flank 200 miles along, where stands the mass of the French Army!"[9]

The French Maginot line, much derided by contemporary opinion, weighed heavily on the German planning. This system of fortifications, running from the southwest corner of Luxembourg south and southeast to the Swiss border, was thought to be impregnable, and so far as history will ever tell us, we must assume it was. Except for one small fort, it held out against the Germans until France surrendered.[10] The Germans were not inclined to attack it in force and they worried that counterattacks from it against the German flank would create a serious threat.

Bock's arguments were unavailing. Just three months before the offensive began, Hitler endorsed the Manstein plan. It worked.

On entering the maximum-security prison in Huntsville, Texas, Professor John J. DiIulio, Jr., was struck by its orderly environment. Inmates were dressed in white uniforms, moved about quietly, and spoke to the guards respectfully, addressing them as "sir" or "boss." Rarely did an inmate accost or speak to DiIulio or any observer. The cells were spartan but clean. The corridors were tidy, the windows unbroken. The food in the mess hall was wholesome and abundant, much of it fresh from the prison farm. In the classrooms where educational programs were conducted, the teacher was clearly in charge, the lesson plans were implemented, and rowdiness was at a minimum. Almost all inmates worked in a prison industry, typically the farm.[11]

By contrast, when he entered the maximum-security prison in Jackson, Michigan, DiIulio encountered a noisy, tension-filled atmosphere. Instead of uniforms, the inmates wore whatever seemed to please them. They moved about at will, and spoke in often threatening and vulgar epithets to the guards. Inmates demanded to know of DiIulio who he was and what he was doing and supplied him with obscene opinions on the genealogy and physical attributes of the warden. The cells were crammed with a variety of personal effects, often piled about in a jumble. In the mess hall, the food was of poor quality. Classroom instruction took place, if at all, in the prison equivalent of a blackboard jungle, in which shouting, aggressive horseplay, and taunting threats aimed at the teacher were more the rule than the exception.

Matters were even worse at the maximum-security prison in Walpole, Massachusetts. DiIulio saw inmates lying in bed with sheets wrapped around them, mummy-style. An officer explained that it was to keep the cockroaches away. One inmate grabbed a stick with a sharp nail protruding from the end and swung it at a guard. Another inmate threatened to throw a guard off the third tier of the cellblock to the concrete floor below. The quality and quantity of food was erratic. On some days, there was not even hot coffee available.

DiIulio's observations were confirmed by those of other outsiders and by statistics supplied by the state correctional authorities. The level of violence was much lower in Texas than in other big-state prisons. Between 1977 and 1979, the homicide rate among Texas inmates was less than one-half of what it was among Michigan inmates and only about one-sixth what it was in California.[12] "Among the larger states," wrote Bruce Jackson, "only Texas prisoners were at less risk in prison than outside of it."[13] A study group from the Rand Corporation concluded that in achieving inmate security, "the Texas system is regarded as the most successful and efficient in the nation. . . . The facilities are extraordinarily clean and free from disturbances."[14] Even though Texas guards have traditionally enforced the rules rigorously and Michigan guards have admittedly overlooked many inmate infractions, the percentage of the inmate population that had acquired at least one disciplinary infraction for a serious matter (making threats, having contraband, inflicting violence, attempting an escape) was far smaller in Texas than in Michigan.[15] The suicide rate was much lower among Texas than among Michigan inmates.[16]

Order in the Texas prisons was not purchased at the price of educational or counseling programs. The state offered a full range of medical and educational services as well as a variety of prison industries, ranging from agriculture to computer programming.

The orderliness of the Texas prisons did not prove to be permanent. Beginning around 1983, the level of violence and disorder increased. Whereas there was no homicide inside a Texas prison in 1978, by 1983 there were ten and in 1984 there were twenty-five. In six years, the murder rate increased six-fold.[17] Other statistics confirmed the unhappy trend. Inmate assaults on prison guards and on other inmates rose dramatically.[18] Corridors that once were spotless became littered, windows that once were clean and intact became dirty or broken. Predatory inmate gangs, organized along racial and ethnic lines, sprang up. The appearance and manner of the inmates deteriorated. But for many years, the Texas prisons were a model for the rest of the nation.

The explanations for this superiority that first come to mind turn out, on close inspection, to be wrong or incomplete. It was not money: State expenditures per inmate were much higher in Michigan (and most other large states) than they were in Texas. It was not manpower: Texas employed fewer guards per one hundred inmates than did Michigan. It was not the amount of training given to guards: In Texas they received 80 hours of formal preservice training; in Michigan they received 640. It was not the absence of crowding: Texas prisons had more inmates per square foot of floor space than did those of Michigan or California. And it was not repression: Though there are some differences of opinion on this, most outside observers, including DiIulio, found little or no evidence of guard brutality. (There is reason to believe that some inmate trustees, called "building tenders," abused their authority and physically coerced other inmates, but the low total level of violence in the prisons suggests that this inmate-on-inmate violence could not, by itself, explain the more orderly nature of Texas prisons.)

Texas inmates are somewhat different from those in California and Michigan. Because Texas judges are more likely to imprison convicted offenders, Texas inmates tend to have less serious criminal records than do those in California and Michigan.[19] This conceivably might make the average Texas inmate more tractable and less violent than his counterpart elsewhere. But as DiIulio points out, we know very little about the relationship, if any, between prior record and inmate behavior. Moreover, when the conditions in Texas prisons began to deteriorate, there had been no significant change in the characteristics of the inmate population. What the Texas system once was able to achieve with a given group of inmates, it no longer was able to achieve with essentially the same group. Most telling, DiIulio describes a California maximum-security prison run Texas-style (but without building tenders) by the brother of a former Texas prison director. Despite being very crowded and housing serious offenders, this facility had lower rates of violence, a neater appearance, and better educational programs than most other similar California institutions.[20] Inmate characteristics, therefore, cannot be the whole story.

Something else—something much more important than money, training, crowding, or inmate traits—was at work. What?

By the 1970s, George Washington Carver High School in Atlanta, Georgia, had become an educational basket case. Located in an all-black, low-income neighborhood, it drew its nine hundred pupils mainly from public housing projects where most of the families were female-headed and on welfare.[21]

The teachers, none of whom lived in the area, were demoralized, and understandably so. The school hallways were dirty and much of the equipment was broken. The students were disorderly and fights were common; not much learning was taking place. By all the standard measures, pupil achievement was low, among the lowest in the city. As Carver High became known as a problem school, other schools in the city tried to transfer problem students there in order to put them out of sight and out of mind. Carver was becoming the dumping ground of the city's educational system. The superintendent was considering closing it.

By the time Carver was visited by Professor Sara Lawrence Lightfoot in the early 1980s, it was hard to believe that anybody had ever considered closing it. The halls and rooms were clean. The equipment worked. The students were neatly dressed and mannerly and they seemed to take pride in their high school. Some teachers had left, but most of those who remained were enthusiastic about what they were accomplishing in the classrooms. Achievement levels had risen, though not by much. Far from being seen as a dumping ground, students from other poor neighborhoods were seeking transfers to Carver.

Carver is not the only inner-city school to have turned itself around. Similar examples can be found in many other cities. Though it is difficult to generalize about what factors were associated with these changes, there is a good deal of evidence from studies comparing good and bad schools about what factors do *not* account for these differences.

At Carver, neither the teaching staff nor the student body changed very much. Essentially the same teachers taught the same students before and after the school's transformation. After the publication in 1966 of the famous Coleman Report (technically, the Equal Educational Opportunity Survey), one would not have expected this. That study of school achievement among hundreds of thousands of pupils in hundreds of American schools found that the characteristics of the students and their families were the best predictors of school achievement. Once those characteristics are held constant, one would expect only small differences in pupil achievement that could be attributed to readily observable differences among the schools.[22]

But other things learned from the Coleman Report are consistent with what happened at Carver. The Coleman group found no significant differences in educational attainment that were associated with the quality of school buildings, the level of expenditures, or the size of classrooms. Similar conclusions have been reached by other researchers. For example, economist Eric A. Hanushek reviewed 130 studies of school outcomes and concluded that the level of resources made no appreciable difference in pupil achievement.[23] In England, Michael Rutter and his colleagues, assessing the differences in educational outcomes among twelve high schools in London, found that these differences bore no significant relationship to the size or age of the school buildings, the number of pupils per 100 square feet of floor space, or the pupil-teacher ratios in the classrooms.[24] At Carver, no new buildings were erected, there was not much of an increase in per pupil expenditures, and the number of children in the average classroom did not change.

But *something* must have changed at Carver and at other schools like Carver. Whatever it was, it is not easily detected in surveys of the "objective" features of school organizations.

This book has begun with brief accounts of the differences among three common and important kinds of government organizations—differences, that is, among bureaucracies. The next chapter will try to explain why these organizations with similar tasks differed in their behavior (or, in the case of Carver, how it changed its behavior) and derive whatever lessons that can be learned from these examples.

The reason for proceeding in this way is not, however, to teach the reader how to run an army, a prison, or a school. Rather, it is to remind ourselves that bureaucracy is a complex and varied phenomenon, not a simple social category or political epithet. In the recurring debate about how large (and presumably how bureaucratic) government should be, all sides tend to treat government agencies as stereotypes. Liberals who want the government to play a large role in society often either minimize the problems created by bureaucratic rule or assume that problems can be solved simply by spending more money, constructing better facilities, hiring better people, or vesting the clients of these agencies with more rights. Conservatives who want the government to play a smaller role in our lives taunt liberals for their misguided optimism about the nature of bureaucratic rule and urge that bureaucracy be curtailed, but often they apply their critique of bureaucracy inconsistently: "Let us have fewer welfare offices but a bigger army."

It is essential that we think seriously about which public goals can best be achieved under public or private auspices, and this book will conclude with some observations on that issue. But however large or small the public sector should be, it is unlikely that this nation will ever decide to do without an army, or choose to turn over the armed services to private enterprise. Possibly prisons and schools can be better managed by private enterprise, but in the foreseeable future this nation, like most, will rely heavily on public prisons and public schools to attain important criminal justice and educational objectives. Private security companies are numerous and growing, but public police departments are here to stay. The State Department may be a rich source of bureaucratic jokes, but conducting foreign affairs is no joke and for the most part can be done only by a public bureaucracy.

There are two ways to look at government agencies: from the top down and from the bottom up. Most books, and almost all elected officials, tend to take the first view. The academic perspective, much influenced by Max Weber (and lately by economic theories of the firm), typically centers on the structure, purposes, and resources of the organization. The political perspective draws attention to the identity, beliefs, and decisions of the top officials of the agency. These are important matters, but the emphasis given to them has caused us to lose sight of what government agencies *do* and how the doing of it is related to attaining goals or satisfying clients.

There are two circumstances under which a top-down view is warranted. Both require us to know what the agency is doing on a day-to-day basis. One circumstance exists when the goals an agency is to serve can be precisely specified in advance and progress toward those goals can be reliably measured by its top officials. In chapter 9 I call such agencies "production organizations" and give as an example the management of the retirement program by the Social Security Administration. The other circumstance occurs when an interest group closely monitors the work of an agency (even one with somewhat vague goals) and reports its judgments in a persuasive manner to the legislature. In chapter 5 I call this condition "client politics" and give as examples the old Civil Aeronautics Board and the present-day Agricultural Stabilization and Conservation Service.

But many, perhaps most, government agencies do not meet either of these conditions, though we sometimes suppose they do. Everyone knows what soldiers, prison guards, and schoolteachers do, so what is interesting about armies, prisons, and schools must be their structures, budgets, and rules. But if that is correct, why then did Carver High School change so dramatically without any change in its structure or budget? Why did the German army defeat the French army without having access to greater resources? The organizational structure of state departments of corrections are pretty much the same, yet very different prisons are run by these departments, in ways that depend very little on their budgets.

In other cases we do not assume we know exactly what the members of a government agency do. We wonder, and sometimes worry, about what the officers of the Central Intelligence Agency or agents of the Drug Enforcement Administration really do. We assume, however, that their behavior results from rules, laws, and organizational structure, and so we can change that behavior by changing the rules, laws, and structures. This view often governs the actions of political leaders who press for government reorganizations. Because of this assumption, these leaders—or the scholars who evaluate their actions—are often surprised to learn that the reorganization did not accomplish their objectives. Several studies have noted the failures of reorganization.[25] Many of these resulted from having looked at the agency in question from the top down.

For example, political scientist Patricia Rachal studied the effort made in the early 1970s to reorganize the federal role in narcotics law enforcement.[26] It involved creating a new agency—the Drug Enforcement Administration—inside the Department of Justice, into which would be merged the old Bureau of Narcotics and Dangerous Drugs (itself the product of a reorganization plan five years earlier) and certain personnel from the Customs Service. The object was to end the duplicative and frequently competitive efforts of Customs and BNDD and to improve the quality of the investigations aimed at major-trafficking organizations. But the interagency rivalries did not end, the investigative strategies did not significantly change, and by 1981 another reorganization was in the offing. Rachal's explanation for this failure was not that the reorganization had only cosmetic, political purposes; not that the people who carried it out were incompetent or wrongly motivated; not that the problems aimed at were imaginary; rather, it failed because its architects did not fully understand what narcotics agents did and why they did it one way rather than another.

By looking at bureaucracies from the bottom up, we can assess the extent to which their management systems and administrative arrangements are well or poorly suited to the tasks the agencies actually perform. By taking this perspective we can explain behavior that otherwise seems puzzling. For example:

- When the Tennessee Valley Authority was created in the 1930s, it was attacked by conservatives because it threatened the well-being of private electric utilities. Within a few decades it was being criticized by liberals because it behaved just like a private utility. Why?
- When Robert S. McNamara was secretary of defense in the 1960s, he raised the military budget but was disliked by the military brass. When Melvin Laird was secretary of defense in the 1970s, he cut the military budget but was liked by the brass. Why?
- For years, the State Department hired Soviet citizens, many if not all of whom were KGB agents, to be cooks, chauffeurs, and repairmen in the American Embassy in Moscow. When it was suggested that it replace the KGB agents with American citizens, the State Department resisted. Why?
- The United States Air Force jealously guards its command of a large fleet of intercontinental ballistic missiles that it regularly seeks to improve. But when the ICBM was first proposed, the air force was indifferent and even hostile to such missiles. Why?
- The United States government has sought to increase the propor-

tion of women working in shipyards. Private shipyards have shown larger such increases than have government-owned shipyards. Why?

- When a new police chief is appointed in order to improve the quality of local law enforcement, the crime rate rarely goes down but the number of traffic tickets issued often goes up. Why?
- When the Environmental Protection Agency was created, economists who had studied the matter argued almost unanimously that the most efficient way to reduce pollution was to assess an effluent charge on polluters. The EPA ignored this advice and instead sued polluters in court. Why?

In the chapters that follow, I try to explain these and other puzzles by offering (for the most part) a bottom-up view of the work of government agencies. I think this is a useful corrective to the perspective common in many political, legal, and academic circles. But such a view, carried too far, can blind us to the important policy and structural choices made by presidents, governors, mayors, legislatures, and courts. The freedom of action of bureaucrats is importantly constrained, and sometimes wholly determined, by the decisions of their political superiors. In Part V I try to make that clear. I also try in other places to specify the conditions under which political dominance of the bureaucracy is more or less likely to occur. By beginning with three important bureaucracies—armies, prisons, and schools—I hope I have made it clear that studying the goals, resources, and structures of an agency is not always a very helpful clue to what it will do. In the next chapter I will suggest some better clues.

CHAPTER 2

Organization Matters

THE GERMAN ARMY, the Texas prisons, and Carver High School did a better job than their rivals because they were, or became, better organizations.

Armies

The key difference between the German army in 1940 and its French opponents was not in grand strategy, but in tactics and organizational arrangements well-suited to implementing those tactics. Both sides drew lessons from the disastrous trench warfare of World War I. The Germans drew the right ones.

By the end of that war, it was evident to all that large frontal assaults by infantry against well-entrenched soldiers manning machine guns and supported by artillery would not be successful. A rifleman who must cross three hundred yards of No Man's Land, slipping and staggering through the countless shell holes made by his own side's artillery bombardment and desperately trying to get over or around barbed-wire barricades, had no chance against the murderous fire of dug-in machine guns. The French decided that under these circumstances the advantage belonged to the defense, and so organized their armies around a squad (or *groupe de combat*) of twelve men whose task it was to fire, serve, and support a machine gun. The rifle was regarded as a subsidiary weapon; only three riflemen were assigned to a *groupe* and their level of training was low. These soldiers, dedicated to the support of the machine gunners, were ideally suited to defend a trench but hopelessly ill-suited to a war of maneuver.[1]

The Germans drew a different lesson. Trench warfare led to stalemate, and Germany, surrounded on all sides by potential enemies with larger manpower reserves, could not afford a stalemate. Therefore, the defensive advantage of entrenched machine gunners had to be overcome. But how? There were only two ways—to make the attacking soldiers bulletproof by putting them in armored vehicles, or to make them hard to shoot by deploying them as infiltrators who could slip through weak points in the enemy's line and attack the machine guns from the rear.[2] When we recall the Panzer divisions with their hundreds of tanks, we may suppose that the Germans chose the first way. They did not. The Panzers were chiefly designed to exploit a breakthrough, not to create one. To create it, the Germans emphasized infiltration warfare.

Their first experiment with this method occurred in 1916 at the battle of Verdun. Abandoning the conventional massed infantry attack preceded by a prolonged artillery barrage (that eliminated surprise and chewed up ground that had to be crossed), the Germans used a brief barrage followed by small groups of infantrymen who probed for weak spots.[3] Gains were made but they were not exploited. A year later a German army used these tactics systematically to attack Riga; the city fell in two days.[4] Further successes along these lines followed at Caporetto.

The Germans sought to use infiltration tactics to produce a *kessel-schlacht* (literally, cauldron battle): a grand envelopment of the opponent's position by turning his flank and spreading out in his rear, exploiting the gains with deep thrusts toward headquarters units (*blitzkrieg*). Under the leadership of General Hans von Seeckt, chief of the army in the early 1920s, this doctrine of maneuver was refined and expounded. It not only fit the lessons of World War I, it fit the realities of Germany's geopolitical position. Under the Treaty of Versailles, Germany was limited to a small professional army that would have to contend with enemies on both the east and the west. It could not match the combined manpower of all of these rivals and it could not afford a war of attrition. Thus, a quick and decisive offensive waged by numerically inferior forces was essential to success.[5]

Such tactics required a certain kind of organization, and the Germans set about creating it. An army that could probe enemy defenses, infiltrate weak points, and rapidly exploit breakthroughs with deep encircling moves could not be an army that was centrally directed or dependent on detailed plans worked out in advance. It had to be an army equipped and organized in such a way as to permit independent action by its smallest units—squads, platoons, and companies. The squad (*gruppe*) should not be tied down to the task of carrying or serving a heavy, water-cooled machine gun. Instead, it should be organized into two sections. The largest (the *stoss trupp*) would consist of seven men armed with rifles and, as resources permitted, with light, rapid-firing machine pistols and submachine guns.

The other, smaller section of four men would service a new, light machine gun weighing only twenty-five pounds.[6]

Designing and equipping such a unit were the easiest tasks. The difficult—and crucial—job was to staff and lead it in such a way that it was capable of intelligent, aggressive, and independent action. This meant that the best soldiers would have to be placed in the squads, especially the *stoss* (or assault) *truppen*, not assigned to headquarters or other rear elements. The officers and noncommissioned officers commanding these small units would have to be given substantial freedom of action. Officers and men alike would have to be given incentives that rewarded fighting prowess, especially that which required them to run risks. Following each battle there would be a rigorous evaluation of the efforts and results. For two decades, the German army devoted itself to solving these organizational problems.

What resulted was a system wholly at odds with the stereotypical view of the German army as composed of fanatical soldiers blindly obeying the dictates of a Prussian general staff. Discipline was severe but it was discipline in service of a commitment to independent action on behalf of combat objectives. In this regard, the post–1920 plans represented a continuation of a military tradition stretching back well into the nineteenth century. The central concept was *auftragstatik*, translated by Martin van Creveld in his brilliant analysis of German fighting power as a "mission-oriented command system."[7] Commanders were to tell their subordinates precisely what was to be accomplished but not necessarily how to accomplish it. The mission must "express the will of the commander in an unmistakable way," but the methods of execution should be limited "only where essential for coordination with other commands."[8] The German army, compared to its rivals (or even to the contemporary American army), had remarkably little paperwork. Orders were clear but brief.

The best German soldiers were expected to be the storm troopers, the best German officers were those that distinguished themselves by leading men in battle. Selecting personnel for specific military specialties (infantry, motor transport, supply, and so on) was not the responsibility of a personnel organization located in the rear but of combat (usually regimental) commanders.[9] In choosing officers, character, especially willpower and a readiness to accept responsibility, counted more than education.[10] Officers at first were chosen by the regimental commanders to whom the candidates had applied; when later this was replaced by a central screening office, the testing focused on physical, pedagogical, and leadership abilities. Even then, the final choice was left in the hands of the regimental commanders.

Soldiers and officers were indoctrinated with the primacy of combat and the central importance of initiative. The 1936 command manual put it this way: "The emptiness of the battlefield demands independently thinking and acting fighters who exploit each situation in a considered, determined, and bold way. They must be thoroughly conscious of the fact that only results matter. . . . *Thus decisive action remains the first prerequisite for success in war.*"[11] Though there were efforts at Nazi indoctrination, they were not centrally managed by Nazi leaders and probably had little effect. The real indoctrination was called "spiritual strengthening" (*geistige betreuung*) and was the responsibility of the commanding officers.

Medals were awarded chiefly for taking successful independent action in combat (Creveld estimates that medals were given much more commonly for this reason in the German army than in other armies). Punishment was often harsh (it is estimated that over eleven thousand German soldiers and officers were executed during the Second World War, many for "undermining the war effort,"[12] but discipline did not fall disproportionately on hapless soldiers. There were almost as many officers and NCOs punished for mishandling subordinates as there were soldiers punished for attacking their superiors.[13] Perhaps because of this, perhaps because German officers (unlike French and American ones) were allowed to fraternize with soldiers when off duty, German soldiers, when interviewed, had a high opinion of their NCOs and officers, describing them as brave and considerate.[14]

To maintain fighting spirit among the squads, platoons, and companies on which combat success so heavily depended, the German army was built up on a local basis. Military units up to the size of a division were formed out of men with the same regional backgrounds—Prussians, Saxons, Bavarians, and so on.[15] When replacements were necessary, they were drawn, so long as wartime exigencies permitted, from the same regions and organized into groups that were then given their final training by a division's field-replacement battalion so as to insure that the new troops would be organized and trained by the men alongside whom they would fight.[16]

The result was an organization well adapted to the task of getting men to fight against heavy odds in a confused, fluid setting far from army headquarters and without precisely detailed instructions. As Creveld summarizes it, the German soldier "fought for the reasons men have always fought: because he felt himself a member of a well-integrated, well-led team whose structure, administration, and functioning were perceived to be . . . equitable and just."[17]

Of course, strategic and technological factors helped. The Manstein plan, despite its risky features, had the advantage of leading to a decisive engagement, not to an inevitable stalemate. The *Stuka* dive bomber was an effective psychological weapon against French troops that had never seen it nor heard its screaming descent. German tanks had radios, French tanks did not. The French advanced too many of their best troops north into Belgium, where the main attack did not come, and too few toward Sedan, where it did. But in war, good tactics can often save a flawed strategy, whereas bad tactics can rarely make even an excellent strategy succeed. The French prepared, tactically as well as strategically, to refight World War I, a war of fixed positions and massed firepower. For such a war they made reasonably good preparations—drawing up detailed mobilization plans, building heavy fortifications, acquiring large quantities of tanks and artillery, organizing their squads around heavy machine guns, and maintaining tightly centralized control over operations. Had they adopted different tactics embedded in a more flexible organization, their strategic errors might not have counted so heavily against them.

Prisons

The Texas Department of Corrections, during the years when it ran what was arguably the best prison system in the United States, based its management of institutions on a clear understanding of the central problem confronting wardens and guards: How do you keep order inside the walls when you are outnumbered and outmuscled by the inmates?

It cannot be done simply by force. Guards can band together to overwhelm a single prisoner, but they cannot do so continuously or against every inmate, yet the threat of unruly behavior is continuous and general. Guards can use weapons to cope with inmate mobs, just as a nation can resort to war to defeat an adversary. But guards, like nations, can only use armed force for the most serious threats, leaving to the imagination and initiative of the prisoners opportunities for misconduct just short of whatever will trigger an armed reprisal.

Some prison authorities believe order can be maintained by encouraging inmates to accept responsibility for their own actions. John DiIulio called this the "responsibility model" and quotes an administrator of the Michigan prisons on how this philosophy shapes the management of that state's prisons: "You have to keep control . . . but we don't have to smother people to keep things under control. We try to show the inmates respect and expect it in return. We are more willing than Texas to give them air [i.e., freedom] and then hold them accountable. . . . We attempt to operate safely in the least restrictive environment possible."[18]

The Michigan philosophy does not condone violence, of course, but provided violence does not erupt, rule enforcement should be minimized. An inmate is classified on the basis of his likely behavior at intake and sent to the least restrictive facility appropriate to his predicted conduct. The rule book reminds guards that "there is no requirement that every rule violation" be handled formally or followed by a sanction, noting that "in many cases verbal counseling or summary action should be the first response to the apparent misconduct."[19]

Inmates should be allowed to move about relatively freely, dress according to their personal tastes, keep many personal effects in their cells, and refuse, if so inclined, to attend educational and rehabilitative programs. Outsiders may telephone and visit frequently with inmates. Inmate organizations are not only tolerated but encouraged "as a means of prisoner self-expression and self-development."[20] Inmates are expected to obey orders, but if they disagree with an order an appeal and grievance procedure exists.

The consequence of this management philosophy, as we saw in chapter 1, was a set of prisons that were disorderly and often violent (though not as violent as those in some other states), where little meaningful work or education occurred, and in which guard morale was low. Security problems were compounded by the amount of personal property inmates were allowed to receive and keep, property that was often used to make weapons or conceal contraband. Because some prisoners were stronger or had more valuables than others, DiIulio observed a convict class system, with certain inmates able to exert authority over or take advantage of others.[21] Given the detailed rules governing prisoner rights, discipline, appeals, and grievances, administrators were inundated with a torrent of paperwork.

The Texas Department of Corrections, under the leadership of its former executive, George Beto, developed a radically different solution to the problem of maintaining order. Known as the "control model," it was based on the assumption that prisoners were impulsive, often dangerous individuals who, left to their own devices, would attempt to take advantage of each other and of the guards. In the eyes of Beto, convicted criminals were persons lacking in an internalized code of discipline, a fact that was evident not only in their criminality but in their indifference to the conventional customs of daily life:

> Observe these inmates. Most of them have simply never known discipline, internal or external. . . . In prison, these men, most of them for the first time in their lives, are made to experience external discipline. They must take a bath every day. They must shave. They must wear fresh clothes. They must wait in lines and be respectful to others.[22]

In this view, inmates were not to be regarded as incarcerated citizens but as convicted criminals. Given the defects in their character, Beto organized his institutions to treat all inmates in a maximum-security setting in which the most minute details of their daily lives were closely regulated. The prisons were governed as paramilitary organizations.

Inmates were required to bathe, shave, and dress in neat uniforms.

Every minute of their day was regulated by a detailed schedule.[23] They arose early, ate breakfast in a mess hall, and walked quietly to their work stations following lines painted on the corridor floors. They were required to address guards as "boss" or "sir." Inmate gangs or associations were forbidden. Even casual groupings in the corridors or yards were broken up.

If they obeyed the rules and behaved properly in classes and at work, inmates earned points that could be exchanged for extra privileges and, most important, for early release. (As of 1982, a prisoner could earn as much as two days off his sentence for every problem-free day served in prison.[24]) If inmates broke the rules, punishment, in the form of extra work duties or time in solitary confinement, was swift and certain. The object of all this was not rehabilitation (though some Texas officials thought the external discipline might help achieve that end) but habituation: making each unruly offender a tractable inmate.

The rules, though clear and detailed, were not extensive and could be listed easily in a small handbook given to each inmate on arrival. The guards and administrators had reports to fill out (all inmate misconduct, for example, was to be promptly reported in writing), but the paperwork was not so onerous as to prevent the administrators, including Beto, from spending a good deal of time in the prison observing the daily routine.

The control model, as DiIulio observed it, was not without its problems. In the hands of a cruel administrator it could become an engine of cruelty. Some of its organizational features were open to abuse. For example, prison administrators selected certain inmates, known as building tenders, to assist them in running the cellblocks. All groups develop leaders, even those in prison; Texas administrators felt it imperative that they, not the prisoners, select the inmate leaders. These building tenders had a certain amount of privilege and authority that without careful selection and control could be used for illicit purposes.

After Beto's retirement, the task of supervising the building tenders became too much for prison administrators who lacked his skill and who confronted an explosive increase in the number of inmates. Some tenders began to abuse their authority, occasionally using violence against other inmates to enforce their demands. The conduct of the tenders became an important issue in the federal court hearings over alleged abuses in Texas prison management. The sweeping order issued by Judge William Wayne Justice in 1980 put an end to the building tender system.[25]

By the mid-1980s, the Texas prisons had lost much of their orderly, violence-free character. There is little agreement on why the change occurred: some blame the intervention of the federal judge, others fault the collapse of external political support for the Department of Corrections, and still others argue that the increase in prison population strained the old order to the breaking point. But most agree that Beto's successors as chief of the Department were unable, for a variety of reasons, to sustain his management system and some of them (such as Raymond Procunier, imported from California to "fix up" the Texas prisons) did not even try.[26] The organizational system and philosophy that had made Texas prisons a model for much of the rest of the nation was scrapped.

Schools

The dramatic change in Atlanta's Carver High School was caused by a dynamic new principal, Norris Hogans. He was an energetic, dominant personality with great willpower and a deep conviction that the school, to be a good school, had first to become a safe and orderly school.

As Sara Lightfoot described the process, Hogans announced a dress code, banned radios and stereos from the hallways and playgrounds, eliminated the graffiti from the walls, and insisted that the hallways and restrooms be kept clean. His managerial system was authoritative, even authoritarian. Teachers and students alike felt his presence; Lightfoot described him as having a "heavy hand and an autocratic style" and projecting a "big-daddy, paternalistic image."[27]

Order was important, but only as a means to an end, not an end in itself. Hogans stressed the importance of education, especially vocational education. He created a new work-study program in which students would spend half their time at school and half working at jobs in the city. To help acquaint them with business and job opportunities, Hogans devised an Explorers' Program whereby students, dressed in white uniform jackets, visited Atlanta firms to meet with their executives. Once a year, Hogans presided over a Free Enterprise Day at which awards were given to students who had completed the work-study program, and exercises were held in honor of "democracy, free enterprise, and capitalism."

Hogans's experiences at Carver High were not unique. There is by now a substantial literature on effective schools and the processes by which schools improve. Gwendolyn J. Cooke describes a disorderly, all-black middle (or junior high) school in which the norm was to "leave the teachers alone and let the students fail."[28] Its transformation by a new principal involved some of the same strategies (though not the same tactics) found at Carver: strong leadership by the principal, a heavy emphasis on creating a safe and orderly environment, and a focus on teaching basic skills in an environment in which learning was expected. Unlike Hogans at Carver, however, this principal tried to share educational leadership with a faculty committee, but soon the teachers sought to have the principal transferred for having exceeded her authority. Instead, the principal saw to it that several dozen teachers were transferred out.

Kenneth Tewel was the principal of the Franklin K. Lane High School in Queens, New York, at the time when it, like Carver, was seen as the leper of the city's school system. He had to get teachers once again to make education a paramount objective and this required him to address their safety and security concerns. His experiences in turning the school around led him to write a doctoral dissertation comparing what he learned with the experience of three other urban high school principals. He concluded that all held identical views of their mission: "to resolve the crisis atmosphere and create the conditions under which students could attend school safely and learn."[29] To accomplish this each principal had to adopt an authoritarian attitude toward the staff and to maintain tight control over the changes. But once the schools were set on a course of orderly progress, a different, more consultative management system seemed preferable.

There is disagreement among scholars on the extent to which "good" schools actually improve the educational achievement of pupils independently of their native abilities and family backgrounds. Some researchers have found significant effects,[30] others have found little or no effect.[31] The most comprehensive and systematic comparisons have been those of James S. Coleman, Thomas Hoffer, and Sally Kilgore in their study of public and private high schools in America.[32] Their conclusions, based on the most elaborate data yet gathered, is that private and Catholic high schools produce greater educational achievement on the average, as measured by standardized tests, than do public high schools after controlling, statistically, for family background.[33]

The reasons for the more impressive results of private and Catholic schools is central to the lessons one might learn from efforts to transform Carver High or Lane High School: "the greatest differences in achievement between private and public schools are accounted for by school-level behavior variables (that is, the incidence of fights, students threatening teachers, and so forth)."[34] In other words, differences in educational attainment crucially depend on differences in order and discipline. The inference one may draw is that creating a secure and fair environment is a necessary precondition to learning. Similar results were obtained by Michael Rutter and his colleagues in their study of twelve London schools.[35] These studies have been criticized, but not supplanted or destroyed. In my judgment, their results may be modified but their central findings will in general be substantiated. There have been several reviews of the burgeoning literature on effective schools and many come to similar conclusions, sometimes described as the "six-factor model": Effective schools tend to have strong principals who provide leadership in instructional matters, to have teachers with high expectations of student achievement, to emphasize learning basic skills, to maintain good order and discipline, to evaluate students on a regular basis, and to devote large amounts of time to study.[36]

There is disagreement about how many of these factors are essential and about the quality of the evidence supporting their importance.[37] But there can be little doubt that, whatever their impact on educational achievement, schools with similar students can and do differ dramatically in their order, atmosphere, and ethos. To most students and parents, these are no small accomplishments.

Some Generalizations

Organization matters, even in government agencies. The key difference between more and less successful bureaucracies, if these three cases are any guide, has less to do with finances, client populations, or legal arrangements than with organizational systems.

Only two groups of people deny that organization matters: economists and everybody else. To many economists, government organizations are like firms: black boxes that convert, at the will of a single entrepreneur, inputs into outputs. Until very recently, the firm had been the atom of economics, the irreducible unit of analysis whose behavior was that of a disembodied intellect calculating the marginal costs and revenues of alternative courses of action. Of late, some economists have become interested in why firms should exist at all and, once they do, how those in charge get their subordinates to do what they consider rational from the firm's point of view. This concern has been elaborated into theoretically interesting (though, as yet, empirically rather arid) arguments about the relationships of principals and agents. This is an issue to which we shall frequently return. But as economists have extended their interest in the firm to include government agencies, they have brought with them, by and large, the conventional view of the firm, that is, somebody (an entrepreneur, a bureau chief) maximizing his or her utility under a set of market or political constraints. That bureaucracies may adopt different organizational arrangements with different consequences is still about as foreign a notion as the possibility that some business firms may act in ways not predicted by marginal-cost economics.

Noneconomists do not need to be told that firms and agencies are complex entities with an internal life far more subtle and changeable than anything that could be described as a maximized utility. But having thrown out the economists' bathwater, they often toss out the organizational baby with it. The most frequent remark I hear from people in all walks of life with respect to organizations is that it's not the organization that's important, it's the people in it.

Now, there is a great deal of truth in the view that people make a difference, just as there is much truth in the view that most of us (most of the time) follow the course of action that will increase our net money benefits. But there are two errors in the "only people matter" view. The first is that people are the products, not only of their biology, family, and schooling, but of their organizational position (or role, as sociologists have put it). As Herbert Simon said many years ago, a person "does not live for months or years in a particular position in an organization, exposed to some streams of communication, shielded from others, without the most profound effects upon what he knows, believes, attends to, hopes, wishes, emphasizes, fears, and proposes."[38] Erich von Manstein and Heinz Guderian, George Beto, Norris Hogans and Kenneth Tewel—these were not simply gifted people who happened to be generals, prison administrators, or school principals; they were people whose views and skills had been shaped by the organizations in which they spent their lives.

Moreover, what they were able to accomplish depended on having the authority and resources with which to act. This is the second difficulty with the view that only people matter. Herbert Simon again:

> If organization is inessential, if all we need is the man, why do we insist on creating a position for the man? Why not let each create his own position, appropriate to his personal abilities and qualities? Why does the boss have to be called the boss before his creative energies can be amplified by the organization? And finally, if we have to give a man some measure of authority before his personal qualities can be transformed into effective influence, in what ways may his effectiveness depend on the manner in which others are organized around him?[39]

Many readers will agree with this and still respond, "yes, but the exact organizational structure surely did not determine the success of Guderian, or Beto, or Hogans." Perhaps. But this view rests on a common error, the confusion of organization with organizational structure. An organization is not simply, or even principally, a set of boxes, lines, and titles on an organizational chart. An organization, in the words of Chester Barnard, is a "system of consciously coordinated activities or forces of two or more persons."[40] The most important thing to know is how that coordination is accomplished.

In the German army, the system of coordination was designed to enhance in lower-ranking soldiers and officers the capacity for independent action toward a general goal and within an overall system of discipline. In the Texas prisons, the system was designed to achieve exactly the opposite effects: not independent action toward general goals, but immediate and reflexive obedience of detailed rules. At Carver High School, the major coordinating effort was aimed at reducing disorder and instilling school spirit and personal self-esteem.

If organization matters, it is also the case that there is no one best way of organizing. Take the question of centralization or decentralization of authority. In the Texas prisons, authority was rigidly centralized and that centralization was regularly made visible by George Beto's frequent walking tours of a prison yard or cellblock. In the German army, authority was equally hierarchical, but the right to give orders or make decisions (which is the essence of authority) was left, to a degree that would have startled French or British generals, in the hands of corporals, sergeants, lieutenants, and captains. At Carver High, there was no doubt who was the boss, but that boss could not run each and every classroom; Norris Hogans had to let teachers teach (which is to say, exercise a great deal of authority). The best he could hope for was that he had instilled a sufficiently strong sense of purpose and could manage a sufficiently powerful set of incentives that the teachers would work hard to use their authority well and on behalf of common purposes. If these first two chapters had included more organizational examples, the variety of coordinating systems would have been even greater. A research laboratory or foreign ministry could not possibly have been run along the lines of the German army or the Texas prisons.

In trying to understand the success of these three organizations, one has to understand how they coped with three organizational issues. First, each had to decide how to perform its *critical task*. By critical task I mean those behaviors which, if successfully performed by key organizational members, would enable the organization to manage its critical environmental problem. For the German army, the problem was the killing power of dug-in machine guns and artillery. The critical task was finding the solution to this problem. There was a technological solution (the tank) and a tactical solution (infiltration). The Germans made use of both, principally the tactical solution. For the Texas Department of Corrections, the critical environmental problem was maintaining order among numerically superior, temperamentally impulsive, and habitually aggressive inmates. The critical task became the elaboration and enforcement of rules sufficiently precise, understandable, and inflexible that inmates would never acquire the opportunity for independent or collective action. For Carver High School the critical environmental problem was the fear, disorder, and low morale among students and teachers. The critical task was to carry out a highly visible, even dramatic attack on these feelings by a relentless program to clean the buildings, keep them safe, and motivate the students.

Notice that I have referred to tasks, not goals. It is often the case that many analysts and executives who wish to improve an organization begin by trying to clarify its goals. Sometimes this is useful. But government agencies, much more than business firms, are likely to have general, vague, or inconsistent goals about which clarity and agreement can only occasionally be obtained.[41] Often any effort to clarify them will result either in the production of meaningless verbiage or the exposure of deep disagreements. The German, French, and British armies all had the same goal—to defeat the enemy. Thinking harder about that goal would not necessarily have led to any deeper understanding of how one defeats an enemy. At some level, the Texas and Michigan prisons may have had similar goals—to keep order, rehabilitate inmates, incapacitate criminals, or deter would-be criminals. But if either organization sought to improve itself by thinking harder about these goals, it probably would have discovered that it did not know how to do some of these things (rehabilitate), could only guess at whether it was able to do others (deter), and would be internally divided over the relative importance or even the meaning of others (order, incapacitation). At Carver High, "educating children" was to some degree a purpose shared by everyone, but if a new principal had devoted himself or herself to clarifying the meaning of education, there would have occurred an interesting seminar but not much change.

Of course, tasks cannot be defined completely without regard to goals. The two are related but in a way that is often complex and uncertain, especially in government bureaucracies. In later chapters I will take up this relationship. I hope for now it is sufficient to assert that on the basis of the three cases considered so far, tasks and goals are not connected in the straightforward way that is implied by the notion that tasks are "means" logically related to "ends."

The second challenge overcome by these three organizations was agreement about and widespread (if not enthusiastic) endorsement of the way the critical task was defined. When that definition is widely accepted and endorsed, we say the organization has a sense of *mission*. (The German army even used a variant of that word—*auftragstatik*—to define what it was trying to achieve.) In all three organizations, members took pride in what the organization was doing and how it was doing it. At Carver High, as with many schools that undergo wrenching change, pride was never universal. Some teachers resisted the changing distribution of authority, others probably disliked the emphasis on order and pageantry. But in time, through persuasion or replacement, Hogans's sense of mission became that of the school.

The third problem that each organization had to solve was to acquire sufficient freedom of action and external political support (or at least non-opposition) to permit it to redefine its tasks as it saw best and to infuse that definition with a sense of mission. Each organization managed to acquire a reasonable degree of *autonomy*. George Beto had the support of key Texas politicians and business leaders. Norris Hogans had the moral, if not financial, support of the Atlanta superintendent of schools. The advocates in the German army of linking flanking and infiltration tactics with *blitzkrieg* penetrations did not get their way unaided; many of them, including Guderian, Rommel, and Manstein, had to overcome the suspicion and even hostility of more traditional German commanders. Cavalry, artillery, and even infantry officers resisted the new doctrines. Adolf Hitler's intervention on behalf of the innovators was decisive.[42]

An Analytical Perspective on Organizations

This book is primarily descriptive: it is an effort to depict the essential features of bureaucratic life in the government agencies of the United States. In Part II, I try to describe how the rank-and-file employees of these agencies decide what to do, in Part III how agency managers decide what to do, and in Part IV how agency executives decide what to do. But it is not merely descriptive. In sorting out the examples, I have been struck by the fact that the concepts useful in explaining what was distinctive about the German army, the Texas prisons, and Carver High School are also useful in explaining how employees, managers, and executives function in police departments, regulatory agencies, the Forest Service and the Park Service, the State Department and the CIA, the Social Security Administration and the Postal Service.

First, rank-and-file employees (or, as I shall refer to them, operators): Why do they do what they do? The formal goals of the organization are sometimes helpful in explaining this, but more often what operators do will depend on the situations they encounter (what they see as the "critical environmental problem"), their prior experiences and personal beliefs, the expectations of their peers, the array of interests in which their agency is embedded, and the impetus given to the organization by its founders. For any distinct bureaucratic unit, these factors combine to produce an organizational culture—a distinctive way of viewing and reacting to the bureaucratic world—that shapes whatever discretionary authority (and it is often a great deal) the operators may have. When that culture is a source of pride and commitment, the agency has acquired a sense of mission.

Second, managers: The further managers are from the day-to-day work of the agency, the more their lives are shaped not by the tasks the operators are performing or the goals the agency is serving but by the constraints placed on that agency by its political environment. These constraints limit their ability to allocate resources, direct workers, and work toward goals. Despite these constraints, managers must try to manage. How they do this will depend on the kind of agency in which they work.

To help simplify the incredible variety of agencies, I describe in chapter 9 four types—types based on the extent to which the goals of the agencies are clear and the work of the agencies' operators is observable. The concrete examples that are the source of my observations are sorted out, to the extent they can be without doing excessive violence to reality, into "production," "craft," "procedural," and "coping" agencies.

Third, executives: Executives, in trying to maintain their agencies (and their own position in them), worry about retaining control over their turf—a popular bureaucratic word for what I call "autonomy." No agency has or can have complete autonomy, but all struggle to get and keep as much as they can. In pursuing their twin goals of maintaining their agencies and maintaining their political position in the larger governmental world, executives follow a variety of strategies (described in chapter 11) and sometimes encourage innovations (described in chapter 12).

After the reader has acquired a worm's eye view of American (especially federal) government agencies, the context in which these bureaucracies work is described in Part V. That context consists of the struggle among the president, Congress, and the courts for control of agency actions. At the end of Part V, all this description is viewed from afar by asking (in chapter 16) how and why public administration in the United States differs from that found in other more or less democratic nations.

The final part describes the chief bureaucratic problems, in particular inefficiency and arbitrariness, of which citizens complain (chapter 17) and then analyzes the major alternatives for coping with those problems—applying rules (chapter 18) and using markets (chapter 19). The final chapter returns to armies, prisons, and schools as a way of seeing what we have learned in the intervening pages and then asks why so few government agencies act as if they had learned and were prepared to apply the lessons that can be drawn from these three examples.

Though this is not a book about how to run a bureaucracy but one about why bureaucracies are run the way they are, I cannot refrain in the final pages from offering some modest suggestions for running them in a somewhat better manner or from indicating why, in my opinion, even these suggestions are unlikely to be heeded. To reassure any bureaucrats who may read this book, the reason why my advice (and theirs, for I have learned many of these ideas from them) is not going to be followed has nothing to do with the limitations or inadequacies of individual bureaucrats and everything to do with the constitutional regime of which they are a part. Readers who want to get immediately to the "bottom line" can spare themselves the hundreds of pages that follow and turn immediately to Federalist Paper number 51, written two centuries ago by James Madison.

PART II

OPERATORS

CHAPTER 3

Circumstances

TO A BUSINESS EXECUTIVE, the importance of tasks and mission is old hat. Figuring out how best to define tasks and motivate workers to perform those tasks is often described as creating the right organizational culture. The voluminous literature about effective firms repeatedly stresses these matters, urging business executives to emulate "the one hundred best firms" or "the Japanese" or "Theory Z" or whatever is currently the fashionable model of well-run enterprises. The literature on public administration, however, rarely mentions these matters. Save for a few celebrated exceptions, books on government agencies hardly refer to organizational culture at all. There will be chapters on structure, planning, decision making, and congressional oversight—all important matters, to be sure—but none on what the organization *does* or the problem of getting people to *want* to do it.

The omission of much discussion of tasks and incentives in these books may partly reflect the academic interests of their authors, but to a large degree it accurately captures the world of the government executive. In the United States, high-level government executives are preoccupied with maintaining their agencies in a complex, conflict-ridden, and unpredictable political environment, and middle-level government managers are immersed in the effort to cope with the myriad constraints that this environment has imposed on their agencies.

Government executives spend much more of their time and energy on handling, face to face, external constituencies than do business executives. One example: The chief executive officer of the New England Electric System (NEES), a firm with assets of nearly $4 billion, revenues of almost $1.5 billion per year, and a work force of over five thousand persons, meets with his board of directors for three or four hours about six times a year;

much of the business is routine, the meetings are invariably amicable, and the CEO almost always gets what he wants. During one period studied by the author, the director of the Federal Bureau of Investigation, an agency with about 22,400 employees and a budget of $1.4 billion, met with his "board of directors"—the several congressional committees having authority over the FBI—more than eighteen times a year.[1] The meetings were often long and acrimonious and the director frequently did not get what he wanted. To finance its projects, NEES could use retained earnings or borrow funds in the bond market; to finance its projects, the FBI could neither retain nor borrow money but had to get appropriations from Congress. The money borrowed by NEES was its own to use for the term of the loan (usually many years); the money obtained by the FBI was available only for one year and then had to be reappropriated. The press rarely investigated NEES but often investigated the FBI.

Government executives must spend so much time coping with their agencies' external environment that they have relatively little time to shape its internal life. Moreover, the typical presidential appointee is only in office for 2.5 years (2.2 years if you exclude regulatory commissioners).[2] As a result, the tasks of a government agency are more likely than those of a firm to be defined by factors other than the preferences of the executive.

Tasks versus Goals

You might think that these limits on leadership are not very important; after all, cannot we infer what an agency will do by looking at its stated goals? If you believe that, open the *United States Government Manual* to almost any page. There you will find statements such as the following:

- Promote the long-range security and well-being of the United States [Department of State]
- Facilitate the full development of the human and natural resource potential of Indian and Alaska Native people [Bureau of Indian Affairs]
- Organize, train, and equip active duty and reserve forces for the preservation of peace, security, and the defense of our nation [Department of the Army]
- Develop viable urban communities by providing decent housing and a suitable living environment [Office of the Assistant Secretary for Community Planning and Development of the Department of Housing and Urban Development]

- Foster, promote, and develop the welfare of the wage earners of the United States [Department of Labor]
- [Achieve] the orderly development and operation of broadcast services [Federal Communications Commission]

All these goals are unclear because reasonable people will differ as to the meaning of such words as "well-being," "potential," "security," "viable," "decent," "suitable," "welfare," "orderly," and "development." Moreover, even if they should agree on the meaning of one goal, they will disagree as to what other goals should be sacrificed to attain them. Should the "full" development of Indians be pursued even if it means the destruction of the native culture of a given tribe? Should "decent" housing be supplied without regard to cost? What balance should be struck between the interests of over-the-air broadcasters, cable broadcasters, and satellite operators in "developing" broadcast services? Should the reserve forces of the army be trained to the extent of calling up reservists for active duty without regard to their civilian occupations and personal preferences?

Many private bureaucracies also have goals that are just as vague and hard to attain as those of public agencies. What is the goal of Harvard College? To educate youth? To preserve and enhance culture? What do these words mean, and how do we achieve whatever state of affairs they supposedly describe? If you cannot answer these questions, how can you decide what professors at Harvard should do? Since nobody can infer professorial tasks from collegiate goals, who defines these tasks, and how? Private colleges, as well as most other private organizations, may not do any better than government agencies in defining their tasks, but being private, they are competitive enterprises supported by the voluntary payments of clients and benefactors. These contributors are free to reward the colleges that please them and shun those that displease them. A government agency, by contrast, is usually a monopoly provider of some service and is supported by a legislative appropriation that is paid for by taxes extracted from citizens who may or may not benefit from that agency. The tasks of operators in private organizations with vague goals become defined through a process of trial and error and internal negotiation that is then tested by competitive natural selection. Some organizations prosper, others merely survive, still others fail. The tasks of operators in government agencies with vague goals are probably set in much the same way, but without a regular test of the fitness of the solution.

To understand a government bureaucracy one must understand how its front-line workers learn what to do. Let us call those workers the operators. (Just who is an operator is not always easy to know, but in general it is a person who does the work that justifies the existence of the organization—teachers in a school, guards in a prison, doctors and nurses in a hospital, patrol officers and detectives in a police department, combat soldiers in an army, check-writers in a disbursing agency, letter sorters and carriers in the Postal Service, grant-givers in a funding agency, diplomats in the State Department, and so on.) The work of the operators is the place to begin because it is their efforts that determine whether the agencies' clients (that is, we the people) are satisfied. Moreover, one cannot say many interesting things about the structure, incentives, and leadership of an agency without first knowing what behaviors are supposed to be organized by those structures, motivated by those incentives, and directed by those leaders.

This is not usually the way government agencies are viewed. As mentioned in the last chapter, there is a tendency among us all to complain about how far the performance of an agency differs from its goals and to speculate about the bureaucratic "pathologies" that may account for this inadequate performance. But that only makes sense if the goals are sufficiently clear that reasonable people can agree on what they mean, and whether the agency has the freedom of action (the authority and resources) necessary to achieve them. A clear goal is an "operational goal."*

Some government agencies do have clear (or operational) goals, and what the front-line workers do can be inferred from them. In the next section, we shall look at some examples. When the agencies have vague or inconsistent goals (as is usually the case), what the workers do will be shaped by the circumstances they encounter at the job, the beliefs and experiences they bring to the job, or the external pressures on the job. Much of this chapter will consider circumstances, especially what I call "imperatives" and peer-group expectations. In the next chapter, we shall look at four factors that are brought to the organization by its members—prior experiences, professional norms, personality, and ideology. In chapter 5 we shall look at forces that are part of the organization's environment—the demands of interest groups.

Defining Tasks: Goals

The Social Security Administration (SSA) has operational goals, at least with respect to the retirement program it administers, and has the freedom and resources with which to pursue them. It is required by law to

*By goal I mean an image of a desired future state of affairs. If that image can be compared unambiguously to an actual state of affairs, it is an operational goal. If it cannot be so compared, and thus we cannot make verifiable statements about whether the goal has been attained, it is a general goal. "Tax adjusted gross incomes at the rate of 28 percent" is an operational goal; "award broadcast licenses so as to serve the public interest, convenience, and necessity" is a general goal. Public agencies rarely have single, clear goals. Their ends are often general and always multiple. For a fuller discussion of these distinctions, see

send a check each month to every eligible retired person in the nation. The amount of the check is determined by an elaborate but exact formula, the eligibility of the recipient by well-understood laws and regulations. The SSA performs this task with remarkable precision, considering that it pays out claims of one kind or another to 35 million people and collects taxes from 110 million more.[3]

Matters are much more complex with respect to its goal of aiding disabled persons because the law is ambiguous as to what constitutes a disability. As a result, there has been more controversy about how the SSA defines its task of helping the disabled than about its task of helping the elderly.[4]

There are, of course, conflicts in the goals of the Social Security *program*. Some think payroll taxes should be set so that each person receives in benefits an amount that reflects how much he or she paid in; if that is done, the rich will get bigger retirement checks than the poor. Others think that taxes should be set so as to put a floor under the benefits of the poor; if that is done, then benefits no longer will be related to what recipients paid in taxes. People disagree over whether benefits should be indexed to inflation and whether people should be entitled to full benefits at ages 62 or 65 or 68. But these policy questions do not of themselves create organizational difficulties in the retirement program: SSA can define its tasks by inferring them from its goals, whichever of these goals is selected.

That SSA can define its tasks by knowing its goals does not mean it will suffer no bureaucratic problems. As we shall see in later chapters, the agency has had a lot of trouble in acquiring and using efficient computers and has been torn asunder by various reorganization schemes. But these problems arise, not from ambiguity about its goals, but from political constraints. These constraints determine how much money is allocated for administration, the salaries it offers to attract key personnel, the identity of the administrator, and the process by which it is allowed to acquire new equipment. The constraints do not affect how it defines its tasks (though in a different political environment they could). In short, SSA is able logically and free politically to define its tasks by reference to (most of) its goals.

That definition traditionally has been this: "Our central task is to pay benefits on time and accurately." Around this simple view has arisen an organizational culture, at least in the field offices of SSA, that emphasizes service. A study by the General Accounting Office (GAO) described "SSA's culture" as involving "face-to-face public service." This culture, in turn,

---

Edward C. Banfield, "Note on Conceptual Scheme," in M. Meyerson and E. C. Banfield, eds., *Politics, Planning, and the Public Interest* (New York: Free Press, 1955), 303ff. Scholars will recognize my heavy indebtedness to Banfield.

implies the maintenance of many field offices each with high staffing levels (even when consolidation and staff reduction might result in substantial savings in administrative costs).[5] A top-level SSA administrator confirmed this to me in an interview in 1987: "Out in the field, the service ethic is very strong," though he added that "consistency" (that is, following the eligibility rules) was as important as "service." This culture is reinforced by congressional insistence that field offices not be reduced in number (there are 1,300 of them, in addition to approximately 4,000 smaller "contact stations"). The service ethic is sufficiently strong that when a new SSA administrator announced that she wanted more field offices to be open during the evening and on weekends and to allow beneficiaries to make appointments (rather than show up and wait in line), the field offices by and large welcomed what many other government agencies would have viewed as an objectionable burden.

The United States Post Office, before it was transformed into the semi-independent United States Postal Service, also had relatively clear goals. Deliver the mail as quickly, cheaply, and accurately as possible. Of course, how much one is willing to sacrifice in cheapness or accuracy to maximize speed of delivery was a matter of dispute. But the goals at least permitted the postmaster general to specify the tasks the Post Office would perform: collect, sort, and deliver mail. But unlike the Social Security Administration, the Post Office did not have the political freedom to define those tasks on its own. Letter carriers had enough power to influence how their jobs were defined, members of Congress had more than enough power to decide how many post offices there would be and where they would be located, the White House would decide when to ask for a rate increase, and organizations representing interested users (publishers, greeting-card manufacturers, direct-mail advertisers) would pressure Congress to keep rates down.[6] Even after the reorganization that produced the Postal Service, some of these constraints on the postmaster general remained in ways that have impeded (though not as much as formerly) the creation of a culture appropriate to achieving the organization's goals.

Defining Tasks: Situational Imperatives

When goals are vague, circumstances become important. Chief among those circumstances are the situations with which operators must cope on a daily basis. Suppose you take a job as a police officer, prison guard, school teacher, State Department desk officer, or inspector in the Occupational Safety and Health Administration. When you report for work the behavior of your clients and the technology available to you will powerfully shape what you do, no matter what the stated goals of the organization may be.

Rookie cops are told this the first day on patrol. "Forget what you learned in the police academy," veteran partners or sergeants will tell them. "I'll show you what police work is really all about." Energetic police administrators often try to prevent this street-corner socialization, but they only succeed within narrow limits, if at all, because the patrol officer, working alone or with one partner, must impose authority on people who are unpredictable, apprehensive, and often hostile. Most of the time when an officer on patrol is summoned, by radio call or passing citizen, he or she can expect to encounter a situation in which great discretion must be exercised over matters of the utmost importance (life and death, honor and dishonor) involving frightened, drunk, quarrelsome, confused, angry, injured, evasive, or violent people.[7] The officer in this situation must exert his or her authority—must "take charge." At least in large American cities (and I suspect elsewhere as well), the uniform and badge do not automatically signify authority to which people will defer. The officer's behavior must supplement and extend such authority as the law may confer. This is especially important when the clients are involved in a quarrel—a domestic dispute, a street-corner brawl, or an argument between landlord and tenant, shopowner and teenagers, etcetera. These circumstances require that order be restored or maintained. But as we have seen, order is a matter of opinion and the methods of maintaining it a matter of art, not science. Though it is the officer's most difficult task, it is also the most common. In one study, nearly a third of all calls for service involved order maintenance, and if accidents (which often involve quarreling motorists) are added to the total, these situations accounted for well over 40 percent of the officer's calls.[8] By contrast, only 10 percent of the calls were matters that clearly involved stopping or solving a crime.

Even when a serious crime has occurred and the goal of the organization is thus reasonably clear ("find and bring to justice the perpetrator"), the circumstances surrounding the investigation are often confused and even chaotic. The officer soon learns that not all victims give a complete or honest account of their losses: The "stolen T.V." may have been taken back by its owner from a "victim" who earlier had "borrowed" it, the "stolen car" may never have existed, or the "assault" may have been started by the victim who then lost the fight.[9] The officer quickly discovers the value of being wary and skeptical. When a suspect is found (and that is not often) he or she will often lie and sometimes try to escape.

All of these circumstances lead the street cop to define the job not in terms of "enforcing the law" but in terms of "handling the situation." To handle the situation, one must first "take charge." Out of the need to take charge, supplemented by a sense of the physical danger inherent in the occupation, the officers develop what Jerome Skolnick has called a "working personality."[10] William Muir has shown that this personality is not always the same: In his superb study of the Oakland Police Department, he found that the officers had different ways (some better, some worse) of taking charge.[11] But take charge they all did, for that was the essence of their task.

Now, it may be objected that a situational imperative such as "take charge" is not much of a job description, especially if there are many different ways of taking charge. That is true. What these difficult, face-to-face situations produce might be described more accurately as an overriding concern with which the operator must somehow cope. The situation defines the outer limits of his or her freedom of action, and thus the outer limits of what will be determined by organizational goals or individual personality. For reasons set forth in chapter 11, the heads of government agencies often ignore these situational factors and thus either allow operators to manage them by instinct or induce the operators to manage them in ways that lead to ineffectiveness, disorder, or corruption. In chapters 11 and 12, a few examples—they are all too few!—will be given of executives who have not only understood situational imperatives but provided a way of handling them which reconciles the operators' desire for survival with the executive's desire for effectiveness.

The employees of prisons and mental hospitals, like police officers, encounter situational factors so powerful as to make formal organizational goals all but meaningless. The stated goals of a prison may include deterring crime and rehabilitating criminals, but the reality of prison life, more than these goals, determines the job of a correctional officer. These realities have been well stated by, among others, Gresham Sykes: Prisoners are typically young, energetic men who have, on the average, committed several crimes before they enter prison for the first time, and many are serving their second or third sentence. They outnumber the guards. In many prisons they have little difficulty fashioning weapons out of shop tools and dining-hall cutlery. From time to time there is a riot, occasionally one of extraordinary savagery (as in New Mexico in 1980). Sometimes there is an escape.

You are a correctional officer. Whatever the administrators may say is the goal of your institution, to you the central imperative is to stay alive and unharmed. If there is a riot or an escape, you will be at best criticized and at worst killed. To avoid that you must control the inmates. *Control*—not deterrence, not rehabilitation—becomes the defining focus of your energies.[12] Precisely how you go about achieving and maintaining control will vary with your personality and the administration of the prison. You could practice terror. You could turn prison management over to powerful con bosses who by force, extortion, and guile manage the inmates in ways that keep them from threatening you. (The con bosses will expect favors from you in exchange for their valuable services—contraband, privileges, power. You will have to pay.) You could give the inmates more rights and freedoms in hopes that this will pacify them. You could attempt to regulate their daily lives by the systematic administration of rewards and penalties. *How* you perform your task will vary depending on how you, in turn, are supervised, but the central problem will be defined, whatever that supervision may be, by the imperatives of the situation you confront daily.

For a long time, attendants in mental hospitals faced a similar imperative. The goals of the hospital might be to cure mental illness or promote mental health, but the institution typically did not have at its disposal the means to produce mental health even assuming its administrators could give a coherent and unambiguous definition of what constituted it. Doctors, psychiatrists, and social workers might do their best to treat the patients in their care, but for you, the ward attendant, the central fact of daily life was that you were in charge of people who engaged in erratic, sometimes bizarre behavior, who did not follow orders as healthy people might, and who were sometimes incoherent, incontinent, and violent. Your task was to manage these people so as to minimize the threats and inconveniences they posed for you. This could be accomplished by restraint, sedation, isolation, electroshock therapy, or the granting and withholding of privileges. The precise means used would be set by hospital policy (albeit with some evasions), but the end toward which these means were directed was determined more by the situation in the wards than by the stated goals of the institution.[13] In this respect, you as an attendant were in much the same position as a prison guard or patrol officer—asserting and maintaining control, even though legally the persons in your charge were not suspects or convicts.

Mental hospitals have changed. The advent of tranquilizing drugs has made it possible to reduce the number of people in these institutions and to control those who remain with more benign, chemical means. This has no doubt improved the quality of life in many hospitals. Whether it has changed fundamentally the task of the attendant is unclear. A mental hospital is different from a general hospital because patients in the latter are ordinarily welcomed back to their homes by their families and friends, and thus it is not necessary to have a core staff of operators whose task it is to control the behavior of people who do not want to be there and whom their families do not wish to take back.

Schoolteachers ordinarily do not have to deal with criminals, convicts, or mental patients, and the goal of their organization, to educate the young, is less ambiguous than that of other client-serving institutions. Though we may argue about what constitutes education, we can agree on certain components of it; learning to read and write, for example, are in almost everybody's view an essential part of education. A teacher is achieving the goal of the organization when he or she teaches these skills and failing to achieve it when he or she does not.

But if learning is, to a degree, an understandable goal, it is not the only concern of the classroom teacher. As Willard Waller pointed out over half a century ago, the teacher faces two tasks: focus student energies to produce learning and control student energies to maintain order.[14] In principle the two tasks are complementary: For learning to occur, order must exist. But in practice the two tasks can diverge sharply. In some circumstances, the preoccupation with order dominates the concern for learning. There is some evidence, for example, that schools in lower-status communities display a greater concern for order than do those in upper-status ones.[15] That relationship might exist because either community expectations or pupil behavior (or both) shape the way teachers define their tasks.

Situational imperatives may seem to have their greatest effect on how operators define their tasks when the organization must deal with uncooperative or threatening clients face-to-face. But the situation may shape tasks even in organizations that are not, in Michael Lipsky's term, "street-level bureaucracies."[16] The United States Department of State does not derive its tasks from some clearly understood goal. Indeed, some critics claim that the men and women who work in State engage in no meaningful tasks at all. Diplomats are caricatured as "cookie pushers," "equivocaters," or "partygoers in striped pants." Needless to say, the foreign service officers who comprise the core of the professional personnel at State do not see themselves in this light. To them, their activities involve work toward a goal of great importance—representing and advancing the interests of the United States abroad. They are engaged in producing "foreign policy." The agency does other things as well—it issues passports and visas and runs educational exchange programs with other nations—but its central activity is to help define foreign policy.[17]

But what is foreign policy? What are the legitimate interests of the United States? No one can answer these questions with any clarity, partly because people disagree about what our interests are and partly because even those who can agree realize that those interests change in unpredictable ways with changing circumstances. Even supposing we can agree on a definition of interests, how do we know what course of action will achieve them? The State Department has goals, but they are so general that no executive can derive from them a clear definition of the department's tasks.

Despite all this ambiguity and conflict, thousands of foreign service officers go to work every day and do something. What is it they do? Why is it they do these things rather than others? What they do is in large measure defined for them by the environment in which they find themselves. Daily they confront a torrent of paper and delegations from other nations. Each piece of paper, every delegation, involves an act of foreign policy. These officers must develop a daily routine by which to manage this torrent in a way that is, arguably, related to the attainment of that vague goal, to "represent and defend national interests." As Donald P. Warwick argues in his insightful study of the State Department, the production of foreign policy involves tasks that occur at all levels and in response to even minor actions within the department. "A consular official's decision to refuse a visa to a student activist in Latin America is as much an expression of U.S. foreign policy as formal proclamations opposing student radicalism."[18] There is no distinction between "policy" and "administration"; almost every administrative act has policy implications and may, indeed, *be* policy whether intended or not.

Foreign service officers "maintain relationships" by the careful exchange of written memoranda with each other and the representatives of foreign powers. "Boiled down to specific tasks, the most direct expression of policy is a written report," Warwick observes. "Words and paper take on enormous importance in the life of the State Department."[19] The central task of diplomats is determined by the need to deliver, respond to, and comment on written reports. A self-evaluation conducted by the department in 1970 confirmed this in language that cannot be improved upon:

> The Service has prized drafting ability above almost all other skills. We emphasize this skill in recruitment and reward it generously in our promotion system. The prize jobs in the service are the reporting jobs. Foreign Service Inspectors habitually examine reporting officers "chron" [i.e., chronological] files to determine whether there has been an adequate volume of production. Little wonder that our ablest and most energetic officers literally seek out opportunities to report, whether the need is urgent or not.[20]

When any action may have policy implications and thus be subject to political criticism after the fact, people taking those actions will have a natural tendency toward caution. Police officers know this and thus, despite a popular impression of over-zealousness fostered by occasional reports of misused authority, tend to proceed cautiously in most instances and, if anything, to underenforce the law.[21] But police work does not invariably leave a paper trail, and so patrol officers are relatively free to use their discretion without worrying that each and every act will be reviewed by people who have regular access to the documents produced by the exercise of that discretion.

The central constraint on those diplomats who perform the reporting task is the constant awareness that the written word *is* policy and thus is subject to close and often hostile scrutiny. As we shall see in later chapters, this task shapes the management system of the State Department and leads to many of the criticisms made of the Department from the outside—criticisms that are often based on a misunderstanding of what diplomats can and cannot reasonably be expected to do. A task defined by situational imperatives leads to the development of an organizational culture that emphasizes caution.

Even when goals are relatively clear, the situation can define the tasks if one way of doing the job seems easier or more attractive. In that case, we say that technology (used broadly to refer to any set of tactics) determines tasks. The Occupational Safety and Health Administration (OSHA) is charged by law with promulgating rules designed to improve worker safety and health. The organizations that pressed for this law were pretty much in agreement that industrial hazards presented a greater threat to worker health than to safety. From time to time workers may be injured by a machine lacking a safety feature or by a poorly designed ladder, but these risks, serious as they are, are not as grave as the prospect of thousands of workers becoming ill or dying as a result of exposure to toxic chemicals. Moreover, both workers and factory managers already have incentives to reduce accidents—such a reduction spares employees obvious pain and suffering, increases productivity, decreases sick leave, and cuts the cost of insurance. By contrast, neither workers nor managers may be aware of health hazards or, if they are aware, they may discount the importance of hazards that will exact their uncertain toll at some distant date.

Given these circumstances, one would expect that most of the regulations issued by OSHA in its formative years would address health hazards. Not so. As John Mendeloff has shown, OSHA has done more to address safety than health concerns.[22] The reason has nothing to do with insidious interest-group pressures or distorted personal values.[23] Regulation-writers find it much easier to address safety than health hazards. The former are technically easier to find, describe, assess, and control than the latter. A worker falls from a platform. The cause is clear—no railing. The effect is clear—a broken leg. The cost is easily calculated—so many days in the hospital, so many days of lost wages, so much to build a railing. The directive is easy to write: "Install railings on platforms." But if a worker develops cancer fifteen years after starting work in a chemical plant, the cause of the cancer will be uncertain and controversial. The cost of the disease will be hard to calculate. The solution will be hard to specify: One can write a directive that says "reduce exposure to chemical X," but medical science will provide only imperfect and controversial guidance to such questions as these: "Reduce by how much?" "Over what length of time?" "With what likely benefits?" As a result of these difficulties, OSHA has been criticized ever since its creation for how slowly it has issued health standards and those that have been issued have been hotly contested.[24]

Wars provide perhaps the most compelling examples of technology determining tasks. An army may allow the existence of a new weapon to determine how it defines and manages the tasks of combat soldiers. Generals are often accused of preparing to fight the last war. That is not a fair criticism. Since no general, at least in modern times, can know with any certainty what the next war will be like, all he has to draw upon in making his preparations are experience and conjecture. Since conjecture is, after all, conjectural, experience inevitably will play a large and proper role in guiding his plans. Successful generals do not ignore the lessons of the past. No one knows in advance what the lessons will be, but some people guess better than others.

As we saw in chapters 1 and 2, French and German generals drew different lessons from World War I. The French believed that artillery and machine guns would dominate the battlefield in the future as they had in the past, and so designed the tasks of infantry around these weapons. The squad was organized to service the machine gun and fixed fortifications were built to protect the infantry. The Germans drew a different lesson: the advantages of artillery and the machine gun could be overcome by maneuver and mobility. The squad was organized to find and exploit, by independent action, weaknesses in the enemy front. The French plans were driven by close attention to technology; the German plans, brilliantly successful, were based on an effort to outwit technology. The command system implied by this distinction in the way tasks were defined led, in the case of the French, to an organization so centralized and inflexible as to be unable to adapt quickly and effectively to the unexpected German tactics. In the case of the Germans, the command system was relatively decentralized and improvisational, and so was able to adapt to almost anything that might transpire.

Some observers believe that the American army might have been more effective in Vietnam had it not been organized around technological innovations that turned out to be inappropriate to the circumstances of the war. The availability of the helicopter, the computer, and sophisticated communications systems made it dangerously easy to centralize control of the war in the hands of distant headquarters. Jobs once performed by sergeants, captains, and majors on the battlefield were now being performed by colonels, generals, and politicians observing the battle from helicopters, hearing about it on radios, or getting data about it from computers.[25]

The critical environment challenge was not simply to defeat the North Vietnamese regular army, but to wrest control of the South Vietnamese villages from the Viet Cong guerrillas. For most of the war, the American army not only did not do this, it did not try very hard. Village defense required sending small detachments to remote places where they would live and work with the natives. In such situations, there was little advantage (and possibly considerable risk) in having massive firepower or advanced technologies.

The critical tasks of the army had been defined previously by the overriding army goal of defending Western Europe against a Soviet armored attack. Most of the units sent to Vietnam had been organized and trained with this in mind. What might work on the plains of Bavaria would not necessarily work in the remote highlands of Vietnam. Interestingly, the one American armed service that tried hard to develop a village defense program was the Marine Corps, a force not organized and trained to fight massive armored battles in Europe. Lightly equipped and with a history of fighting in small wars, the marines in Vietnam quickly developed a village-oriented tactic (the Combined Action Platoons) whereby small units would move into a South Vietnamese village and stay there, committed to defending it against enemy attacks while helping the natives to develop the ability to defend themselves. By all accounts, the marines succeeded in providing greater security to Vietnamese villages at lower casualty rates than did the army.

The army's reaction, according to Andrew F. Krepinevich, was "ill-disguised disappointment, if not outright disapproval."[26] It made only halfhearted efforts to emulate the marines' tactics, preferring (at least until General Creighton Abrams assumed command late in the war) to rely on search-and-destroy missions involving massive attacks by large units against such Vietnamese forces as could be lured into major battles. Scholars disagree as to why army doctrine did not change in response to the realities of war in Southeast Asia. The initial doctrinal emphasis clearly came from having the tasks and structure of the army determined by the need to defend Western Europe and to do so by deploying heavy firepower and advanced technologies that would minimize human losses. In Vietnam that emphasis was probably reinforced by political constraints at home—the perceived need to win battles, inflict heavy (and measurable) losses on the enemy, and generally follow a strategy that might produce a quick victory (and thus avoid the slow erosion of political support). Defenders of the army doctrine argue that the U.S. did not have the forces to follow a village strategy, at least while large units from the North Vietnamese regular army were operating in the south. Critics claim that there were sufficient forces to fight both a village and a large-unit war. What is clear is that for whatever reason tasks were defined more by available technology and prior experiences than by a clear understanding of what kinds of tasks were appropriate to the conditions of war in Vietnam.

Defining Tasks: Peer Expectations

War is the greatest test of a bureaucratic organization. A government agency recruits a large number of poorly paid young men, sends them to some distant and hostile land, and exposes them to the murderous attacks of an unknown foe. It is hard to decide which kind of combat is the most terrorizing—standing erect in drill formation while musket fire rips through your ranks, huddling in a foul and soggy trench while artillery shells drop down upon you, walking through dense jungle not knowing when you will fall into a fatal ambush, or charging across an open field in the face of devastating machine-gun fire. Those who argue that the behavior of an organization is nothing more than the sum of the behaviors of its rationally self-interested members cannot account for an army at war. By almost any standard, the rationally self-interested behavior for a soldier facing the prospect of imminent death or injury is to break and run. As the great military historian John Keegan puts it, "inside every army is a crowd struggling to get out."[27]

There are, of course, rewards and penalties that can be used to induce an army to stand and fight. A soldier who deserts under fire can be caught, court-martialed, and punished. But if soldiers desert en masse, there will be no one to catch them. And even if many were caught and punished, any given soldier might decide rationally that the uncertain prospect of a delayed penalty is less fearsome than the immediate prospect of a painful death. Sergeants and captains can threaten to shoot deserters on the spot, and on occasion they have done just that. But what then keeps the sergeants and officers from running? It is not likely to be the prospect of being shot by colonels and generals who are few in number and (often) distant from the battle scene. In past times, the prospect of loot gave soldiers an interest in winning the battle. But like a court-martial, the prospect of loot is distant and uncertain while the enemy's fire is immediate and palpable. Moreover, while loot may have been important in past battles when small armies fought for dynastic and material objectives, it is of little significance in modern wars in which mass armies struggle for political goals. In 1916, no British soldier could have imagined that there was any loot in Bapaume that was worth his marching into the German machine-gun fire at the battle of the Somme. To some extent, the rational instinct to run, or at least hide, may be overcome with drugs: Keegan notes that at Waterloo and at the Somme, many soldiers got drunk just before the battle, but anyone so drunk as to not know the dangers he faced was probably also so drunk as to be unable to stand and fight. Yet stand and fight they did.[28]

Nor can the willingness to fight be explained by general beliefs about one's nation, the war as a whole, or one's place in the army. During the Second World War, many observers supposed that soldiers with low morale (that is, they didn't like being soldiers in general or being in this war in particular) would be less effective in combat than those with high morale. In fact, as Samuel Stouffer and his colleagues showed in their classic study, *The American Soldier*, there was during World War II no correlation between morale and combat effectiveness.[29]

What does matter are the rewards a soldier receives from other soldiers. At the battle of Waterloo, soldiers who flinched in the face of the enemy were reproved by other soldiers. This was facilitated by deploying the troops in formations that made each man constantly aware of the men on either side of him. To desert meant to disgrace oneself in the eyes of a comrade. Moreover, the tight formations had the paradoxical effect of making each man *feel* safer though in fact he was not. After all, if he left the formation, the enemy was not likely to waste a shot at him, whereas if he remained in the formation he was certain to be the object of concerted fire. It was group solidarity that was decisive in keeping the ranks intact.[30]

This solidarity was reinforced by the leadership, example, and coercive powers of the officers. But what kept the officers fighting? They were not drawn up in tight formations and there were no pistols at their backs. At Waterloo, the answer was honor. "Officers . . . were most concerned about the figure they cut in their brother officers' eyes. Honor was paramount."[31] A century later, at the battle of the Somme, when soldiers no longer fought standing in close ranks and officers were no longer drawn from the nobility, the same factors—a degree of coercion, greatly supplemented by group solidarity and a sense of honor and reputation—kept the British Army intact in the face of fearful losses.[32]

Soldiers fight when the men next to them expect them to fight. Soldiers fight well when they are members of cohesive small groups and led by officers they trust; they fight poorly when the group lacks cohesion and the officers cannot inspire trust. Their generalized attitudes and political views—how they feel as individuals about soldiering, patriotism, or the war—seem much less important.

Making peer expectations serve organizational needs is difficult at best and requires at a minimum that peers stay together for long periods. If the membership of the small group frequently changes, there will be a decline in the value individuals assign to the opinion of others; the new people will be emotionally less important than the old ones. Many critics have argued that the policy of replacing American combat soldiers on an individual rather than on a group basis weakens the cohesion of the group to which the individual replacements are assigned.[33] In Vietnam, small-group cohesion often broke down almost completely, as evidenced by the abnormally high rates of desertion, grenade attacks on officers ("fraggings"), and refusals to go into battle.[34] Though reasons for this crisis in discipline are complex, frequent personnel rotations appears to have contributed to it. Soldiers had less confidence in their oft replaced peers and leaders. This social instability became especially acute just before an individual soldier was scheduled to return to the United States; having weak ties to his comrades in any event, he was especially loath to take risks when in a month or two he would be on his way home. The evidence suggests that a soldier's discipline was especially weak during the period just preceding his departure for the States.[35]

When an organization that exposes its members to mortal dangers does a poor job of managing small-group cohesion, those groups will start to define tasks independently of the organization. The U.S. Army in Vietnam pursued a search-and-destroy strategy, but platoons and companies in which group cohesion had broken down would often informally pursue a "search-and-evade" strategy: nominally going out to engage the enemy, actually going out to avoid him.[36] The phenomenon is not limited to armies. In Alvin Gouldner's classic study of a gypsum plant, one group of workers, the miners, would sometimes defy the company's managers because their jobs involved physical dangers so acute that they would refuse to accept certain orders. "Down here we are our own bosses," the miners would say, and accordingly they would refuse to work in places where they believed the risks were too high.[37] Note, however, that great as the dangers were, peer-group solidarity was sufficient to get men to work in the mines. Peer expectations are both a source of motivation and a force defining what are acceptable and unacceptable tasks.

If the expectations of peers can be so important in the desperate conditions of combat or lurking hazards of mining, we should expect them to have some effect under ordinary circumstances as well. Take narcotics investigators. The goal of reducing the availability of dangerous drugs does not unambiguously imply a clear set of tasks. If dangerous drugs are imported and distributed by large criminal organizations, then the best strategy would seem to be to identify and investigate those organizations until a legally sound case can be brought against them. But to establish that a dangerous drug is being illegally sold, it is first necessary for an undercover officer to buy that drug from an illegal dealer. One way to build a case against the criminal organization is to arrest the dealer, persuade him to become an informant in exchange for dropping the charges, and then use his information to identify and arrest higher-level dealers, thereby working one's way up to "Mr. Big." But another way is to use intelligence leads to identify higher-ups in the organization and investigate them by means of surveillance, wire taps, and the collation of documentary evidence.

The leaders of the Drug Enforcement Administration (and its predecessors, the Bureau of Narcotics and Dangerous Drugs and the Federal Bureau of Narcotics) from time to time have emphasized one or the other of these two strategies, but the operators—the street agents—have tended to define their jobs as one of making undercover buys and lower-level busts. The reason for their resistance to defining their jobs as intelligence gatherers and document readers is that the culture of the street agent rewards officers who are skilled at making buys and busts. As one administrator put it, they feel that "there is something wrong with a guy who will pass up the buy tonight."[38] Undercover work is dangerous and requires strong nerves and considerable skill. To sustain themselves in these tasks, the agents depend on the respect of their fellow agents. But that respect comes in time to form a set of expectations that resists change, and so it is no easy matter to convert street agents into document readers.

That peer groups affect task performance will hardly be news to anyone familiar with the classic studies done at the Hawthorne plant of the Western Electric Company. There, as every student of organization knows, men who wired together the electrical connections in telephone equipment restricted their output to conform to a group norm, thereby producing less than the amount of work that would have maximized their wages.[39] To a degree, peer rewards were sufficiently important to offset money rewards.

I am making a somewhat different point: Peer expectations not only affect how hard people work at their jobs, they can affect what they decide the job *is.* Soldiers will stand and fight rather than cut and run (here peer expectations induce rather than limit performance); miners will dig in dangerous—but not too dangerous—places; narcotics agents will buy and bust rather than watch and wait; police officers will decide when and how to use force and make arrests.

Conclusions

Given these great differences in how the work of government agencies actually gets defined, it is foolish to speak about bureaucracy as if it were a single phenomenon. When tasks can be inferred freely and unambiguously from the stated goals of a government agency, they can be defined by the agency's executive and, given proper leadership, can become the basis of a strong organizational culture. The Social Security Administration is an example. When goals are relatively unambiguous but the agency lacks the political freedom to convert those goals into tasks, the formation of a suitable culture becomes much harder. The Post Office was an example. When the goals are too vague or ambiguous to permit them to become a ready basis of task definition, the tasks often will be shaped not by executive preferences but by the incentives valued by the operators. This is especially true in government, where the need to acquire and maintain external support for an agency is so great as to divert all but the ablest and most energetic executives from careful task definition. Moreover, for reasons to be explained in chapter 8, government executives have limited influence over subordinates because the incentives controlled by managers are weak and hard to manipulate. Thus in a public bureaucracy the tasks of its key operators are likely to be defined by naturally occurring rather than by agency-supplied incentives.

Among these naturally occurring incentives are the imperatives of the situation (especially important when clients are subjected to unwanted controls in low-visibility circumstances, as with the police, mental hospital attendants, and schoolteachers, or when the organization has embraced a dominant technology, as has been the case with some military organizations) and the expectations of peers (especially important when the organization exposes its members to dangerous circumstances, as is the case with miners, narcotics investigators, and combat soldiers).

These incentives emerge from within the organization. A skillful executive can sometimes shape them in ways that lead the workers to define their tasks as the executive wishes, a matter that will be explored in chapter 6. But workers may bring to the organization attitudes, predispositions, and preferences that will make them responsive to incentives over which the organization has relatively little control. That is the subject of the next chapter.

CHAPTER 4

Beliefs

WHEN RICHARD NIXON became president in 1969, he was worried that the federal bureaucracy would sabotage his administration's plans. To Nixon, the government agencies over which he nominally presided were staffed by liberals recruited by past Democratic administrations who would resist his conservative policies. Richard Nathan, a political scientist, has given us a vivid account of the efforts made by the Nixon White House to control or bypass what were often described as "New Deal bureaucrats."[1]

Nixon's worries were nothing new. When the Labour party came to power in Great Britain in 1945, its leaders suspected that the British civil service, most of whose members had been hired by Conservative administrations, would sabotage Labour plans to expand the welfare state and nationalize major industries. To make matters worse, the higher echelons of the British bureaucracy had been recruited from among the graduates of the elite British universities, chiefly Oxford and Cambridge, and these institutions were thought to be bastions of Tory privilege and seedbeds of Tory opinions. A book reflecting these fears had been published shortly before the Labour victory. In it, J. Donald Kingsley argued that democratic control over government was weakened to the extent that the administrators of government programs were unrepresentative of the people at large.[2]

Attitudes and Behavior

Both liberals and conservatives fear that the attitudes of bureaucrats will determine how they define and perform their tasks. Such concerns will strike most people as reasonable. In our daily lives we often explain the behavior of a spouse or child, friend or co-worker, as reflecting his or her attitude. If a family member performs a household chore reluctantly or moodily, we account for this by saying that he or she has an uncooperative or sulky attitude. If politicians favor higher welfare payments, we explain this by saying that they are liberals; if they want to cut those payments, we take this as a sign that they are conservatives. Given these common experiences, the preceding chapter may strike many readers as beside the point, if not plain wrong. Why talk about situational imperatives and formative experiences when what diplomats, police officers, or antitrust lawyers do is the result of their attitudes?

If that is your view, it may come as a surprise to learn that psychologists do not find much evidence that behavior is explained by attitudes. "Reports of rather low or insignificant relations between attitudinal predictors and behavioral criteria have been accumulating for more than 40 years," conclude two scholars after an exhaustive summary of the literature.[3] "The present review provides little evidence to support the postulated existence of stable, underlying attitudes within the individual which influence both his verbal expression and his actions," concludes another scholar after finishing his review of the available studies.[4] And in one of the most dramatic tests of a social science prediction, the fears of the Labour party and of J. Donald Kingsley turned out to be unfounded: The Labourites came to power, passed laws enlarging the welfare state and nationalizing industries, and the supposedly reactionary British civil servants faithfully carried out the new policies.

Why do these common beliefs about the power of attitudes seem to be so wrong? An attitude is a person's evaluation of some entity (a policy, an object, another person) in his or her environment. The assumption that attitudes explain behavior is equivalent to saying, for example, that how we behave toward our job depends on how we evaluate it (whether we like or dislike it). But our behavior toward an object will be influenced not only by our evaluation of it but by the rewards and penalties associated with alternative courses of action. These influences include not only those controlled by persons in authority (our parents, our boss) but also those controlled by co-workers (for example, their approval or disapproval). When we realize that attitudes must compete with incentives for influence over our behavior, it is not surprising that attitudes often lose out to the rewards we seek or the penalties we try to avoid.

Consider intake workers in welfare offices. They interview applicants for Aid to Families with Dependent Children or General Relief and determine their eligibility. Many observers believe that what welfare workers do is governed by their attitude toward welfare recipients: Liberals often think the workers are nosy skinflints; conservatives often suppose them to be mush-headed do-gooders. To judge from the working atmosphere in welfare offices, one might infer that the liberals are right. The offices are unattractive, even intimidating. Jeffrey Prottas, who spent many months observing work in several local offices of the Massachusetts Department of Public Welfare, described them this way:

> Welfare applicants frequently have to wait several hours before they are seen by a worker. The surroundings are not congenial. Waiting areas are always crowded and dismal. No one can (or will) provide the least clue to the probable length of the wait or what will happen next. There are always some applicants who leave before seeing a worker.[5]

But if we conclude from these facts that welfare workers handle clients in this way because the former have a negative attitude toward the latter, we shall be very much mistaken. For one thing, the people hired as welfare workers are not substantially different from those hired to work in hotels, insurance companies, and real estate offices, where one encounters a very different atmosphere—typically, one that is bright, cheery, and helpful. The reason has little to do with attitudes and almost everything to do with incentives. In the welfare office, workers are trying to ration scarce resources among needy clients seeking a "free" good (a welfare check); the business firms, by contrast, are trying to induce customers to make a voluntary purchase.

For another thing, differences in the way affairs are conducted among different welfare officers are largely unrelated to the attitudes of the workers. Tana Pesso compared two welfare offices in Massachusetts and found that in one, the intake clerks treated the clients with more respect and consideration than in the other. In the first office, the workers met with the clients behind closed doors, spoke to them in friendlier terms, and gave them a bit more help as they struggled to understand the document they were about to sign; in the second, there was little privacy, fewer explanations, and no extra assistance. The offices had workers with similar backgrounds. The differences were the result of how the offices were managed: in the first, supervisors stressed that workers be considerate; in the second they did not.[6]

But the differences between the two offices were much less significant than their similarities. All workers valued convenience and equity over accommodation and responsiveness. That is to say, the welfare workers acted so as to minimize both the burdens of handling a clientele that was often complicated, demanding, and uncooperative and the likelihood that their decisions would later be described as unfair or unjustified. The price of convenience and equity (or justifiability) was unresponsiveness to individual wants.[7] This is fully in accord with what Prottas found. The more amenable and deferential the client, the more helpful the worker. The more aggressive, demanding, and knowledgeable the client, the less helpful was the worker. Put another way, when the client cooperated with the worker so as to minimize the latter's costs, the latter provided better service; when the client refused to cooperate and thus raised the worker's costs, the latter provided less service.[8]

In short, the imperatives of the situation more than the attitudes of the worker shape the way tasks are performed in welfare offices. The key imperative is to reconcile the wants of a variegated and somewhat suspect group of petitioners with the organizational need for achieving equity and managing the large case load.

Welfare workers, of course, must labor under the eyes of their supervisors, and accordingly we might expect their attitudes to have only a modest influence on their behavior. But many public employees work alone or in pairs outside the purview of supervisors. Surely in these cases individual attitudes will shape behavior. Consider police officers on patrol in a racially mixed city. In 1966, sociologists Donald Black and Albert Reiss interviewed such officers in three large northern cities about their racial attitudes. Most white officers expressed critical views of blacks. Some of these officers were, by any standard, bigoted. Black and Reiss also arranged to have these officers observed while on patrol. Despite their views, the officers arrested black and white suspects in comparable circumstances at about the same rate.[9] Here, an important aspect of task definition—deciding whether to use an arrest to handle a situation—was made on grounds having little to do with the race of the suspect, and thus presumably little to do with the racial attitudes of the officers. Attitudes may have affected how the police spoke to citizens (Black and Reiss had no data on that), but they did not define the job itself, i.e., the circumstances under which an arrest was appropriate. That seemed to be defined by the circumstances of the moment (for example, whether there was a victim present who wanted an arrest) and by some shared understanding among the officers as to what constituted grounds for an arrest.

Individual attitudes may not even determine whether in the heat and fright of a tense moment the police shoot their guns at citizens. James Fyfe studied police shootings in New York City. He compared the rate at which blacks were shot by black officers and white officers, and found that black officers were about twice as likely to shoot at black civilians as were white officers. When the duty assignment of these officers (e.g., what kind of precinct they worked in) was held constant, black and white officers were about equally likely to use deadly force.[10] Given this finding, it is hard to believe that racial attitudes were the sole or even the most important determinant of police behavior.

Even when attitudes do make a difference, it is possible for organizations to change behavior without changing attitudes. In the early 1970s, the rate at which police officers shot civilians (who were disproportionately black) in Birmingham, Alabama, was over four times greater than the rate at which they shot them in Washington, D.C., even though the crime rate in Washington was more than twice as high as in Birmingham. In Detroit, police used deadly force (again, disproportionately against blacks) at a rate twice that of the police in Oakland, California, even though the two cities had comparable crime rates and populations. But when new police administrators took office in Birmingham and Detroit, the rate at which the police used deadly force dropped dramatically even though the crime rates were increasing.[11] It is hard to imagine that these sharp differences and dramatic changes in behavior were the result of great differences or sudden changes in attitudes. It is more likely that they were the result of managing rewards and penalties.

Similar findings by the dozen have come from the inquiries of industrial psychologists and sociologists. If attitudes determine behavior, then employees with poor morale or little job satisfaction would display higher rates of absenteeism and lower rates of productivity then those with high morale and much job satisfaction. In fact, there seems to be little, if any, relationship between satisfaction and absenteeism or productivity.[12] This is not to say that there are no individual differences related to productivity; as we shall see in chapter 8, some traits *do* predict job performance, but these do not include generalized attitudes.

Attitudes (and ideology) will influence how a job is performed if the job is weakly defined—that is, there are few clear rules specifying how it should be done and few strong incentives enforcing those rules. Voting in any election is a weakly defined "job" (or role, to use the sociologists' term). As a result, people are free to vote their beliefs. Playing second base for the Boston Red Sox is a tightly defined job. The position and moves of that man are shaped by very precise rules and understandings and reinforced by powerful incentives—an umpire's call, a manager's fine, an owner's contract, a crowd's applause. No serious baseball fan would waste much time trying to learn about the attitudes or political opinions of second basemen.

The roles that can be played in a government agency range from those that are almost as highly defined as that of a second baseman to those that are only slightly more structured than that of a voter. People who sit at computers all day and type in data on social security earnings are performing tasks so mechanical that one can imagine their being replaced some day by a machine. But other tasks, like those of a police officer or schoolteacher, are quite unroutinized. What these people do importantly depends on varying and unpredictable circumstances. The role of an antitrust lawyer or a foreign service officer lies somewhere in between. Personal beliefs can have a large effect on how tasks are defined when the role to be played is not highly specified by laws, rules, and circumstances and when the operator playing that role receives relatively weak rewards from the organization itself.

Many government agencies are filled with operators performing loosely defined roles—lawyers, scientists, engineers, diplomats, physicians, criminal investigators, forest rangers, and administrative law judges, to name but a few. Some of these people also receive money wages from their agencies that are less than what they could receive doing similar tasks for private firms. To varying degrees, all of these operators bring to their work predispositions about how the job ought to be done. These predispositions come from their prior experiences, their sensitivity to professional standards, their political ideology, and perhaps their personality characteristics. When such operators play a role that is weakly defined, they will tend to play it in ways consistent with these predispositions.

Defining Tasks: Prior Experiences

When a government agency is created, it is not assembled out of people who are blank slates on which the organization can write at will. Except for young employees getting their first jobs, the operators will have worked for other organizations, often other government agencies. Indeed, most new agencies are formed out of bits and pieces of old ones—the Department of Energy absorbed employees from the Interior Department, the Federal Power Commission, and the Atomic Energy Commission; the Department of Education acquired former members of the Department of Health, Education, and Welfare; the Drug Enforcement Administration inherited investigators from the Customs Service and the Bureau of Narcotics and Dangerous Drugs. These people had learned certain ways of doing things. If a new agency has ambiguous goals, the employees' prior experiences will influence how its tasks get defined.

When the Economic Cooperation Administration (ECA) was created in 1948 to implement the program of assistance to Europe popularly known as the Marshall Plan, it had, in Herbert A. Simon's phrase, a "prenatal history."[13] Determined to get off to a fast start, the first administrator, Paul Hoffman, borrowed personnel from other government agencies. But he did not borrow them to perform tasks that were already well understood; the nation had never run a Marshall Plan before, and no one was quite certain how to do so.

As a consequence, the tasks of the ECA were defined, at least at the outset, by people who had learned how to do things in other agencies. In the State Department there already existed a group providing interim aid to France, Greece, and a few other countries. There were also people in the departments of Agriculture, Commerce, and the Interior who knew how to find commodities and ship them overseas. These people brought with them to the ECA a conception of foreign aid that involved figuring out what kinds of commodities (wheat, oil, and so on) were needed by what countries and in what amounts and then approving or disapproving particular shipments.[14] Because *something* had to be done, and quickly, these people were allowed to decide, without much supervision or direction from the executives of the ECA, what to do and how.

But there were other ways of running a foreign aid program. One was to encourage economic cooperation among European nations so as to rationalize its war-torn industry and open up larger, continent-wide markets. Some people from the State Department brought this conception with them. Another was to loan money to these countries on the basis of the estimated economic value of particular projects and then let the Europeans use this capital to produce their own commodities and services. People entering ECA from the Export-Import Bank brought this approach with them. A third was to use American money to help improve the European balance of trade. Estimates would be made of what Europe would consume and produce and of the shortfall, if any, between consumption needs and production possibilities. Economists brought this methodology with them.

As Simon makes clear, no one thought through in advance what the tasks ought to be and the organization that was created to house these tasks was designed with little regard for the work that would be done in it. "If the name of the agency had been taken off the [Budget Bureau's] proposed organization chart, it would have been extremely difficult to determine whether the organization was to engage in foreign assistance, salt mining, or the practice of law."[15]

As time passed and experience was gained, some definitions of the task prospered and others waned. The key factors that determined the survival of a given task definition was, first, how workable it was (could people in fact get the job done) and how strongly it was supported by external allies (other agencies and groups in Congress). Initially, the commodity approach prevailed—there were people at their desks who knew how to ship goods abroad and they had allies in other agencies. The economic cooperation approach did not make much headway. No one knew how to produce "cooperation," and if it were produced at all it would have to be done overseas, in the Paris office of the ECA, rather than in Washington. Thus, this approach was not likely to dominate thinking at agency headquarters. In time, the economists working on the balance-of-trade approach began to win out over the pure commodity specialists.

Experiences in other agencies also helped define what tasks the newly formed Central Intelligence Agency (CIA) would perform. When it was created (first by executive order in 1946, then by statute in 1947), the CIA was intended to be a coordinating mechanism that would synthesize the foreign intelligence produced by other agencies, in particular the State Department and the military services. Its tasks were supposed to be "coordination, planning, evaluation, and dissemination."[16] Today people forget that the Director of Central Intelligence has two functions: he directs the CIA and also makes recommendations for the coordination of the *entire* intelligence community.

But what does one do when one "recommends ways to coordinate"? That is a question to which we shall return in later chapters; it suffices for now to say that given the realities of turf wars among government agencies the answer is not much, and that only with great difficulty. What the CIA in fact would do was powerfully influenced by the people it hired. Some of these people were specialists in writing intelligence reports—something akin to the synthesizing and coordinating roles the agency was supposed to perform. But once the government decided to have a clandestine service capable of gathering information and carrying out covert operations, there was no other obvious bureaucratic home for it but the CIA. It was a momentous change, for it brought into the agency many people who had formerly worked for the Office of Strategic Services (OSS), the wartime agency that had not only done research but managed spies and conducted covert operations behind enemy lines.

The OSS alumni transferred to the CIA a conception of intelligence work that they had learned in an activist, highly secret, can-do organization: produce your own intelligence by clandestine information gathering and advance U.S. interests by taking covert actions on behalf of friends and against enemies. By 1947, possibly one-third of the CIA's employees had come from the OSS.[17] Their influence was even greater than their numbers might suggest. A history of the agency prepared for a Senate committee investigating its activities in 1976 concluded that "in large part, CIA's functions, structure, and expertise were drawn from the OSS."[18] In particular, "although the Agency was established primarily for the purpose of providing intelligence analysis to senior policymakers, within three years clandestine operations became and continued to be the Agency's preeminent activity."[19]

This shift did not occur surreptitiously nor was it the case of the tail wagging the dog. The OSS operational veterans brought to the CIA experiences that constituted an alternative definition of that organization's central task. The choice confronting the agency was (in oversimplified form) "to coordinate" and "to act." Nobody was quite certain what the first meant but everybody was aware that, if done at all, this task would make the CIA a rival of other intelligence organizations that would naturally resent and resist being guided, interpreted, or synthesized by some upstart bureau. OSS veterans knew exactly what the second task involved, because they had done it for many years.[20] Other intelligence agencies might resent a rival clandestine collection effort, but that was easier to tolerate than a coordinating effort. And the other groups, especially State, were not eager to take on one kind of secret work—covert operations—abroad.

The OSS alumni brought with them a clear, workable task; the Agency soon saw that this task helped it solve its organizational maintenance problem. The Agency's political superiors, deeply worried about Soviet expansion in Eastern Europe and Soviet-sponsored civil wars in Western Europe, were delighted to have at their disposal an agency that could do something about these things.[21] And do it they did: The CIA helped finance elections in Italy, organize revolution in Guatemala, and direct counterrevolution in Iran.

The impact of organizational experience on the definition of tasks is perhaps most vivid in the joint military commands that bring together officers from the army, navy, and air force. Everyone recognizes, of course, that members of a military service, or any organization, will try to defend and advance the interests of their parent organizations whenever they are placed in an interorganizational setting. That is a matter to be explored more fully in the chapter on autonomy and turf. I am here arguing a different point: that prior organizational experiences affect how new organizational tasks are defined even when there is no desire to engage in turf wars.

Arthur T. Hadley, a journalist with extensive military experience, has remarked on how a military service, especially in wartime, gives to its members a distinctive way of looking at new tasks.[22] An army officer learns to be part of an organization that can do nothing without extensive coordination of human efforts. The smallest self-contained fighting unit is a division (or a reinforced regiment) consisting of thousands of personnel performing a myriad of specialized tasks. Tanks, artillery, infantry, antiaircraft, signals, engineering, and intelligence must operate on the basis of a common plan. But even this unit can only survive if it moves in concert with other regiments and divisions. Moreover, army officers are open to constant inspection by higher-ranking officers. The army experience produces people who can accept, more easily than representatives of other services, the coordinating tasks that are the reason for existence of joint military commands and staffs.

The young naval officer has a different experience. A ship is a self-contained unit that can be maneuvered independently of other units. On board ship, hierarchy is powerful and actions are constantly monitored, but *among* ships there is a freedom of action and degree of isolation from the rest of the military (and society at large) that is much greater than what a typical army officer experiences. Air force pilots acquire the greatest tendencies toward independence. Flying a jet aircraft is a solitary and exuberant activity that requires exceptional physical skills. Those proficient at it tend, in Hadley's view, to be somewhat intolerant of those who are not, especially those who haven't even tried. Hadley's characterization of the consequences of military experience, which he admits is overdrawn, may help explain why navy and air force officers may *tend* to do less well in managing interservice coordinating tasks than their army counterparts.

Defining Tasks: Professional Norms

During a typical week, the Federal Trade Commission (FTC) in downtown Washington, D.C., receives several dozen letters from individuals and firms complaining about what the writers believe are the unfair business practices of certain enterprises. These letters are screened by an Office of Evaluation consisting of several attorneys. Many of the letters are simply gripes about behavior that does not violate any federal law; others contain accusations that may involve a violation; and still others call attention to what appear to be clear cases of wrongdoing. While these letters are being reviewed, the Office also learns from newspaper stories about planned corporate mergers. If the merger is a large one, the firms involved must notify the FTC directly. Meanwhile, economists in the FTC make recommendations for the investigation of certain industries that seem to be dominated by a small number of large firms or that appear to be making abnormally high profits. All of these sources of information go to an Evaluation Committee that recommends to the top officials of the FTC which cases should be investigated and which should not.

In reaching these decisions, the FTC gets rather little guidance from the statutes. These are the Federal Trade Commission Act and the Clayton Act. They make it illegal for firms to engage in "unfair" or "deceptive" methods of competition, practice certain forms of price discrimination, or buy (or merge with) other firms if the effect of this "may be to substantially lessen competition or tend to create a monopoly." As political scientist Robert A. Katzmann and others have pointed out, these words are too vague to provide clear guidelines for deciding what to do. The FTC has produced an *Operating Manual*, but it does not tell the Evaluation Committee exactly what these statutory words are supposed to mean or how to decide what cases to bring.[23] Yet cases are brought and lawyers go to work on them. Somehow, the tasks of the FTC get defined with sufficient clarity to enable its staff to know what to do.

What does tell the employees of the FTC what to do is, to a significant degree, the professional norms that they have learned and the career opportunities those professions hold out to them.

Medicine, nursing, engineering, economics, the law—these and countless other occupations are popularly referred to as professions. People engaged in a profession often get more respect, income, and deference than do people who work at "ordinary" jobs. But a popular label is not a useful definition. What is distinctive about members of a profession, at least for purposes of explaining organizational behavior, is not how much status, income, or deference they receive but the sources of these rewards. A professional is someone who receives important occupational rewards from a reference group whose membership is limited to people who have undergone specialized formal education and have accepted a group-defined code of proper conduct. The more the individual allows his or her behavior to be influenced by the desire to obtain rewards from this reference group, the more professional is his or her orientation. Thus, not every member of an occupation whom we think of as a professional may in fact be a professional. An attorney who serves a client even when that service is likely to incur the displeasure of the bar association and law school professors is not a professional (though he or she may be an excellent attorney); by the same token, a physician who follows the procedures recommended by other physicians and by medical school professors even when it is not in the best interests of the doctor is highly professional.

In a bureaucracy, professionals are those employees who receive some significant portion of their incentives from organized groups of fellow practitioners located outside the agency. Thus, the behavior of a professional in a bureaucracy is not wholly determined by incentives controlled by the agency. (We might define a bureaucrat as someone whose occupational incentives come entirely from within the agency.) Because the behavior of a professional is not entirely shaped by organizational incentives, the way such a person defines his or her task may reflect more the standards of the external reference group than the preferences of the internal management.

The tasks performed by employees of the Federal Trade Commission crucially depend on whether they are lawyers or economists. As Robert Katzmann has shown, attorneys prefer to pursue a case in which there is clear evidence that the conduct of some firm violates the law. They are prosecution-minded. This orientation reflects both their training in the law and court procedures and (in many cases) their desire to use the skills they develop at the FTC to land a job with a well-paying, prestigious law firm. They evaluate potential cases on the basis of the strength of the evidence and the reigning interpretation of antitrust law. Economists, by contrast, are trained to evaluate potential cases in terms of their likely impact on consumer welfare. To them, an easily prosecuted case of business misconduct may have no impact on the prices consumers pay or the quality of goods they receive, and so economists argue against taking on these cases and in favor of finding cases that involve large concentrations of economic power that if broken up might unleash competitive forces which will make consumers substantially better off.[24] Moreover, the FTC economists are disproportionately drawn from among those who studied at or were influenced by the University of Chicago. "Chicago economics" emphasizes the social benefits of free markets.

The lawyers reply that economists, especially Chicago ones, are prone to pick cases on the basis of economic theory rather than legal reality, cases that are difficult to investigate and may find little support in the courts. At the extremes, a lawyer is happiest with an allegation that two companies have illegally conspired to fix prices, while an economist is happiest with the discovery that the size and market power of the Exxon corporation may reduce competition in the oil industry.

Differences within the FTC over what the agency's job should be are not simply professional preferences about policy choices; they are competing visions, sometimes invested with a good deal of emotion, as to how best to discharge a public responsibility. Lawyers sometimes refer to economists as "case killers," "dogmatic" people engaged in "God-playing." For their part, economists see themselves as social scientists—as "dispassionate searchers for truth"; lawyers, on the other hand, are seen as people less interested in truth than in finding facts to support a predetermined case.[25]

The government lawyers' professional orientation toward prosecution was also noted by Arthur Maass in his study of federal investigations of state and local political corruption. Federal law provides no clear justification for the many heavily publicized cases brought by U.S. attorneys against mayors, judges, city councilmen, and state legislators. Nor can the desire for partisan advantage explain the sharp growth in such cases since the mid-1970s: prosecutors in both Republican and Democratic administrations have pressed these investigations. What drives the program, Maass concludes, "is the prosecutorial mentality" coupled with the personal career benefits that come from having sent some corrupt local official to prison.[26]

But lawyers are not wholly professional in their outlook. They are, after all, trained to serve the interests of a client and may do this with little regard for what other lawyers think. Even in the FTC, some lawyers endorsed the shift toward investigating large structural cases of the sort that, beginning in the 1970s, many FTC commissioners favored. And personal advantage, such as getting a job in a big firm or laying the groundwork for a campaign for governor, reinforces their occupational bias toward vigorous prosecution.

Engineers, on the other hand, rarely benefit personally from bringing the norms of the engineering profession into government service. When they define vague or ambiguous tasks in ways that conform to engineering predilections, it is usually without the added incentive of enhanced opportunities for winning elective office. This strong professional orientation helps explain why the National Highway Traffic Safety Administration

(NHTSA) has acted as it has in discharging its responsibility to reduce death and injury on the highways. By law, NHTSA could have chosen to improve the skills and habits of drivers, enhance the design of roads, or eliminate the defects in the autos; to some extent, it has done all three. But to a remarkable degree, it has favored changing the automobile rather than the driver or the highway. Charles Pruitt explains this as the result of the decision to staff the agency predominantly with engineers. In part this decision was made knowing—and wanting—its consequences.

Born in a crisis atmosphere after a bruising congressional attack on the auto manufacturers, NHTSA felt it had to take immediate, highly visible action to improve auto safety. Educating people to drive more safely was a policy that would have taken years to produce results (if in fact it would have produced any results at all); redesigning the car to meet federal standards could be done much more quickly. The redesign that could be made the fastest was one intended to make the car more "crashworthy"—for example, less likely to impale a driver on a steering column or light switch. No doubt cars have become more crashworthy in part as a result of NHTSA rules, thereby vindicating the initial hiring decisions. But the decision to staff the agency with crash engineers (instead of specialists in driver education, alcohol abuse, or highway design) had long-term consequences that may not have been intended.* These engineers worked persistently and enthusiastically to require the installation of air bags (devices that, in the event of a crash, deploy automatically to protect the occupants), despite the intense political controversy engendered by this proposal. Moreover, NHTSA resisted demands from other federal agencies that it devote more attention to human and environmental factors in highway safety.[27]

The impact of the engineering profession on the work of the National Aeronautics and Space Administration (NASA) has been frequently remarked. When the space shuttle Challenger exploded, killing its crew, there was a review to find out what happened. The engineers in NASA and the firms supplying NASA were a gifted and dedicated group that had accomplished extraordinary feats. But their approach to their work may have created blind spots. Engineers value quantitative data and distrust personal opinions. Thus, the anxieties that some may have felt about the readiness of the shuttle to be launched were not as forcefully expressed as they might have been or attended to as seriously as they should have been because they were perceived as hunches, not facts or numbers. One engineer working on Challenger put it this way: "I have been personally chastised in flight readiness reviews at Marshall [Space Flight Center] from using the words 'I feel' or 'I think,' and I have been cruci-

*Hiring scientists and engineers shapes private firms as well as public agencies. For an early insightful account, see Tom Burns and George M. Stalker, *The Management of Innovation* (London: Tavistock, 1961), 174–76.

fied . . . because 'I feel' and 'I think' are not engineering-supported statements, but they are just judgmental."[28]

Even in a highly bureaucratic welfare office, some of the intake workers have acquired, by virtue of their training and experience, a quasi-professional attitude toward their clients. As a consequence, though the situation presses them to treat clients equally and distantly (as explained previously), a few operators whom Prottas observed tried to think of themselves not as intake clerks but as social workers. Contrary to the views of those who believe that welfare workers seek to degrade or punish applicants, many of these bureaucrats wished to use what little discretion they had to help clients, or at least those who seem to be "deserving." To the extent circumstances permitted (which given the case loads and organizational requirements was not much), "they look[ed] forward to opportunities to behave as social workers, which means an opportunity to do something more than the routine processing of simple cases."[29]

Nowhere is the influence of professional norms more evident than in the contrasting histories of two otherwise similar agencies: the Forest Service and the Park Service. The former, created in 1905, and the latter, created in 1916, each manage vast tracts of public lands, many of which are so similar as to be indistinguishable. The two agencies, with roughly comparable functions, often have been bitter bureaucratic rivals. But the Forest Service from the first committed itself to develop and be guided by a doctrine of "professional" forestry, by which was meant the scientific management of forests in order to produce a sustained yield of timber and other natural resources. Though this utilitarian focus was later modified, the commitment to professional education and research never changed. By the time Herbert Kaufman studied it in the 1950s, 90 percent of all rangers were trained foresters, meaning that they had at least a bachelor's and sometimes a master's degree in forestry or some related subject.[30] Most are members of the Society of American Foresters.[31] The Forest Service provided the impetus for much of this professional education and, in turn, is now molded by the doctrines developed in those schools and societies. In recent years, many Forest Service practices, such as clear-cutting and below-market timber sales, have become controversial. However, right or wrong, these policies are not the result of having caved in to economic interests; they reflect beliefs about what good forest management requires. To change the way Forest Service tasks are performed today would require equivalent changes in forestry doctrine that is probably beyond the capacity of the Forest Service to dictate: the parent has become hostage of the child.

By contrast, the Park Service inherited many of its lands, including Yellowstone, from the army, and saw its job as balancing the need to preserve the wilderness with the popular desire to enjoy it.[32] These goals seemed to require law-enforcement and engineering skills—law enforcement to set down and apply rules for campers, engineering to build facilities for them. The task became defined as managing *people* more than managing parks. There was never an effort to develop a park ranger profession that was rooted in science and higher education. Even today, the main career track in the Park Service is the "ranger" track, by which is meant experience in visitor protection and safety, and not the naturalist track, which includes research. The ranger track, reports Alston Chase, a Park Service critic, is officially classified as nonprofessional, with no educational prerequisites beyond a high-school diploma.[33] The few scientists in the service have little influence.[34] In 1985 the Park Service, which manages over three hundred parks, spent about $16 million on research, less than the budget of one Forest Service experiment station.[35]

One consequence of these differences in operator values can be found in how the two services manage visitors. Craig W. Allin found that even in comparable areas attracting comparable visitors, the Forest Service gives less emphasis to regulating visitor use than does the Park Service.[36] The Park Service, like the Forest Service, has been deeply embroiled in controversy, especially since a vast brush fire ravaged Yellowstone Park in 1988. At issue are the age-old questions of popular access versus wilderness preservation; managing the wildlife versus deferring to natural forces; and fighting fires by "letting them burn" versus practicing controlled burning.[37] Each agency handles its controversies in characteristic ways: the Forest Service engages in extraordinarily detailed planning and research activities designed to defend its view of correct forest management;[38] the Park Service searches for external allies and engages in periodic changes of direction.*

Politicians and interest groups know that professionals can define tasks in ways that are hard for administrators to alter, and so one strategy for changing an organization is to induce it to recruit a professional cadre whose values are congenial to those desiring the change. We have seen already how the supporters of highway safety worked to insure that crash engineers were hired by NHTSA, thereby giving that agency at birth a distinctive focus. By the same token, the tendency (explained in chapter 3) of the Occupational Safety and Health Administration (OSHA) to work harder on improving safety than on health standards began to give way to a greater concern for health matters as OSHA began to hire more and more research scientists and public health experts. These professionals were less concerned with finding the bureaucratically easiest task and more concerned with focusing agency efforts on what their professional techniques identified as hazards and their professional norms taught them to take seriously.[39]

*That I have described the Forest Service as a professional organization and the Park Service as a nonprofessional one does not mean that I think the former is good and the latter bad. Professionalism and nonprofessionalism each can lead to good or bad outcomes.

Even established bureaucracies with strong professional traditions already in place can be altered by inserting a new profession. The Army Corps of Engineers and the Forest Service both have changed the way in which they approach certain tasks because they were obliged to hire a large number of persons who identify with the emerging environmentalist professions. The National Environmental Policy Act (NEPA) requires federal agencies to take into account the environmental impact of their projects. To do this they must prepare (among other things) environmental impact statements (EIS), and therefore must hire people skilled at preparing such reports—biologists, ecologists, biochemists, and the like. In 1984, when Serge Taylor published his account of the EIS process, the two agencies employed between them several hundred of these new professionals.[40] In this way, attention to different values was institutionalized in ongoing organizations, but at a price: having tasks defined by rival professions weakened the ability of the agencies to develop and maintain a shared sense of mission.

The Forest Service, for example, was an organization dominated by a single professional culture when Herbert Kaufman studied it in the 1950s. By the 1980s it had become divided into many different professional cultures. Today foresters have to contend with engineers, biologists, and economists, among others. The foresters dislike the tendency of engineers to elevate mechanical soundness over natural beauty, of biologists to worry more about endangered species than about big game, and of economists to put a price on things foresters regard as priceless.[41] This is a topic to which we shall return when we discuss the sense of mission in agencies (chapter 6).

Political Ideology

In the United States the higher levels of the federal government are staffed by bureaucrats who are more liberal than the population at large and certainly more liberal than business executives. Stanley Rothman and S. Robert Lichter interviewed two hundred top-level career administrators in a variety of federal agencies. Over half described themselves as politically liberal and said they had voted for George McGovern for president in 1972; nearly two-thirds voted for Jimmy Carter in 1976. Overwhelmingly they supported a woman's right to an abortion and agreed that environmental problems are serious. On the other hand, they displayed no generalized antipathy toward American society: the great majority believed that private enterprise is fair to workers and that less regulation of business would be good for the country; only a tiny fraction thought the nation should move toward socialism.[42]

There were important differences among senior bureaucrats depending on the kind of agency for which they worked. Those employed by "activist" agencies (such as the Environmental Protection Agency, the Consumer Products Safety Commission, and the Department of Health and Human Services) were significantly more liberal than those employed by "traditional" agencies (such as the Departments of Agriculture, Commerce, and the Treasury). In the activist agencies, bureaucrats were more likely than their counterparts in traditional agencies to say that women and blacks should get preference in hiring, that poor people are the victims of circumstances, and that U.S. foreign policy has aimed at protecting business.[43]

Essentially the same conclusions were reached by Joel Aberbach and Bert Rockman in their survey of senior bureaucrats holding office at the time Richard Nixon was president. They found evidence that Nixon was correct in his perception of bureaucratic ideology—that the officials were more liberal than he—and that the most liberal of all were in the social service agencies. Over 90 percent of the Democrats in these activist agencies were classified by Aberbach and Rockman as on the left. By contrast, only 25 percent of the Democrats in traditional agencies were leftists.[44]

These findings show that liberals who worry that high-level bureaucrats will have conservative opinions are wrong. In retrospect, it is clear that Kingsley was mistaken to think that because they are unrepresentative of the public at large, bureaucrats will prefer the status quo. Conservatives who fear the liberalism of bureaucrats do have grounds for concern, but exactly how much concern is not at all clear. We really don't care what bureaucrats think, we care what they do. Does ideology determine behavior? There is no systematic evidence bearing on this question.

From what already has been said about attitudes and behavior, we would expect ideology to make little difference in routinized or highly structured roles. There is no liberal or conservative way to deliver the mail or issue a driver's license. The example of police arrest and shooting practices suggests that there are even limits to how much difference personal beliefs can make in relatively ambiguous roles. But that still leaves a lot of ground to cover.

What some of that ground may look like is suggested by Jeremy Rabkin's account of the development of the Office for Civil Rights (OCR).[45] Created in 1965 to implement various civil rights laws, the OCR had a great deal of latitude in defining its own task. It is charged with insuring that no "program or activity receiving federal financial assistance" shall practice discrimination with regard to race, color, sex, handicap, or national origin. If discrimination were shown, the guilty organization could lose its federal funding. It was left to OCR to decide what constituted a "program or activity," whether the federal assistance had to be received directly or need only be received indirectly in order to bring the entity under the law, and what constituted evidence of discrimination.

After some initial fumbling and uncertainty, the OCR staff began to issue regulations that took an expansive view of the reach and force of the law. Discrimination was forbidden in any part of a school or other organization receiving federal aid, not merely in those parts that were directly supported. For example, if a school library bought books with federal aid, the cafeteria staff and the sports programs could not discriminate, even if they received no money. Discrimination was broadly defined to include any case in which a school district employed (for example) blacks in a lesser proportion than their representation in the community, whether or not anyone had produced evidence of discrimination. In perhaps its most controversial decision, OCR issued orders banning father-son and mother-daughter banquets at schools, orders later reversed by Congress in response to a public outcry.

There were several reasons for OCR taking this expansive view of its powers. Civil rights and feminist organizations often attacked it for "dragging its feet." Schools and universities were not effective in lobbying against the regulations. Cabinet officials and congressional committees did rather little to restrain OCR. But in part the agency acted as it did because it attracted people who had "considerable enthusiasm for its mission."[46]

The OCR is not alone in this regard. When the National Labor Relations Board (NLRB) was created in 1935, it attracted pro-labor lawyers to its staff who gave that agency a distinctive ideology until later events muted or ended the ideological enthusiasms of the staff.[47] The Office of Surface Mining Reclamation and Enforcement (OSM), an agency created to regulate strip-mining in the coal fields, attracted dedicated environmentalists to its staff who went well beyond the letter of the law in drawing up mining regulations.[48]

Why did ideology seem to influence the behavior of the staff of OCR, the lawyers in the NLRB, and the environmentalists in OSM, but not the arrest decisions of police officers? The answer, I conjecture, is to be found in the differing environments in which these bureaucrats work. The OCR, NLRB, and OSM were newly created policy-making bodies operating in a political environment shaped (if not dominated) by like-minded partisans in Congress and the supporting interest groups. Attitudes—whether ideology in the OCR, prior experiences in the ECA, or professional norms in the FTC—are most likely to influence the performance of weakly defined roles, especially when the attitudes are reinforced by other incentives. The jobs in a new agency charged with designing new policies are about as vaguely defined as one can imagine; moreover, a newborn agency is surrounded by its political parents—people and groups eager to applaud behavior that is consistent with the zeal of those who won the fight to create the agency.

Police officers have a great deal of discretion, but that does not mean that their tasks are vaguely defined. It only means that what they do is not clearly defined by formal organizational rules. Their work is shaped by informal understandings that are the product of daily, street-level contact with clients and years of on-the-job experience. These contacts and experiences tell police officers how to handle unruly citizens, when to use deadly force, what demeanor will win the approval of more senior colleagues, and which arrests will both stand up in court and be rewarded by promotion boards. The outside observer may not notice these sources of task definition and thus suppose that officers are free to do whatever they want; but that conclusion is wrong—and when it leads to ill-considered efforts to change behavior by writing rules, it is mischievous.

This perspective on ideology suggests that the formative years of a policy-making agency are of crucial importance in determining its behavior. As with people, so with organizations: Childhood experiences affect adult conduct. This means, as will be argued at length in chapter 6, that one must study history.

Agencies, like adults, learn from experience, and so the formative childhood years are only part of the story. Bureaucracies will in time acquire a distinctive personality or culture that will shape the attitudes of people who join these organizations; this also is discussed in chapter 6. When critics of an older agency complain that bureaucrats with the "wrong attitude" are determining its behavior, they are often reversing the causal process. The agency is in fact producing certain attitudes in its members.

There is a good deal of evidence that the political views of bureaucrats tend to correspond to their agency affiliation more than they reflect their social status. Kenneth Meier and Lloyd Nigro looked at the beliefs of a sample of higher-level federal civil servants and found that the social origins of these officials explained only about 5 percent of variance in their opinions; agency affiliations, on the other hand, explained much more.[49] Bernard Mennis compared foreign service officers and military officers performing similar jobs, mostly having to do with managing foreign political and international-security affairs. He found that their policy views differed sharply in the way one would expect: The foreign service officers were more liberal, the military officers more conservative. But these differences existed despite the fact that the social backgrounds of the two groups of officials were about the same.[50] As Charles Goodsell summarized these studies, "the agency positions in which bureaucrats 'sit' have much to do with where they 'stand.'"[51]

Defining Tasks: Bureaucratic Personality

Even if specific attitudes do not always determine bureaucratic behavior, many people think that those who work for government agencies have a distinctive personality. As with attitudes, opinions differ along political lines as to what that distinctive personality is. Liberals sometimes describe bureaucrats as cautious, conformist individuals loath to take risks. Conservatives sometimes describe them as zealous empire-builders determined to expand their power at the expense of the public. And there are probably some who think that bureaucrats are both conformists and zealots, simultaneously.

Robert K. Merton, a sociologist, was the foremost exponent of the view that a bureaucratic personality exists. He did not assert that bureaucrats are born with such a disposition, only that the logic of work in a bureaucratic organization tends to foster—or perhaps create—such an outlook. In a large, complex organization, operators tend to value means over ends: That is, they worry more about following the right rule than about achieving the ultimate goal. Merton called this "goal displacement," a process by which, as he put it, instrumental values become terminal values.[52]

There are aspects of organizational life that make people risk averse. Indeed, it would be surprising if they did not, since organizations are created in the first place to reduce uncertainty and risk. All organizations by design are the enemies of change, at least up to a point; government organizations are especially risk averse because they are caught up in a web of constraints so complex that any change is likely to rouse the ire of some important constituency. But political and organizational pressures for conformity are very different from the presumed tendency of bureaucracies to either recruit or be especially attractive to individuals with risk-averse, conformist personalities. Insofar as we can tell from the few studies that have been done, the presumption is untrue.

In 1963, W. Lloyd Warner and his collaborators published a study of nearly thirteen thousand career federal civil servants, mostly in civilian agencies, holding the rank of GS-14 and higher. As part of the survey, the authors administered a Thematic Apperception Test (TAT) to 257 of the federal managers. The TAT, as many readers will know, consists of a series of pictures of commonplace scenes (e.g., an older man talking to a younger man in an office) for which the interviewee must supply a story. These stories are then scored in accordance with rather well-established criteria. The bureaucrats revealed a personality disposition that on the whole was idealistic and strongly oriented toward achievement. There were individual differences, of course, but as a group the civil servants did not turn out to be conformist or cautious.[53]

A similar study was carried out by Melvin Kohn in the 1960s and published in 1971. The data in this research came from answers to interview questions rather than from the interpretation of TAT stories, and the subjects were drawn from a somewhat different sample—about three thousand men employed in a variety of civilian occupations. The degree to which their employing organization was bureaucratic was scored by counting the number of hierarchical levels in it. The results suggest that men employed in the more bureaucratic organizations were more likely to display intellectual flexibility and value self-direction and new experiences than was the case of men employed in less bureaucratic organizations. One reason for this finding may be that the employees of bureaucratic organizations tended to have more schooling than those of other kinds of organizations, and education (or the individual traits that correlate with education, such as intelligence) may produce those qualities detected in the survey.[54]

Charles Goodsell has reviewed a number of studies of the same sort as Kohn's, and most produce the same results.[55] There are exceptions. An experiment in which business managers and public-school administrators played a game involving choices between big payoffs with high risk and low payoffs with small risk revealed that the businessmen were more likely to accept risk than the school officials.[56] Given the greater rewards in a successful business career and the greater security in many (but not all) government careers, it would be surprising if there were no differences in the kinds of people found in each. But there is as yet no strong, consistent evidence that the two careers attract different personalities.

Conclusions

Prior experiences and professional norms (and their attendant career opportunities) certainly influence the behavior of rank-and-file bureaucrats; political ideology may have an effect, but we do not have enough evidence to speak confidently about this. Experience, professionalism, and ideology are likely to have their greatest influence when laws, rules, and circumstances do not precisely define operator tasks.

For decades, the number of agencies conferring broad discretion on operators steadily increased. Driven by an optimistic belief in the ability of nonpartisan experts effectively to manage complex economic affairs, Congress told many regulatory agencies with respect to some problem to do whatever would serve "the public interest." In these cases, the powers of the state were turned over, at least initially, to appointed officials who could make choices based on their beliefs and professional norms. Moreover, more professionals were hired to staff the government partly because agencies were now performing more complex tasks for which special training was thought to be necessary, partly because the work force came to consist of a higher proportion of people with some professional training, and partly because the employment of professionals seemed to lend credibility and legitimacy to agency activities. The FTC in 1914, the NLRB in 1935, the CIA in 1947, the ECA in 1948, the OCR in 1965, and OSHA in 1970 would have offered opportunities for personal beliefs to shape tasks simply because they were new; the agencies had choices to make and little in their statute specified what choices should be made. In addition, these agencies reflected the Progressive confidence that good people would define tasks in the right way, even without statutory guidance. But the "right way" is a matter of some dispute about which lawyers, economists, diplomats, engineers, spies, and civil rights activists have very different views.

As we shall see, an effort began in the 1970s to avoid making these broad grants of discretionary power to the new agencies that were then being created. This change was not, however, prompted by a desire to reduce the power of the professionals or the ideologues but rather by the belief that agencies having wide discretion were more likely to be captured by outside interest groups. It is important, therefore, to assess the extent to which professional norms (and possibly political ideology) can withstand external pressure. It is to that subject that we now turn.

CHAPTER 5

Interests

WHEN the Tennessee Valley Authority (TVA) was created in 1933, it was hailed by liberals as evidence of a new national commitment to regional planning linked with grass-roots democracy. When he sent the TVA bill to Congress, President Franklin Roosevelt described it as involving "national planning for a complete river watershed" that would address "all forms of human concern."[1] David Lilienthal, a member of the first TVA board of directors and later its chairman, wrote rhapsodically about his experience in a book entitled, *Democracy on the March.*[2] To him, the TVA was the crown jewel of the New Deal era because it would address comprehensively a variety of ills—ruinous floods, rural poverty, and economic backwardness—by means of a semiautonomous program of conservation, flood control, power production, agricultural development, and regional planning. The enthusiasm of liberals was matched by the anger of conservatives who believed that all this talk of planning was nothing less than the beginning of "creeping socialism."

Within three decades the positions had reversed. Now liberals were attacking the TVA as a ruthless and insensitive power company that in its single-minded devotion to generating electricity was despoiling the environment and that in its obsession with nuclear power was risking catastrophe. One journalist lamented that the TVA had lost "the aggressive, idealistic fervor of the early days."[3] Environmentalists complained of the pollution caused by the TVA's coal-burning power plants and fought the agency's plan to build the Tellico Dam on a river inhabited by the snail darter, a fish on the endangered-species list. Many liberals felt that a dream had been betrayed: The TVA had nothing to do with grass-roots democracy on the march.[4]

What had happened? The most widely accepted explanation for the apparent change in TVA's behavior was the pressure of interest groups. In this view, the agency had a broad and promising legal mandate, but its tasks were actually defined by powerful interests in the Tennessee Valley region. Sociologist Philip Selznick called this co-optation. In his classic study, *TVA and the Grass Roots,* he argued that in order to survive politically, the TVA had to abandon its commitment to planning and turn over the implementation of its agricultural programs to the powerful land-grant universities and farmer organizations in the area.[5] In particular, the TVA used the Extension Service of the U.S. Department of Agriculture as its operating arm. That service was deeply embedded in local courthouse politics and closely allied with the American Farm Bureau Federation, an organization representing the more affluent farmers in the region. This relationship in turn created within the TVA a group that was sympathetic to the Extension Service and thus disinclined to pursue ambitious planning and land reform programs.[6]

Selznick's landmark study is cited to this day by people who worry that any government agency that vests its operators with much discretion will have the tasks of these operators defined by the pressures of external organized interests. This is especially likely in the United States, where political authority is so divided and decentralized as to leave any newborn agency naked and helpless, lacking effective protection against lateral pressures. To these people, the story of the TVA is duplicated by that of the Forest Service, the Bureau of Land Management, the Food and Drug Administration, and countless other agencies that must cope with powerful private groups. In short, tasks are not defined by situations, norms, experiences, directives, or ideology, but by interests.

But there is another, very different explanation for what happened to the TVA. In this view, the agency had its tasks defined by law, experience, and professional norms, not by sinister private interests. First, the law: The New Deal rhetoric about the TVA did not, except by inference, find its way into the actual statute authorizing it. The law empowered the TVA to build dams and generate power; planning was nowhere explicitly authorized.[7] Second, the formative experience: The political expectations and statutory language clearly envisaged the building of dams, and so dams were built. In fact, dams were inherited; when the TVA was formed in 1933, there was already a government-owned dam and power plant at Muscle Shoals that the TVA took over. From the beginning the agency found itself in the hydroelectric business. Within a year, the agency was building two more dams and had purchased transmission lines from private utilities in the area. By 1941, the TVA had quadrupled its generating capacity, thereby becoming the sixth largest utility company in the nation. When World War II vastly increased the demand for electricity, the Authority quickly and effectively responded—by the end of the war, it had more than doubled its power production, becoming the single largest utility in the country.[8] And finally, professional norms: To take over and run existing hydroelectric plants and to build and operate new ones the TVA had to hire hundreds of engineers. These "power people" quickly became the largest occupational group in the Authority, bringing with them a clear view of their task—namely, to build the most efficient generating plants possible. Since the cost of a kilowatt of power declines (up to a point) the more power one produces, the most efficient power plants will be the largest. In turn, a large power plant requires many customers in order to pay for itself. Thus, the norm of engineering efficiency led those who shared it to define the tasks of the TVA in this way: Build large, efficient generators to serve many customers.[9] The TVA's general manager described his agency's task succinctly: "Thou shalt supply power at the lowest possible cost consistent with financial soundness."[10] In an organizational environment dominated by this occupational culture, it is hard to imagine how people favoring rural planning or environmental protection would make much headway. They did not. As the hydroelectric potential of the rivers became exhausted, the TVA began building coal-fired plants; as coal became costly, it began planning nuclear power plants.[11] Though its relations with local interest groups may have had some effect, it seems clear that the evolution of the TVA would have been much the same had they never existed.

At the time Edward Mansfield wrote about it, the Federal Maritime Commission (FMC) had a richly deserved reputation in Washington for failing to serve the goals set by Congress: to prevent ocean-shipping companies from charging rates that were discriminatory (i.e., they favored one shipper or port over another) or unreasonable (e.g., the rates were too high).[12] In fact, the FMC almost always approved every rate the shipping companies submitted and when it did not it was usually because of some technical error in the submission, not because the rates were judged too high.[13]

There were several reasons for what one congressional committee called a pattern of "regulatory neglect." For example, the people selected to be FMC commissioners were often incompetent political hacks. But Mansfield suggests that leadership failures were as much a consequence as a cause of agency failures. The key to the FMC's difficulty was that "the agency must administer a vaguely worded statute in a political environment dominated by the carriers [that is, the regulated industry]."[14] About thirty law firms represented these carriers; only one represented the shippers that used the carriers. As one shipping firm official put it, "the carriers have had an overwhelming input."[15] The steamship companies were well-organized and effective because the rates they were allowed to charge were crucial to their profitability. The large shippers could negotiate directly with steamship companies to get good rates and did not need the help of the FMC. The small shippers were poorly organized and ineffective. Thus, the very group the law was intended to protect—the small shipper—in fact was not protected.

Some observers would say that the FMC had been captured by the industry it was supposed to regulate. But "capture" does not quite describe what happened. The maritime industry did not bribe FMC staffers or offer them lucrative post-government jobs; rather, it took advantage of a situation that gave to the carriers an insuperable advantage. The number of proposed shipping rates was so large that the FMC staff members had to routinize their work. When a high-volume task is routinized, vague statutory language must go uninterpreted (such as the statement that a price-setting agreement shall not be "unjustly discriminatory" or "contrary to the public interest" and that a proposed rate shall not be "unreasonably low or high"). There was neither the time nor the resources to assign meaning to these ambiguous words when coping with the flood of documents entering the FMC offices. The FMC staff member thus was led to take a reactive view of his or her task: If the proposed rate was not challenged by a shipper, it must be reasonable. Shippers only occasionally had an incentive to protest. As a result, most proposed rates went into effect.[16]

Here we have two agencies—the TVA and the FMC—that seemed equally vulnerable to interest-group influence. In both cases the agencies were created by statutes that were sufficiently vague as to confer substantial discretion on each of the staffs. In both cases the agencies were placed in political environments in which a few key groups had a big stake in the outcome and thus an incentive to organize to affect that outcome. But in the case of the TVA the agency had its tasks defined chiefly by its formative experiences (the need to operate an existing dam) and its professional culture (the values of the power engineers it hired); in the case of the FMC, the agency had its tasks defined by the imperatives of the situation (the need to manage a large flow of paperwork in an environment in which one set of interests but not its rival had an incentive to organize and to act). No mechanistic theory of capture can do justice to what in fact happened.

Agencies and Interests

If two agencies that seem equally liable to capture have such different experiences, then agencies that are different in their statutory origin and political environment are even more likely to have different experiences. There is no doubt that some agencies have their tasks powerfully shaped by external interests. Sometimes this happens because Congress intended it that way: it told the agency to serve certain private interests or arranged the agency's procedures so that these interests in fact would be served. How often this occurs will be discussed in chapter 14. Other agencies may be heavily influenced by outside interests even when that was not intended; this might correctly be called capture. And still other agencies may behave in a way that leads the affected interests to complain bitterly about "runaway," "zealous," and "short-sighted" bureaucrats who "overregulate" certain industries or occupations.

Clearly, some distinctions are in order. The influence of outside interests on an agency will depend, in the first instance, on the way those interests are arrayed in the agency's environment. To oversimplify, a government agency can occupy one of four kinds of political environments: It can confront (1) a dominant interest group favoring its goals; (2) a dominant interest group hostile to its goals; (3) two or more rival interest groups in conflict over its goals; or (4) no important interest group. Which kind of environment they face will shape the forces working on operators as they try to define their tasks.*

In the first case, the agency is the product of *client* politics. Client politics occurs when most or all of the benefits of a program go to some single, reasonably small interest (an industry, profession, or locality) but most or all of the costs will be borne by a large number of people (for example, all taxpayers). In other words, client politics occurs when the benefits have a high per-capita value and the costs have a low per-capita value. Because the recipients' benefits are large, they have an incentive to organize and press for the law; since the costs to those who pay them (per person) are low and perhaps hidden, they have no incentive to organize to oppose the law.

The Civil Aeronautics Board (CAB) for much of its history was an example of client politics. Created in 1938, it was intended to protect and enhance the infant civil aviation industry by reducing "destructive competition" and providing subsidies in the form of contracts to carry air mail. The airlines stood to gain a great deal by the creation of an agency that would restrict entry into the industry and set prices at a level that would almost guarantee profits. The airline passengers who would pay these prices had no way of knowing that the regulated prices would be higher than those set by market competition, but even had they known this the difference in price to each of them probably would have been too small to care about. As a result, the airline companies enthusiastically supported the bill and virtually no one opposed it. Other examples of client politics include the Federal Communications Commission (FCC), created to secure the property rights of radio (and later television) stations in the electromagnetic frequency on which they broadcast; and the Commodity

*The conceptual scheme presented here draws on work earlier published in James Q. Wilson, ed., *The Politics of Regulation* (New York: Basic Books, 1980), chap. 10; and Wilson, *American Government*, 4th ed. (Lexington, Mass.: D. C. Heath & Co., 1989).

Credit Corporation, created to pay farmers the difference between what their products are worth on the open market and what Congress thinks the farmers should earn.

The opposite of client politics is *entrepreneurial* politics. Here, the costs are heavily concentrated on some industry, profession, or locality but the benefits are spread over many if not all people. Because costs have a high per-capita value, the affected group has a strong incentive to oppose the proposed law. Because benefits have a low per-capita value, the recipients have little incentive to press for its enactment. Creating an agency or passing a law under these circumstances obviously will be difficult, yet it does occur. The formation in 1966 of the National Highway Traffic Safety Administration (NHTSA) is an example. The keys to its creation were the existence of a skilled policy entrepreneur (Ralph Nader), a scandal that embarrassed his industry opponents (the clumsy attempt by General Motors to investigate Nader), several politicians who were looking for an issue around which to campaign (Senator Abraham Ribicoff and others), and a number of reporters and editors who were receptive to the stories Nader was producing.[17] Nader's arguments coupled with the political and media impact of the scandal and the ensuing congressional hearings were sufficient to throw industry opponents of the measure on the defensive and to convert a policy issue ("what is the responsibility of government for highway safety?") into a moralistic crusade ("who dares oppose a plan to punish the insensitive and destructive auto industry?").

The passage of laws intended to regulate pharmaceuticals, control toxic substances, purify the air and water, and prevent the sale of flammable clothing to children have followed similar patterns. There may be a scandal—for example, a drug that led to the birth of deformed infants, a chemical that harmed the health of workers, a child who died from being burned by a nightgown, or an oil spill that washed up on a California beach. But even without a scandal, skillfully conducted congressional hearings can paint the industry opponents of regulation in bad light—for example, pharmaceutical manufacturers who admitted to making very high profits on new drugs. The hearings will be conducted by a politician who, ambitious for higher office, seeks a reputation for being a tribune of the people; for example, Senator Edmund Muskie toughened his proposed clean-air act to meet Ralph Nader's charges that he had "sold out" to industry.[18]

An agency created or empowered as a result of entrepreneurial politics will face, at least initially, a hostile interest group—those who disproportionately bear the costs of its actions. But many of the founding members of the new agency will be drawn from the social movement that helped to create it and they will have the aid of watchdog groups composed of political allies. For a while these forces will be able to fend off the pressures of the cost-bearing interest and even to impart a degree of regulatory zeal to the agency's work. But such an agency will be very much at risk: when the zeal of their early allies flags, it may find itself confronting an environment where much of the information it needs and many of the political resources to which it must respond will be in the hands of an interest fundamentally hostile to its purposes.

In the third case, an agency will be neither the tool nor the victim of an outside interest if it is the object of offsetting pressures from rival interest groups. These opposed forces will, so to speak, hold the agency erect. This pattern of *interest-group* politics occurs when the program of the agency produced both high per-capita costs and high per-capita benefits. Both the likely beneficiaries and the likely cost-payers have a strong incentive to organize and press their competing claims.

The Occupational Safety and Health Administration (OSHA) was formed in 1970 after a struggle between organized labor and organized business over the proper governmental response, if any, to the hazards employees encounter in the workplace. The fight in Congress over the language of the bill pitted labor and management against one another; the struggle before the agency over the contents of specific regulations continues to pit labor against management. In the same way, the creation of the National Labor Relations Board (NLRB) in 1935 came after a struggle between labor and business and, as with OSHA, the fight continued long after the agency was born.[19] The Interstate Commerce Commission was created in 1886 out of a struggle between many interests—long-haul railroads that wanted high prices and less competition, farmers and oil companies that wanted lower prices and more competition from the railroads, and various cities that wanted to be served by the railroads.[20]

Finally, some agencies operate in an environment in which no important interest group is continuously active. This occurs when the bureau and its program appear to offer widely distributed benefits and impose widely distributed costs. Because the benefits have a low per-capita value, no one organizes to seek them; because the costs have a low per-capita value, no one organizes to avoid them. We call this *majoritarian* politics.

The passage of the Sherman Antitrust Act in 1890, leading to the creation of the Antitrust Division of the Justice Department, was an example of majoritarian politics. As Suzanne Weaver wrote, the Sherman Act was "a response not to industry's desire to obtain federal protection from the uncertainties of competition, but rather to a popular sentiment that large corporations were gaining too much power over the lives of individual citizens."[21] The popular press at the time was filled with stories exposing the industrial trusts and their real or imagined abuses. Politicians moved to capitalize on inflamed public sentiment. At the same time however, no particular firm or industry felt especially threatened by the agitation, for the antitrust law was not aimed specifically at any business; indeed, given the ambiguity of its language (it banned "combinations in restraint of trade"), it was not exactly clear what it *was* aimed at. There were opponents of the law, but they argued on constitutional rather than economic grounds: the Constitution does not give to the federal government sufficient authority over commerce to sustain Senator Sherman's statute. The critics lost, but not because an industry had been outvoted.

Interests and Operators

The extent to which the tasks of operators are shaped by the pressures of external interests will vary depending on which of the four political environments surround the agency.

CLIENT AGENCIES

A client agency will have to struggle mightily to avoid having its work influenced by the single, organized group with which it must deal on a daily basis. Many do not succeed, a few do not even try. There need be nothing corrupt nor sinister about this. The employees of the Federal Maritime Commission received almost all of their information from steamship companies that wanted their rate-setting agreements approved and their individual prices upheld. Usually there was no one to tell the FMC analysts whether these agreements and rates were good or bad for the consumer or the economy as a whole. For much of its history, the Civil Aeronautics Board learned almost everything it knew about civil aviation from the airline industry itself. Rivalry between carriers might give the CAB a chance to make an informed choice on a specific case as when, for instance, American Airlines and United Airlines competed for the right to fly from Chicago to Honolulu. But that rivalry was limited to the market conditions in two specific cities, and so the information gleaned was limited to these matters. Such competition ordinarily would not tell the CAB analysts much about the effect on air fares generally of the oligopolistic cartel that agency had helped to create.[22]

In some cases, the dependence of an agency on its private-sector clients is formalized. The Agricultural Stabilization and Conservation Service (ASCS) oversees the federal programs that pay farmers subsidies. The work of the service is closely monitored by a network of over three thousand county committees, each composed of three farmers elected by their fellow farmers in their county. These farmers would bristle at being told they are an interest group in the same way as are the steamship companies for the FMC, and in a sense they are right: The farmers' role in making agricultural policy was officially sanctioned by Congress, whereas the role of the steamship companies is a product of circumstance. But in another sense, the farmers have made the ASCS their client agency because of their political influence; it so happens that this influence was strong enough to produce a formal rather than an informal clientelism.

Client relationships are not confined to agencies that deal with the economic sector. Until President Reagan altered its leadership after a bruising fight with Congress, the Civil Rights Commission was heavily influenced by civil rights organizations that constituted almost the only active groups in its political environment. Not surprisingly, the work of the commission tended to reflect the views of these groups. The National Academy of Sciences and the National Science Foundation reflect the preferences of their major constituency, professors interested in research.

ENTREPRENEURIAL AGENCY

An agency created as the result of entrepreneurial politics is in a precarious position: since it was born out of an attack on the interests it is now supposed to regulate, its employees must worry that the social movements that created their tasks may desert the fledgling agency because of shifting interests or waning passions, leaving it to confront a hostile interest group alone and unprotected. There are cases where something like this has happened. The Food and Drug Administration (FDA), created out of popular revulsion against injuries and deaths caused by certain drugs and patent medicines, was expected to prevent the distribution of unsafe or ineffective drugs. But each drug scandal, such as the deaths attributed to elixir of sulfanilamide in 1937 or the infant defects caused by thalidomide in 1961, would be followed by a period during which consumer and medical groups lost interest in the FDA. Of course the drug manufacturers never lost interest in the FDA because their profitability depended crucially on the speed and certainty with which the agency would approve new drugs for marketing. Moreover, the FDA could not offer sufficient pay or research opportunities to attract many top-flight scientists to its ranks. Though many of its operators were quite competent, few were outstanding.[23] And the people it did employ had a daunting task: to evaluate new-drug applications, each of which might contain as many as two hundred volumes of information, within the statutory limit of 180 days and with awareness of the possibility that the new drug might save lives. The people with whom the FDA dealt on a daily basis were usually industry representatives, rarely critics of drug approvals. Under these circumstances it would be easy for many operators to resolve all doubts in favor of industry. Occasionally this may have happened. In the late 1950s and early 1960s the FDA had the reputation of being rather passive, perhaps even pro-industry, in its outlook.[24]

But much of the time, FDA operators define their jobs in a quite different way. Despite the pressures of their daily work, their overriding fear, as Paul Quirk has shown, is the scandal that would occur if they approved a new drug that later caused death or injury. Though scandals might be rare, the memory of them lasts a long time.[25] This memory is reinforced by the awareness that one disaffected employee could blow the whistle by leaking a story about poor review work to Congress or the press.

In short, agencies born of entrepreneurial politics are at risk of capture, but capture is not inevitable. Later in this chapter we shall review a number of factors that have operated in recent years to minimize the ability of the cost-bearing interest group to define the agency's tasks.

INTEREST-GROUP AGENCY

Operators in agencies confronting interest-group politics might seem to have an easy time of it: with their environment split among contending groups they can pick and choose how they define their tasks, secure in the knowledge that somebody out there is likely to be their ally. But in fact it is not so easy. For one thing, anything they do will be criticized by somebody and, like most people, bureaucrats don't enjoy criticism. For another, their political superiors in the executive branch and Congress will tilt, depending on the political winds, first toward one interest group and then toward another. Under these circumstances it will be hard to know what one is supposed to do; things that were once rewarded now are penalized, and vice versa.

The Occupational Safety and Health Administration faces this problem every day as it make rules and inspects workplaces. In doing these things OSHA rarely can please both industry and labor. Often they cannot even please their own superiors. Under Morton Corn (appointed by President Ford) OSHA had a reputation for zealously promulgating new safety and health rules; under Eula Bingham (appointed by President Carter) it was known for being committed to strong standards but cautious about antagonizing its critics; under Thorne Auchter (appointed by President Reagan) it acquired a reputation for being more concerned with the costs than the benefits of regulations.[26] Rules and enforcement efforts that were praised by one administrator were damned by the next, and this made a difference in what the agency did.[27]

David P. McCaffrey has traced the history of OSHA in an effort to discover whether its behavior is best explained by industry capture, interest group pressures, or organizational necessities. His subtle analysis deserves careful study, but in general he finds that interest-group pressures coupled with changing agency executives explain most of OSHA's conduct. In the early years organized labor was the most active interest group because it had played a key role in creating the agency. Having this head start, labor was able to influence many of OSHA's first decisions—for example, getting tough standards on coke oven emissions and the use of various dangerous chemicals, such as polyvinyl chloride. But as business learned more about OSHA, it improved its representational effectiveness.

As a consequence, some of the early standards that business thought overly stringent were loosened and OSHA became reluctant to act quickly or without careful analysis in proposing new standards.[28]

Interest-group pressures set the (changing) outer limits of what OSHA would do, but within those limits the personnel of the agency were able to define their tasks in accordance with professional norms (see chapter 4). As Steven Kelman has observed, "the most important factor explaining OSHA decisions on the content of regulations has been the pro-protection values of agency officials, derived from the ideology of the safety and health professional[s] and the organizational mission of OSHA."[29] The clearest example of these norms at work was the decision by agency officials to insist upon reducing workplace exposure to loud noises by redesigning the machinery used in the workplace rather than by relying on the much less costly method of requiring workers to wear ear plugs.

MAJORITARIAN AGENCIES

The majoritarian politics that created the Antitrust Division left it confronting an environment devoid of important interest groups. Its vigor or laxness would be almost entirely the result of the character of its head and the kind of backing he received from the president. The Sherman Act was broad and vague enough to permit the agency to behave in ways that would not stimulate the formation of a hostile interest group. The division avoided taking on entire industries that then would comprise an active interest group with a stake in defeating the division; rather, it proceeded on a case-by-case basis, taking up and acting on complaints from an individual firm that one of its competitors was behaving illegally.[30] A firm that was the complainant in one case might be the accused in another, and vice versa. Sometimes a particular firm threatened by an antitrust prosecution will try to use political influence to block the case (as in 1971, when ITT offered a large campaign contribution to the Nixon administration in return for an end to its antitrust prosecution), but one-shot, single-firm efforts of this sort pose a much weaker threat to an agency's autonomy than the continuous intervention of a large, well-organized group. And in the ITT case, there is no evidence that the division acted improperly.[31]

What can happen when an agency created by majoritarian politics behaves in a way that arouses an organized foe is illustrated by the Federal Trade Commission. Charged with enforcing antitrust laws rather similar to those administered by the Antitrust Division, the FTC through most of its history followed the division's practice of handling specific complaints on a case-by-case basis. But in the 1970s, pursuant to explicit congressional authorization it began issuing rules governing the conduct of entire industries. The Funeral Industry Practice Rule would have required the item-by-item disclosure of the price of each component of a funeral (the casket, the vault, the undertaker's services, and so on), prices that traditionally had been hidden in a lump-sum charge for the casket. The Used Car Rule would have required the dealer to conduct a detailed inspection of each car offered for sale and post the results on the car window. Undertakers and used-car dealers were outraged by these proposed rules. Very quickly, members of Congress discovered just how many undertakers and car dealers they had in their districts and how well-connected they were. The FTC suddenly had activated large, hostile interests who were successful in getting Congress to force the agency to back down.[32]

Restraints on Capture

Reality has a way of outrunning opinion. About the time many political observers had concluded that government agencies get captured by private interests, the political system had changed to make such capture much harder. Several things were responsible for this.

LOWER COSTS OF POLITICAL ORGANIZATION

It always had been hard to organize and direct the concerns of people who have a small personal stake in a public policy. When the costs or benefits of a program have a low per-capita value, most people who are affected by the program may be unaware of it, feel that the burdens of getting involved in politics are much greater than the small gains the involvement may produce, and believe (rightly) that their individual contribution to any such effort will not affect its chances for success. In short, citizens are either ignorant of their stake in a policy or inclined to be "free riders" on the activities of others.

Technological advances in the arts of direct-mail solicitation and the emergence of large foundations prepared to make financial contributions to causes they favor have combined to lower the cost of creating a political organization that can serve as a watchdog over an entrepreneurial agency. By sending dramatic appeals ("Save the whales!" "Right to bear arms!") to carefully selected mailing lists, an "organization" can be formed. Of course, it is not a conventional organization in the sense of a group of people who meet and coordinate activities; rather, it is an organization of a few leaders supported by money contributed by a large following. To these contributions can be added grants from foundations that believe in the cause (traditionally most of these foundations have had a liberal outlook, but a growing number now exist to support conservative causes). Between 1970 and 1987, foundations gave an estimated $100 million to liberal public-interest law firms; the Ford Foundation alone gave approximately $21 million to them.[33] Occasionally these groups raise additional money by marketing services directly to "members" (actually, customers): Organizations representing retired people, for instance, sell by direct mail insurance and health products. Whatever the source, the funds are available to hire publicists, lawyers, and analysts.

The results of this can be seen at the Environmental Protection Agency. Industries that bear the costs of coping with air and water pollution do not have the lobbying field to themselves. Even though the average citizen who is worried about pollution has little incentive to join an organization that will lobby on his or her behalf before the EPA, groups such as the Environmental Defense Fund can claim to speak plausibly on behalf of many such people. This is not to imply that the distribution of political resources has been equalized among all relevant interest groups, only that it is now rare to find an agency that can deal in a purely clientele relationship with a single affected group.

Of course, not all government policies lend themselves to direct-mail solicitation or arouse the interest of foundations. It would be tough to write a letter about the work of the Federal Maritime Commission that would move thousands of people to send in $25 checks to some watchdog organization. The slogan "bring down the cost of shipping plywood!" does not have quite the same punch as "save the baby dolphins!"

Sometimes the government itself acts as the vicarious representative of unorganized constituencies. The Antitrust Division of the Justice Department has intervened before other federal agencies when it felt that they were not acting in ways that enhanced market competition. The division argued against Federal Maritime Commission rate agreements that the ATD felt were anticompetitive[34] and it pressed the Civil Aeronautics Board to move toward less regulation of the airlines.[35] The advantage of having the ATD play this role is that unlike the average citizen it may take seriously the cost of shipping plywood.

REDISTRIBUTION OF POLITICAL ACCESS

A remarkable transformation in American politics occurred in the middle decades of the twentieth century: There was a redistribution of political resources without an equivalent redistribution of economic resources. Access to government became more widely distributed because the number of points through which the system could be entered multiplied and the number of points through which privileged groups enjoyed exclusive access declined. This is not to say that it became easier to alter government policy; greater access meant more voices were heard, and the result was sometimes babel rather than decision.

Much of this change happened by design, the result of a belief among key political elites that in the past access had been too restricted. These people—members of Congress and their staffs, journalists and editorial writers, professors and social activists—had been taught that government, far from being pluralistic, was readily captured by interests, especially business interests. This belief had a large element of truth in it, though it was far from the whole truth.[36] Acting on this view, new programs were embedded in structures and surrounded by procedures intended to prevent capture, and old procedures where possible were modified to achieve the same end.

Many of the newer regulatory agencies such as the Environmental Protection Agency and the Occupational Safety and Health Administration were placed specifically under the direction of a single administrator rather than a multi-member commission in order to reduce their vulnerability to business pressures.[37] If there were no commission, there would be neither opportunity nor justification for having the overseers of the agency be representative of affected interests. The job of a single administrator was not to represent but to decide, and in a way that would fix responsibility on him or her.

The campaign finance laws were toughened to limit contributions to candidates in any federal election to $1,000 from individuals and $5,000 from political action committees. In theory this would prevent greedy interests from buying the support of a politician who could then control a regulatory agency in a manner convenient to those interests. At the same time the decentralization and individualization of Congress was creating a situation that reduced the opportunity for any given member, bought or unbought, to have unchallenged influence over an agency. This decentralization led to a proliferation of subcommittees with overlapping jurisdictions over executive agencies, increasing the odds that any given agency would have overseers with opposed views as to how it should behave.

The Food and Drug Administration, for example, has been the object of almost continuous investigation by senators and representatives—Estes Kefauver, Gaylord Nelson, Edward M. Kennedy, Lawrence Fountain, Paul Rogers, and others—critical of the FDA's decision to approve some new drug. One FDA administrator was moved by this barrage of criticism to complain that no member of Congress ever seemed to care whether the agency erred in the opposite direction—that is, failing to approve a new drug that should have been made available.[38] The EPA also gets heavy political flak. If it fails to approve the use of a pesticide, congressional committees representing farmers attack it; if it does approve the pesticide, other committees representing environmentalists attack it. Watchdog groups can almost always find a sympathetic member of Congress to take up their cause.

Access to the courts also has been broadened. By statute and court decision, "standing"—the right to bring suit in court—has been given to a far wider array of interests than was once the case. Congress has authorized private parties to sue the government over many matters on which the government formerly had been immune from suit, and the parties that can bring the suit now may include people who have only a distant and indirect rather than immediate and palpable stake in the outcome. It is also easier to bring class-action suits on behalf of large groups of affected parties. Finally, the private party's legal costs in many cases must be paid by the government agency that is sued if that agency loses in court. As a result of these changes it is hard to imagine a decision of any consequence made by the EPA that would not be challenged in court by somebody.[39]

These efforts to reduce privileged access and broaden competitive access has brought to the work of all but the dullest federal agencies a degree of contentiousness that would have been unimaginable in the 1930s or 1940s. Of course, none of these changes guarantee that an entrepreneurial group will defeat a client agency, but they do contribute to an environment in which it is increasingly unlikely that an agency will confront but a single source of information and incentives.

BELIEFS

In chapter 4 we have seen countless examples of how certain beliefs—professional norms—help shape the way tasks are performed in agencies. A skeptic might rejoin that what shapes tasks are not the beliefs of professionals but their aspirations for lucrative post-government employment with the firms they once regulated. If law firms hire government attorneys and pharmaceutical companies hire government scientists, would not these lawyers and scientists perform their tasks in ways that enhance their post-government employment prospects?

Possibly. But two things must be borne in mind. First, some professionals may not desire private jobs because the material and nonmaterial satisfactions of public service may equal or exceed those of private employment. We do not know how many people this describes, but it describes some, for there are many professionals in fact who stay in government throughout their careers. Second, the kind of government work that will impress a potential private employer is not necessarily that which favors industry but that which conveys evidence of talent and energy. An attorney working for the FTC or the ATD displays talent and energy by aggressively and successfully enforcing the law.[40] A law firm wishing to hire a government attorney who knows antitrust law will not hire a person who has lost a case against a big client of that firm, it will hire somebody who won such a case. William Ruckelshaus was a pro-environment EPA administrator; after he left government, his law firm was hired by a plastics industry that was worried about EPA regulations. Ruckelshaus was hired because he was competent, not because he was pro- or anti-industry.[41] The central issue is whether a government employee is valuable to industry because he or she "knows how to pull strings" and "thinks our way," or because that person "knows the law" and "can win cases." The more professional the orientation toward work, the more likely it will be skills rather than contacts that make that employee an attractive candidate for recruitment.

In the TVA, professional power engineers worked in ways that eased the fears of conservative critics of the TVA's planning mission because they wanted to generate power efficiently, not because they wanted to curry favor with the Farm Bureau. And in the Civil Aeronautics Board we see a case of professionalism defining a job in ways directly contrary to industry interest despite the fact that the CAB was functioning in an environment conducive to client politics.

CAB economists were among the first group inside the government to begin pressing for the deregulation of prices and conditions of entry into the civil aviation business. A five-person staff task force issued a report in 1975 saying that "protective entry control, exit control, and public-utility type price regulation under the Federal Aviation Act are not justified by the underlying cost and demand characteristics of commercial air transportation."[42] In reaching this conclusion (later reinforced by other staff studies), the CAB economists were taking a position consistent with that of fellow economists in academia and in opposition to the clearly expressed preferences of the airline industry.[43] In their magisterial study of the politics of deregulation, Martha Derthick and Paul Quirk show how some CAB economists had always thought this way (the "dissidents"); others changed their minds (the "converts"); and still others were hired because they were convinced already of this view (the "newcomers").[44] The views of this growing phalanx of staff members caused the commissioners and members of Congress to sit up and take notice. Deregulation was not accomplished until many other actors—two presidents, other federal agencies, several senators and representatives—had played their parts; but the decisive initial steps were taken by staff members who chose to act as if their agency was not in a clientele relationship with industry.

Given what happened in the CAB, under what circumstances will similar professionals in similar agencies act in this way? If the staff led the deregulation movement in the CAB, why did it not do so at the Interstate Commerce Commission (ICC)? The short answer is that we do not know. Derthick and Quirk offer some speculations. The CAB was an elite agency with a larger fraction of truly professional staff members than was the ICC. At the CAB, the chairman used personnel powers in ways that encouraged antiregulation economists; at the ICC, such powers were either unused or nonexistent. In addition, the imperatives of the situation differed in the two agencies. The CAB staff had to handle relatively few rate cases each year; by contrast, the ICC staff (like that of the FMC) had to cope with a flood of paperwork generated by the rail and trucking industry (the ICC received over five thousand applications for operating rights each year).[45]

Broader political beliefs also may affect the environment in which the agencies work. At one time, the daily business of a government agency was of no interest to the media unless there was a juicy scandal or a grant to the hometown folks. The emergence of a new generation of reporters with a more adversarial stance toward government has changed that somewhat. Now, "whistle-blowers" can claim the attention of journalists more easily. Members of Congress and their staffs once believed that regulating prices and conditions of entry into an industry was the right thing to do; now many are inclined to believe that where competition exists prices are best set by the market. The risks of accident and disease in the workplace were always matters for the individual employee to worry about; today these risks are also a matter of government concern. At one time, a manufacturer was responsible for defects in its products only if they were the result of negligence; today many firms are liable even if there was no negligence. This changed political and intellectual environment has altered the balance of forces with which the members of an agency must cope.

Conclusions

Government agencies are not billiard balls driven hither and yon by the impact of forces and interests. When bureaucrats are free to choose a course of action their choices will reflect the full array of incentives operating on them: some will reflect the need to manage a workload; others will reflect the expectations of workplace peers and professional colleagues elsewhere; still others may reflect their own convictions.

And some will reflect the needs of clients; that is, those people or groups that are affected disproportionately by the actions of the agency. The impact of organized interests on agency behavior will depend on at least four factors: the extent to which the legislature wants and expects there to be an impact; the degree of discretionary authority possessed by agency members; the array of interests in the agency's environment; and the relationship between desired behavior and client incentives.

If Congress wants an agency to tend to the needs of a group, it usually makes that preference clear. If it seems not to care, or some parts of Congress want an interest helped and others do not, the agency is likely to be given a lot of discretion that will then be used in a (usually vain) effort to stay out of trouble. How it uses that discretion will be influenced by whether the costs and benefits of its policies are distributed so as to create an environment consisting of clients, entrepreneurs, interest groups, or nothing at all. The rewards offered by clients may make the agency's behavior serve the interests of the client or the interests of its rival, depending on whether those rewards are mediated by professional standards. A lawyer may behave one way if what is done simply pleases or displeases a client and in quite another way if what is done first must satisfy a judge or jury.

CHAPTER 6

Culture

FOR DECADES, the State Department has employed foreign nationals to do much of the work in American embassies. They have served as chauffeurs, telephone operators, messengers, housekeepers, receptionists, and the like. This meant that in Moscow, several hundred people working in the American embassy were under the control of, if not in the employ of, the KGB. The ambassador's chauffeur, for example, was a Soviet agent. One might think that the State Department would be alarmed about having so many hostile intelligence officers working in one of its most sensitive diplomatic missions and in close proximity to its key officials. Not at all. When an effort was made in Washington to get the Soviet nationals replaced by American citizens, State strenuously resisted, claiming that the Soviets provided valuable services that Americans were unable or unwilling to perform (one U.S. official said he depended on his KGB chauffeur to help him find his way around Moscow and get him tickets for the Bolshoi Ballet). Moreover, embassy morale would suffer if Americans had to do the jobs once done for them by Soviet personnel. Congress threatened to pass a law requiring the State Department to replace these foreign nationals with Americans. Just when the issue was coming to a head, the Soviet government withdrew its citizens from the embassy in retaliation for the arrest by the FBI of a Soviet spy in New York.

When the U.S. built a new embassy in Moscow, Soviet companies were hired to do much of the work. In the mid-1980s, after the building was almost complete, it was learned that it had been assembled in such a way as to greatly enhance the collection of intelligence. The plans and construction techniques had been approved in advance by the State Department office in charge of construction. As construction proceeded, U.S.

inspectors failed to detect just how badly compromised the new building was until it was almost ready for occupancy.

Moscow is not an isolated case. Over a period of years, the United States repeatedly found evidence of Soviet penetration of its embassies abroad.[1] Hidden listening devices were uncovered, often quite by accident. Inspection teams sent out to study the situation brought back reports of unprotected embassies. Alarm systems were inadequate, doors poorly guarded, and visitor movements not closely monitored.

Outside the State Department, various advisory bodies had pressed throughout the 1980s to get State to improve embassy security, but to little avail. Matters finally came to a head when a marine guard assigned to our embassy in Moscow admitted that he had been romantically involved with a Soviet woman who worked there. She almost certainly was a KGB agent. Though the State Department had been told almost six months earlier of a similar incident, nothing had been done. The marine was later convicted of espionage. When the General Accounting Office (GAO) looked into the matter it found that the office in the State Department charged with investigating possible security breaches was disorganized and overworked, did not stay in touch with other agencies, and provided no serious counterintelligence training to diplomats.[2]

A reader with a conspiratorial cast of mind might think that these lapses were the result of sinister influences at work within the U.S. government. But there is no evidence of that at all. Instead what occurred was the result of an organizational culture that simply did not assign a high value to security. Not assigning much value to security, it did not allocate many resources to the task or reward people who worked at it.

Organizational Culture

Every organization has a culture, that is, a persistent, patterned way of thinking about the central tasks of and human relationships within an organization. Culture is to an organization what personality is to an individual. Like human culture generally, it is passed on from one generation to the next. It changes slowly, if at all.

In business, "corporate culture" is a hot topic.[3] Popular books abound with accounts of how IBM or Hewlett-Packard emphasize teamwork and excellence in ways that gave them a competitive advantage over their more mechanistic and individualistic rivals. The theme has been taken up by scholars who have begun to set forth competing (and usually highly abstract) definitions of organizational culture and look for ways of describing it more precisely.[4] Though now much in vogue, the concept is at least a half century old. In 1938 Chester Barnard wrote about the "moral ele-

ment" in organizations and the "moral factor" in leadership. By moral he did not mean merely obeying the law or following the rules, but "the process of inculcating points of view, fundamental attitudes, loyalties, to the organization . . . that will result in subordinating individual interest . . . to the good of the cooperative whole."[5] Two decades later Philip Selznick likened the creation of "organization character" to character formation in an individual: A viable organization is not merely a technical system of cooperation (any more than an individual is merely a mechanism processing food and sensations); it is an institution that has been "infused with value" so that it displays a "distinctive competence" (or a distinctive incompetence!).[6] An organization acquires a distinctive competence or sense of mission when it has not only answered the question "What shall we do?" but also the question "What shall we be?"

There are some difficulties with viewing organizations as culture. One mistake is to assume that an organization will have *a* culture; many, perhaps most, will have several cultures that are often in conflict. The culture of the United States Navy is very different depending on whether you are assigned to submarines, aircraft carriers, or battleships. Another is to give so much emphasis to culture—that is, to the subjective states of organization members—that one loses sight of the objective conditions of organizational participation. The best-known study calling attention to what we now call culture (the famous inquiry at the Western Electric factory into the way in which group norms determined worker output) badly overstated the effect of beliefs and understated the influence of money payments, supervisory controls, and prevailing economic conditions.[7] A third problem has been the failure of theorists of organizational culture to state and rigorously test hypotheses about culture; as a result, many critics argue that culture is little more than a mushy word used to dignify the hunches and intuitions of softheaded writers who produce journalism in the guise of scholarship.[8]

This last criticism is partially correct but fundamentally mistaken. Organizational culture admittedly is a vague concept, but no less real than concepts such as national culture or human personality. We find it hard to explain how exactly Italians differ from Germans or introverts from extroverts, but we do not doubt that there are important differences. Recall the examples in chapter 1: The German army, Carver High School, and the Texas prisons did not differ from their less successful rivals because they paid their workers more money but because they had managed to discover a rational definition of their core tasks and induce their members to share and act on that definition. They had created an organizational culture appropriate to their critical environmental challenge and generated enthusiasm among the operators about taking that culture seriously.

Human personality consists of those enduring traits among individuals that lead them to respond differently to the same stimuli.[9] When faced with aggression, some of us retreat, some fight back, and some are paralyzed with fear. When faced with a risky chance to make money, some of us seize it, some ignore it, and some anguish over it. Organizational culture consists of those patterned and enduring differences among systems of coordinated action that lead those systems to respond in different ways to the same stimuli. When faced with changed environmental conditions, some organizations persist in traditional ways of behaving and others will adopt new ways of behaving. When criticized, some organizations hunker down and others conduct a searching self-examination.

All organizations have one or more cultures just as all people have a personality. An agency's culture is produced in part by those factors discussed in the preceding three chapters. We can summarize them by saying that the predispositions of members, the technology of the organization, and the situational imperatives with which the agency must cope tend to give to the organization a distinctive way of seeing and responding to the world. This is especially the case when the organization's stated goals are vague. When, as is often the case, these factors produce different definitions of core tasks for different people (or, more typically, different subunits), the organization will have several cultures. Sometimes, however, all or most members agree as to what the organization's central tasks are and how they should be performed; then the organization has a single culture.

A Second Look at the State Department

The core tasks of the State Department have been defined as maintaining relationships and replying to documents (see chapter 3). This definition has generated an organizational culture that values diplomacy above all else. To a foreign service officer diplomacy implies communication, and communication implies openness. In this view, security is the enemy of openness. One could rejoin that there is in fact no conflict between diplomacy and security; indeed, one could argue that effective diplomacy requires good security. But many diplomats believe that a secure embassy is one that seems closed, uninviting, forbidding. Security means saying little; diplomacy means saying a lot, albeit carefully. Security means keeping foreigners at arm's length; diplomacy means getting to know people by, among other ways, employing them. Some diplomats do not bother to argue the point; they give lip service to security but regard the people, technical devices, and organizational procedures that make up a security system as a bothersome encumbrance that often makes ridiculous demands.

In such a culture one would predict that security specialists will not win rapid advancement (especially if they are in competition with diplomats) and security concerns will not win out in struggles over scarce resources. That is exactly what happened in State. The people and offices in charge of security were kept in subordinate positions, denied their own budget and personnel authority, and forced to wait their turn for new resources. After heavy prodding by outside task forces, over the years State upgraded its security apparatus and hired more security professionals, but never with enthusiasm. Every outside committee that looked at the matter concluded that the department was dragging its feet.[10]

The elite corps of professional diplomats that, though constituting a minority of all State employees, dominates its culture had its modern origin in the Rogers Act of 1924. This law defined a career diplomatic service that would be "semi-independent" of its host agency, the State Department, and of the civil service system.[11] Until the law was modified in 1980, the Foreign Service consisted chiefly of generalists, not specialists, who would engage in political reporting and negotiation. Members would be rotated among assignments to insure that they did not become specialists and would be promoted on the basis of reporting to make certain they did not become administrators.

In business firms and many government agencies promotion is based on the display of administrative skill coupled with specialist knowledge. The Foreign Service was created with different expectations and, though circumstances have modified the formative experience, it still displays a faint contempt for both specialization and administration.[12] These attitudes are reinforced by, and help shape the response to, the circumstances in which diplomats find themselves: Inundated with incoming messages, they are pressed to respond with messages of their own.

Foreign service officers place a high value on "the diplomatic approach," and that means "subtlety, skill in negotiation, cultural sophistication, and good manners."[13] That also means caution, an aversion to bold language or action, and a desire for consensus.[14] Some have argued that these are the traits of the social class from which diplomats are drawn or result from an effort to ape the style of European diplomats. There may be something to this, but I doubt there is very much. Take a person of reasonable intelligence from almost any background, expose him or her to this task environment—the situational demands, the foreign service ethos, and the incentives that reward those who manage those demands and conform to that ethos—and I predict that he or she would act pretty much as other diplomats act. Circumstances require that paper be processed; organizational culture leads it to be processed by generalists rather than by specialists. Skill in processing paper is rewarded; skill in other things—embassy security is one and management generally is another—are not. Secretary of State George Shultz attempted to change this culture somewhat by fixing on each ambassador responsibility for embassy security, but with only limited effect.

Since every organization has a culture, every organization will be poorly adapted to perform tasks that are not defined as part of that culture. The State Department is not alone in this regard. The Tennessee Valley Authority for a long time had (and may still have) an engineering culture that values efficient power production and undervalues environmental protection. Universities have a culture that rewards professorial research more than classroom teaching. Later in this chapter we shall consider in more detail the defects of an organizational culture. But first it is important to appreciate its strengths. That is easiest to do when an organization takes pride in an explicit, often consciously created culture.

Organizational Mission

When an organization has a culture that is widely shared and warmly endorsed by operators and managers alike, we say the organization has a sense of *mission.** A sense of mission confers a feeling of special worth on the members, provides a basis for recruiting and socializing new members, and enables the administrators to economize on the use of other incentives. As we shall see in the chapter on compliance, having a sense of mission is the chief way by which managers overcome the problem of shirking in organizations that (like most government bureaus) cannot make the money wages of operators directly dependent on the operators' observed contribution to attaining the goals of the organization.

Able administrators will not want to let their agencies' culture be formed by the chance operation of predispositions, professional norms, interest-group pressures, or situational imperatives. Such executives will try to shape that culture by plan in order to produce not only a widely shared but warmly endorsed culture—in short, a sense of mission.

No administrator finds it easy to create a sense of mission; government executives find it especially difficult. When agency goals are vague, it will be hard to convey to operators a simple and vivid understanding of what they are supposed to do. Thus tasks will get defined in ways over which administrators have only limited control, with the result that the definition adopted by the operators may be one that the executive does not intend and may not desire. Since government agencies often have more than

*"Mission" is sometimes used by bureaucrats to refer to the principal goal of their agency. I am using the word here in a somewhat different way to mean what Philip Selznick calls "distinctive competence"[15] or Morton Halperin calls "essence."[16] Among the other scholars who have made use of the term are Jonathan Bendor,[17] Jerry Mashaw,[18] Robert F. Durant,[19] and Martha Derthick.[20]

one goal and thus engage in more than one kind of task, they will have many competing cultures that cannot easily be fused into a shared sense of mission. Since government administrators are hemmed in by a variety of legal and political constraints, they usually will lack the power to impose their own sense of mission on the organizations of which they are nominally the head. And since developing a sense of mission is easiest when an organization is first created, the fact that most administrators take up their duties in organizations that have long histories sharply reduces their opportunities for affecting the culture at all, much less making it into a strong and coherent sense of mission.

But sometimes an organization is endowed with a sense of mission despite ambiguous goals, personal predispositions, group pressures, and situational imperatives. This usually occurs during the formative experience of the organization, an experience shaped and interpreted by a founder who imposes his or her will on the first generation of operators in a way that profoundly affects succeeding generations.* Borrowing a term from ethology, John R. Kimberly calls this a process of "imprinting."[23] The imprint is deepest and most lasting when the founding executive has a strong personality and a forcefully expressed vision of what the organization should be.

Herbert Kaufman has given us a classic account of the many ways by which the Forest Service controls the activities of its far-flung representatives. No more important control technique exists than the method created by Gifford Pinchot for recruiting and training foresters.[24]

When Pinchot assumed command (no weaker term will do) of the Bureau of Forestry in 1898, he made it clear that he expected it to do more than study forests and educate people as to their uses. He expected the bureau to *manage* the forests. He began a program to train personnel in forest management so that by 1905, when he succeeded in wresting control of federally-owned forests from the Interior Department, he was ready to put operators who shared his vision in charge of these vast lands.

From the first, Pinchot saw to it that his agency would have the feel of an elite service. He stressed to prospective recruits the dangers and hardships of life in the forests and the need to conform to the strict code of conduct and the strong hierarchical controls of the organization.[25] During most years the service rejected far more applicants than it accepted (in 1940, 18 percent were taken), and as many as 15 percent of those accepted dropped out within the first three years.[26] Today, even graduates of forestry schools go through rigorous in-service training, much of it designed to inculcate the values of professional forestry as much as the practical

*The social structure and prevailing ideology of the historical period in which an organization is founded can also shape its mission. I will not here pursue this intriguing but difficult line of inquiry. Arthur L. Stinchcombe opened up the topic in a famous essay[21] and I have since tried to develop it with respect to voluntary associations.[22]

techniques of forest management. When they take up their posts, the rangers are aware that they are under the watchful eye of a corps of inspectors, created by Pinchot in 1905. The inspection system is a comprehensive and continuous process of evaluating everybody in the organization with "blunt and hard-hitting" reports.[27]

The result of these formative experiences was the creation of a cadre of foresters who deeply believed in what Paul J. Culhane has called "progressive conservation": the expert, nonpartisan, and professional management of the national forests for the benefit of many different kinds of users.[28] If that seems obvious to us now, consider how differently the fledgling agency might have evolved had it gone through a different formative experience. A decentralized organization with operators working alone in isolated outposts might well have decided that its task was to please whatever dominant and politically influential group existed in local communities. The situational imperative in Boise might have led foresters to defer wholly to mining interests, in Portland wholly to timber interests, and in Santa Barbara wholly to nature-lovers. Something different happened, and Pinchot helped make the difference.

J. Edgar Hoover had a similar impact on the newly created Federal Bureau of Investigation, and by means not very different from those employed by Pinchot in the Forest Service. The old Bureau of Investigation in the Department of Justice had acquired a sorry reputation for actively fomenting the Red Scare, organizing mass deportations, and spying on the political enemies of the Harding administration. Hoover had been part of this early history as Attorney General A. Mitchell Palmer's right-hand man during the Red Scare years.[29] A lesser man might have been broken by the criticisms that eventually descended on the old bureau or might have continued to pursue the political causes that had come to taint it. But Hoover learned from experience and when he accepted the directorship of the bureau from Attorney General Harlan Fiske Stone in 1924 he was determined that the new organization would make none of the mistakes of the old.

The old agents were cleaned out and there was no partisanship in the choice of replacements. The anti-radical focus was played down. The newly christened Federal Bureau of Investigation was to limit itself to gathering facts about possible violations of federal laws. Policy advocacy at least formally was foresworn. A personnel system was put in place outside the normal civil service system, one that gave Hoover almost unlimited authority to hire and fire, promote and demote. A training academy was organized and a corps of inspectors set up to check on the most minute details of an agent's work. The elaborately cross-indexed files that Hoover had begun when he ran the General Intelligence Division (the group charged with keeping track of radicals) were enlarged and extended to cover ordinary criminals. Thus began the legend of the spit-and-polish

FBI agent, defined by detailed orders about dress, grooming, and conduct. The slightest hint of corruption or misuse of authority was grounds for instant punishment. Hoover made it appear (and appearances were not far from the truth) that he personally oversaw every detail of the FBI's work. "For the average FBI agent," Sanford J. Ungar was later to write, "the Bureau became his extended family, his source of many political and social values, his most enduring fraternal connection."[30]

As we shall see, this organizational system had its costs and in time changing political circumstances made the Hoover methods a liability even before he died in 1972.[31] But when it began it was a memorable formative experience for the organization's new members. Hoover left no doubt about it: The job of an FBI agent was to conduct interviews with citizens in ways that would enhance citizen confidence in the bureau, meticulously record and cross-index those interviews in ways that would obtain prosecutorial support, and make arrests in ways that would be immune to legal challenge.[32]

The United States Army Corps of Engineers is the largest engineering and construction organization in the world and, as Mohammad Al-Saud has shown, it is widely regarded as the best such agency in the federal government.[33] It designs and oversees the construction of civil projects in this country and military projects for this and other governments around the world. To manage its far-flung enterprises, the corps sends its field representatives throughout the United States, Latin America, Europe, Africa, the Middle East, and the Far East. Though given wide discretion and left without close headquarters supervision, these field representatives in the opinion of almost every observer have performed admirably, insuring that local contractors build the projects in accordance with specifications, within budgets, and without scandal. As we shall see in a later chapter, the formal personnel control mechanisms of the corps cannot by themselves explain this enviable record.

What does account for its success is the strong sense of mission (what Al-Saud calls a "professional ethos") with which corps members are imbued.[34] The origins of that ethos can be traced back to the founding of the corps as an elite engineering unit in the U.S. Army by Sylvanus Thayer, when he became superintendent of the United States Military Academy at West Point. Thayer set about devising a rigorous curriculum of engineering education patterned after the Ecole Polytechnique in France, where Thayer had been educated. Recruitment and promotion in the Corps of Engineers were based strictly on merit.

Secretary of War John C. Calhoun extended the influence of the corps by centralizing and regularizing the management of army construction projects. After the Civil War, the Academy became a school for the training of all officers, not just engineers, but the top graduates from West Point were customarily assigned to the Corps of Engineers, thereby confirming and enlarging its status as an elite unit. By 1910, when Congress authorized the corps to hire large numbers of civilians to manage its growing list of projects, the tradition of being part of a unit with high performance standards and strict codes of integrity was so widely accepted that the organization could become overwhelmingly civilian in composition without losing the sense of mission developed out of its military ancestry. Reinforcing this sense was the organizational folklore about the legendary projects for which the corps had been responsible: the Washington Monument, the Library of Congress, the Panama Canal, the Pentagon, and the Manhattan Project.

Like the Forest Service and the FBI, the corps recruits and trains new members with an eye chiefly on the maintenance of its sense of mission. The corps advertises itself as a prestige organization with exacting standards and difficult duties. A prospective member is told that he or she may be sent to some remote part of the world, and then, before he or she can establish a comfortable life there, suddenly is uprooted and sent to a new post in another distant location. At the same time the corps emphasizes that it will take care of its own, working hard to guard against any personnel layoffs owing to budget cuts and going to great lengths to get field representatives who have completed a project reassigned to other projects of equivalent importance.[35]

Forest rangers, FBI agents, construction engineers—by government standards, these are glamorous, often exciting jobs. It is easy to assume that "mission" is really nothing more than "excitement." Not at all. An organization can have a strong sense of mission—that is, a widely shared and endorsed definition of the agency's core tasks—when the tasks are prosaic, even dull. Take the Social Security Administration (SSA).

As we have seen, its work could not be more routine: assessing eligibility, determining benefits, writing checks. But when the Social Security system was founded in 1935, key leaders, especially Arthur J. Altmeyer and John G. Winant, pressed hard and successfully for winning an exemption from standard civil service rules so that they could hire especially talented persons, usually with a social-science background, who shared the liberal commitment to a universal retirement system in which benefits would be guaranteed to all contributors as a matter of right and without a means test.[36] To be sure, these goals were firmly embedded in the statute. But it is easy to imagine creating an organization that would implement the statute in accordance with a very different ethos. The founders could have said: "Our job is to protect the taxpayers and save money. Thus, every person claiming a retirement benefit should be viewed with suspicion and his or her claim inspected with lengthy, painstaking care. Moreover, when Congress considers changes in the statute, the SSA should at most remain neutral and perhaps devote itself to finding fault with any proposed benefit increases."[37]

Instead, the founders of the SSA created an organization with what Martha Derthick, like many others, has called a "client-serving ethic."[38] Altmeyer and Winant devoted many hours to handpicking the managers of local field offices to insure that they were fully imbued with the client-serving ethos. Recruitment and training programs emphasized not just the procedures but the "philosophy" of Social Security (by which was meant the commitment to serving beneficiaries).[39]

SSA was given a relatively simple task that was carefully defined by law. The founders of SSA did not have to define the task nor counter situational factors that might lead to other definitions (after all, the clients *wanted* what SSA had to offer, unlike the "clients" of the FBI). But the founders were not content with simply presiding over a technical machine that efficiently converted claims into benefits; they wanted SSA to be an institution that in large part would run on its members' commitment to providing service.

That commitment was alive and well for almost half a century. In bureaucracy as in life, however, no good deed goes unpunished. Congress, appreciative of SSA's accomplishments but (apparently) ignorant of the reasons, gave to that agency two tasks that threatened to subvert SSA's sense of mission—administering Supplemental Security Income (SSI) and Disability Insurance (DI). SSI is a federal program that supplements the incomes of poor, blind, aged, and disabled persons; DI is one that pays benefits to disabled workers regardless of income. The tasks required by these programs were fundamentally different from those entailed by the older retirement program. Retirement benefits went to everybody who had paid taxes into the Social Security trust fund and who had reached a certain age. Everyone was treated alike on the basis of clear national standards. SSI required the SSA to decide who was needy—that is, to design and impose a means test. DI required SSA to decide who was disabled sufficiently to prevent them from working—that is, to evaluate medical evidence.

In her penetrating account of SSA's efforts to cope with these tasks, Martha Derthick showed how both very nearly overwhelmed the agency. For many years, SSA was able to finesse one of these difficulties by relying on the states to decide who was disabled. But when Congress and the president ordered a tightening of standards and the withdrawal of benefits from people who were not truly disabled, SSA had to look behind the state administrations and evaluate the evidence itself. The result was near chaos. SSI required creating a massive computer and administrative system to judge "need"; DI required empowering hundreds of administrative law judges to hear complaints from people who claimed their benefits had been unfairly terminated. To administer these programs SSA had to abandon its commitment to benefits awarded as a matter of right and on the basis of national standards in favor of benefits awarded on the basis of need and in accordance with complex court rulings and ambiguous claims. The SSA not only experienced a managerial nightmare, it "suffered an incalculable loss of prestige, morale, and self-confidence."[40] Its members found themselves in conflict with clients who once had been supportive, in conflict with Congress and the courts which had once kept hands off, and in conflict with each other.

The Effects of Culture: Some Generalizations

The benefits of a strong sense of mission are clear from the SSA case. The widely shared and strongly endorsed commitment to service on the basis of nationally determined rights made it easier to manage that vast agency. People did not always have to be told what to do; they knew what to do, and what is more important, wanted to do it well. (The SSI and DI controversies were a blow to the agency's mission.) Other examples of the positive effects of culture will be discussed in the next chapter. But this gain may be purchased at a price: First, tasks that are not part of the culture will not be attended to with the same energy and resources as are devoted to tasks that are part of it. Second, organizations in which two or more cultures struggle for supremacy will experience serious conflict as defenders of one seek to dominate representatives of the others. Third, organizations will resist taking on new tasks that seem incompatible with its dominant culture. The stronger and more uniform the culture—that is, the more the culture approximates a sense of mission—the more obvious these consequences.

SELECTIVE ATTENTION

The State Department is hardly a unique example of organizational culture determining which tasks are regarded as most important. Within the Central Intelligence Agency there have been two dominant cultures, each organized into its own directorate. One emphasizes the analysis of intelligence on the intentions and capabilities of other nations, the other the clandestine gathering of intelligence and the conduct of covert operations abroad.[41] There has been a good deal of rivalry between the "white" (analytical) and "black" (clandestine) sides of the agency, but the latter has always been dominant. As a result, certain tasks have been neglected. Two examples: counterintelligence and defector management.

Counterintelligence means, loosely, defending one's agency or nation against the activities of a hostile intelligence service. One way to accomplish this is to identify and neutralize efforts to penetrate the CIA with spies and double agents. Counterintelligence (CI) officers are trained skeptics who often question the sincerity of a Soviet intelligence officer who says he is willing to defect to this country or to work for the CIA while remaining in the KGB; they worry that he is actually a plant or a double agent. Intelligence officers, by contrast, are rewarded for recruiting Soviet agents or inducing them to defect. The CI officers always seem to be saying no to colleagues who want them to say yes. It is important not to exaggerate these differences in orientation. Intelligence officers usually go to great lengths to be certain the person they are recruiting is the real thing and not a plant; the CI officer often will decide that the alleged defector is a real defector. But when conflict arises, culture shapes the outcome. In the CIA, intelligence has always won out over counterintelligence.[42]

There was one period when CI seemed to have the upper hand, a period recalled with great bitterness by almost everyone who lived through it. That was when James Jesus Angleton was the chief of counterintelligence. To his admirers, Angleton was a gifted intellect who made a valiant but ultimately unsuccessful effort to keep the KGB from planting moles and double agents inside the CIA. To his critics, he was a paranoid believer in nonexistent conspiracies whose false and reckless charges prevented the CIA from recruiting authentic Soviet defectors and ruined the careers of some CIA officers. Angleton and his old CI staff drove intelligence officers half crazy with their endless, suspicion-laden accusations about the bona fides of alleged defectors and their oft-expressed fears that the CIA had been penetrated by a Soviet mole. But intelligence officers drove Angleton half crazy with what he regarded as their naive eagerness to believe anybody who claimed to be a defector and their reluctance to doubt the "secrets" they thought they had uncovered. In 1974, William Colby, then director of central intelligence, fired Angleton.

But even when Angleton was at the height of his powers, counterintelligence was organizationally a stepchild in the CIA. His influence was personal, not structural, and his fall from power was as much the result of personal failings as of any organizational weakness. His CI staff was never able to dominate the culture of the CIA; they were (at best or at worst, depending on your perspective) organizational guerrillas waging war on the operations directorate. Professor Robin Winks has observed, correctly, that CI "had always been vulnerable within the agency" because it seemed to get in the way of what intelligence officers wanted to do—namely, to discover secrets and recruit defectors.[43] Whatever the source of his power, however, the firing of Angleton and the breakup of his CI staff confirmed the organizational power and perceived correctness of the dominant culture. Almost immediately, Colby sent written instructions to the field encouraging them to recruit Soviet officials instead of regarding them all as provocations.[44]

Every culture has a blind spot, and so every organization pays some price for its culture. For over two decades—including the years when Angleton was in office—the Cuban intelligence services were able to plant double agents in the CIA and monitor virtually every detail of CIA activities in that country.[45]

Defector management has suffered from the same cultural orientation. Even when everyone in the CIA agrees that, say, a KGB colonel who has sought asylum in a U.S. embassy is a genuine defector, the resettlement of that defector in this country has been done in ways that reveal how poorly regarded this task has been within the CIA culture. Working on defector resettlement means attending to the mundane details of housing, drivers' licenses, bank accounts, and job opportunities, often on behalf of people who are frightened, petulant, and demanding. Doing these things is not, in bureaucratic language, "career enhancing." In plain language, nobody rises far in a culture that stresses cunning and derring-do by proving himself to be a talented babysitter. Under these circumstances, one would predict that many able CIA officers would resist assignment to defector work, and so that work would suffer. We know that some defectors have complained publicly. Unfortunately, the core tasks of the dominant organizational culture—learning secrets—require that defector management be done well in order to make defecting to this country attractive to the members of hostile intelligence services. In short, the skewing of an organization's reward system by the existence of an organizational culture can make it difficult for those who are part of that culture to do their work well.

Examples could be multiplied indefinitely. We have already seen in chapter 5 how the power engineers created the dominant organizational culture in the TVA, with the result that other TVA goals—for example, regional planning and environmental protection—suffered. A similar story can be told about the Washington, D.C., mass transit system. When the system was being developed in the 1960s and 1970s, the agency responsible for the job (the Washington Metropolitan Area Transit Authority, or "Metro") was organized in a way that made the design and management of rail transit the core task and the source of the organization's culture. But Metro also was supposed to run bus service in the area. Operating buses required a different culture, but the Metro created no special organizational niche in which that culture could develop. Bus service deteriorated as a result, and for a long time the organization seemed unable to cope with the problem. The bus was the step-child of the organization. (For example, though there was more crime on buses than on subways, for years all of the security guards were assigned to train and rail stations and none to buses or bus stops.) Here, as with defector management in the CIA, different tasks will be done well only if given enough organizational autonomy so that distinctive, self-supporting cultures can develop and claim their share of resources.[46]

A tragic example of the risks to which an organization with a strong sense of mission may be exposed can be found in the inquiry into the accident on January 28, 1986, that destroyed the space shuttle *Challenger* and claimed seven lives. The National Aeronautics and Space Administration (NASA) was imbued with an engineering culture that had so captured the imagination of its adherents and had been responsible for so many extraordinary accomplishments that few if any doubted its value. The mission, as described by the Rogers Commission that investigated the accident, was a "can-do" attitude based on the diligent and systematic application of hard work and engineering principles.[47] The engineers' brilliant achievements in launching the Apollo capsules, the moon-landing vehicle, and the first space shuttle led NASA to accept each new challenge with fresh zeal—but with a steady drain on resources, human energies, attention to detail, and careful planning. "NASA's attitude historically has reflected the position that 'We can do anything,' " the Rogers Commission later wrote, "and while that may essentially be true, NASA's optimism must be tempered by the realization that it cannot do everything."[48]

Several engineers had grave reservations about the design of the shuttle rockets, in particular the part where two sections of the fuel tanks were joined together. They worried that the joints might separate under heavy stress or during very cold weather—precisely what happened in 1986, with fatal results. One of those engineers, Roger Boisjoly, employed by a NASA contractor, Morton Thiokol, later told the Rogers Commission that he was diffident about expressing his concerns:

> I have been personally chastised in flight readiness reviews . . . for using the words "I feel" or "I think," and I have been crucified to the effect that that is not proper presentation because "I feel" and "I expect" are not engineering-supported statements, but they are judgmental. . . . And for that reason, nobody [raises objections] without a complete, fully documented, verifiable set of data.[49]

Of course, engineers did not kill crew members. There were many contributing factors: pressures to move quickly with the launch schedule, budget cuts that resulted in a shortage of spare parts, unwise reductions in quality-assurance inspectors, and management decisions to accept ever-higher risks because "nothing had gone wrong the last time."[50] Warnings that should have been heeded were not. Organizational checks and balances designed to enforce safety rules were ineffective. But these contributing factors may have been tolerated in part because of the confidence a highly mission-oriented organization had that it could meet any challenge, overcome any difficulty. Government agencies, contrary to folklore, are not invariably collections of nay-sayers; sometimes they are collections of yea-sayers. The challenge for executives is to strike the right balance between them.

MULTIPLE CULTURES

Many government agencies have multiple, competing cultures. Some manage the competition well, some do not. A major responsibility of an executive is not only, as Selznick has put it, to infuse the organization with value, it is also to discover a way by which different values (and the different cultures that espouse those values) can productively coexist.

Ever since Morton H. Halperin wrote *Bureaucratic Politics and Foreign Policy*,[51] students of government agencies have been acutely aware of how organizational cultures (Halperin called them organizational essences) shape the behavior of the military services. The culture of the United States Air Force for a long time expressed the primacy of flying combat aircraft capable of carrying nuclear weapons. The Second World War brought glory and power to bomber pilots; after the war, the USAF became culturally a fraternity of bomber pilots. Bomber pilots rose to most of the top jobs in the service. This meant that officers who flew other kinds of aircraft—fighters, transport planes, or infantry-support tactical aircraft—discovered that they were not part of the dominant culture. What this meant can be grasped from Arthur T. Hadley's observation that from the creation of the air force until 1982 no fighter pilot ever had become air force chief of staff.[52] Even more subordinate has been the Military Airlift Command, a unit that suffers not only from having to fly transport planes instead of bombers but transport planes designed to carry *army* personnel to distant battlefields. (By an interservice agreement, to be discussed in a later chapter, the army was denied the right to have its own fleet of troop transports.) Operating a "bus service" for the army is not a highly rewarded task in the USAF.

The principal challenge to the dominant USAF culture came not from fighters or transports but from missiles. As we shall see in a later chapter, in the early 1960s the air force was not eager to have the new intercontinental ballistic missiles (ICBMs). These gadgets threatened the supremacy of the bomber and, to be fair, in fact no one knew whether they would work. Besides, as Halperin put it, "sitting in silos just cannot compare to flying bombers."[53] But the decision was not the air force's to make. Civilians decided to acquire missiles and the air force faced an awkward choice: either preserve the culture at the cost of letting the army and navy have what may turn out to be the weapon of the century, or get on the bandwagon at the cost of modifying the culture. The air force got on the bandwagon, albeit reluctantly. It has accommodated the new missile technology (and accompanying missile culture) well enough to become a strong advocate of building more advanced ICBMs as existing ones become outmoded. But still it insists on the crucial role of the bomber, and so has campaigned incessantly for ever more advanced bombers, first the B1, then the B1B, then the Stealth bomber.

The United States Navy has at least three organizational cultures each symbolized by the kind of shoe the officers wear. The "black shoe" navy is the navy of battleships, cruisers, and destroyers—ships of the line, built to protect the sea lanes and bombard enemy shores. The "brown shoe" navy is the navy of aircraft carriers and carrier-based aircraft. Naval aviators wear brown shoes; even the captains of the carriers traditionally have an aviator background. The "felt shoe" navy is the world of the submariners (they wear cloth shoes to reduce noise and so help defeat enemy listening devices). Since the Second World War the carrier, or brown-shoe, navy has been the dominant culture, but not as dominant as the strategic bomber force has been in the air force. Carrier admirals usually have won the allocative struggles, but not always; the submariners have powerful external allies in Congress and public opinion (Admiral Hyman Rickover, founder of the nuclear submarine navy, until his death was a popular and political hero). Even the battleship, once relegated to the role of a floating museum for schoolchildren, has made a comeback owing to support from the Reagan administration. The greater balance among rival cultures in the navy than those in the air force suggests that the problem of having multiple cultures can be managed without having one culture win out over another.

The uneasy balance among brown-, black-, and felt-shoe officers may be healthy, but also it is incomplete. At least two other tasks that the navy performs—shipping military cargo ("sealift") and sweeping mines—have received relatively little organizational support. When in 1987 the navy began escorting oil tankers in the Persian Gulf to protect them against Iranian attacks, it discovered to its embarrassment that it did not have a sufficient fleet of minesweepers to protect the convoys from the ancient mines put in the sea lanes by the pathetically small Iranian Navy. Commanding a minesweeper was not as career enhancing as commanding a carrier or a submarine; not surprisingly, very few minesweepers had been built.

Some government agencies have been endowed with so strong a sense of agency-wide mission that they do a better job than others in managing the tensions among rival occupational subcultures. The National Security Agency (NSA), the organization that intercepts messages from other nations and tries to break their codes, thinks of itself as an elite intelligence agency. Its goals are so clearly defined that its core tasks are well-understood; as a result, the cultural differences that exist among different occupational groups within NSA do not materially get in the way of coordinating activities. At worst, these groups form a prestige hierarchy, with the "crippies" (the theoretical mathematicians and cryptanalysts) at the top, closely followed by the "computer jocks" and the linguists. Status differences may be important but they do not seem to threaten goal attainment precisely because the goals are so clear and well-understood.

The Forest Service also has had a strong sense of mission, but one that contained more ambiguities than the precise goals of NSA. Achieving "multiple use and sustained yields" from forests was a sufficient description of service tasks when the details of those tasks were filled in by the professional foresters who made up the organization. But as new demands on the agency led it to bring in new occupational and professional groups, the ambiguities became more important and divisive. The "yield" of a forest was very different depending on whether you spoke to a biologist, an economist, an engineer, or a forester. Evidence of these different perspectives were the colloquial and not always flattering names each group acquired. For example, rangeland specialists were known as "cowpunchers," architects as "landscrapers," conservationists as "hysterical conservationists," and wildlife biologists as "moose-and-goosers."[54]

Christopher Leman described how the Forest Service has been able to accommodate many of these new cultures. The remoteness of many of the posts to which service members are assigned forces different specialists to spend time with each other rather than with professional colleagues elsewhere in the organization or outside of it. This leads to greater mutual tolerance and respect than would be the case if each was confined to a separate organizational unit.[55] Some of the tasks of service members (e.g., surveying) can be performed independently of the tasks of other specialists; since close coordination is not needed, struggles for dominance are less common. And the mission traditions of the service often lead members to value their association with the service as a whole as much or more than they value their affiliation with fellow specialists.

But this accommodation only works up to a point. Leman also reports that the multiplication of occupational specialties has taken its toll. As mentioned in chapter 4, economists, engineers, conservationists, and foresters struggle to impose their definition of core tasks on the service. The result has been a measurable drop in organizational loyalty. A 1981 survey found that the majority of service employees believed the service had declined in morale and in the strength of the mutual bonds among employees. The annual turnover rate in 1983 was nearly twice what it had been in the 1970s.[56]

RESISTING NEW TASKS

The sense of mission inside the FBI is and has been very strong; for decades it was strong enough to lead the bureau to resist tasks that seemed to threaten the core culture. Accordingly, the FBI did not become involved in the investigation of organized crime or narcotics trafficking despite the fact that these matters were violations of federal law that the bureau, had it actually been as imperialistic as some of its critics alleged, easily could have brought under its jurisdiction. There were several reasons for staying clear of such investigations, but one was that these cases seemed to require FBI agents to behave in ways that judged by the standards of the bureau's culture were deemed too risky.

The investigation of a bank robbery or kidnapping begins with a complaint: the bank president or the kidnap victim's relatives call the bureau with a plea for help. It can easily be determined that a law has been broken. A case file is opened. Agents are assigned to interview victims and witnesses. To find leads the dossiers of likely suspects are studied and criminal informants are contacted. If a suspect is found he or she is questioned. If the case is solved and an arrest is made, it is usually because of the ability of FBI agents to conduct productive interviews, supplemented by a combination of luck and laboratory analyses of physical evidence.[57] All this can be done, and by and large had been done, in accordance with the strictest rules governing arrests, searches, and interrogations and in ways that permitted the agent to conform precisely to the image (that is, mission) of the FBI that J. Edgar Hoover had been at such pains to develop—clean-cut, aboveboard, nonpartisan.

Investigating consensual crimes such as narcotics trafficking is another matter. No victim files a complaint. There is no obvious criminal incident to investigate. If the existence of a crime, much less its perpetrators, is to be established, then the agent must either participate in an illegal transaction (by posing as a drug buyer) or penetrate the criminal enterprise (by posing as a gangster). Undercover work is not only risky for the agent, it is risky for the bureau—it exposes it to the possibility that in going undercover an agent will break the law, become corrupted, or otherwise create embarrassment or controversy for the FBI.

For decades the culture of the bureau led many of its key officials to oppose using undercover methods and for that reason (among others) to oppose investigating narcotics cases. The many scandals that occasionally had tarnished the image of the agencies that did take on drug cases—originally the Federal Bureau of Narcotics, then later the Bureau of Narcotics and Dangerous Drugs and the Drug Enforcement Administration—only confirmed FBI members in their desire to stay away from these threatening activities. Ultimately the FBI did take over general responsibility for drug enforcement for reasons and with results that will be discussed in a later chapter.

The United States Department of Agriculture for many years has had responsibility for running the Food Stamp program whereby persons with low incomes receive certificates enabling them to buy food at greatly reduced prices. People who believe that "bureaucrats are imperialists" would expect Agriculture jealously to guard its control of the rapidly growing Food Stamp program. They would be surprised to learn that in fact Agriculture has repeatedly tried to get rid of it.

In the early 1970s, President Richard Nixon submitted a reorganization plan that called for the transfer of the Food and Nutrition Service (FNS), which ran Food Stamps as well as other programs, out of Agriculture and into the Department of Health, Education, and Welfare (now Health and Human Services). He did so with the blessing and encouragement of the secretary of agriculture. Agriculture was in the business of helping farmers grow things and paying farmers not to grow things. Contradictory as these goals may seem, they at least were managed by an organizational culture that saw itself as in the "food business," serving as the farmer's friend. Food Stamps were part of the "welfare business." The main Agriculture bureaus dealt with farmers and county farm organizations; the FNS had to deal with state and local welfare offices. Aid to farmers was calculated by using clear formulas based on crop prices; aid to the poor was based on determining "need." Marc Tipermas, who studied the plan, found that department representatives believed the continuation of FNS in Agriculture would "undermine the department's ability to deal effectively with all its other programs."[58]

FNS, a senior Agriculture spokesman complained, was "pulling resources away from my office—in terms of management attention, like audits, computer analysts, financial analysts, and the Secretary's personal time."[59] This explanation is a bit hard to accept at face value. The agricultural subsidy program is vast, complex, and extremely expensive. But no secretary of agriculture has ever proposed transferring it out because of these "burdens" on his time and resources. What made Food Stamps burdensome was not simply its cost, but its nature; it required Agriculture to perform tasks very different from those it was used to performing, and this was seen as a distraction, as it was. Administrators can handle very complex and expensive programs if they involve a small or at least compatible set of tasks. Managing complex and expensive programs is much harder if they involve highly disparate tasks. Agriculture saw this and wanted to rid itself of the interloper. It failed, and still has responsibility for FNS to this day.

Culture and Mission: A Summary

Every organization has a culture, many have several. When a single culture is broadly shared and warmly endorsed it is a mission. The great advantage of mission is that it permits the head of the agency to be more confident that operators will act in particular cases in ways that the head would have acted had he or she been in their shoes. There are fewer distortions in the flow of information because both the sender and the recipient of the message share common understandings. FBI agents behaved as if J. Edgar Hoover were looking over their shoulders in part because the agents believed that was the right way to behave. Field representatives of the Army Corps of Engineers, office managers in the Social Security Administration, and district rangers in the Forest Service also act as they do in part as if they felt the ghosts of Sylvanus Thayer, Arthur Altmeyer, and Gifford Pinchot looking over their shoulders. Of course, there are no ghosts; indeed, many members of these agencies may never have heard of these people. But the ethos shaped by these men has been embodied in the expectations of living coworkers and superiors, thereby giving organizational life to long-dead and dimly remembered founders.

The importance of that ethos becomes clearest when it begins to decay. This may happen because of the arrival of groups in the organization that have a different occupational or professional culture (for example, the Forest Service), or it may result from the decisions of new leaders who by plan or by accident destroy the old sense of mission or attempt to replace it with one that may not be well-adapted to organizational needs or cannot elicit the enthusiasm of the operators. As we saw in chapter 2, the sense of mission of the Texas Department of Corrections barely outlasted the departure of George Beto.

The advantages of a clear sense of mission are purchased at a cost. Tasks that are not defined as central to the mission are often performed poorly or starved for resources. Subordinate cultures may develop around these peripheral tasks, but promotional opportunities for members of these cultures may be so restricted that the ablest members will avoid assignment to these subunits because service in them is "NCE" (Not Career-Enhancing). As we shall see in later chapters, a strong sense of mission may blind the organization to changed environmental circumstances so that new opportunities and challenges are met with routinized rather than adaptive behavior. But even short of occasions for major organizational change, the perceptions supplied by an organizational culture sometimes can lead an official to behave not as the situation requires but as the culture expects.

PART III

MANAGERS

CHAPTER 7

Constraints

BY THE TIME the office opens at 8:45 A.M., the line of people waiting to do business at the Registry of Motor Vehicles in Watertown, Massachusetts, often will be twenty-five deep. By midday, especially if it is near the end of the month, the line may extend clear around the building. Inside, motorists wait in slow-moving rows before poorly marked windows to get a driver's license or to register an automobile. When someone gets to the head of the line, he or she is often told by the clerk that it is the wrong line: "Get an application over there and then come back," or "This is only for people getting a new license; if you want to replace one you lost, you have to go to the next window." The customers grumble impatiently. The clerks act harried and sometimes speak brusquely, even rudely. What seems to be a simple transaction may take 45 minutes or even longer. By the time people are photographed for their driver's licenses, they are often scowling. The photographer valiantly tries to get people to smile, but only occasionally succeeds.[1]

Not far away, people also wait in line at a McDonald's fast-food restaurant. There are several lines; each is short, each moves quickly. The menu is clearly displayed on attractive signs. The workers behind the counter are invariably polite. If someone's order cannot be filled immediately, he or she is asked to step aside for a moment while the food is prepared and then is brought back to the head of the line to receive the order. The atmosphere is friendly and good-natured. The room is immaculately clean.

Many people have noticed the difference between getting a driver's license and ordering a Big Mac. Most will explain it by saying that bureaucracies are different from businesses. "Bureaucracies" behave as they do because they are run by unqualified "bureaucrats" and are enmeshed in "rules" and "red tape."

But business firms are also bureaucracies, and McDonald's is a bureaucracy that regulates virtually every detail of its employees' behavior by a complex and all-encompassing set of rules. Its operations manual is six hundred pages long and weighs four pounds.[2] In it one learns that french fries are to be nine-thirty-seconds of an inch thick and that grill workers are to place hamburger patties on the grill from left to right, six to a row for six rows. They are then to flip the third row first, followed by the fourth, fifth, and sixth rows, and finally the first and second. The amount of sauce placed on each bun is precisely specified. Every window must be washed every day. Workers must get down on their hands and knees and pick up litter as soon as it appears. These and countless other rules designed to reduce the workers to interchangeable automata were inculcated in franchise managers at Hamburger University located in a $40 million facility. There are plenty of rules governing the Registry, but they are only a small fraction of the rules that govern every detail of every operation at McDonald's. Indeed, if the DMV manager tried to impose on his employees as demanding a set of rules as those that govern the McDonald's staff, they would probably rebel and he would lose his job.

It is just as hard to explain the differences between the two organizations by reference to the quality or compensation of their employees. The Registry workers are all adults, most with at least a high-school education; the McDonald's employees are mostly teenagers, many still in school. The Registry staff is well-paid compared to the McDonald's workers, most of whom receive only the minimum wage. When labor shortages developed in Massachusetts during the mid-1980s, many McDonald's stores began hiring older people (typically housewives) of the same sort who had long worked for the Registry. They behaved just like the teenagers they replaced.

Not only are the differences between the two organizations not to be explained by reference to "rules" or "red tape" or "incompetent workers," the differences call into question many of the most frequently mentioned complaints about how government agencies are supposed to behave. For example: "Government agencies are big spenders." The Watertown office of the Registry is in a modest building that can barely handle its clientele. The teletype machine used to check information submitted by people requesting a replacement license was antiquated and prone to errors. Three or four clerks often had to wait in line to use equipment described by the office manager as "personally signed by Thomas Edison." No computers or word processors were available to handle the preparation of licenses and registrations; any error made by a clerk while manually typing a form meant starting over again on another form.

Or: "Government agencies hire people regardless of whether they are really needed." Despite the fact that the citizens of Massachusetts probably have more contact with the Registry than with any other state agency, and despite the fact that these citizens complain more about Registry service than about that of any other bureau, the Watertown branch, like all Registry offices, was seriously understaffed. In 1981, the agency lost 400 workers—about 25 percent of its work force—despite the fact that its workload was rising.

Or: "Government agencies are imperialistic, always grasping for new functions." But there is no record of the Registry doing much grasping, even though one could imagine a case being made that the state government could usefully create at Registry offices "one-stop" multi-service centers where people could not only get drivers' licenses but also pay taxes and parking fines, obtain information, and transact other official business. The Registry seemed content to provide one service.

In short, many of the popular stereotypes about government agencies and their members are either questionable or incomplete. To explain why government agencies behave as they do, it is not enough to know that they are "bureaucracies"—that is, it is not enough to know that they are big, or complex, or have rules. What is crucial is that they are *government* bureaucracies. As the preceding chapters should make clear, not all government bureaucracies behave the same way or suffer from the same problems. There may even be registries of motor vehicles in other states that do a better job than the one in Massachusetts. But all government agencies have in common certain characteristics that tend to make their management far more difficult than managing a McDonald's. These common characteristics are the constraints of public agencies.

The key constraints are three in number. To a much greater extent than is true of private bureaucracies, government agencies (1) cannot lawfully retain and devote to the private benefit of their members the earnings of the organization, (2) cannot allocate the factors of production in accordance with the preferences of the organization's administrators, and (3) must serve goals not of the organization's own choosing. Control over revenues, productive factors, and agency goals is all vested to an important degree in entities external to the organization—legislatures, courts, politicians, and interest groups. Given this, agency managers must attend to the demands of these external entities. As a result, government management tends to be driven by the *constraints* on the organization, not the *tasks* of the organization. To say the same thing in other words, whereas business management focuses on the "bottom line" (that is, profits), government management focuses on the "top line" (that is, constraints). Because government managers are not as strongly motivated as private ones to define the tasks of their subordinates, these tasks are often shaped by the factors described in the preceding four chapters.

Revenues and Incentives

In the days leading up to September 30, the federal government is Cinderella, courted by legions of individuals and organizations eager to get grants and contracts from the unexpended funds still at the disposal of each agency. At midnight on September 30, the government's coach turns into a pumpkin. That is the moment—the end of the fiscal year—at which every agency, with a few exceptions, must return all unexpended funds to the Treasury Department.

Except for certain quasi-independent government corporations, such as the Tennessee Valley Authority, no agency may keep any surplus revenues (that is, the difference between the funds it received from a congressional appropriation and those it needed to operate during the year). By the same token, any agency that runs out of money before the end of the fiscal year may ask Congress for more (a "supplemental appropriation") instead of being forced to deduct the deficit from any accumulated cash reserves. Because of these fiscal rules agencies do not have a material incentive to economize: Why scrimp and save if you cannot keep the results of your frugality?

Nor can individual bureaucrats lawfully capture for their personal use any revenue surpluses. When a private firm has a good year, many of its officers and workers may receive bonuses. Even if no bonus is paid, these employees may buy stock in the firm so that they can profit from any growth in earnings (and, if they sell the stock in a timely manner, profit from a drop in earnings). Should a public bureaucrat be discovered trying to do what private bureaucrats routinely do, he or she would be charged with corruption.

We take it for granted that bureaucrats should not profit from their offices and nod approvingly when a bureaucrat who has so benefited is indicted and put on trial. But why should we take this view? Once a very different view prevailed. In the seventeenth century, a French colonel would buy his commission from the king, take the king's money to run his regiment, and pocket the profit. At one time a European tax collector was paid by keeping a percentage of the taxes he collected. In this country, some prisons were once managed by giving the warden a sum of money based on how many prisoners were under his control and letting him keep the difference between what he received and what it cost him to feed the prisoners. Such behavior today would be grounds for criminal prosecution. Why? What has changed?

Mostly we the citizenry have changed. We are creatures of the Enlightenment: We believe that the nation ought not to be the property of the sovereign; that laws are intended to rationalize society and (if possible) perfect mankind; and that public service ought to be neutral and disinterested. We worry that a prison warden paid in the old way would have a strong incentive to starve his prisoners in order to maximize his income; that a regiment supported by a greedy colonel would not be properly equipped; and that a tax collector paid on a commission basis would extort excessive taxes from us. These changes reflect our desire to eliminate moral hazards—namely, creating incentives for people to act wrongly. But why should this desire rule out more carefully designed compensation plans that would pay government managers for achieving officially approved goals and would allow efficient agencies to keep any unspent part of their budget for use next year?

Part of the answer is obvious. Often we do not know whether a manager or an agency has achieved the goals we want because either the goals are vague or inconsistent, or their attainment cannot be observed, or both. Bureau chiefs in the Department of State would have to go on welfare if their pay depended on their ability to demonstrate convincingly that they had attained their bureaus' objectives.

But many government agencies have reasonably clear goals toward which progress can be measured. The Social Security Administration, the Postal Service, and the General Services Administration all come to mind. Why not let earnings depend importantly on performance? Why not let agencies keep excess revenues?

I am not entirely certain why this does not happen. To some degree it is because of a widespread cultural norm that people should not profit from public service. If that is the case, then in other cultures (and in our own in earlier times) we should see examples of bureaucrats in large part being paid from fees they get from clients or excess revenues they retain in the agency. Max Weber describes many such cases in his magisterial history of administration under patriarchal—that is, princely—rule.[3]

But in part it is because we know that even government agencies with clear goals and readily observable behavior only can be evaluated by making political (and thus conflict-ridden) judgments. If the Welfare Department delivers every benefit check within 24 hours after the application is received, Senator Smith may be pleased but Senator Jones will be irritated because this speedy delivery almost surely would require that the standards of eligibility be relaxed so that many ineligible clients would get money. There is no objective standard by which the tradeoff between speed and accuracy in the Welfare Department can be evaluated. Thus we have been unwilling to allow welfare employees to earn large bonuses for achieving either speed or accuracy.

The closest we can come to supplying a nonpolitical, nonarbitrary evaluation of an organization's performance is by its ability to earn from customers revenues in excess of costs. This is how business firms, private colleges, and most hospitals are evaluated. But government agencies cannot be evaluated by this market test because they either supply a service for which there are no willing customers (for example, prisons or the IRS) or are monopoly suppliers of a valued service (for example, the welfare department and the Registry of Motor Vehicles). Neither an organization with unwilling customers nor one with the exclusive right to serve such customers as exist can be evaluated by knowing how many customers they attract. When there is no external, nonpolitical evaluation of agency performance, there is no way to allow the agency to retain earnings that is not subject to agency manipulation.

If neither agencies nor their managers can appropriate surplus revenues for their own benefit, few agencies will try to produce surpluses by economizing on expenditures; instead, one would expect them to be spendthrifts. Within the limits of their appropriations and other applicable laws, they are. Grant-giving and contract-letting agencies in particular spend furiously every September. Economist William Niskanen, among others, has generalized this observation into a theory of bureaucratic behavior. He assumes that bureaus wish to maximize the size of their appropriations and that the legislature, though it does not want to spend any more than it has to, has no way of knowing how much it actually costs the bureaus to produce each additional unit of output (for example, dollars per additional letter delivered, bomb dropped, or crime prevented). As a result, each bureau will get a much bigger appropriation than it "needs"—that is, a bigger one than a well-informed legislature would supply. Thus, bureaucratic government means expensive government.[4]

In chapter 13 we shall look more closely at these assumptions. For now it is enough to note the many and obvious exceptions to the Niskanen prediction. The Massachusetts Registry of Motor Vehicles does not have lavish offices, large staffs, nor expensive computers. In comparison to even a small insurance company, its facilities are spartan. The Social Security Administration occupies a large office-building complex, but the interior appointments are modest and the office spaces cramped. In almost every state, prisons are overcrowded. In Boston, the police occupy the same headquarters building in which they have worked since 1925; meanwhile, all about it there have risen new and luxurious office buildings to accommodate business firms. In the Pentagon, major generals sit in offices that the chief teller of a small bank would regard as claustrophobic. Having taught at both public and private universities, there is little doubt in my mind that the latter supply their faculty with nicer offices and more amenities than the former.

One wonders why Niskanen thinks bureaucrats are so desirous of maximizing their budgets if they can enjoy so few of the fruits. As we have already seen, they cannot put any surplus revenues into their own pockets; their salaries do not increase with the size of the budget (salaries are set by legislatures and have nothing to do with the size of the employing agency); and now it even appears that they cannot even expect to occupy big offices with thick rugs on the floor and nice views of the city. We shall leave the question of whether bureaucrats maximize anything at all to a later chapter; for now, we note that the political environment in which they work powerfully inhibits them from converting their management of a bureau into material gain.

Critics of government agencies like to describe them as "bloated bureaucracies," defenders of them as "starved for funds." The truth is more complicated. Legislators judge government *programs* differently from how they judge government *bureaus.* Programs, such as Social Security, have constituencies that benefit from them. Constituencies press legislators for increases in program expenditures. If the constituencies are found in many districts, the pressures are felt by many legislators. These pressures ordinarily are not countered by those from any organized group that wants the benefits cut. Bureaucrats may or may not be constituencies. If they are few in number or concentrated in one legislative district they may have little political leverage with which to demand an increase in numbers or benefits. For example, expenditures on Social Security have grown steadily since the program began in 1935, but the offices, pay rates, and perquisites of Social Security administrators have not grown correspondingly.

If the bureaucrats are numerous, well-organized, and found in many districts (for example, letter carriers in the old Post Office Department or sanitation workers in New York City) they may have enough leverage to insure that their benefits increase faster than their workload. But even numerous and organized bureaucrats labor under a strategic disadvantage arising from the fact that legislators find it easier to constrain bureaucratic inputs than bureaucratic outputs. The reasons are partly conceptual, partly political. Conceptually, an office building or pay schedule is a tangible input, easily understood by all; "good health" or a "decent retirement" or an "educated child" are matters of opinion. Politically, legislators face more or less steady pressures to keep tax rates down while allowing program benefits to grow. The conceptual ambiguities combine neatly with the political realities: The rational course of action for a legislator is to appeal to taxpayers by ostentatiously constraining the budget for buildings, pay raises, and managerial benefits while appealing to program beneficiaries by loudly calling for more money to be spent on health, retirement, or education. (Witness the difficulty schoolteachers have in obtaining pay increases without threatening a strike, even at a time when expenditures on education are growing.) As a result, there are many lavish programs in this country administered by modestly paid bureaucrats working on out-of-date equipment in cramped offices.*

*Elsewhere, government officials may enjoy generous salaries and lavish offices. Indeed, in some underdeveloped nations, travelers see all about them signs of public munificence and private squalor. The two may be connected.

The inability of public managers to capture surplus revenues for their own use alters the pattern of incentives at work in government agencies. Beyond a certain point additional effort does not produce additional earnings. (In this country, Congress from time to time has authorized higher salaries for senior bureaucrats but then put a cap on actual payments to them so that the pay increases were never received. This was done to insure that no bureaucrat would earn more than members of Congress at a time when those members were unwilling to accept the political costs of raising their own salaries. As a result, the pay differential between the top bureaucratic rank and those just below it nearly vanished.) If political constraints reduce the marginal effect of money incentives, then the relative importance of other, nonmonetary incentives will increase. We saw in Part I what those other incentives will be—professional reputation, personal ideology, interest-group demands, and situational imperatives.

That bureaucratic performance in most government agencies cannot be linked to monetary benefits is not the whole explanation for the difference between public and private management. There are many examples of private organizations whose members cannot appropriate money surpluses for their own benefit. Private schools ordinarily are run on a nonprofit basis. Neither the headmaster nor the teachers share in the profit of these schools; indeed, most such schools earn no profit at all and instead struggle to keep afloat by soliciting contributions from friends and alumni. Nevertheless, the evidence is quite clear that on the average, private schools, both secular and denominational, do a better job than public ones in educating children.[5] Moreover, as political scientists John Chubb and Terry Moe have pointed out, they do a better job while employing fewer managers.[6] Some other factors are at work. One is the freedom an organization has to acquire and use labor and capital.

Acquiring and Using the Factors of Production

A business firm acquires capital by retaining earnings, borrowing money, or selling shares of ownership; a government agency (with some exceptions) acquires capital by persuading a legislature to appropriate it. A business firm hires, promotes, demotes, and fires personnel with considerable though not perfect freedom; a federal government agency is told by Congress how many persons it can hire and at what rate of pay, by the Office of Personnel Management (OPM) what rules it must follow in selecting and assigning personnel, by the Office of Management and Budget (OMB) how many persons of each rank it may employ, by the Merit Systems Protection Board (MSPB) what procedures it must follow in demoting or discharging personnel, and by the courts whether it has faithfully followed the rules of Congress, OPM, OMB, and MSPB. A business firm purchases goods and services by internally defined procedures (including those that allow it to buy from someone other than the lowest bidder if a more expensive vendor seems more reliable), or to skip the bidding procedure altogether in favor of direct negotiations; a government agency must purchase much of what it uses by formally advertising for bids, accepting the lowest, and keeping the vendor at arm's length. When a business firm develops a good working relationship with a contractor, it often uses that vendor repeatedly without looking for a new one; when a government agency has a satisfactory relationship with a contractor, ordinarily it cannot use the vendor again without putting a new project out for a fresh set of bids. When a business firm finds that certain offices or factories are no longer economical it will close or combine them; when a government agency wishes to shut down a local office or military base often it must get the permission of the legislature (even when formal permission is not necessary, informal consultation is). When a business firm draws up its annual budget each expenditure item can be reviewed as a discretionary amount (except for legally mandated payments of taxes to government and interest to banks and bondholders); when a government agency makes up its budget many of the detailed expenditure items are mandated by the legislature.

All these complexities of doing business in or with the government are well-known to citizens and firms. These complexities in hiring, purchasing, contracting, and budgeting often are said to be the result of the "bureaucracy's love of red tape." But few, if any, of the rules producing this complexity would have been generated by the bureaucracy if left to its own devices, and many are as cordially disliked by the bureaucrats as by their clients. These rules have been imposed on the agencies by external actors, chiefly the legislature. They are not bureaucratic rules but *political* ones. In principle the legislature could allow the Social Security Administration, the Defense Department, or the New York City public school system to follow the same rules as IBM, General Electric, or Harvard University. In practice they could not. The reason is politics, or more precisely, democratic politics.

The differences are made clear in Steven Kelman's comparison of how government agencies and private firms buy computers. The agency officials he interviewed were much less satisfied with the quality of the computers and support services they purchased than were their private counterparts. The reason is that private firms are free to do what every householder does in buying a dishwasher or an automobile—look at the past performance of the people with whom he or she previously has done business and buy a new product based on these judgments. Contrary to what many people suppose, most firms buying a computer do not write up detailed specifications and then ask for bids, giving the contract to the lowest bidder who meets the specifications. Instead, they hold conversations with a computer manufacturer with whom they, or other firms like them, have had experience. In these discussions they develop a sense of their needs and form a judgment as to the quality and reliability of the people with whom they may do business. When the purchase is finally made, only one firm may be asked to bid, and then on the basis of jointly developed (and sometimes rather general) guidelines.

No government purchasing agent can afford to do business this way. He or she would be accused (by unsuccessful bidders and their congressional allies) of collusion, favoritism, and sweetheart deals. Instead, agencies must either ask for sealed bids or for competitive written responses to detailed (*very* detailed) "requests for proposals" (RFPs). The agencies will not be allowed to take into account past performance or intangible managerial qualities. As a result, the agencies must deny themselves the use of the most important information someone can have—judgment shaped by personal knowledge and past experience. Thus, the government often buys the wrong computers from unreliable suppliers.[7] But as we shall see in a moment, Congress—whatever it may claim—values "fairness" over effectiveness.

Constraints at Work: The Case of the Postal Service

From the founding of the republic until 1971 the Post Office Department was a cabinet agency wholly subordinate to the president and Congress. As such it received its funds from annual appropriations, its personnel from presidential appointments and civil service examinations, and its physical plant from detailed political decisions about the appropriate location of post offices. Postal rates were set by Congress after hearings dominated by organized interests that mail in bulk (for example, direct-mail advertisers and magazine publishers) and influenced by an awareness of the harmful political effects of raising the rates for first-class letters mailed by individual citizens (most of whom voted). Congress responded to these pressures by keeping rates low (though never low enough to mollify the competing interests) and making up the difference between what the department earned from rates and paid in expenses by providing heavy subsidies drawn from general tax revenues (it was easier politically to hide larger appropriations that usually were not accompanied by a tax increase than higher rates that of course were translated immediately into prices customers had to pay). The wages of postal employees were set with an eye on the political power of the unions representing those employees: Congress rarely forgot that there were hundreds of organized letter carriers in every congressional district.

In 1971, the Post Office Department was transformed into the United States Postal Service (USPS), a semiautonomous government corporation. The USPS is headed by an eleven-member board of governors, nine appointed by the president and confirmed by the Senate; these nine then appoint a postmaster general and a deputy postmaster general. It derives its revenues entirely from the prices it charges and the money it borrows rather than from congressional appropriations (though subsidies still were paid to the USPS during a transition period). The postal rates are set not by Congress but by the USPS itself, guided by a legislative standard (the USPS must break even and each class of mail it handles must bear its proportionate share of the service's costs) and an independent advisory body (the Postal Rate Commission, which makes recommendations as to what the rates should be). No longer—in theory—are the prices charged for one class of mail (say, first-class letters) used to subsidize the rates charged for another class (say, second-class books and magazines). The USPS has its own personnel system, separate from that of the rest of the federal government, and bargains directly with its own unions.

Having loosened some of the constraints upon it, the Postal Service was able to do things that in the past it could do only with great difficulty if at all. John Tierney has described the changes. When it was still a regular government department, a small local post office could only be closed after a bitter fight with the member of Congress from the affected district. As a result, few were closed. After the reorganization, the number closed increased: Between 1976 and 1979, the USPS closed about twenty-four a year; between 1983 and 1986, it closed over two hundred a year.[8] The service developed a formula by which to allocate costs to various classes of mail (and thus to allocate prices to various classes of users); despite interest-group opposition the Supreme Court has upheld the formula.[9] When the old Post Office, in the interest of cutting costs, tried to end the custom of delivering mail to each recipient's front door and instead proposed to deliver mail (at least in new suburban communities) either to the curbside or to "cluster boxes,"* intense pressure on Congress forced the department to abandon the idea. By 1978 the USPS had acquired enough autonomy to implement the idea despite continued congressional grumblings.[10] Because the USPS can raise its own capital by issuing bonds it has been able to forge ahead with the automation of mail-sorting procedures. It now has hundreds of sophisticated optical scanners and bar-code readers that enable employees to sort mail much faster than before. By 1986 optical character readers were processing 90 million pieces of mail a

*A cluster box is a metal structure containing twelve to one hundred mailboxes to which mail for a given neighborhood is delivered.

day. Finally, despite political objections, the USPS was slowly expanding the use of the nine-digit zip code.

In short, acquiring greater autonomy increased the ability of the Postal Service to acquire, allocate, and control the factors of production. More broadly, the whole tone of postal management changed. It began to adopt corporate-style management practices, complete with elaborate "mission statements," glossy annual reports, a tightened organizational structure, and an effort to decentralize some decisions to local managers.

Though Congress loosened the reins, it did not take them off. On many key issues the phrase *quasi-autonomous* meant hardly autonomous at all. Congress at any time can amend the Postal Reorganization Act to limit the service's freedom of action; even the threat of such an amendment, made evident by committee hearings, often is enough to alter the service's programs. The nine-digit zip code was finally adopted but its implementation was delayed by Congress for over two years, thus impeding the efforts of the USPS to obtain voluntary compliance from the business community.

When the USPS, in a move designed to save over $400 million and thereby avoid a rate increase, announced in 1977 that it planned to eliminate Saturday mail deliveries, the service was able to produce public opinion data indicating that most people would prefer no Saturday delivery to higher postage rates. No matter. The House of Representatives by an overwhelming vote passed a resolution opposing the change, and the USPS backed down. It seems the employee unions feared that the elimination of Saturday deliveries would lead to laying off postal workers.[11]

Similarly, when the USPS in 1975–76 sought to close many rural post offices it had as an ally the General Accounting Office. A GAO study suggested that twelve thousand such offices could be closed at a savings of $100 million per year without reducing service to any appreciable extent (many of the small offices served no more than a dozen families and were located within a few miles of other offices that could provide the same service more economically). The rural postmasters saw matters differently, and they found a sympathetic audience in Congress. Announcing that "the rural post office has always been a uniquely American institution" and that "service" is more important than "profit," senators and representatives joined in amending the Postal Reorganization Act to block such closings temporarily and inhibit them permanently.[12] As John Tierney notes, the year that the USPS timidly closed 72 of its 30,521 offices, the Great Atlantic and Pacific Tea Company closed 174 of its 1,634 stores, and "that was that."[13] The USPS even as a "quasi-autonomous government corporation" is powerfully constrained; A&P, a *fully* autonomous private corporation, by comparison is unconstrained.

My argument is not that all the changes the USPS would like to make are desirable, or that every vestige of politics should be removed from its management. (The extent to which public services should be supplied by private organizations will be taken up in a later chapter.) Rather, it is that one cannot explain the behavior of government bureaucracies simply by reference to the fact that they are bureaucracies; the central fact is that they are *government* bureaucracies. Nor am I arguing that government (or more broadly, politics) is bad, only that it is inevitably (and to some extent desirably) sensitive to constituency demands.

The argument is that political supervision of the factors of production leads managers to become constraint-oriented rather than task-oriented. If political superiors (for example, the president and Congress) were confident that they could observe and evaluate the outputs of an agency, and if achieving the desired outputs were the only concern of these superiors, then an agency might be given a budget and a goal and left free to apply the resources to achieving that goal. For example, if Congress had been content to ask of the old Post Office Department that it deliver all first-class mail within three days at the lowest possible cost, it could have let the department arrange its delivery system, set its rates, locate its offices, and hire its personnel in whatever way it wished—provided that the mail got delivered within three days and at a price that did not lead mail users to abandon the Post Office in favor of a private delivery service. Managers then would be evaluated on the basis of how well they achieved these goals.

Of course, Congress had many goals, not just one: It wanted to please many different classes of mail users, satisfy constituency demands for having many small post offices rather than a few large ones, cope with union demands for wage increases, and respond to public criticism of mail service. Congress could not provide a consistent rank-ordering of these goals, which is to say that it could not decide on how much of one goal (e.g., keeping prices low) should be sacrificed to attain more of another goal (e.g., keeping rural post offices open). This inability to decide is not a reflection on the intelligence of Congress; rather, it is the inevitable consequence of Congress being a representative body whose individual members respond differently to different constituencies.

Neither Congress nor the postal authorities have ever supported an obvious method of allowing the customers to decide the matter for themselves—namely, by letting private firms compete with the Postal Service for the first-class mail business. For over a century the Post Office has had a legal monopoly on the regular delivery of first-class mail. It is a crime to establish any "private express for the conveyance of letters or packets . . . by regular trips or at stated periods over any post route."[14] This is justified by postal executives on the grounds that private competitors would skim away the most profitable business (for example, delivering business mail or utility bills in big cities), leaving the government with the most costly business (for example, delivering a Christmas card from Aunt

Annie in Eudora, Kansas, to Uncle Matt in Wakefield, Massachusetts). In time the Post Office began to face competition anyway, from private parcel and express delivery services that did not deliver "by regular trips or at stated periods" (so as not to violate the private express statute) and from electronic mail and fund-transferring systems. But by then it had become USPS, giving it both greater latitude in and incentive for meeting that competition.

Faced with political superiors that find it conceptually easier and politically necessary to focus on inputs, agency managers also tend to focus on inputs. Nowhere is this more evident than in defense procurement programs. The Defense Department, through the Defense Logistics Agency (DLA), each year acquires food, fuel, clothing, and spare parts worth (in 1984) $15 billion, manages a supply system containing over two million items, and administers over $186 billion in government contracts.[15] Congress and the president repeatedly have made clear their desire that this system be run efficiently and make use of off-the-shelf, commercially available products (as opposed to more expensive, "made-to-order" items).[16] Periodically, however, the press reports scandals involving the purchase of $435 hammers and $700 toilet seats. Some of these stories are exaggerated,[17] but there is little doubt that waste and inefficiency occur. Congressional investigations are mounted and presidential commissions are appointed to find ways of solving these problems. Among the solutions offered are demands that tighter rules be imposed, more auditors be hired, and fuller reports be made.

Less dramatic but more common than the stories of scandals and overpriced hammers are the continuing demands of various constituencies for influence over the procurement process. Occasionally this takes the form of requests for special favors, such as preferentially awarding a contract to a politically favored firm. But just as important and more pervasive in their effects are the legal constraints placed on the procurement process to insure that contracts are awarded "fairly"—that is, in ways that allow equal access to the bidding process by all firms and special access by politically significant ones. For example, section 52 of the *Federal Acquisition Regulation* contains dozens of provisions governing the need to give special attention to suppliers that are small businesses (especially a "small disadvantaged business"), women-owned small businesses, handicapped workers, or disabled and Vietnam-era veterans, or are located in areas with a "labor surplus."*[18] Moreover, only materials produced in the United

*For example, the law requires that a "fair proportion of the total purchases and contracts" shall be "placed with small-business enterprises" and that "small business concerns owned and controlled by socially and economically disadvantaged individuals, shall have the maximum practicable opportunity to participate in the performance of contracts let by any Federal agency." [15 *U.S. Code* 637(d)(1)] In pursuance of this law, it is the government's policy "to place a fair proportion" of its acquisitions with small business concerns and small business disadvantaged concerns (*Federal Acquisition Regulation*, 19.201a). A "socially and

States can be acquired for public use unless, under the Buy American Act, the government certifies that the cost is "unreasonable" or finds that the supplies are not available in this country in sufficient quantity or adequate quality.[19]

The goal of "fairness" underlies almost every phase of the procurement process, not because the American government is committed heart and soul to fairness as an abstract social good but because if a procurement decision is questioned it is much easier to justify the decision if it can be shown that the decision was "fairly" made on the basis of "objective" criteria. Those criteria are spelled out in the *Federal Acquisition Regulation*, a complex document of over six thousand pages. The essential rules are that all potential suppliers must be offered an equal opportunity to bid on a contract; that the agency's procurement decision must be objectively justifiable on the basis of written specifications; that contracts awarded on the basis of sealed bids must go to the contractor offering the lowest price; and that unsuccessful bidders must be offered a chance to protest decisions with which they disagree.[20] However, consistent with the government's frequently expressed interest in improving the quality and reliability of what it purchases, other provisions of the law authorize agencies to take into account factors in addition to price. When two firms compete for a contract without sealed bids, the agency is instructed to award the contract to a "responsible source" whose proposal is "most advantageous to the United States," considering price and "other factors included in the solicitation" (such as, presumably, reliability, quality, and past performance).[21]

To understand the bureaucratic significance of these rules, put yourself in the shoes of a Defense Logistics Agency manager. A decision you made is challenged because someone thinks that you gave a contract to an unqualified firm or purchased something of poor quality. What is your response—that in your judgment it was a good buy from a reliable firm? Such a remark is tantamount to inviting yourself to explain to a hostile congressional committee why you think your judgment is any good. A much safer response is "I followed the rules." Those rules give you vague guidance on what constitutes quality (a subjective matter) but clear guidance on how to solicit bids and award contracts—let everybody compete (especially small and disadvantaged firms) and base the award on price, an "objective" criterion. If the complaint is that the supplier made too much money on the contract even though the supplied material was of adequate quality, as DLA manager you could respond by saying that "profits are their business, not mine." But that is tantamount to an invitation to ex-

---

economically disadvantaged individual" includes, but is not limited to, a black American, Hispanic American, Native American, Asian-Pacific American, or Asian-Indian American (Ibid., 52.219.2).

plain to another hostile committee why you are indifferent to firms making "windfall profits at the public's expense." A much better defense is to say that you audited the supplier's books and made him follow every clause in a detailed contract.

If despite all your devotion to the rules Congress uncovers an especially blatant case of paying too much for too little (for example, a $3,000 coffee pot), the prudent response is to suggest that what is needed are more rules, more auditors, and more tightly constrained procedures. The consequence of this may be to prevent the buying of any more $3,000 coffeepots, or it may be to increase the complexity of the procurement process so that fewer good firms will submit bids to supply coffeepots, or it may be to increase the cost of monitoring that process so that the money saved by buying cheaper pots is lost by hiring more pot inspectors. Or it may be all three (see chapter 17).

The need to publicly justify procurement decisions to a legislature will induce rational managers to base their decisions on the most defensible criteria. To a large degree that means referring not to the achievement of the goal (did the hammer work?) but to the satisfaction of the more objective, quantifiable, and visible constraints on hammer selection.

Various critics of this process from time to time have noted that constraint-driven management may be the enemy of goal-oriented management. But it is very difficult to find ways to change things when it is easier for political superiors to observe whether you are obeying constraints than whether you are achieving goals. Thus, one cannot be too optimistic about suggestions such as the following, taken from an otherwise excellent analysis of the problems of managing the DLA procurement: "Attract and retain the calibre of procurement personnel necessary to make the kinds of subtle distinctions among products that will be necessary to ensure value."[22] Not only is it difficult for the government to recruit and retain talented engineers and experienced contract administrators (a GAO study found that 41 percent of the supervisors in the DLA had less than three years of experience),[23] it is hard to imagine why even talented and experienced personnel would run the risk of making "subtle" (and thus hard to defend) judgments instead of following the rules in the most literal fashion.

The extent to which managers are constraint-oriented will vary depending on how easily observed and readily evaluated are the agency's efforts to attain its stated goals. One can well imagine managers in the Postal Service or the Social Security Administration being more concerned with stated goals than those in, say, the State Department. But even in agencies with clear goals (as our review of the USPS should have made clear) constraints on allocating the factors of production are difficult to avoid.

Managers learn by watching other managers. They will judge the significance of a constraint by observing what has happened in the agency to a person who violated it. The greater the costs of noncompliance, the more important the constraint. Thus, managers (and employees generally) will learn what their vulnerabilities are and respond accordingly. They will become averse to any action that risks violating a significant constraint. The more such constraints there are, the more risk averse the managers will be. The acquisition of these learned vulnerabilities is another way by which the organization's culture is formed.

Contextual Goals

An agency's primary goal may be clear or vague, but its primacy usually is not in dispute. "Educate children," "prevent crime," "maintain relations with other nations"—ambiguous as these objectives may be, they nonetheless justify the existence of school systems, police forces, and the State Department.

But these primary goals are not the only ones an agency is expected to serve. In addition it must serve a large number of contextual goals—that is, descriptions of desired states of affairs other than the one the agency was brought into being to create. For example, a police department not only must try to prevent crime and catch criminals, it must protect the rights of the accused, safeguard the confidentiality of its records, and provide necessary health services to arrestees. These other goals define the context within which the primary goals can be sought.

The number and importance of contextual goals has risen dramatically in recent years. The Administrative Procedure Act (APA), passed in 1946, requires most federal agencies to observe certain standards of procedural fairness. They cannot adopt a new rule or policy without first giving written notice of their intention to do so (usually by publishing a "notice of proposed rulemaking" in the *Federal Register*) and soliciting comments from interested parties. If the agencies hold hearings, they must allow interested parties to appear and introduce evidence. In 1981, President Reagan required that the regulations an agency proposed to adopt also would have to be submitted to the Office of Information and Regulatory Affairs in the Office of Management and Budget. OMB had the power to block regulations if in its judgment the costs exceeded the benefits.

The Freedom of Information Act (FOIA), passed in 1966–67 and amended in 1986, gives citizens the right to inspect almost all government records with the exception of military, intelligence, trade secrets, and those files the disclosure of which reasonably could be expected to constitute an invasion of privacy or compromise a law-enforcement investigation.[24] Even these exceptions are not absolute. For example, in response to an FOIA request the FBI must supply all of the requested documents after blacking out those specific words and sentences containing protected information, but a shrewd reader often can infer the deleted material from the context. To reduce even further the chances that an agency can manipulate the FOIA to its own advantage, the law requires the agency to prove that it need not release the information (rather than requiring the citizen to prove that it should release it). The Privacy Act, passed in 1974, created elaborate safeguards for insuring the confidentiality of the files the government keeps on individual citizens, such as Social Security, law enforcement, and personnel records.[25] The open-meeting or "Government in the Sunshine" act, passed in 1976, requires that "every portion of every meeting of any agency shall be open to public observation" unless certain specified matters (such as military or trade secrets or private personnel records) are to be discussed.[26] The National Environmental Policy Act (NEPA), passed in 1969, requires all federal agencies (and many others as well) to take into account the environmental consequences of their actions by preparing, among other things, an environmental impact statement before undertaking "any major Federal action significantly affecting the quality of the human environment."[27]

During the 1970s, various federal agencies were required by law to pay some or all of the costs of groups that wished to intervene in their decision-making processes. For example, groups wishing to get the Federal Trade Commission to restrict the amount and kinds of advertisements that television broadcasters could include in the Saturday morning cartoon shows watched by children not only had the right to appear before the FTC; the costs of that appearance would be paid by the FTC. This intervenor funding program was sharply cut back during the 1980s.

Many other contextual goals exist that are never embodied in statute. Instead they are defined and enforced by congressional committees that make approval of an agency's budget contingent on the bureau serving some goal that the committee values. For example, the Park Service may be obliged to fix up certain national parks dear to the hearts of key members of Congress (and possibly less dear to the hearts of the Park Service) as a condition of getting its appropriation approved. The agreement will be entirely informal, but no less binding for that.

A European observer would be baffled by all this. As Steven Kelman has observed, "few countries require anything resembling the openness of the American process."[28] There may be consultation in European governments, but it tends to be informal and behind the scenes. Foreign government agencies need serve far fewer contextual goals than their American counterparts. A European would be astonished to learn that in the United States citizens can read many government files but the government can read few citizen files. In Europe it tends to be just the opposite. (The reasons for these differences will be discussed in chapters 13 and 16.)

These contextual goals have two principal, and somewhat different, motivations. The first is a desire to insure procedural fairness. (For example: "Give notice." "Hold hearings." "Encourage participation." "Consider evidence." "Reveal records." "Allow arrested persons a chance to talk to a lawyer.") The second is a desire to favor certain interests over others. (For example: "Buy American." "Buy from small businesses owned by women.") The first motive might be described as an effort to produce a level playing field, the second as an effort to tilt the playing field.

The Effects of Constraints and Context

The existence of so many contextual goals and political constraints has several consequences for the management of public agencies. First, managers have a strong incentive to worry more about constraints than tasks, which means to worry more about processes than outcomes. Outcomes often are uncertain, delayed, and controversial; procedures are known, immediate, and defined by law or rule. It is hard to hold managers accountable for attaining a goal, easy to hold them accountable for conforming to the rules. Even when a bureau's primary goals are clear and progress toward them measurable, the managers of the bureau cannot be content with achieving them with the least use of resources; they also must worry about serving the contextual goals of the agency. These contextual goals are defended by powerful interests or by individuals and groups with access to important centers of power—the courts and congressional committees. The Army Corps of Engineers can describe exactly how a dam should be built and verify that it was built that way, but woe betide it if it goes ahead with the dam without extensive public consultation and close attention to environmental issues.[29]

Second, the multiplicity of constraints on an agency enhances the power of potential intervenors in the agency. Every constraint or contextual goal is the written affirmation of the claim of some external constituency. Thus the agency has weak boundaries and a large, variegated "membership" consisting of all who have a stake in the maintenance of one or more constraints. In the United States, where courts have great authority and access to them is relatively easy, the multiplication of constraints enhances the power of the courts over bureaucratic processes. If an agency is bound by a procedural rule, such as the obligation to hold hearings, people affected by that agency's decisions can enforce the procedural rule by going to court. The rules have conferred rights; courts exist to enforce rights.

If an interest (say, the clean-air interest) has acquired special legal status, then that claim to a special status can be enforced by appeal to the courts. Between 1963 and 1983, the number of appeals from the decisions of federal administrative agencies heard by U.S. courts of appeal nearly tripled.[30]

Third, equity is more important than efficiency in the management of many government agencies. This follows from the first two consequences: if managers must follow the correct procedures and if courts exist to enforce those procedures, then a procedural rule often will be defended by claiming that it is essential to the fair or equitable treatment of agency members or clients. Equity issues always seem easier to judge than efficiency issues: We cannot easily say whether the pupils were educated, the streets made safer, or some diseases prevented; but we can say whether every pupil got the same textbook, every citizen got the same police response, and every patient got the same vaccine.

Some consequences of allowing equity issues to govern bureaucratic decisions can be seen in the differences between public and private agencies that handle juvenile delinquents. David Street, Robert Vinter, and Charles Perrow studied three institutions of each kind and found that public institutions had much greater difficulty in controlling their inmates than private ones. The reason was that the public institutions had to take any delinquent referred to them by the courts, whereas the private ones were free to select the kinds of delinquents they would accept. (They used this freedom to reject "difficult" cases: One excluded sex offenders and another violent ones.) The consequence of the differences in intake could be traced through every aspect of the management of the institutions. Given their heterogeneous, somewhat dangerous clientele, the public agencies emphasized custody and discipline and gave managerial power to staff members whose duty it was to maintain control. With their more homogeneous and tractable inmates, the private agencies emphasized therapy and rehabilitation and gave managerial power to members of the treatment staff.[31] (The study is silent on whether the emphasis on rehabilitation actually produced any; judging from studies of other programs it is unlikely.)

Fourth, the existence of many contextual goals, like the existence of constraints on the use of resources, tends to make managers more risk averse. Police administrators rarely lose their jobs because the crime rate has gone up or win promotions because it has gone down. They can easily lose their jobs if somebody persuasively argues that the police department has abused a citizen, beaten a prisoner, or failed to answer a call for service.[32] School administrators rarely lose their jobs when their pupils' reading scores go down or win promotions when scores go up. But they can lose their jobs or suffer other career-impeding consequences if students are punished, controversial textbooks assigned, or parents treated impolitely. Under these circumstances it is hardly surprising that police captains spend a lot of their time trying to make certain that their officers follow the rules and that school principals spend a lot of their time cultivating the goodwill of parents.

Fifth, standard operating procedures (SOPs) are developed in each agency to reduce the chance that an important contextual goal or constraint is not violated. All large bureaucracies have SOPs; public bureaucracies have many more because in addition to the managerial problems that arise out of size and complexity they must conform to the politically enforceable constraints asserted by external constituencies. As we shall see in later chapters, rules can multiply to the point where no action at all is possible if every action must conform to every rule. Nonetheless rules persist, both as a written commitment to respect the claims of constituencies and as a device to punish operators who upset those constituencies.

Sixth, public agencies will have more managers than private ones performing similar tasks. More constraints require more managers to observe and enforce them. Mark A. Emmert and Michael M. Crow compared forty-one governmental research and development (R&D) laboratories with forty-six private ones. The R&D labs were about the same size and age, but the ratio of administrators to total staff was much higher (almost twice as high) in the public than in the private ones.[33] Government bureaucracies are more "bureaucratic" than industrial ones in large part because we—the people and our political representatives—insist that they be.

Finally, the more contextual goals and constraints that must be served, the more discretionary authority in an agency is pushed upward to the top. In most organizations, front-line operators are in a better position to exercise judgment about operating problems than upper-level managers, who can know of a problem, if at all, only through delayed and much-condensed reports. It is easier to allow front-line operators to exercise discretion when only one clear goal is to be attained. The greater the number and complexity of those goals, the riskier it is to give authority to operators. Thus, public agencies, though often they acknowledge the principle of decentralization, more often act on the principle of centralization. If the administrator is going to get into trouble for what an operator does, the former will find ways of making the decision for the latter. The history of the Postal Service is consistent with this: While management was still the Post Office Department it was highly centralized; as the semiautonomous USPS, the reduction in the number of constraints permitted it to move toward more decentralized management.[34] Some public agencies, however, perform tasks the management of which cannot be centralized—police departments, for example, or public schools. The tension in such bureaucracies between the necessity of letting operators decide what to do and the inevitability that managers will be blamed when something is done wrong is a major source of the mutual suspicion with which operators and managers view one another.

Public versus Private Management

The late Professor Wallace Sayre once said that public and private management is alike in all unimportant respects.[35] This view has been disputed vigorously by many people who are convinced that whatever problems beset government agencies also afflict private organizations. The clearest statement of that view can be found in John Kenneth Galbraith's *The New Industrial State*. Galbraith argues that large corporations, like public agencies, are dominated by "technostructures" that are governed by their own bureaucratic logic rather than by the dictates of the market. These corporations have insulated themselves from the market by their ability to control demand (through clever advertising) and set prices (by dominating an industry). The rewards to the technocrats who staff these firms are salaries, not profits, and the goals toward which these technocrats move are the assertion and maintenance of their own managerial autonomy. The corporation has become a self-governing center of power rather than a market-driven firm.[36] As such, it seems to have more in common with a government agency than with a competitive capitalist.

Professor Galbraith's book appeared at a time (1967) when American businesses were enjoying such unrivaled success that its beautifully crafted sentences seemed to capture some enduring truth. But the passage of time converted many of those eloquent phrases into hollow ones. Within ten years, it had become painfully obvious to General Motors that it could not, in Galbraith's words, "set prices for automobiles . . . secure in the knowledge that no individual buyer, by withdrawing its custom, can force a change."[37] Competition from Toyota, Nissan, and Honda had given the individual buyer great power; coupled with an economic slowdown, that competition led GM, like all auto manufacturers, to start offering cash rebates, cut-rate financing, and price reductions. And still the U.S. firms lost market share despite the "power" of their advertising and saw profits evaporate despite their "dominance" of the industry.

But Galbraith's analysis had more serious flaws than its inability to predict the future; it led many readers to draw the erroneous conclusion that "all bureaucracies are alike" because all bureaucracies employ salaried workers, are enmeshed in red tape, and strive to insure their own autonomy. The large corporation surely is more bureaucratic than the small entrepreneur, but in becoming bureaucratic it has not become a close relative of a government agency. What distinguishes public from private organizations is neither their size nor their desire to "plan" (that is, control) their environments, but rather the rules under which they acquire and use capital and labor. General Motors acquires capital by selling shares, issuing bonds, or retaining earnings; the Department of Defense acquires it from an annual appropriation by Congress. GM opens and closes plants, subject to certain government regulations, at its own discretion; DOD opens and closes military bases under the watchful guidance of Congress. GM pays its managers with salaries it sets and bonuses tied to its earnings; DOD pays its managers with salaries set by Congress and bonuses (if any) that have no connection with organizational performance. The number of workers in GM is determined by its level of production; the number in DOD by legislation and civil-service rules.*

What all this means can be seen by returning to the Registry of Motor Vehicles and McDonald's. Suppose you were just appointed head of the Watertown office of the Registry and you wanted to improve service there so that it more nearly approximated the service at McDonald's. Better service might well require spending more money (on clerks, equipment, and buildings). Why should your political superiors give you that money? It is a cost to them if it requires either higher taxes or taking funds from another agency; offsetting these real and immediate costs are dubious and postponed benefits. If lines become shorter and clients become happier, no legislator will benefit. There may be fewer complaints, but complaints are episodic and have little effect on the career of any given legislator. By contrast, shorter lines and faster service at McDonald's means more customers can be served per hour and thus more money can be earned per hour. A McDonald's manager can estimate the marginal product of the last dollar he or she spends on improving service; the Registry manager can generate no tangible return on any expenditure he or she makes and thus cannot easily justify the expenditure.

Improving service at the Registry may require replacing slow or surly workers with quick and pleasant ones. But you, the manager, can neither hire nor fire them at will. You look enviously at the McDonald's manager who regularly and with little notice replaces poor workers with better ones. Alternatively, you may wish to mount an extensive training program (perhaps creating a Registration University to match McDonald's Hamburger University) that would imbue a culture of service in your employees. But

*In the revised edition of his book, Galbraith responded to his many critics who argued that he had advanced no persuasive evidence that large corporations had insulated themselves from the market by controlling demand and prices. His response was to "stand on my argument—and appeal . . . to the evidence of the eye" (p. xv). That "evidence" consisted largely of the fact that corporations spend a lot of money on advertising. He does not trouble himself to ask what, if anything, corporations buy with that expenditure. By the late 1970s American auto manufacturers were buying a declining market share and lower profits. Perhaps if they had doubled their advertising budgets they could have purchased zero market share and bankruptcy.

unless the Registry were so large an agency that the legislature would neither notice nor care about funds spent for this purpose—and it is not that large—you would have a tough time convincing anybody that this was not a wasteful expenditure on a frill project.

If somehow your efforts succeed in making Registry clients happier, you can take vicarious pleasure in it; in the unlikely event a client seeks you out to thank you for those efforts, you can bask in a moment's worth of glory. Your colleague at McDonald's who manages to make customers happier may also derive some vicarious satisfaction from the improvement but in addition he or she will earn more money owing to an increase in sales.

In time it will dawn on you that if you improve service too much, clients will start coming to the Watertown office instead of going to the Boston office. As a result, the lines you succeeded in shortening will become longer again. If you wish to keep complaints down, you will have to spend even more on the Watertown office. But if it was hard to persuade the legislature to do that in the past, it is impossible now. Why should the taxpayer be asked to spend more on Watertown when the Boston office, fully staffed (naturally, no one was laid off when the clients disappeared), has no lines at all? From the legislature's point of view the correct level of expenditure is not that which makes one office better than another but that which produces an equal amount of discontent in all offices.

Finally, you remember that your clients have no choice: The Registry offers a monopoly service. It and only it supplies drivers' licenses. In the long run all that matters is that there are not "too many" complaints to the legislature about service. Unlike McDonald's, the Registry need not fear that its clients will take their business to Burger King or to Wendy's. Perhaps you should just relax.

If this were all there is to public management it would be an activity that quickly and inevitably produces cynicism among its practitioners. But this is not the whole story. For one thing, public agencies differ in the kinds of problems they face. For another, many public managers try hard to do a good job even though they face these difficult constraints. In the next chapter we shall look more closely at what managers do.

CHAPTER 8

People

ONE DAY IN 1977, a personnel specialist at the United States Navy's Naval Ocean Systems Center (NOSC) in San Diego visited an electronics engineer working on torpedo designs. "I'm here to classify your job," the engineer was told. "What do you do?" The engineer, irked by this unwelcome intrusion, muttered that he "invented things." The personnel specialist wrote down this fact and returned to her office. She took from a shelf the volume entitled *Position Classification Standard for Electronics Engineering, Series GS-855*, published in 1971 by the United States Civil Service Commission, which described the skills that engineers at various levels are supposed to have. At the time, the engineer was in grade GS-15 (the U.S. civil service system classifies all employees in eighteen grades, from GS-1 at the bottom to GS-18 at the top).* She decided that "inventing things" was not part of the job description of a GS-15 engineer but that it might be part of the assignment of a GS-13. She advised the engineer's supervisor that the job should be downgraded to the lower level.

The supervisor erupted in anger. The engineer as it turned out was the world's leading expert on the logic systems of torpedo guidance devices. Without him the torpedo development program at NOSC would be crippled. If his job were downgraded he probably would quit.

The incident was one of many that had generated what one manager called "extreme animosity" between government personnel officers and government managers at NOSC and elsewhere. Line managers regarded personnel specialists as ignorant busybodies who couldn't tell the difference between an engineer and an elevator operator. The specialists regarded line managers as loose cannons who did not understand that jobs

*"GS" stands for "General Schedule."

had to be classified in order to insure the fair, equitable, and nonpolitical treatment of public employees. In the words of another official, running NOSC was an "arm-wrestling exercise" between line managers and position classifiers.

Up at the China Lake Naval Weapons Center (NWC) matters were even worse. At least NOSC was able to hire competent engineers because so many people wanted to live and work in San Diego. But China Lake is located in the midst of the California desert, miles not only from the beach but from anything resembling a city. The government's inflexible pay system made it hard to offer attractive salaries or to reward employees who did good work. By the time a junior engineer had learned enough on the job to do the job, he or she would leave for a better-paying post with industry and life in an attractive suburb. "We were becoming not the Naval Weapons Center but the Naval Aerospace Engineering Training Grounds," lamented one China Lake executive.[1] Reassigning a worker from one job to another required a pile of complex paperwork; demoting a worker was regarded as next to impossible.

The personnel specialists did not enjoy being the object of all this hostility. Their job supposedly was to help recruit and keep good employees; in fact, their job was to preside over a mountain of paperwork containing job descriptions and classifications, paperwork that, once completed, was filed and forgotten. The position classification for the NOSC torpedo engineer took five or six single-spaced pages. "The first job I ever classified at China Lake was a GS-13 mathematician," recalled one personnel specialist. "It took nine months to finalize. That's totally outrageous!"[2]

When the government decided to reduce the size of its work force (called a Reduction in Force, or RIF), the absurdity of some of the rules became indisputable. Eight months after the merger of two navy research laboratories into the new Naval Ocean Systems Center, an RIF was ordered, which meant that 150 employees had to be laid off. Under the RIF rules enforced by the (then) Civil Service Commission, who got laid off was determined primarily by seniority, not merit. This meant that if one employee was "RIFfed," he or she (if qualified) could bump a less senior person who then could bump a less senior one, right on down the line without regard for occupational specialty. In theory an engineer could bump the commanding officer's secretary who then could bump the plumber.

Faced with all these constraints, line managers struggled to devise ways to get around the system. Instead of transferring an employee from one job to another, a process that took days of shuffling papers, the employee would be "loaned" (technically, detailed) to the new post. Instead of firing incompetent workers they would be given undesirable assignments in hopes they would quit; if they didn't, at least they were out of the way. If a manager wanted to promote an engineer but discovered that the higher grade only could be given to a person with supervisory duties, a new subunit—say, a Widget Branch, consisting of three people—would be created so that the promoted engineer could "supervise" it.

The Personnel System

The foregoing description of NOSC and China Lake is written in the past tense because in those places things have changed. But for most of the federal personnel system (and for many state systems that are modeled on the federal rules) not much has changed. That system, begun in 1883 with the passage of the Pendleton Act, has three goals: to hire public employees on the basis of merit rather than political connections, to manage these employees effectively, and to treat equal employees equally.

ENTRY: WHAT DOES "MERIT" MEAN?

Merit is established on the basis of an open examination. For a long time the examination was a test that usually combined some measure of general ability and knowledge with some measure of the skills relevant to a particular job. Such tests still are used for clerical jobs such as stenographer and file clerk. Applicants take a typing test and display their ability to alphabetize. But candidates can be examined in ways that do not involve a test—by assessing their education, training, and experience, for example. Scientific, technical, and engineering personnel are "examined" by evaluating their college education and work history.

The main problem in examining people has involved applicants for administrative positions. Unlike candidates for clerical jobs who are tested by watching them do a sample of the actual work, there is no economical way to watch managers perform a representative sample of their actual work. Moreover, the purpose of the examination is to identify people who have the ability to *become* managers, not to find people who already have been managers. Unlike scientific and engineering jobs, managerial skills are not necessarily learned in college (if they can be learned at all!). Beginning in 1939 the Civil Service Commission designed a series of tests intended to assess the general abilities of potential managers who would enter government service at the rank of GS-5 or GS-7. The goal was to find a relatively simple and economical way of measuring abilities that would predict later performance in a wide variety of jobs. In 1974 this effort culminated in the Professional and Administrative Career Examination, or PACE, a test designed to evaluate candidates for over one hundred federal jobs, mostly of a managerial or administrative nature. Twenty-four research psychologists spent five years developing it.

The selection process operated this way: Persons taking the PACE had to be graduates of four-year colleges or have three years of professional experience (in fact, almost everybody was a college graduate). The lowest possible score was 40; to be considered for a federal job it was necessary to earn a 70. (If you had an outstanding grade record in college your test score was increased by a formula that guaranteed your final score would be at least 70.) If you passed, veteran's preference points would be added to your test score (five for any veteran, ten for those with a service-connected disability).* The Office of Personnel Management (OPM), the present-day successor of the old Civil Service Commission, then prepared a rank-order listing of all candidates who had passed. All veterans with service-connected disabilities automatically went to the top of the list; other veterans were ranked along with non-veterans, except that in the case of tie scores the veteran's name always appeared first. A federal agency that wanted to hire somebody from this list had to choose from among the top three names on it. No federal agency was obliged to use the PACE exam; it could fill an administrative or specialist job by internal promotion (for example, by promoting a secretary).

The PACE was a test of general mental abilities and as such had many of the same qualities as other similar tests, such as the Armed Forces Qualification Test (AFQT), the General Aptitude Test Battery (GATB) used by the United States Employment Service, and even the Scholastic Aptitude Test (SAT). Such tests are valid to the extent that they accurately predict performance on the job (or in the case of the SAT, in school). No test is perfectly valid; that is, no test predicts job performance precisely. The key question is how well a test predicts compared to other ways of making such predictions, such as job interviews, reference checks, or amount of experience.

For a long time industrial psychologists believed that no single test could predict performance across a wide variety of jobs, and so heavy reliance was placed on tests developed for a specific job as well as on interviews and experience. Recent research had shown this view to be false. By combining the results of thousands of studies done on a great variety of jobs, scholars have been able to show that tests of general mental ability are better predictors of job performance (as measured by such criteria as supervisors' ratings) than any job-specific tests.[3] The research also indicates that ability tests of any kind are more valid than other evaluation methods, such as interviews.

During the first five years the PACE was used, nearly three-quarters of a million people took it and over thirty-five thousand were hired from among those who passed it. Then a federal judge brought the process to

*The mothers and spouses of deceased or disabled veterans may also be eligible to get ten bonus points. Veteran's preference does not apply to scientific and professional positions at rank GS-9 or above.

a halt. In January 1979, lawyers representing black and Hispanic plaintiffs alleged that the PACE discriminated against members of minority groups in violation of Title VII of the Civil Rights Act of 1964. A sample of 1978 PACE test takers showed that whereas 42 percent of the whites scored 70 or above (before augmenting the scores with veteran's preference points), only 5 percent of the blacks and about 13 percent of the Hispanics earned a 70 or higher.[4]

The suit never went to trial. The federal government and the plaintiffs' lawyers negotiated for two years and on January 9, 1981, eleven days before Ronald Reagan assumed the presidency, the Carter administration entered into a consent decree under which the PACE would be abolished over a three-year period. OPM agreed to replace PACE with a series of different selection procedures that would "eliminate adverse impact against blacks and Hispanics as much as feasible" and that would "validly and fairly test the relative capacity of applicants to perform PACE occupations."[5] Judge Joyce Green approved the proposed consent decree.

With the demise of the test, entry-level administrators were recruited in three ways. First, job-specific tests were written for certain occupations. But it takes a great deal of time and effort to produce a valid test, and so only a few occupations (sixteen by 1988) had them. To get such tests for the hundred or so remaining administrative jobs would have taken decades. Second, government agencies were allowed to appoint people to professional jobs directly, without tests. There were several ironies in this. A court decree intended to increase the hiring of minorities abolished a procedure (the PACE test) that did not allow agency heads to rely on their personal preferences and prejudices and led to the adoption of a procedure, the so-called Schedule B appointments, that gave agency heads the opportunity to use any standards they wanted, or no standards at all. And in a suit brought by the National Treasury Employees' Union another federal court declared that the Schedule B procedure was illegal. Third, agencies filled managerial or specialist jobs by internal promotion.

Publicly, OPM denied that the abolition of PACE created serious problems. Privately, several top officials said that it was leading to a drop in the quality of entry-level managers. One executive described the decline in quality as a "death spiral." Some agency heads disagreed. In fact, OPM had no way of telling whether the federal work force was getting better, getting worse, or staying the same. Though it was created to help recruit people on the basis of merit it had gathered no data and done no studies that would indicate whether there were any changes in the meritoriousness of the people it recruited.[6] But OPM officials and most research psychologists who addressed the matter believed that since PACE was a proven predictor of job performance its loss meant the federal government had no way of insuring that able candidates were hired in preference to the not-so-able. And a 1986 survey of over 21,000 federal employees revealed that far more bureaucrats thought the quality of recent applicants for jobs had declined than thought it had improved.[7]

Agency heads, by contrast, were pleased with the new freedom they enjoyed after the abolition of PACE. Many believed that the Schedule B system allowed them to hire faster with less red tape and to go aggressively after people they wanted. And the decentralized system led to the hiring of a higher percentage of blacks and Hispanics.[8]

The search began for a new selection procedure. Announced in June 1988, it had several components. First, written tests would be administered for clusters of similar jobs. Though it was too expensive to design a test for each of more than one hundred occupations, tests could be written for groups of closely related occupations. Second, the candidates' character would be evaluated by an Individual Achievement Record, a questionnaire that attempts to measure what candidates have been able to accomplish with the opportunities they have had. It assesses work habits, work history, grades by field, and extracurricular activities. Third, agencies would be free to hire outstanding scholars. Any college graduate with a satisfactory grade point average (as of 1989, OPM had not yet decided whether that would be 3.0 or 3.25) could be hired without him or her having to take a test. Studies by OPM suggest that the Individual Achievement Record and the college grade-point average were moderately good predictors of job performance.[9]

MANAGING PEOPLE: THE CLASSIFICATION, APPRAISAL, AND PAY SYSTEM

Having a career in the federal bureaucracy means working one's way up through as many as eighteen pay grades (GS-1 to GS-18) in an occupation described in great detail in OPM manuals. Describing a position is usually done not by managers who hire and supervise employees but by personnel officers trained to apply the OPM manuals. This may not present much difficulty when it comes to describing and classifying typists or file clerks, but it creates all manner of problems when it involves people who perform complex tasks, as suggested by the experiences of the two navy labs.

One has to read an actual position classification standard to appreciate the mysteries of the personnel profession. GS-11 electronics engineers whose starting salary (in 1989) is $33,169 "apply broad knowledge of diverse engineering concepts and procedures." GS-12 electronics engineers whose starting salary is $37,294 "apply deep and diversified knowledge to atypical or highly difficult assignments." GS-13 electronics engineers whose starting salary is $41,121 "are highly knowledgeable specialists in their subject-matter areas" who are "innovative and original."[10] It would defy the talents of a biblical scholar to explain the difference between "broad,

. . . diverse" knowledge and "deep and diversified knowledge," or to clarify why a GS-13 engineer's ability to be "innovative and original" is worth $3,827 more than a GS-12 engineer's ability to handle "atypical" assignments.

Within a grade (for example, GS-12) pay increases occur in "steps." Theoretically, moving up these steps requires obtaining a good performance rating, but in practice almost everybody gets a fully satisfactory rating and so moving up the steps tends to reflect the passage of time. Once a person has accumulated enough seniority to use up all the step pay increases within a given grade, further pay increases require that he or she be promoted to the next higher grade (except, of course, for any changes in the entire pay schedule). But that requires getting the personnel office to approve a higher classification for that person, and that brings us back to the vague (but lengthy) language of the position classification standards.

If a manager wants to move an employee to another job, the manager first must make certain that the new job is classified at the same level (say, GS-12) as the employee's existing job, or the manager must prove to the personnel office that the employee deserves a promotion to GS-13. To do that the manager must find language in the position classification standard that will justify the promotion. This means that managers spend much of their time memorizing verbal abstractions, honing their skills at drafting flowery memos recommending promotions, and arguing with position classifiers.

In 1978, Congress passed the Civil Service Reform Act (CSRA), designed in part to make it easier to base pay (within a single grade) on merit rather than seniority and to move senior bureaucrats from one job to another. The CSRA created a category of government employees, the Senior Executive Service (SES), made up of career and noncareer officials drawn from the three highest civil-service grades (GS-16, GS-17, and GS-18) and from other equivalent positions. Career SES members may earn up to 20 percent of their base salary in performance bonuses each year. (Total bonuses paid by an agency may not exceed 3 percent of its career SES payroll.) In addition, a few presidentially designated "meritorious" or "distinguished" career executives may annually receive bonuses of $10,000 or $20,000. Finally, the CSRA authorized merit pay for middle-level managers (GS-13, GS-14, and GS-15). Before 1978, pay at these ranks reflected time in grade almost to the exclusion of other considerations. Now part of a manager's annual pay increase could reflect performance on the job.

There is little evidence that either the bonus or merit-pay system has had much effect on agency behavior. For one thing, bonuses have been based chiefly on individual rather than on agency performance.[11] An SES member may be performing his or her individual assignment well but the agency may be doing poorly. By contrast, many firms link individual bonuses to organizational achievement so that the payments, while based in part on individual effort, also depend on the firms' earnings. Moreover, SES members do not think that even the individual performance standards are fair or meaningful. A 1982 report by the Weatherhead School of Management at Case Western Reserve University revealed that most SES members in the agencies studied were indifferent to or cynical about the bonuses, believing that they were awarded either randomly or as "payoffs" to favored managers. Part of the problem may have been that agency heads often gave small bonuses to many people rather than large ones to a few, a result of a desire to minimize disgruntlement and of the difficulty in evaluating employee performance in organizations with vague and complex goals.[12] Similarly, a 1982 survey by the Institute for Social Research at the University of Michigan found that most middle-level managers were skeptical of the benefits of the merit-pay program. Very little money was involved and the pay differential between ordinary and outstanding performers was very small. As with the SES bonuses, most eligible managers received small merit increases.[13]

These difficulties in linking pay to performance are exacerbated by the fact that both employees and managers, though they sometimes approve of merit pay in principle, tend to dislike it in practice. Though NOSC employees have come to accept merit pay, many other government workers prefer that pay be based on seniority and that promotions be based on "objective" tests of merit rather than on the evaluations of supervisors. Schoolteachers regularly oppose merit pay; police officers regularly insist that promotions be based on written examinations and seniority and not on the opinions of police chiefs and captains. Everywhere one looks one finds public employees using such influence as they have (and often it is very great) to minimize managerial authority over compensation plans. One suspects that they would do this in private firms as well (and to the extent that compensation is based on union contracts they do), but firms do not serve as legislatures in which their employees have influence. Moreover, firms often can demonstrate how certain compensation plans (e.g., bonus systems) do in fact achieve savings or sales.

Many managers also dislike certain aspects of performance-based compensation. Though they would prefer to promote subordinates on the basis of merit, distributing pay on that basis is risky. It means making hard-to-defend distinctions among many people with whom they must continue to work. Anyone who has filled out an employee evaluation form knows how great is the temptation to check the box labeled "excellent" or "very good" when asked to rate the subordinate (just as every professor knows how tempting it is to use such language when recommending a graduate student for a job). Almost all of us want to be liked; we dislike unpleasant scenes or dirty looks (remember, the employees are shown their evaluation forms). Favorable evaluations are easy to make when it costs us nothing to make them—when our salary and our department's budget are not adversely affected by this bias toward generosity. Of course, if keeping on or promoting poor quality employees hurts us—as it may if our organization is competing for business or we ourselves are having our pay determined by how efficient our department is—then usually we will find the courage to make the tough choices. In government the inability to evaluate the agency as a whole affects every part of it; and so rules replace performance as a basis for managing personnel.

DISMISSALS

Contrary to popular view, it is not impossible to fire a government employee. But it is very difficult.

Most federal workers in the competitive service have the right to appeal adverse actions by the agency for which they work, including a decision to fire them, demote them, deny them within-grade pay increases, or suspend them without pay for any substantial period. These appeals are usually made to a local office of the Merit Systems Protection Board (MSPB), which assigns the case to an administrative judge (AJ). The AJ attempts to resolve the dispute; failing that, the aggrieved employee (the appellant) has the right to a hearing at which evidence is presented and witnesses are examined under oath. The AJ renders a decision within 120 days. Either the worker or the agency can appeal that ruling to the MSPB (consisting of three presidential appointees), which may decide to hold a new hearing and issue its own decision. The appellant then can appeal the MSPR decision to the United States Court of Appeals for the federal circuit (or if the case involves alleged discrimination, to the Equal Employment Opportunity Commission*).

In the year ending September 30, 1987, the administrative judges at the MSPB heard about 6,500 cases. They dismissed about one-third of them (usually for lack of jurisdiction); of the remainder, they settled about one-third (usually by negotiations between the appellant and the agency). This left about 2,500 cases that were formally adjudicated; of these the appellant won less than one-fourth. Many of the losers appealed to the full MSPB and again most of them lost. Many of those losers appealed to the federal court; again most lost. Statistically, the agency that fires or demotes an employee has a good chance of having that decision upheld.[14]

But the cost and time of this lengthy appeal process means that agency executives are discouraged from taking an adverse action against any employee with a litigious personality, unless the employee's misconduct or

*Employees who allege discrimination on the basis of race, ethnicity, sex, or personal handicap can appeal an agency personnel decision to the Equal Employment Opportunity Commission (EEOC), where an examiner will conduct a hearing with evidence and witnesses. The employee can appeal to the courts.

bad performance is so serious as to make the effort worthwhile. It takes an average of 75 days for the AJ to reach a decision and, if appealed, another 149 days for the MSPB to reconsider the case. There are no data on how many days it takes the courts to decide, but it is probably a substantial number.[15]

Costly behavior tends to be rare behavior, and so not many employees are the object of adverse actions. In 1987 about 2,600 employees who had passed their probationary period were fired for misconduct, poor performance, or both. (Another 2,500 resigned in lieu of an adverse action.[16]) No one knows exactly how many employees are entitled to MSPB protection, but it is probably at least two million, which means that fewer than two-tenths of 1 percent were fired.

Changing the System

A little-noticed provision of the Civil Service Reform Act of 1978 authorized the OPM to conduct "demonstration projects" to see if changes in the personnel system would improve federal management. Not more than ten such experiments could be conducted, none could last more than five years, and each could affect a maximum of five thousand employees.

The provision might have remained unnoticed had not the personnel officers at the Naval Weapons Center and the Naval Ocean Systems Center been desperate. The former could not recruit enough good engineers, the latter was embroiled in a bureaucratic fire fight with line managers over how to rewrite position descriptions and classifications when NOSC was being formed out of two once-separate laboratories.

The result was the Navy Demonstration Project, usually called, after the location of the Naval Weapons Center, the "China Lake experiment."[17] Its goal was to give line managers greater authority over assigning, promoting, and rewarding their subordinates. This was done by grouping all the jobs at the labs into five broad career paths (professional, technical, specialist, administrative, and clerical) and lumping the eighteen GS grades into (depending on the path) four, five, or six broad pay levels (or "bands").* About five thousand employees at the two labs, mostly but not entirely scientific, professional, and technical persons, participated in the demonstration project.

The managers benefited in several ways. At NOSC they were given simplified, one-page descriptions of each career path to replace the de-

*For example, all engineers in grades GS-9, GS-10, and GS-11 were grouped together into Band II. A new GS-9 engineer who did outstanding work could be given pay raises within that band which earned him or her the pay equivalent of a GS-11 without having to be assigned to a new job, given managerial responsibilities, or promoted to a new rank.

tailed, multi-page descriptions of each occupation. To classify a position they had to do little more than make a photocopy of the simplified description and attach it to a form on which they checked a few boxes. When they recruited a new person they had the flexibility to meet market-determined entry pay levels. The managers could increase the pay of outstanding individuals within each pay band without having to justify promoting them to a higher grade or transferring them to a managerial position. Funds were given to all managers out of which they could distribute incentive pay increases and award one-time performance bonuses. The amount of money in these funds and the rules governing their use made it impossible to give pay increases or bonuses to everybody; thus the managers were forced to make choices based on performance. Should there be a reduction in force (none has yet occurred at NOSC or NWC), higher-ranking employees would only be allowed to bump persons within their own career path; moreover, the right to bump would be determined chiefly by performance ratings and only secondarily by seniority.

The experiment was immediately popular with the managers and has grown in popularity with the workers.[18] The guerrilla warfare between personnel offices and line managers ended. The former no longer had to be cops telling managers what they could not do; the latter no longer had to manipulate or evade rules to get their job done. Unlike the general merit-pay program authorized by the Civil Service Reform Act, the two navy labs *really* based pay on merit in ways that rewarded good performers but not poor ones.

The enthusiasm in the field was supported by the evaluations conducted by the Office of Personnel Management. OPM compared what happened over an eight-year period in the two California labs with the experience of two similar navy labs located on the East Coast. It found that the NWC at China Lake was able to compete more effectively for engineers by offering them higher starting salaries and quicker opportunities for advancement. During the first five years of the demonstration project the turnover rate at the West Coast labs declined, while at the East Coast labs it remained the same.[19] More important, there was a change in *who* was likely to leave. In both experimental and control labs the high-performing employees were less likely to quit than the low-performing ones, but the experimental labs did better than the control labs in this regard.[20] Managers at the navy lab in San Diego (NOSC) were unanimous in saying that the demonstration project was helping them maintain or improve the quality of the skilled work force.

All this cost money. The payroll at the California demonstration labs went up faster than it did at the east coast control labs.[21] But that should not be surprising. If an organization's only objective were to minimize the size of its payroll it would hire low-priced talent, get rid of senior people as soon as they started to earn a lot of money, and replace them with more recruits. Of course, quality would suffer. To maintain quality one would hire the best people and keep them as long as possible, even after their paychecks became fat. That is what the California labs did.

Resisting Change

Since the more flexible personnel system is praised by managers, employees, and OPM, one would think the federal government would rush to adopt it nationwide.

OPM submitted legislation that would permit but not require other agencies to adopt a version of the China Lake–San Diego plan. Congress did not act. The bill or something like it may yet pass, but it first must overcome the opposition of several groups. The Federal Managers Association polled its twenty thousand mid-level civil servants and found that 70 percent were opposed to extending nationally the merit-pay principle of the China Lake–San Diego project.[22] Many unions of federal employees are opposed. A person from the General Accounting Office who studied the demonstration projects said, "I'm not so sure there's anything really wrong with our current system."[23]

Part of the resistance may reflect simple inertia. As one personnel specialist at San Diego put it to me, "The old-school, professional classifiers are wedded to the old system." These officials are opposed to decentralization; to them the federal personnel system should be run centrally, otherwise it is not a system. (Of course, making it a centrally run system requires issuing a six-thousand-page personnel manual.) But more than inertia or old habits are at work. Employee unions are skeptical about, if not downright hostile to, the idea of merit pay. Pay based on seniority is safer because it minimizes the authority of managers. Some members of Congress worry that a decentralized system would lead to pay inequality—engineers, for example, would be paid different amounts in different parts of the country. They are right, of course; wage rates vary across local markets. But what is understandable to a business executive is a threat to Congress because its members feel especially vulnerable to any complaints of unequal treatment from their constituents. Finally, the decision of the Reagan administration that any new personnel system must be "cost neutral"—that is, not cost any more than the existing system—was seen by many as meaning that if Mary Smith were given a performance bonus it would have to come out of the pocket of John Jones. Such a zero-sum game is not good politics.

Bureaucratization versus Professionalization

The central dilemma of any public personnel system involves the choice between a bureaucratized and a professionalized service. The former consists of a set of rules that specify who are to be hired, how they are to be managed, and what they are to do; the latter consists of rules that specify who are to be hired but that leave great discretion to the members of the occupation, or to their immediate supervisors, to decide what they are to do and how they are to be managed. A profession, as we saw in chapter 4, is an occupation in which the conduct of its members is importantly influenced by an external reference group of fellow specialists who prescribe training, evaluate practice, and set standards. Physicians, economists, and engineers are for the most part professionals; clerks, investigators, and contract officers are not. Professionals are expected to put the well-being of their clients or the search for truth above their own interests. Society invests heavily in the training of professionals in part because the clients—medical patients, for example—are unable to evaluate the quality of the procedures to which they are subjected.

In government agencies professionals occupy an anomalous position. On the one hand, many professionals are hired because they bring esoteric knowledge to their tasks—they know how to do things that must be done that others cannot easily be taught—and because they are expected to regulate their own behavior on the basis of professional norms. On the other hand, democratic government requires bureaucratic accountability, and that means that no one wholly can be trusted to make important choices free of legal and administrative constraints.

This anomaly usually is resolved by hiring professionals for their expert knowledge but denying them the right to use that knowledge as they see fit. Government undertakes many tasks the performance of which cannot be specified in advance and it produces certain outcomes the quality of which cannot be judged even after the fact. We cannot tell the GS-15 engineer at the Naval Ocean Systems Center how to design a torpedo guidance system, but at least we can tell if the system he or she does design will guide torpedoes. We cannot tell a professor of philosophy at the University of California how to teach philosophy and we cannot tell after the teaching is done whether it was good, bad, or indifferent.

The biggest struggles in the federal personnel system have been over autonomy—allowing local managers to make decisions and allowing actual or quasi-professionals to do their jobs. If the government consisted of nothing but clerks (as it once did), we would not be having a controversy over whether the China Lake experiment should be adopted nationwide (though even the management of clerks might improve if managers had greater authority to hire and fire them). A personnel system created in the nineteenth century when we did have a government of clerks now has to cope with a government of engineers, scientists, lawyers, physicians, economists, auditors, and teachers.

Teachers are an especially difficult case. They are trained in institutions of higher education to perform a task of supreme importance but one that cannot be easily observed or accurately evaluated. Many critics doubt that what they learn in those institutions is adequate to the job they must do or that how they do the job can be left to their own judgment or to the supervision of their professional peers. In the opinion of many, teachers are at best a quasi-profession, and therefore must be managed as if they were bureaucrats.

In this country the pendulum swings back and forth between efforts to bureaucratize and efforts to professionalize public-school teaching. Private-school teaching, by contrast, has been left almost entirely to the market: Individual private schools have been free to hire whomever they wished, and the clients of these schools (the parents) have been free to select whichever school they wished (subject to the constraint that each school must meet certain minimum state standards).

As the public-school movement arose in the early nineteenth century, Horace Mann and others sought to professionalize teaching.* The first "normal" or teacher-training school was established in 1839. By the turn of the century the Progressive movement began to press for making teaching a profession akin to law and medicine; to this end it supported creating schools of education within the universities. But teaching never acquired the status of law or of medicine. It was always under attack inside the university for lacking the intellectual content of either the liberal-arts curriculum or the other professional schools.[24] Moreover, since the graduates of schools of education were chiefly employed by local governments (whereas most lawyers and doctors were employed in private enterprise), there was always a powerful institutional pressure to treat teachers as bureaucrats—that is, as people whose jobs could be centrally specified and controlled.

The periodic attempts to do this arose as a consequence of national crises or shifts in elite moods.† The Soviet launching of Sputnik in 1957 prompted a greater emphasis on mathematical, scientific, and foreign-

*In what follows, I have drawn heavily on and am much indebted to the several studies at the Rand Corporation by Linda Darling-Hammond, Barnett Berry, Arthur E. Wise, Milbrey W. McLaughlin, Richard F. Elmore, and Harriet T. Bernstein.

†These elite enthusiasms sometimes led to kooky efforts to bureaucratize teaching. In 1910, the Carnegie Foundation for the Advancement of Teaching hired Morris L. Cooke, a disciple of efficiency expert Frederick W. Taylor, to investigate university teaching. His report recommended that professors use standardized lecture notes in order to make universities more productive. One commentator said Cooke's report "reads as if the author received his training in a soap factory." See Samuel Haber, *Efficiency and Uplift* (Chicago: University of Chicago Press, 1964), 65–66; and Raymond E. Callahan, *Education and the Cult of Efficiency* (Chicago: University of Chicago Press, 1962).

language training; the crisis over school integration in the late 1950s and early 1960s led to federal legislation aimed at improving teaching in schools that enrolled disadvantaged and minority-group pupils; the decline in college entrance scores in the late 1960s stimulated a demand that the public schools get "back to basics"; the growing concern for immigrants and disabled people resulted in a requirement that schools supply bilingual and "special needs" education; popular unrest about crime in the schools led to the imposition of new mechanisms for either managing security, enhancing student rights, or both. All of these pressures had in common "a tendency to substitute external authority—social science methods, university experts, regulatory requirements, and legal principles—for the authority and expertise of educational practitioners."[25]

Teachers were being bureaucratized because state and national governments, and their public supporters, distrusted the professional judgment of teachers. But as Richard Elmore and Milbrey McLaughlin note, such distrust creates a dilemma: "the fate of the reforms ultimately depends on those who are the object of distrust."[26] That bureaucratization took the form of specifying not only who might be a teacher but what teachers were to do. They were to test students more frequently, teach from new math and science curricula, report in greater detail on their activities, and alter their classroom procedures (by using computers, team teaching, foreign languages, or whatever). Linda Darling-Hammond and Barnett Berry report that between 1969 and 1974, state legislatures enacted at least sixty-six laws requiring or encouraging new school management, budget, planning, evaluation, and testing procedures. By 1983, thirty-eight states had authorized tests of student competency as a requirement for graduation and all fifty states had done something by way of setting new standards for public schools.[27]

In the mid-1980s, however, the pendulum began swinging in a different direction. Alarmed by predictions that the nation was running out of good teachers, state legislators began passing bills designed to attract more teachers and upgrade the quality of the teachers already employed. The attractions included higher salaries, enhanced status and authority, and more substantive certification requirements. By mid-1986, forty-six states were using or developing statewide tests of teacher competency and teacher salaries had increased by more than 35 percent since 1980. Twenty-six states had implemented policies requiring certain minimum grades or test scores as a prerequisite for admission into teacher-education programs. And dozens of states had increased the number of hours that must be devoted to studying subject-matter or "academic" courses by would-be teachers, especially in the liberal arts.[28] Some states even considered requiring prospective teachers to first earn a baccalaureate degree in a four-year liberal-arts college before beginning teacher training. A few states now limit a teacher's credential to the subject matter (for example, mathematics or physics) in which they are proficient rather than to grant them a broad, all-purpose credential.[29]

All but four states now require teacher competency tests. One such test, the National Teacher Examinations (NTE), is in use in at least twenty states. As with the PACE test, minorities have not done as well as whites on the NTE, leading to court challenges to its use. Moreover, organized teachers complain that the tests have been developed by government agencies or testing organizations rather than by members of the profession itself, as with the tests administered to veterinarians or architects. In response, some states are considering establishing teacher boards to devise and administer the exams.[30]

Once certified, new teachers increasingly are being asked to go through a probationary period in which their performance on the job is assessed. Once having passed the performance assessment they are less likely than formerly to receive a permanent or lifetime certificate; instead, thirty-two states now require that they renew their certificates by further education or in-service training.[31] While all of this has been going on, educational reformers such as the Carnegie Forum on Education and the Economy and the National Governors' Association have been urging that more autonomy be given to school principals and classroom teachers.[32] This new wave of reform reflects the belief that teaching ought to be professionalized rather than bureaucratized. This implies that what teachers do will be left more to the discretion of teachers and their first-line supervisors, the principals.

The change has been summarized felicitously by Darling-Hammond and Berry this way: "The second wave reformers suggest greater regulation of teachers . . . in exchange for the deregulation of teaching."[33] The reason for the switch is the recognition that "reforms concentrating on specific content and instructional strategies can influence practice only at the margins."[34]

But there is no more reason to believe that the pendulum will remain at the professional end of its swing now than there was to suppose it would in the 1950s. Public-school teaching always will be under the control of politicians sensitive to popular beliefs; this means that teacher discretion always will be constrained by whatever interests can claim to speak for the public—bilingualism, the new math, computer literacy, crime control, sex education, or whatever.

The fragility of the present enthusiasm for decentralization, professionalism, and teacher empowerment is revealed by the great difficulty public schools have had in implementing performance or merit pay. Arthur E. Wise and his colleagues surveyed teacher evaluation practices in thirty-two school districts and did not find many success stories. The common problems were the hostility of teachers and the incompetence of principals.[35] The four districts in which they found success stories worthy of close examination had unusually skillful and strongly motivated educational leaders who in collaboration with supportive teachers designed a performance evaluation system well-suited to the particular circumstance of the community and its schools.[36] In short, well-run public schools are possible when talented, dedicated people are at work in sympathetic communities. It is good to know that this occurs; it is too much to expect that it will occur everywhere.

Conclusions

The people who work for government will always want the freedom to do their work without excessive constraints but they will resist efforts to evaluate and reward them on the basis of that work. This problem has become more acute of late with the recruitment of so many professionals and quasi-professionals into government service and the multiplication of legislative and judicial constraints on government work. As the tasks become more complex, workers will want more freedom; as the constraints multiply, they will be less and less trusting of their managers (who are in charge of enforcing the constraints) or of the political process (that has created the constraints).

When bureaucrats become defensive about or hostile to the pressures on them, politicians and interest groups confuse their defensiveness with timidity and their hostility with subversion, and so are tempted to engage in bureaucrat-bashing: deriding bureaucrats as narrow-minded, self-serving, or incompetent drudges. Naturally the objects of this bashing will resent it, not least because the caricature so often is untrue.[37]

The managers are caught in the middle between workers and politicians. The challenge they face and how they cope with it is the subject of the next chapter.

CHAPTER 9

Compliance

GIVEN THE CONSTRAINTS on the managers of public agencies, it is a wonder that there is any management at all. Managers are supposed to coordinate the work of operators in order to attain organizational goals. For managers to do this properly the goals must be known, the work must contribute to their attainment, and the powers of the managers must be sufficient to produce the needed coordination. I trust that the preceding chapters will have persuaded the reader that these conditions rarely are met in public agencies; often, goals are hopelessly vague, activities sadly ineffectual, and powers sharply limited.

Nonetheless, managers do make things happen. When people call the police, the police (usually) come; when children go to school, teachers are there with study plans in hand; when forest fires break out, forest rangers respond; when workers retire, Social Security checks start arriving; when soldiers are ordered into combat, they fight. Even in Watertown, a person who waits in line long enough at the Registry will get a driver's license.

If you believe that all bureaucrats are wholly self-interested individuals desirous only of maximizing their own welfare, much of this should never happen. Why shouldn't a schoolteacher avoid work by letting the students play games or loaf in class? Most students have little incentive to complain to their parents that they are having fun instead of studying hard, and even if they do complain the school administrators can only with great difficulty fire the teacher or lower the teacher's salary. Why shouldn't soldiers run instead of fight? Their desertion will be known only to officers near enough to the scene of combat to have an understandable desire to run as well. Why shouldn't police officers ignore the citizen's story about a stolen car? Their superiors have no way of knowing other than from the officers' report whether a car was stolen at all and what, if anything, was done to find it. Of course, some teachers don't teach, some police don't investigate, and some soldiers don't fight. But most do.

When employees do not exert themselves to achieve the goals of their organization they are shirking. Of late, economists have turned their attention to the problem of shirking and developed theories showing why the problem will be very common and describing the conditions under which it can be avoided.[1] They are called principal-agent models, meaning that they address the question of how a principal (for example, the owner of a firm or the manager of a government bureau) can arrange the incentives confronting an agent (for example, a worker or lower-ranking manager) so that the latter does what the former desires. The problem of shirking does not arise when the principal can directly observe and control the agent's actions; it arises when those actions cannot be observed or when the agent has information about the work that can be withheld from his or her principal. When a company president cannot watch what a plant manager is doing, the latter may not work as hard and thus produce as much profit as the president would like. This may occur for one or both of two reasons. First, the person who applies for the job of plant manager may conceal a lack of qualifications but be hired anyway because the president wrongly thinks he or she is qualified.* Or the plant manager may decide that since income is not dependent on how profitable the factory is he or she need not work as hard as the president would like.† Either way, the president gets less effort (and less profit) than is wanted.

The economists' solution to this problem is to design clever employment contracts that, for example, guarantee the plant manager a minimum fixed salary (otherwise he or she would not take the job at all) plus a bonus contingent on achieving a certain level of profitability. This is not as easy as it seems, because so many things besides the manager's actions will influence profitability—the weather, the cost of raw materials, technological change—that it is hard to know how much of the profit if any should be credited to the manager's efforts. (More technically, it is very hard to measure the marginal product of individual effort.) That is why most people are paid largely or entirely by salaries rather than with a share of profits.

The problem of shirking is in principle even greater in a government agency. Not only do many employees work out of sight of their bosses, often they produce nothing that can be measured after the fact. Suppose a police officer walking a beat makes no arrest. That can mean either that no crime occurred or that the officer could solve none of the dozens of crimes that in fact did occur. Of course in some agencies the output of operators can be observed and measured. In the Postal Service, managers

*In technical terms this is the problem of "adverse selection."
†In technical terms this is the problem of "moral hazard."

know how much mail the clerks are sorting and how fast they are sorting it. (The USPS uses the Origin and Destination Information System, or ODIS, to measure the time it takes to deliver first-class mail.) But the constraints on government managers make it almost impossible to design an employment contract that would base compensation on an employee's performance even assuming (a big if) that there was some way to link how fast the mail was delivered to the actions of a given employee or manager.

The difficulties of avoiding shirking in a government agency go well beyond the problems of meeting the prescriptions of the standard principal-agent theory. First, the output of an agency may not only be unobservable, it may be unknowable. If the agency's goal is so vague as to be meaningless (for example, "advancing the interests of the United States") the administrator often will not know what to do and thus cannot be expected to tell the subordinate what to do, much less judge the work after the fact. Second, every agent in a government bureau is likely to have many principals—not only a bureau supervisor, but also superiors in the Office of Management and Budget, the White House, the courts, and several congressional committees. Moreover these superiors will frequently change as elections come and go. Third, the agents—diplomats, doctors, engineers, pilots, police officers, schoolteachers, antitrust lawyers, and public health officers—will bring their own political preferences, professional standards, and prior experiences to their jobs. Other things being equal they would prefer more pay to less, but other things are rarely equal and the prospect of a pay increase often is linked more to seniority than to performance. As we saw in Part I, bureaucrats have preferences and these include definitions of how the job *ought to be done* as well as how much it ought to pay. For every manager who complains that an employee is doing too little (shirking), there is another who complains that an employee is doing the wrong thing (subverting).[2] Under these conditions of vague or conflicting goals, multiple principals, and bureaucrats with policy preferences it is hardly surprising that economists have not made much progress in finding even theoretical solutions to the problem of shirking. What is surprising is that bureaucrats work at all rather than shirk at every opportunity.

How can this be? In part the answer is that even in government service managers to some extent can control the material rewards of their subordinates. It may be hard to fire or demote anybody, but it is not too hard to give people attractive or miserable job assignments or to speed up or slow down their prospects for promotion.[3] And the answer can in part be found in the problem itself: Bureaucrats have preferences. Among them is the desire to do the job. That desire may spring entirely out of a sense of duty, or it may arise out of a willingness to conform to the expectations of fellow workers and superiors even when there is no immediate financial advantage in doing so.

Recall (from chapter 3) why a soldier fights: It is not because a clever economist has designed an employment contract that leads him to risk his life in order to maximize his income; it is because he does not wish to let down his buddies or appear cowardly in their eyes. Both the Union and the Confederate armies during the Civil War were notoriously undisciplined: officers often were elected by the soldiers, and even when appointed they received little deference; orders were hard to enforce; desertion was common; military trials and formal punishments were so unpopular as to be hard to employ. But in battle the men fought, sustained by a sense of honor and small-group loyalties reinforced by the fact that in so many companies the soldiers came from the same towns and villages.[4] Police officers who go to the scene of a family quarrel are running a risk: The disputants may turn violently against the officers. Once there, what the officers do, barring some gross misconduct, will never be known to their superiors. A rationally self-interested officer either would not go to the scene or, once there, do as little as possible. Yet many officers go to great lengths to calm the disputants and counsel the victim.* They do so because it is expected of them, the situation seems to demand it, and their partners would think less of them if they did not show they could "handle the situation."

Mission and Compliance

It is a commonplace that people do not live by bread alone, but it is one often forgotten by scholars seeking to find the most parsimonious explanation of human action and the most elegant prescription for how best to induce that action. In business, where one might suppose that money incentives are the whole story, great efforts have been made by the most productive firms to supplement those incentives with a sense of mission based on a shared organizational culture. The managers of government agencies, whose control of pecuniary rewards is much less than that of their business counterparts, presumably would have an even greater stake in making use of nonmaterial rewards. There are three kinds of such rewards: a sense of duty and purpose, the status that derives from individual recognition and personal power, and the associational benefits that

*They do these things despite evidence that if they merely arrested the alleged assailant and left, both parties would be better off. Richard Berk and Lawrence Sherman have shown in a brilliant experiment that future victimizations of women are less likely when the man is arrested than when he is counseled or cooled off. (See Lawrence W. Sherman and Richard A. Berk, "The Specific Deterrent Effects of Arrest for Domestic Assault," *American Sociology Review* 49 [1984]: 261–72.) Here the police behave in a certain way despite the fact that an alternative is not only substantively better, it will lead to recognition from superiors (an arrest statistic).

come from being part of an organization (or a small group within that organization) that is highly regarded by its members or by society at large. Purpose, status, and solidarity; these are the elements out of which a sense of mission might be fashioned.

But some public managers find that it is very hard to use those elements to create, by plan, such a sense. The Immigration and Naturalization Service (INS) has been conspicuous for its weak sense of mission and low morale.[5] The chief reason is that it has vague and competing goals: "Keep out illegal immigrants, but let in necessary agricultural workers"; "carefully screen foreigners seeking to enter the country, but facilitate the entry of foreign tourists"; "find and expel illegal aliens, but do not break up families, impose hardships, violate civil rights, or deprive employers of low-paid workers." No organization can do all of these things well, especially when advocates of each have the power to mount newspaper and congressional investigations of the agency's "failures." The conflict over goals has resulted in starvation for funds; the INS workload has increased far faster than its resources.[6] The INS is an extreme case, to be sure, but it is not a unique one: Prison systems are supposed to both confine and rehabilitate; the State Department is supposed to represent both this country to other nations and other nations to this country. No organization can develop a sense of mission when it cannot even in principle decide what single, main thing it is supposed to do.

But a sense of mission can be found in some public agencies. A few have been mentioned in earlier chapters: the Army Corps of Engineers, the FBI, NASA (before the *Challenger* disaster), the Marine Corps, and many field offices of the Social Security Administration. Clearly, the problem of achieving compliance with organizational purposes has been solved in some agencies. And even in bureaus that have no obvious sense of mission, most operators usually work toward organizational goals without major problems of shirking. Agencies must differ with respect to managing compliance. Some of those differences can be stated systematically.

Types of Agencies

From a managerial point of view, agencies differ in two main respects: Can the activities of their operators be observed? Can the results of those activities be observed? The first factor involves *outputs*—what the teachers, doctors, lawyers, engineers, police officers, and grant-givers do on a day-to-day basis. Outputs consist of the work the agency does. The second factor involves *outcomes*—how, if at all, the world changes because of the outputs. Outcomes can be thought of as the results of agency work. The outputs (or work) of police officers are the radio calls answered, beats walked, tickets written, accidents investigated, and arrests made. The outcomes (or results) are the changes, if any, in the level of safety, security, order, and amenity in the community.

Outputs—work—may be hard to observe because what the operator does is esoteric (for example, a doctor performing a diagnosis or a physicist developing a theory) or because the operator acts out of view of the manager (for example, a police officer handling a family quarrel or a ranger supervising a forest). If operator actions are esoteric or unobserved, the problem of moral hazard arises: the operator may shirk or subvert. Outcomes—results—may be hard to observe because the organization lacks a method for gathering information about the consequences of its actions (for example, a suicide-prevention agency may actually prevent suicides but it has no way of counting the number of potential suicides that did not occur); because the operator lacks a proven means to produce an outcome (for example, prison psychologists do not know how to rehabilitate criminals); because the outcome results from an unknown combination of operator behavior and other factors (for example, a child's score on a test reflects some mix of pupil intelligence, parental influence, and teacher skill); or because the outcome appears after a long delay (for example, the penalty imposed on a criminal may lead to a reduction—or even an increase—in the offender's behavior five years later). I realize, of course, that what constitutes an outcome is a matter of judgment. Is the outcome of the work of the U.S. Employment Service referring an unemployed person to a job, having any employer actually hire the person, or helping the person develop a meaningful, long-term career? In what follows I shall refer chiefly to effects that approximate the most operational (or least vague) statement of the agency's goals.

Observing outputs and outcomes may be either difficult or easy. Taking the extreme cases produces four kinds of agencies: Agencies in which both outputs and outcomes can be observed; agencies in which outputs but not outcomes can be observed; agencies in which outcomes but not outputs can be observed; and agencies in which neither outputs nor outcomes can be observed. For reasons that I hope will become clear as we proceed, I have called the first kind of agency a *production* organization, the second a *procedural* organization, the third a *craft* organization, and the fourth a *coping* organization.*

PRODUCTION ORGANIZATIONS

Where both outputs (or work) and outcomes are observable, managers have an opportunity to design (within the limits established by external

*In developing this typology I have been influenced by (though I have not followed) the distinctions suggested by Henry Mintzberg in *The Structuring of Organizations* (Englewood Cliffs, N.J.: Prentice-Hall, 1979), especially part IV. My classification is a crude effort to sort out some important differences. It is hardly a theory and many agencies do not fit its categories. Use with caution.

constraints) a compliance system to produce an efficient outcome. The Internal Revenue Service (IRS) can observe the activities of its clerks and auditors and can measure the amount of money collected in taxes as a result of their efforts. It can estimate with some accuracy the additional amount of tax monies that will be produced by increasing the proportion of certain classes of tax returns that are audited. The United States Postal Service can observe the actions of its letter sorters and other operators and can calculate how closely they are meeting the organization's delivery standards, such as getting 95 percent of all zip-coded first-class mail from Boston to Los Angeles within three days.[7] The Social Security Administration can (and does) measure the speed with which retirement (OASI) claims are paid to beneficiaries. In these cases I am assuming that the preferred outcomes of the IRS are to maximize taxes collected per employee; of the USPS to achieve mail delivery goals with the lowest possible expenditure; and of the SSA to get as many checks out on time and in the proper amount as possible given available resources.

The existence of observable outputs (the activities of auditors, letter sorters, and claims processors) and observable outcomes (taxes collected, mail delivered, checks received) simplifies the managerial problem. But that is not to say that managing these agencies is easy. Though the OASI work of the SSA in principle is simple and measurable, the law and rulings that it administers are incredibly complex. When it started out, SSA had to assign a unique identifier (a Social Security number) to every eligible person in the country, create and maintain lifetime earnings records for all of these people, and decide what would constitute proof of age and identity. The problems caused by people who change the way they spell their names or who have no valid birth certificates were, at least initially, staggering.

SSA has solved these problems and in the process infused many of its field employees with a strong sense of mission—the "service ethic." To maintain this ethic it has taken advantage of changes in the civil service laws that permit it to reward high-ranking employees with performance bonuses and has tried to promote and assign people in a way that rewards good work.

The existence of conditions conducive to production-oriented management does not guarantee that such management will occur. Issuing drivers' licenses at the Registry of Motor Vehicles is an activity with observable outputs (clerks working) and observable outcomes (licenses received). The differences between the efforts to produce efficiency in the USPS and IRS and service in the SSA, on the one hand, and the lack of equivalent efforts on behalf of efficiency or service in the Registry, on the other, have many explanations, some of which will be addressed in later chapters. They include cultural differences between politics in Massachusetts and politics in Washington, D.C., and the fact that political superiors get large benefits from having taxes collected and retirement checks mailed out but much smaller benefits from having drivers' licenses issued.

A problem that confronts the managers of all production agencies is that by plan or inadvertence they may give most of their attention to the more easily measured outcomes at the expense of those less easily observed or counted. There is a kind of Gresham's Law at work in many government bureaus: Work that produces measurable outcomes tends to drive out work that produces unmeasurable outcomes. Consider the IRS. It wishes to get the maximum amount of tax revenues from the work of its auditors. It is therefore tempted to judge auditors solely on the basis of how much money they produce from each audit and how many audits they conduct. This can lead the auditors to become so zealous in auditing that they annoy taxpayers who feel they are being treated unfairly or hounded about minor errors.

Similarly with intake workers in a welfare office. Certain aspects of its work—the number and accuracy of claims processed—are readily observable. Being observable, welfare-office managers may press their operators to maximize the number of claims or to minimize the number of errors. (Doing both simultaneously is no easy trick; more claims requires speedy clerks, fewer errors requires careful clerks. Careful, speedy clerks are in short supply.) But another, less easily observed outcome thereby will be neglected—being helpful to clients. If careful, speedy clerks are in short supply, careful, speedy, friendly clerks are even harder to find. And when they are found, numbers-oriented managers can lead the clerks to emphasize speed or accuracy at the expense of kindness and civility.[8]

In his study of a state employment agency, Peter Blau observed that when managers counted the number of applicants referred to employers by each interviewer, both good and bad things happened. Because interviewers were judged by how many unemployed persons were informed of job openings, any tendency the (predominately white) interviewers had to discriminate against black applicants was suppressed: a black referral counted for just as much as a white one. At the same time, however, clerks would refer even unqualified applicants to employers, where their chances of getting or keeping a job were poor, because a marginal referral counted for as much as a qualified one. There was no incentive to spend a lot of time on hard cases. In addition, clerks competed with each other for placements, sometimes concealing from each other the existence of a job opening.[9]

The employees of production-oriented agencies are not indifferent to the management systems with which they must cope. They will try on occasion to fudge the numbers by which they are evaluated, either out of a desire to shirk (that is, minimize effort) or subvert (that is, produce outcomes other than the measured one). John Tierney recounts instances of postal clerks and lower-level managers manipulating the ODIS system that was used to measure how fast the mail was delivered. In some cities, late mail was removed from delivery units before the mail was sampled to measure how long it had taken to get that far.[10]

In no agency was the "stat game" played with greater zeal than in the FBI during J. Edgar Hoover's tenure as director. Agents were expected to produce ever higher numbers of arrests, recoveries (for example, of stolen cars), apprehended fugitives, and savings (that is, money the U.S. government did not have to pay to a citizen who had filed a claim against it). Before the bureau changed under Director Clarence Kelley, every agent was under enormous pressure to produce these "stats." This resulted in FBI agents getting lists from local police departments of stolen cars that had been found so that the agents could claim them as "recoveries" even though the agents had done little or nothing to find the cars.[11] The number of fugitives apprehended could be maximized by concentrating on deserters from the armed forces (most of whom were found at home) rather than on major felons who had gone underground to escape serious punishment. By the 1970s, a bureau survey disclosed that 60 percent of the cases that the FBI presented for prosecution to local U.S. attorneys were being declined. In many cases the reason for the declination was that the case was too trivial to warrant prosecutorial effort.[12]

The error made by the IRS, the state employment office, and the FBI was to define outcome too narrowly, so that only some but not all of the desired results were being observed and counted. In the IRS and the employment agency this may have been inadvertent; in the FBI it was quite deliberate, part and parcel of Hoover's strategy for maintaining his organization in the good graces of Congress (see chapter 11). This error is made all too easily in any organization, but especially in government agencies where outcomes are not measured by sales in a market of voluntary transactions. Private express services do not have the same problem in measuring performance as did the old Post Office Department (and to some extent the present-day Postal Service); if Purolater Courier starts losing customers to Federal Express or United Parcel Service, it knows it has a management problem.

Before one can properly manage a production agency, first one must be certain that it *is* a production agency. This means being reasonably confident that all the important outcomes are being observed. SSA and USPS can do this more easily than the IRS or the employment service, and the latter two can do it more easily than the FBI. To its credit, in the mid-1970s the FBI finally decided that the quality of cases was more important than their quantity and changed its management system accordingly. That the change was bitterly resisted by many FBI managers is testimony to how powerful is the lure of purely statistical management systems.[13]

PROCEDURAL ORGANIZATIONS

When managers can observe what their subordinates are doing but not the outcome (if any) that results from those efforts, they are managing a procedural organization. The administrators of a mental hospital can learn what the medical staff is doing but cannot easily (if at all) observe the results of many kinds of treatment, either because there is no result or because it will occur in the distant future. At a juvenile reformatory the work of the counselors can be observed but not whether the work has had a positive effect; only time will tell, and by then the youngsters will be out on the street. Managers at the Occupational Safety and Health Administration (OSHA) know or can easily find out what their safety and health inspectors are doing, but only with great difficulty can they learn whether those activities have materially improved safety and health at the factories that they inspect (indeed, in the case of health they may never know since the gestation period for many illnesses caused by industrial poisons is years or decades).[14]

Perhaps the largest procedural organization in the government is the United States Armed Forces during peacetime. Every detail of training, equipment, and deployment is under the direct inspection of company commanders, ship captains, and squadron leaders. But none of these factors can be tested in the only way that counts, against a real enemy, except in wartime. This is especially true of those weapons systems designed to deter nuclear war. Since 1945, none ever has been fired in anger; one hopes none ever will be. By taking samples of these nuclear missiles, disarming them, and firing them, the fact that they fly can be verified and their accuracy can be estimated. But none of this tells us in fact what we really need to know: Do these weapons deter enemy aggression and, if fired, will they explode as planned on enemy targets? Military leaders often are criticized for preparing to fight the last war, but given their inability to test their preparations on a real enemy in advance of the next war, the criticism is a bit unfair.

The conditions that define a procedural bureaucracy seem to make it ripe for management in ways that encourage the development of professionalism. What better way, one might ask, to manage organizational activities, the outcomes of which cannot be observed from any administrative perch, than by recruiting professionals to do the work in accordance with the highest professional standards? These standards would constrain the practitioners to put the client's interests ahead of their own and to engage in behavior that is most likely to produce the desired outcome. This sometimes happens (as in the case of better-run mental hospitals), but more often it does not. The reason, I believe, is that a government agency cannot afford to allow its operators to exercise discretion when the outcome of that exercise is in doubt or likely to be controversial. Public management, as we saw in the last chapter, is constraint driven. Sometimes those constraints can be loosened if a manager can say convincingly, "see here, what we're doing really works." If the manager cannot justify on the grounds of results leaving operators alone to run things as they see fit, the manager will have to convince political superiors that the rules governing government work are being faithfully followed. Putting the fig leaf of professionalism over the nakedness of unknown outcomes will not fool anybody.

In short, because it is constraint driven, management becomes means-oriented in procedural organizations. *How* the operators go about their jobs is more important than whether doing those jobs produces the desired outcomes. Recall the state employment agency: Peter Blau observed that managers were preoccupied with finding ways of controlling exactly what their clerks and interviewers did. Perhaps they were under the erroneous impression that the agency was a simple production organization (that is, it could easily observe its outcomes) when in fact it was not. More likely they knew full well that they could not tell unambiguously whether they were attaining their goals; all that they could be sure of was trouble if they violated important procedural constraints such as overspending or discrimination on the basis of race.

In a procedural organization, standard operating procedures (SOPs) are pervasive. Popular accounts of service in the peacetime army or navy are replete with stories about rules and procedures. ("If it moves, salute it; if it doesn't move, pick it up; if it is too big to pick up, paint it.") As we shall see in a later chapter, in recent decades the U.S. Army has devoted much of its peacetime efforts to elevating SOPs to the level of grand tactics by trying and then discarding various war-fighting doctrines. But when war breaks out, SOPs break down. The reason is obvious: outcomes suddenly become visible. Staying alive, taking real estate, and killing the enemy are such important outcomes that the only SOPs which continue to have much force are those that contribute directly to producing those outcomes. At least that is almost true. Some SOPs, such as those that seem central to the mission of the organization, continue to exert an influence even though they are actually getting in the way of producing good outcomes. The U.S. Army in Vietnam tried to apply doctrines and SOPs designed for large conventional wars in central Europe to the unconventional war of the Vietnamese villages.[15] Because they were facing the enemy at close range, the smallest organizational units—the squads, platoons, and companies—were the first to see the error in this. Some managed to change doctrine even when larger units—divisions and corps—led by men far from the scene of battle adhered to the old view.

CRAFT ORGANIZATIONS

In wartime, many army and navy units change from procedural to craft organizations. Whereas formerly their members acted under the direct gaze of managers (marching on parade, practicing on the rifle range, maneuvering in convoys), now they fight in the haze, noise, and confusion of distant battlefields. Commanders who in peacetime knew the whereabouts and activities of every soldier are in wartime lucky to know the location and actions of entire battalions. This is part of the "friction" of war of which Clausewitz wrote so compellingly.[16] But wartime commanders do learn (usually rather quickly) whether those battalions won their engagements. A craft organization consists of operators whose activities are hard to observe but whose outcomes are relatively easy to evaluate.

Examples of craft organizations are not limited to the drama of war. Peter Blau described a "federal enforcement agency" (almost surely the Wage and Hour Division of the U.S. Department of Labor) in which the key operators, called "compliance officers," spent much of their time working away from their offices, unobserved, investigating complaints that employers have violated federal laws governing the pay and hours of work of their employees.* These officers interviewed employers and employees (often in their homes), inspected records, and negotiated compliance agreements with the employers that included a promise of future good behavior and, sometimes, a bill for back wages that had to be paid. Defiant employers were referred to federal attorneys for legal action.

The day-to-day activities of the Wage and Hour employees were much less minutely regulated than those of the workers in the state employment agency that Blau also studied. The reason was clear: The former could be judged on the basis of the results they achieved in a way that the latter could not.[17] The compliance agreements and legal complaints brought in by the Wage and Hour officers could be reviewed for legal accuracy and substantive completeness. The law and agency rules clearly described what constituted a correct outcome, and that outcome could be observed. The compliance officers either produced that outcome or they did not. No law or rule prescribed with equal clarity for the employment service interviewer what constituted the right outcome (A referral? A job obtained? A job held for a year? A career begun?) and in any case there was no way for the agency to observe any outcome other than a referral. Because of

*The principal law is the Fair Labor Standards Act, which specifies the minimum wage that must be paid and the maximum number of hours that may be worked in covered industries. The division also enforces provisions of the Davis-Bacon Act (governing pay on federal works projects). Until 1978, when jurisdiction was transferred to another agency, it enforced the Equal Pay Act (which bans pay discrimination on the basis of sex), and the Age Discrimination in Employment Act (which offers protection to workers over the age of forty from discrimination in hiring, firing, and compensation).

these differences management in the Wage and Hour Division was goal-oriented; management in the employment service was means-oriented.

Many investigative agencies practice goal-oriented management. Detectives in a police department are evaluated on the basis of crimes solved, not procedures followed. Attorneys in the Antitrust Division of the Justice Department exercise substantial independence in initiating and developing cases. The division can afford to give them this freedom because higher-level managers review the final report and decide whether it constitutes grounds for prosecution. As Suzanne Weaver observed, these decisions are usually routine (the initiating attorney's judgment is ratified), but even when they are difficult the division managers have fairly clear grounds for evaluating the outcome; given the evidence produced and the current rulings of federal courts, is the division likely to win if it decides to prosecute?[18]

There are scarcely any operators in any federal agency whose daily work is harder to observe than the field representatives of the Army Corps of Engineers. They work for a year or two in remote locations, overseeing the building of military bases or other facilities. When Mohammad Al-Saud studied the corps in 1986, one of its largest projects was deep in the interior of Saudi Arabia. And that was only one of over four thousand projects costing over $6 billion and spread over Africa, Europe, Latin America, the Middle East, the Far East, and, of course, the United States. Though managers did make inspection trips, by and large "the field representative receives little instruction concerning how to administer his task"; indeed, "he is scarcely looked over and surveyed by his supervisors at all."[19] It was not only distance that made detailed oversight rare, it was the nature of the task itself. No one could say in advance exactly how one might insure that an air base was built on time, within budget, and according to specifications. Outputs—the daily work of the engineers in the field—could not be centrally directed. But outcomes could be evaluated: It was easy to learn whether the air base was built on time and within budget, and it was not too difficult to decide whether it was built according to specs.

Perhaps the best-known study of a government agency trying to manage the behavior of operators working in remote places is Herbert Kaufman's *The Forest Ranger.*[20] Kaufman asked how managers in the Washington headquarters of the Forest Service could overcome the centrifugal tendencies of nearly eight hundred district rangers who supervised national forests located (in many instances) in distant places. His answer was the multiplication of formal controls: detailed rules spelled out in a multi-volume *Forest Service Manual*; reporting requirements that obliged district rangers to account for how they spent virtually every minute of every day; policy guidelines (what Kaufman called "preformed decisions") covering many eventualities, frequent inspections and in-service training programs;

and the rotation of foresters among different posts to forestall the development of excessively localistic perspectives.

Kaufman's fascinating account of how a dispersed bureaucracy achieves policy integration may seem to refute the argument of this section—that where observing outputs is hard and outcomes easy, management will not try to control the daily activities of its operators. After all, the amount of logging or tourism in a national forest is not hard to observe; even the condition of the wildlife there is observable to some degree. If that is true, why shouldn't the managers of the Forest Service have evaluated the district rangers on the basis of the outcomes they produced and forgotten the burdensome efforts to know what the rangers did with their every waking hour? The answer, I think, is that outcomes in a forest are not in fact as easily observed as are those in the Corps, or the Antitrust Division, or the detective division of a police department. It takes a long time for a tree to grow. The ecology of a forest develops gradually and can change for reasons that a forester may or may not be able to affect. It has not been easy to judge whether or not a given ranger's work has contributed to the service's general goal of managing forests to achieve "maximum use and sustained yield." For these reasons, I believe, the Forest Service is an interesting mixed case. The results of a ranger's work can be observed only up to a point—one can tell whether he or she managed to put out a forest fire or build a road but not whether the forest in twenty years will have a hardy stand of trees or sustain an abundant range of wildlife. Thus, the service has managed its members by a combination of procedural controls and outcome evaluations.

The service is, however, like other craft organizations in one important respect: It relies heavily on the ethos and sense of duty of its operators to control behavior. In the case of lawyers in the Antitrust Division, engineers in the Army Corps, and many of the foresters in the Forest Service, this ethos derives from an internalized set of professional norms. In the case of non-engineers in the corps, compliance officers in the Wage and Hour Division, many police detectives, and soldiers in wartime, this ethos derives not from a profession but from a job-derived tradecraft articulated, if at all, only within the intimate settings of small work groups.

It is just this combination of self-taught or professionally indoctrinated skills and group- or profession-induced ethos that justifies calling such agencies craft organizations. It was Arthur Stinchcombe who first used the concept of a craft to distinguish the relatively decentralized, procedurally self-regulating organizations of the sort I have been describing from conventional bureaucracies. His example was the construction industry, where carpenters, plumbers, electricians, and others come together with minimal central control to produce a building on the basis of "work processes governed by the worker in accordance with empirical lore."[21] The quality control on their work derived from the ability of a contractor or owner to assess the value of the finished structure with the added strength of the commitment of the various craft members to do a "good job" as each other would define it.

Agencies that can evaluate their members by the outcomes produced rather than by the procedures followed are rarely content to do only that. Public management—or at least good public management—is not so relentlessly utilitarian as to think that only results matter. One reason for this is that every public agency produces many kinds of outcomes—not just progress toward the primary goal of the agency, but also conformity to the contextual goals and constraints in which the agency is enmeshed. Take the case of investigators, whether detectives, Wage and Hour officers, or Antitrust lawyers: Each has many opportunities to abuse his or her authority by taking bribes, using excessive force or improper investigative methods, or engaging in political favoritism. Though managerial checks will prevent some of this, most of it will have to be controlled by the sense of duty of the operators themselves. Blau noted that the Wage and Hour officers often were offered bribes, that the offer of a bribe was almost never reported, but that insofar as he could tell bribes were rarely if ever accepted.[22] Weaver found no hint of abuse of authority among the Antitrust Division lawyers. Some police detectives are corrupt but most are not; some police departments have experienced pervasive corruption, most have not. How much corruption occurs will depend on a variety of factors, including important cultural ones. Successful managers in skills-oriented agencies not only try to develop the right skills in their employees, they also try to encourage the adoption of a shared commitment as to what constitutes duty and good work.

COPING ORGANIZATIONS

Some agencies can observe neither the outputs nor the outcomes of their key operators. A school administrator cannot watch teachers teach (except through classroom visits that momentarily may change the teacher's behavior) and cannot tell how much students have learned (except by standardized tests that do not clearly differentiate between what the teacher has imparted and what the student has acquired otherwise). Police officers cannot be watched by their lieutenants and the level of order the officers maintain on their beat cannot readily be observed or, if observed, attributed to the officers' efforts. Some of the activities of diplomats (for example, private conversations with their counterparts in a foreign government) are not observed and many of the outcomes (for example, changes in foreign perceptions of U.S. interests or in foreign attitudes toward U.S. initiatives) cannot easily be judged.

The managers of these agencies must cope with a difficult situation. They can try to recruit the best people (without having much knowledge about what the "best person" looks like), they can try to create an atmosphere that is conducive to good work (without being certain what "good work" is), and they can step in when complaints are heard or crises erupt (without knowing whether a complaint is justified or a crisis symptomatic or atypical).

Every dean of faculty at a private college is quite aware that these difficulties are not unique to government agencies. How do you improve your educational product when you can neither describe the product nor explain how it is produced? The headmasters of private schools face the same fundamental problem as do the principals of public schools, and the managers of private security services confront many of the same problems as the lieutenants in charge of patrol forces in police departments. But the management of private coping organizations is different in two important respects from that of comparable public agencies: First, private organizations must survive by attracting clients and contributors. A loss of either is a signal that something is wrong. The managers may not know just what *is* wrong, owing to poor information about outputs and outcomes, but the market signal usually will initiate a search for information and motivate a desire to use it. By trial and error if not by plan the organizations will change. Second, private organizations face far fewer constraints in using or disposing of capital and labor than do public organizations (see chapter 7).

Moreover, *something* that managers do in coping organizations seems to make a difference. We have already reviewed the findings of James Coleman and colleagues that private and parochial schools do a better educational job than public schools. Eric Hanushek's summary of the research on public schools concludes that some teachers do a much better job than others and good principals are those who are somehow able to find, keep, and motivate the good teachers; the problem is that there seem to be no objective, readily observed measures that systematically distinguish good teachers from bad or explain how good principals are able to identify and motivate the good ones.[23]

Where both outputs and outcomes are unobservable there is likely to be a high degree of conflict between managers and operators in public agencies, especially those that must cope with a clientele not of their own choosing. The operators will be driven by the situational imperatives they face—the teachers' need to keep order in the classroom or the officers' desire to create order on the street or restore order in the quarreling family. The managers will be driven by the constraints they face, especially the need to cope with complaints from politically influential constituencies. Complaints can be rejected when the manager can show that the complained of behavior did not occur or they can be partially deflected when the manager can argue that the outcomes achieved justified the action in question. But coping agencies are precisely those that do not know with confidence what behavior occurred and cannot show with persuasiveness what outcomes resulted. And so managers, depending on their personal style, cope with the complaints as best they can. In doing so they must strike a delicate balance: If they take the complaint seriously, the operator will feel that he or she has not been "backed up"; if they take the complaint lightly, the citizen will feel that the agency is "insensitive." Teachers do not like principals who fail to back them up in conflicts with pupils or parents. Police officers do not like captains who fail to back them up in conflicts with citizens and lawyers.[24]

For many years the dominant doctrine of police professionalism was based on the view that the police administrator had to get control of his department to prevent corruption or abuse of authority and to bring to bear on the crime problem the methods of rapid response, scientific investigation, and complete record keeping. This led police managers to treat their departments as if they were production agencies: Officers were asked to follow standardized procedures, keep careful records of what they did, stay close to the police radio always to be on call, and generate statistical evidence of their productivity. This in turn led the officers to emphasize those aspects of their job that were most easily standardized and recorded, that could be directed by radio transmissions, and that generated statistics. These included writing reports of crimes (mostly thefts and burglaries that occurred in the past) and making easy arrests (for example, handing out tickets for traffic violations and making arrests for such "on view" offenses as public drunkenness and disorderly conduct). It led them to de-emphasize managing family or barroom quarrels and handling rowdy street youths. In short, one part of the police job, order maintenance, was sacrificed to another part, law enforcement.[25] The difficulty was that for many citizens order maintenance was more important than law enforcement and for many officers the bureaucratic supervision was an impediment rather than an aid to solving crimes.

Because of increased citizen dissatisfaction with the disorderliness of the urban environment some police departments began moving to redress the balance by involving their officers more deeply in order-maintenance activities. Officers were instructed to walk beats rather than ride in cars, report broken street lights or abandoned cars as well as crime, and handle the homeless and the disorderly as well as the truly criminal. But many police managers resisted for quite understandable reasons. Order-maintenance work (such as coping with rowdy youngsters or handling quarrelsome families) produces few if any statistics, puts the officer in conflict-ridden situations, and increases the risk of complaints about officer misconduct from people who disagree with the officer as to what constitutes an acceptable level of order or how best to achieve it.[26] The order-maintenance role of the police is threatening to many police managers, and so many departments are split between managers (and many officers) who believe that the dominant mission ought to be law enforcement and those who believe it ought to be order maintenance (or community service or problem solving).

In coping organizations as in procedural, management will have a strong incentive to focus their efforts on the most easily measured (and thus most easily controlled) activities of their operators. They cannot evaluate or often even see outcomes, and so only the brave manager will be inclined to give much freedom of action to subordinates.

The subordinates, of course, are not without their own resources. Some will conform their behavior to whatever is being measured ("they want stats, we'll give 'em stats"); others will subvert the management strategy by ignoring the measured activities (thus jeopardizing their own chances for advancement) or by generating enough stats to keep management happy while they get on with their own definition of what constitutes good work.

Compliance and Equity

Anybody who has served in the military, the foreign service, the CIA, or many other far-flung government agencies knows that you can expect frequent rotation in duty assignments. Some of this occurs because of your desire to move on, some despite your desire to stay in one place. During the war in Southeast Asia military officers typically were assigned to Vietnam for one-year tours of duty. No sooner did a battalion commander learn his way around and begin to become effective than he was shipped back to the states or off to Europe. State Department diplomats and CIA station chiefs often are uprooted from one post just about the time they have begun to learn the language and local routines and sent to another post where they have to cope with a new language and set of customs. Why do U.S. government agencies distribute assignments in ways that seem to minimize the chance for key employees to become expert in their tasks?

Ask these agencies and you will be told that they wish to develop well-rounded personnel capable of doing any job in the organization. No doubt there is an advantage in having broadly experienced employees. But there is also an advantage in having highly expert employees, especially in a nation, such as this one, that is notorious for the failure of its educational system to give its students a deep grounding in foreign languages, geography, and history. Government personnel systems in agencies with far-flung responsibilities generally are biased toward frequent rotation at the expense of lengthy exposure. But it would be a mistake to attribute this policy entirely to the unthinking preferences of the agencies' managers. In fact, the employees prefer it to the alternative.

Whenever duty assignments vary greatly in attractiveness, employees naturally will prefer the more to the less attractive. Diplomats will prefer Paris to Kabul, naval officers will prefer the Mediterranean to the Arctic Circle, army officers would rather be in Hawaii than in Seoul. If merit and organizational need were the sole criteria for allocating duty assignments then good battalion commanders would have been kept in Vietnam for three or four years and poor ones sent back to the states, and skilled diplomats would be kept in Moscow or Beijing rather than rotated out to Lisbon or Rome. But employees demand that they be given a fair chance at the choice postings, and fair in government agencies usually means equal. Since almost everybody from top to bottom wants nice assignments, almost everybody has a shared stake in maintaining a system that maximizes the frequency with which they are redistributed.

The same principle operates with respect to those assignments that are career enhancing. A career-enhancing post may be a certain geographical assignment, training school or program, or task. In the army, Ranger school, the Staff and Command College, or the Training and Doctrine Command at various times have been regarded as career-enhancing postings; so also has service on the staff of the National Security Council. In the navy, getting command experience on the right kind of ship (a destroyer, submarine, or aircraft carrier) is important; getting stuck on oilers or minesweepers is to be avoided. Obtaining a career-enhancing assignment is often called getting your "ticket punched."

This is especially important when the number of career-enhancing assignments is small relative to the demand. Suppose that it is very important in the army to have commanded a maneuver battalion. That is a job ordinarily given to a lieutenant colonel. But there are far more lieutenant colonels than there are battalions for them to command. If the army kept the best commanders in battalions for long tours of duty the units would probably perform better, but the promotion opportunities of all the other lieutenant colonels would be reduced. In striking a balance the army leans in the direction of frequent rotation, as evidenced by the fact that the typical battalion commander only serves for eighteen months and sometimes (as in Korea) only twelve months. Even so, only a minority of all eligible lieutenant colonels are selected for command. If the tours of duty were doubled in length (as one army chief of staff, Eugene Meyer, tried to do) the selection ratio would be cut in half. As a result, the plan to have thirty-month tours did not survive.

Managing any organization means not only finding incentives of high value and distributing them so as to reward the proper behavior but also providing access to them in ways that comport with the members' sense of equity. In government agencies, especially those that are procedural or coping organizations, there are powerful pressures to convert equity into equality; that is, to make rewards equally available to all rather than equally available to the most talented.

Styles of Management

So far I have been discussing managers as if they were all alike. Obviously that is not the case. Managers have personalities, and personality makes a difference. Unfortunately, however, the study of public management so far has produced only labels for types of managers, rather than data on how many of each kind there are, why some are more common than others, what factors lead a person to adopt one style and not another, and what consequences different styles have for organizational effectiveness.

Anthony Downs, an economist, has described five kinds of bureaucrats: climbers, conservers, zealots, advocates, and statesmen.[27] Hugh Heclo has written about program bureaucrats, staff bureaucrats, reformers, and institutionalists.[28] I have tried to distinguish among careerists, politicians, and professionals.[29] There are no doubt other classifications. The meaning of each label can be inferred from the words without much difficulty. But other than to generate the lists, all of which have a certain intuitive plausibility, not much has been accomplished.

Personal style does make a difference, as anyone who has ever worked for anybody else will gladly testify. That we cannot say much systematically about these differences is unfortunate, and probably reflects the hostility to the study of individual differences that has afflicted so much of social science, especially those parts that have taken up the study of organizations. However, style does not spring entirely from personality. There is a temptation among all of us to describe as personal traits what are in fact organizational roles. If we encounter a Postal Service manager preoccupied with increasing efficiency by getting an optical scanner to work better we may think we are watching the "engineering mentality" at work. If we watch a company commander endlessly drilling his troops on the parade ground we may mutter about "tin soldiers." If we observe a supervisor in the Antitrust Division approve the cases developed by a staff attorney we may think of her as a "rubber stamp." If we find a police captain worrying over whether his precinct has made enough arrests last month we will refer knowingly to a "bean counter." But the manager, the commander, supervisor, and captain are not necessarily by nature engineers, tin soldiers, rubber stamps, or bean counters; they are persons playing roles in organizations whose core tasks profoundly shape what it is that managers can and will do. People matter, but organization matters also, and tasks matter most of all.

The principal challenge facing public managers is to understand the importance of carefully defining the core tasks of the organization and to find both pecuniary and nonpecuniary incentives that will induce operators to perform those tasks as defined. Shirking is minimized by making certain that the proper performance of core tasks both enhances the careers of operators and confers upon them the esteem of their co-workers. The latter requires building a supportive culture around those core tasks. In William Ouchi's terminology the problem of "performance ambiguity" is managed by making the operating units of the organization into a "clan": a group having "organic solidarity" that is sustained by intensive socialization, both formal and informal.[30] This is not easily done, which is why many public agencies have no sense of mission. But it can be done, even in agencies that lack any way of closely monitoring the behavior of key operators.

Summary: Achieving Compliance

Managers in public agencies have only a few incentives with which to induce operators to comply with agency rules, and the use of these incentives is highly constrained. In each of the four kinds of agencies described here a somewhat different mix of incentives will be employed. In production organizations managers are able to observe both the work and its results and so will be in a position to evaluate workers on the basis of their contribution to efficiency. They can ask whether a given result is being achieved with the minimum use of resources (or a given level of resources is producing the greatest valued outcome). Whether in fact they produce an efficient operation will depend of course on whether the agency is given the freedom and resources to do so. A production agency that could work more efficiently if it had good computers might be denied by a parsimonious legislature the funds with which to buy them. Or political superiors may not wish to achieve efficiency; they may desire instead to have the agency give favored treatment to politically privileged clients. Members of Congress may say they want an efficient Internal Revenue Service but in fact they want one that is efficient only up to a point—the point at which voters begin complaining that they are being harassed.

In procedural organizations the general bureaucratic tendency to manage on the basis of process rather than outcome is much magnified because processes can be observed and outcomes cannot. Since the work of the operators can be watched, it is watched all the time. Managers use many forms of continuous surveillance to insure conformity to correct procedures, ranging from direct observation to periodic statistical reports. The life of a soldier or sailor in peacetime is one of incessant scrutiny and the repetition of seemingly pointless tasks. The great risks in procedural organizations are that morale will suffer (operators may resent the surveillance, believing they know—even if they cannot show—how to do the job right) and that the surveillance will bias the work of the agency (by inducing operators to conform to rules that detract from the attainment of goals).

In craft organizations managers can evaluate and reward operators on the basis of the result they achieve even if the former do not know how the latter are achieving it. But they have to worry that the freedom of action enjoyed by unobserved workers will permit a few of them to act improperly or even illegally. Wage and Hour inspectors may take bribes, police detectives may extort confessions, field engineers may wink at construction irregularities. Results can be observed, but often not until it is too late to correct any errors. The most successful agencies of this type are those that develop among their workers a sense of mission, a commitment to craftsmanship, or a belief in professional norms that will keep unobserved workers from abusing their discretion.

In coping organizations effective management is almost impossible. Of course some work can be observed some of the time and some examples of results achieved do occasionally come into view (though no one can be certain how representative of all outcomes these examples are). A police sergeant periodically sees a patrol officer working the street; a police captain from time to time will be told of a barroom fight well handled or a suspected offender wrongly shot. Managers of police patrol officers, like managers of operators in any coping organization, try to achieve compliance by attending to alarms—periodic signals that something has gone wrong. Punishing those workers who set off the alarms by their apparently wrongful action sends a message to all workers. (Commending those employees whose good conduct happens to come to light also sends a message, but since citizens have more incentive to complain of the abuses they have suffered than to praise the virtues they have seen there tend to be more punishments than commendations issued by coping managers.) Since the alarms are set off randomly, the behavior that triggered them may not be an accurate sample of how operators ordinarily work and so the punishments may not be perceived as fair. Consequently, operators in coping organizations often feel they are treated unfairly by managers who don't "back them up" or who are "always getting on their case."

PART IV

EXECUTIVES

CHAPTER 10

Turf

DURING THE SEVEN YEARS he was secretary of defense, Robert S. McNamara presided over a dramatic growth in military spending, from $195 billion in 1961 to nearly $225 billion (in constant dollars) in 1968. In just his first year in office McNamara added over $6 billion to the defense budget. Yet by the time he had resigned he had become to the military brass one of the most unpopular secretaries since the creation of that office in 1947.[1]

During the four years he was secretary of defense, Melvin R. Laird helped cut the defense budget by 28 percent, from $243 billion in 1969 to $175 billion (in constant dollars) in 1973. The army lost divisions, the navy lost ships, and total military personnel declined by about one-third. But despite these cuts, Laird was a very popular secretary among the military services.[2]

Morton H. Halperin, who first noted this puzzle, explained it by observing that bureaucracies "are often prepared to accept less money with greater control than more money with less control."[3] This is because of the high priority they attach to autonomy, or turf. McNamara had little respect for the autonomy of the separate military services; Laird had a great deal. When the former took office he began immediately to centralize defense decision making in the office of the secretary of defense where crucial decisions about weapons and operational doctrine were made by "whiz kids"—young defense intellectuals skilled in the methods of quantitative analysis, whom McNamara had brought with him. When Laird took office he cut the defense budget (the war in Vietnam was winding down), but he left the services free to make the cuts as they wished. Laird had no whiz kids working for him and was careful to consult with the generals and admirals about important decisions that affected their respective services.[4] Each armed force under Laird retained control over the definition of its critical tasks.

This concern for autonomy is not limited to the military. For years members of Congress tried to persuade J. Edgar Hoover that the FBI should take over federal responsibility for investigating drug trafficking. If he had agreed it would have meant a big increase in the FBI's budget. Hoover would have none of it. He insisted that the job be left with the Federal Bureau of Narcotics, then in the Treasury Department. Even after Hoover's death most top key FBI officials continued to resist congressional and Justice Department pressure to take on the narcotics problem.[5] It was not until the Reagan administration that the FBI was finally induced to exercise supervisory authority over the Drug Enforcement Administration (DEA), and even then many FBI executives—including the one put in charge of the DEA—opposed a full merger of the two agencies.

For many years Hoover also resisted enlarging the FBI's activities to include the systematic investigation of organized crime. He justified this with the simple expedient of denying that there was any such thing as organized crime, whether it be called the Mafia, the syndicate, the outfit, or the mob. This denial sounded hollow after a sergeant of the New York State Police stumbled upon a meeting of dozens of gangland figures at the home of Joseph Barbara in Apalachin, New York, in 1957. But Hoover continued to resist until evidence gathered by his own agents clearly identified the members of the national crime commission and after Mafia hoodlum Joseph Valachi became an FBI informant.[6]

The State Department for years resisted the transfer to it of the United States Information Agency and the Agency for International Development.[7] In the late 1940s the United States Army sought to divest itself of its air units.[8] The Department of Agriculture proposed in 1973 and again in 1974 to transfer the Food and Nutrition Service (FNS), the agency responsible for the food stamp program, out of Agriculture and into the Department of Health, Education, and Welfare (HEW).[9] When the White House in 1968 proposed transferring the Bureau of Drug Abuse Control out of HEW and taking the Volunteers in Service to America (VISTA) program away from the Office of Economic Opportunity (OEO), HEW and OEO did not object.[10] Marc Tipermas, who studied five major federal reorganization plans in the late 1960s and early 1970s (including the three just mentioned), was able to characterize twenty-five agency reactions to the prospect of gaining or losing an important subunit. In fifteen cases, the agency sought to grow or hold on to what it had; in ten cases it declined a chance to grow or actually approved of losing a subunit.[11]

These examples and Tipermas's data offer very little support for the widespread notion that government agencies are imperialistic, always seeking to grow by taking on new functions and gobbling up their bureaucratic rivals. In particular, the facts are inconsistent with the theory advanced by Gordon Tullock and William Niskanen (among others) that bureaucrats desire to maximize their agency's size.[12] There are, to be sure, plenty of examples of imperialistic agencies headed by growth-oriented executives, but there are also many examples of reluctant agencies headed by cautious, skeptical executives. We hear more about the former than of the latter because expansionist agencies make noise (often the noise of smaller agencies being gobbled up), whereas the latter go about their daily business quietly.

Executives and Autonomy

That daily business involves performing agency tasks in a way that minimizes the effort needed to maintain the organization. Organizational maintenance is the special responsibility of the executive.[13] Maintenance means assuring the necessary flow of resources to the organization. In a business firm that support chiefly takes the form of capital and labor. If business competition were not restrained by laws prohibiting monopolistic practices, maintaining a firm also might involve eliminating competition for resources and markets. In a government agency, maintenance requires obtaining not only capital (appropriations) and labor (personnel) but in addition political support. Moreover, government agencies are not restrained by the antitrust laws; therefore, maintenance can and often does involve eliminating or otherwise coping with the threats posed by rivals.

Political support is at its highest when the agency's goals are popular, its tasks simple, its rivals nonexistent, and the constraints minimal. Ideally, a government bureau would like to be the only organization in town curing cancer and would like to have no limitations on how it goes about achieving that cure. The typical bureau is in a much less happy state of affairs. It must do something that is unpopular (e.g., collecting taxes) or difficult (e.g., managing foreign affairs) and that a half dozen other agencies are doing (e.g., gathering intelligence or catching drug dealers), and it must do these things under the watchful and critical eyes of countless subcommittees, interest groups, and journalists. It faces inadequate budgets, complex tasks, several rivals, and many constraints.*

*In the language of organization theory, government agencies suffer from "high resource dependence." Business firms may be dependent on external sources for resources, but they can reduce this dependence by mergers and vertical integration and by financing investments out of retained earnings. Moreover, though the external stakeholders who provide resources to a firm retain certain property rights in the resource, unlike legislatures they ordinarily do not obtain any managerial authority. Cf. Jeffrey Pfeffer and Gerald R. Salanick, *The External Control of Organizations: A Resource Dependence Perspective* (New York: Harper & Row, 1978), 261, 272. For a pioneering analysis of the external or constituency-related causes of turf-enhancement, see Matthew Holden, Jr., " 'Imperialism' in Bureaucracy," *American Political Science Review* 60 (1966): 943–51.

The view that all bureaus want larger budgets ignores the fact that there is often a tradeoff between bigger budgets on the one hand and the complexity of tasks, the number of rivals, and the multiplicity of constraints on the other. All else being equal, big budgets are better than small. But all else is not equal. Part of the "all else" I call autonomy.

Philip Selznick defined autonomy as a "condition of independence sufficient to permit a group to work out and maintain a distinctive identity."[14] There are two parts to Selznick's definition, an external and an internal one. The external aspect of autonomy, independence, is equivalent to "jurisdiction" or "domain." Agencies ranking high in autonomy have a monopoly jurisdiction (that is, they have few or no bureaucratic rivals and a minimum of political constraints imposed on them by superiors). The internal aspect of autonomy is identity or mission—a widely shared and approved understanding of the central tasks of the agency.

Budget increases that threaten to reduce agency autonomy are often but not always resisted. The armed services did not like Robert McNamara because he reduced their autonomy by reducing their authority to make key decisions about weapons and doctrine. The fact that McNamara gave them more money did not make up for the loss of independence with respect to their mission.

The Agriculture Department did not like having to run the food stamp program in part because issuing food stamps involved a very different set of tasks from those making up the traditional mission of Agriculture (namely, helping farmers) and in part because being responsible for food stamps meant being accountable to those congressional committees and interest groups concerned with welfare programs (as opposed to agricultural programs). Perhaps if the food stamps program had been small, Agriculture would not have worried; but in the early 1970s the secretary of agriculture realized to his horror that the program would soon account for two-thirds of all the expenditures of the entire department. What this meant in practical terms was expressed by one department official this way: "We had to follow up on complaints of fraud, civil rights violations, etcetera, and this was taking up all our time and people."[15] One suspects it was the political as much as the financial costs of these complaints that worried him.

The FBI did not want to get involved in either narcotics or organized crime because the organization costs seemed so high. An agency whose freedom from political constraints depended in large measure on its reputation for integrity and efficiency would be exposed to the potential for corruption inherent in drug and Mafia investigations and the prospect that the bureau would be blamed for not "solving" narcotics trafficking in the way it traditionally had solved kidnappings and bank robberies. Moreover, the mission of the FBI—carefully controlled investigations based on interviewing citizens—might be compromised by having to take on new tasks, such as making undercover drug buys and posing as Mafia members, in ways that would make the internal management of the organization more difficult or even threaten the existence of its shared sense of mission. Suppose, for example, that the FBI had accepted full responsibility for investigating drug dealers. There was a good chance that some of its agents might be bribed (leading to public scandals); there was an excellent chance that the drug problem would get worse no matter what the FBI did (leading to public questioning); and there was some chance that FBI agents who were drug specialists would start competing inside the bureau for funds and promotions against agents who were not drug specialists (leading to internal friction). All in all it looked like a bad investment.

To a government executive an increase in the autonomy of his or her agency lowers the cost of organizational maintenance by minimizing the number of external stakeholders and bureaucratic rivals and maximizing the opportunity for agency operators to develop a cohesive sense of mission. Foregoing certain new tasks and their associated budget increases seems like a reasonable price to pay for these benefits.*

This is not to say that all executives always will act in autonomy-enhancing ways. Secretary of State George Shultz fought hard and successfully to keep as part of the State Department the bureaus concerned with building American embassies and providing security for those facilities. He did so despite the embarrassing revelations throughout the 1980s of major weaknesses in embassy security and serious deficiencies in the department's building program (see chapter 6). These events made it more costly for State to stay in the business of overseeing embassy construction. The firestorm of congressional criticism aimed at State's management of embassy construction and security would have led many secretaries of state to conclude that the department would be better off giving these lightning rods to some other government agency. Moreover, morale in both the foreign missions building office and the bureau of security was at a low ebb, as one might expect given the fact that the culture of the department rewarded diplomats, not building supervisors or security of-

*An earlier version of my discussion of autonomy was criticized by Herbert Kaufman on the grounds that autonomy, defined as "freedom to do all that they [the bureau chiefs] wished," can never exist in politics. And of course he is right. But by autonomy I mean not freedom of action but relatively undisputed jurisdiction. Bureau chiefs know that they cannot be free of legislatures and elected executives, but they try, whenever the circumstances permit it, to maintain as much control as they can over that range of tasks that define the bureaus' jurisdictions. Three of the six bureaus Kaufman studied—the Internal Revenue Service, the Social Security Administration, the Food and Drug Administration—never had to face a challenge to their jurisdiction; and two others—the Customs Service and the Forest Service—had gone through bruising struggles over jurisdiction (the former with the Bureau of Narcotics and Dangerous Drugs, the latter with the Park Service) before Kaufman studied them in 1978. See Herbert Kaufman, *The Administrative Behavior of Federal Bureau Chiefs* (Washington, D.C.: The Brookings Institution, 1981), 161–64.

ficers. For both external and internal reasons, therefore, it might have seemed prudent to let other government agencies that specialized in construction or security take on these controversial activities. But no; Secretary Shultz, described by a fellow cabinet member as "the most turf-conscious man I've ever met," insisted on keeping these functions. Shultz's position was viewed by many Washington insiders as just another example of agency executives tenaciously defending their turf at whatever the cost. But his behavior was not typical, as is shown by the willingness of the secretary of agriculture to let go of food stamps, of OEO to let go of VISTA, of HEW to let go of BDAC, and of the army to let go of the air force. Giving up a bureau in order to enhance an agency's autonomy is the extreme (and thus especially revealing) case. More common is the effort to define one's existing mission in such a way as to deny to bureaucratic rivals the opportunity to intrude on core tasks.

When Gifford Pinchot got control over the national forests transferred out of the Interior Department and into the Agriculture Department, where Pinchot's Forest Service was located, it was a masterstroke aimed at protecting the autonomy of his service. That it occurred at all, given the traditional (and plausible) claims Interior had to the forests, was testimony to the extraordinary political skill of Pinchot. He mobilized lumber and cattle interests in support of his raid on Interior, arguing that if the forests were in the Agriculture Department it would be easier to turn them to economic uses. (Later the lumber and cattle people learned to their disappointment that Pinchot intended to impose tight controls on their access to the forests.) When Pinchot's friend and patron, Theodore Roosevelt, suddenly became president after the assassination of William McKinley, luck was added to skill, and the Transfer Act of 1905 became law.[16]

David Lilienthal's careful propagation of the myth of "grass-roots democracy" as a central feature of the mission of the newly created TVA was, according to Erwin Hargrove, a key element in his strategy to keep the TVA from being absorbed by the Interior Department.[17] The slogan "grass-roots democracy" was meant to suggest that the TVA, unlike Interior, would work directly with and for the people in the Tennessee Valley region. The slogan was based on the notion that the TVA would allow farmers to participate in the selection of farms on which new soil-conservation and crop-development projects would be tested. If the TVA had publicly defined its mission as consisting chiefly of building dams and generating power (which in fact was what the TVA mostly did), then there would have been no obvious reason why the Interior Department (which had a long history of building water projects) could not have taken it over.

Next to J. Edgar Hoover and David Lilienthal, no more skillful practitioner of turf-building ever walked the halls of power than Admiral Hyman G. Rickover. The brilliant but cantankerous naval officer, by virtue of close relations with Congress and private contractors, managed to acquire authority over the development of *all* nuclear power plants for military purposes and in time over the entire nuclear-powered submarine force.[18] In the ordinary course of bureaucratic politics, anything so promising as nuclear propulsion would have been taken up by all manner of civilian and military agencies. The result would have been that one agency did the research, another ordered reactors, a third installed them in ships of various kinds, and a fourth (and fifth and sixth) would recruit, train, and command the personnel who sailed the ships. Instead one man was able to create a single entity that came to be called "Rickover's Navy," over the objections of many naval superiors. He did it by carefully attending, from the very first, to acquiring autonomy before he acquired resources.

"Unifying" the Military Services

Struggles over autonomy are especially visible when the organizations involved have similar tasks, as do the armed forces. We take the quarreling among these services as a fact of life. What we sometimes forget is that serious plans were laid after the end of the Second World War to unify the armed forces. The motives of both proponents and opponents were chiefly the preservation or enhancement of autonomy.

The key proponent was the army. The War Department offered a plan whereby the army, navy, and air force would be placed under the control of a single military chief of staff who would report to a secretary of defense. With the war at an end, the army feared that it would suffer a disproportionate cut in its resources as soldiers returned to civilian life. By contrast, the navy and the air force operated ships and airplanes; the need to keep at least some of these weapons operating would enable these services to resist cuts as deep as those the army would experience. Moreover, the nuclear bombs possessed by the air force seemed to offer a cheap form of defense: Who needs lots of soldiers when a few bombers (and later, ballistic missiles) easily can deter any potential aggressor? The army's fear was well-grounded; whenever the defense budget is to be cut, it usually turns out to be easier to cut people than to cut equipment. A single, unified commander, presumably drawn from the army—would "balance" the needs of the three services (i.e., protect the army's role).[19]

The army plan was supported by the air force because this seemed to offer the best guarantee of the latter's autonomy. Military aviation had begun and grown up as part of the army under the title of the Army Air Force (AAF). The AAF was eager to become a separate service, an ambition that enjoyed a great deal of public support. The army was willing to let this happen, in part because the nominally subordinate air force had become so big and popular that the army feared being dominated by the AAF if both services remained united and in part because infantry generals did not like the idea of sharing power with AAF generals.[20] In short, both the army's and the air force's interest in autonomy would be furthered by separation. But the army attached a condition to air force independence: All three services would be joined at the top under the authority of a single military commander. President Harry Truman strongly endorsed the War Department plan.

The opponent of unification was the navy and again the reason was autonomy. The navy in a sense is a miniature defense department not only with its own ships but also its own infantry (the Marine Corps) and its own air force (naval aviation). It is therefore especially vulnerable to any reorganization plan. The proponents of efficiency and unification might well decide that the "rational" organizational form would be one in which the navy's ground-forces—the Marines—were transferred to the army and its air units transferred to the air force. Led by Secretary of the Navy James Forrestal, the navy fought the army plan, offering in its place a proposal that would simply establish two coordinating committees—the Joint Chiefs of Staff, composed of the top military commanders, and a council (which became the National Security Council) that would bring together the key civilian officials concerned with defense.

In time a compromise was reached. A single Defense Department was created (as the army wanted) but the secretary of defense would have few powers (as the navy wanted). There would be no single military commander (as the army wanted) but instead a Joint Chiefs of Staff (as the navy desired); as a concession to the other services the navy agreed to a separate air force. James Forrestal, who had fought unification, was appointed the first secretary of defense and soon came to realize how many jurisdictional problems remained to be solved and how little authority he had to solve them. For example, the navy and the air force both wanted to play a role in strategic deterrence, and so the former sought to build large aircraft carriers and the latter to build big bombers, all at a time of shrinking defense budgets. The newly independent air force was eager to control all military aviation while the army insisted on retaining some aviation units of its own. In 1948 Secretary Forrestal convened a conference at Key West, Florida, at which the services were supposed to settle their differences. It produced only a paper agreement, though one with unanticipated consequences.

One provision of the Key West agreement was that the air force would procure and control all aircraft designed to support army infantry operations. To insure that the army complied with this clause it was specifically precluded from buying any fixed-wing aircraft that weighed more than five thousand pounds.[21] The Korean War revealed the weakness of the agreement. The air force culture was based on flying high-performance fighters and long-range bombers, especially the latter. As a result the air force invested rather little in the kind of aircraft suitable for close support of infantry operations—slow-moving, well-armored planes carrying large payloads—and was opposed to letting these aircraft be controlled by army commanders. When the army sought congressional approval to buy such aircraft for itself, the Key West Accords were invoked and the plan blocked. But a few years later a clever army general noticed that the Key West Accords referred only to *fixed-wing* aircraft. They said nothing about helicopters. And so the army began to acquire armed helicopters to perform the close-support function that the air force was reluctant to perform. The Vietnam War accelerated this build-up, and soon the army had a massive helicopter fleet. But military opinion remains divided over whether the helicopter performs the close-support task as well as fixed-wing aircraft might. The argument has not been settled on the merits, however, but on the basis of each service's deeply felt desire for autonomy. Richard Stubbing, a former analyst of the military budget, summarizes the problem this way:

> The Air Force continues to give minimal attention to close air support and buys just enough attack aircraft to protect its claim to the close-air-support mission. Meanwhile, the Army, unsure that it can rely on Air Force support when it is needed, purchases a vast fleet of attack helicopters which, while more expensive than attack planes and potentially far more vulnerable, can be placed under direct Army command.[22]

These and other examples of military turf wars are sometimes mistakenly described as cases of organizational imperialism—the drive to have more for the sake of more, motivated by the belief that bigger is better. That is a superficial understanding of the matter. What the armed forces are doing is attempting to match mission and jurisdiction. Having a strong sense of mission is important to any organization, but especially to a military organization in which a willingness to confront danger and perform selflessly often is the product of a shared commitment to the ethos or culture of the service. A strong sense of mission implies an organizational jurisdiction coterminous with the tasks that must be performed and the resources with which to perform them. For example, army officers do not want to control tactical (or close-support) air units simply because they like the idea of owning aircraft but because experience has taught them that planes that strafe and bomb targets directly in front of advancing infantry units must be coordinated with exquisite precision if the strafing is to occur exactly when needed and the bombs are to fall on enemy troops. By the same token, air force officers do not object to flying slow ground-support aircraft because they disdain strafing enemy troops but because experience has taught them that slow-moving aircraft are vulnerable to attack by fast, maneuverable enemy fighters. Thus, they want tactical aircraft that can defend themselves by flying as fast and turning as quickly as the enemy they may encounter. The problem is that fast, maneuverable planes are not very good at ground-support missions.

Because the mission interests of the two services are based on plausible, serious concerns, finding an organizational form that will reconcile mission and jurisdiction is not easy. Though the original law creating the Defense Department has been amended several times for the purpose of reducing service rivalry, finding the right match between mission and jurisdiction is still as elusive as ever.

Eliot Cohen has described this matching problem in another context, that of antisubmarine warfare during World War II. At issue was which service would control land-based aircraft used to search the sea-lanes for enemy submarines. The navy wanted to control these planes in order to help escort the convoys of naval vessels and merchant ships that were attempting to evade the German submarines. Since the navy was responsible for the convoys' safety and since navy personnel manned many of the ships, naturally they wanted the airplanes to stay close to the convoys. The army air force, on the other hand, had no responsibility for convoys. Its interest was in finding and attacking German submarines. Air force officers thus wanted to use the planes not to stick tight to convoys but to range widely over the seas, hunting for submarines wherever they might be found.[23] Finally, the army air force relinquished control over land-based antisubmarine planes to the navy. It was a wise decision. The mission-jurisdiction match was of vital importance to the navy but of lesser importance to the air force. Moreover, surrendering control over the planes meant that air force pilots no longer would have to take orders from naval commanders when escorting convoys.[24]

Achieving Autonomy

No agency head can ever achieve complete autonomy for his or her organization; politics requires accountability, and democratic politics implies a particularly complex and all-encompassing pattern of accountability. The best a government executive can do is to minimize the number of rivals and constraints.

The best time to achieve a mission-jurisdiction match is when the organization is created. An organization is like a fish in a coral reef: To survive, it needs to find a supportive ecological niche. Sometimes that niche is specified by law, as when the Social Security Administration or the Internal Revenue Service were created. But often the law is sufficiently vague as to give the founding executive a chance to seek out a niche. In doing this certain rules of thumb are worth following.

First, seek out tasks that are not being performed by others. Prison administrators have no difficulty following this rule since hardly anybody else wants to take on this thankless task. But the first directors of the Central Intelligence Agency faced plenty of rivals—the military services as well as the State Department had active intelligence services. This fact, along with the prior experiences of the founding members of the CIA, led it to define a new role for itself in the area of covert operations. Though intelligence was also done, operations became the culture-defining task of the CIA. This continued until the advent of the overhead reconnaissance satellites, with their power to photograph in extraordinary detail from altitudes of four or five hundred miles the military and industrial facilities of other nations. The obvious question then arose, who would control these devices?

The air force had the rockets with which to put the satellites into orbit and a deep interest in learning what they might reveal about Soviet rockets. The CIA also had an interest in the program; it promised to reveal more things than even an army of spies could possibly discover. A bitter struggle erupted between the CIA and the air force over control of the program. In time it was resolved by creating the National Reconnaissance Office (NRO) under the secretary of the air force and giving it the task of launching and controlling the satellites. A CIA officer was made second in command. To oversee the NRO and to select targets for coverage, a complex array of coordinating committees was created. The interagency quarrels continued, of course, but in time (according to some observers of this highly secret world) the quarreling lessened as the NRO began to acquire its own sense of mission and professionalism.[25]

The FBI's opposition to any involvement in narcotics investigation was based not only on a fear of corruption but also on a desire to avoid taking on a task already performed by other organizations that would then become its rivals. Even if the old Federal Bureau of Narcotics had been completely taken over by Hoover, the Customs Service, the Border Patrol, and the Immigration and Naturalization Service all played roles in drug-law enforcement. When the FBI finally did enter the drug enforcement area, it discovered that managing these organizational rivalries was a major headache.

Second, fight organizations that seek to perform your tasks. The air force unsuccessfully sought to prevent the navy from building big aircraft carriers, and the Navy unsuccessfully sought to block the building of big bombers. At stake was the interest each service had in maintaining its ability to deliver nuclear weapons against distant adversaries. The FBI successfully fought to keep the Office of Strategic Services (OSS) from playing the dominant role in counterespionage. J. Edgar Hoover distrusted the OSS and its ambitious head, William "Wild Bill" Donovan. He feared (correctly as it turned out) that the OSS would attempt to operate inside the United States as well as overseas. Domestic counterespionage was the FBI's job and it went to great lengths to defend it. For example, when some OSS officers were attempting to burglarize a foreign embassy in Washington, Hoover learned of it and sent some FBI agents to prevent it. Donovan complained to Roosevelt, but Hoover won and these tasks were confirmed as solely within the FBI's jurisdiction.[26] When Roosevelt gave Hoover the job of gathering intelligence in Latin America, Hoover was especially alert to make certain the OSS did not try to horn in.[27]

Third, avoid taking on tasks that differ significantly from those that are at the heart of the organization's mission. The Army Corps of Engineers cherishes its reputation as an organization that can reliably, on schedule and within budget, design and construct ports, bridges, dams, and complex water-resource development systems. Beginning in the 1970s new kinds of issues gained strong congressional backing—programs to dispose of toxic wastes, improve urban water distribution systems, and enhance the management of coastal areas. The casual observer might suppose that these new programs would provide a happy hunting ground for corps engineers eager to expand their agency's work and increase its budget. In fact, many senior engineers opposed corps participation in these new programs. They did so precisely because they were *programs*, not projects. A project involves designing and building a structure for a client. The corps knew how to manage a project. By contrast, a program, such as cleaning up toxic wastes or improving a city's water system, involves negotiating agreements with state and local agencies, providing technical assistance to a variety of political jurisdictions, managing grant-in-aid programs, and inducing firms to use fewer toxic substances or cities to conserve water. As Arthur Maass and Myron Fiering pointed out, the corps has refused to participate in many of these programs even though this has meant a decline in its construction budget.[28] Mission was more important than budgets.

Fourth, be wary of joint or cooperative ventures. The FBI for many years was reluctant to assign its agents to interagency task forces created to mount a coordinated attack on organized crime.[29] Hoover feared that the FBI's reputation might suffer if it had to share responsibility for mistakes caused by the bad judgment of other task force members not controlled by the FBI.* For the same reason, the Army Corps of Engineers has had a "no detailing" rule that forbids assigning corps members to other government organizations, even other parts of the military. As one

*One might ask why other law enforcement agencies were willing to participate in these strike forces. I am not certain, but I believe it was because they had a weaker sense of mission and of the political benefits of maintaining that mission.

corps executive told Mohammad Al-Saud, "We don't think our reputation is enhanced by doing pieces of jobs where it [the work] could get lost and become a poor job because of something somebody else does."[30] If the corps takes on a project it wants exclusive authority for it. For example, someone proposed that the Environmental Protection Agency (EPA) should contract with the corps to oversee the removal of certain toxic wastes. The corps refused to take the job because, as one corps official put it, "if we don't design it, if we are not the contracting officer, if we do not have the authority . . . we're just working for the EPA. . . . Then, something goes wrong, and we have headlines in the newspaper, 'Corps of Engineers Fails.' "[31]

Fifth, avoid tasks that will produce divided or hostile constituencies. Like most states, California and Wyoming have state fish and game departments with jurisdiction over many forms of wildlife within their boundaries. These departments have the task of protecting species of wildlife from illegal hunting or fishing; in addition, they restock certain lands and waterways with game. The core constituencies of these departments are the hunters and fishermen in the state; it was they who first took the lead in creating the departments in the nineteenth century and it is they who now support the fish and game departments before the legislatures. That support has been so effective that the departments have managed to acquire a good deal of autonomy even from legislative control by the simple expedient of setting the fees for fishing and hunting licenses at a level adequate to make the departments self-supporting. Thomas H. Hammond studied how these departments have reacted to opportunities to take on new tasks.[32] In general they have tried to shun any task that would produce a divided constituency. As a result, in both states the fish and game departments have sought to avoid getting involved in controlling predators such as wolves and coyotes, since the issue pits farmers who want predators killed to protect their livestock against ecologists who want them protected because they think these species are endangered. So successfully did the Wyoming department duck the issue that the legislature assigned the task to the Department of Agriculture.*

Sixth, avoid learned vulnerabilities. Every organization, like every person, learns from experience what behavior will create big problems; but compared to people, organizations have longer memories and are more risk averse. Once burned, forever shy. Learned vulnerabilities are for the FBI, corruption; for prisons, escapes and riots; for the Department of Defense, a $435 hammer; and for the Food and Drug Administration, approving a food additive that might be carcinogenic. When something

*Hammond also notes that to fully explain what tasks the departments took on or avoided one also must understand the professional norms of the operators in the departments, a conclusion consistent with the argument made in chapter 4.

goes badly wrong at a high political cost the incident enters the agency's memory as a legendary horror story. A great deal of the time and energy of agency officials is devoted to creating mechanisms designed to insure that the horror never recurs. Sometimes the mechanisms are extreme. For example, one of the many (possibly true) stories about J. Edgar Hoover is his insistence that FBI agents not drink coffee in public while on duty. The reason: to avoid any chance that a citizen spotting agents drinking coffee would complain to a member of Congress about "government bureaucrats loafing at the taxpayers' expense."

The advantage of avoiding a learned vulnerability is that it minimizes the power of external stakeholders over the agency. As the next chapter will make clear, government executives often cannot take credit for accomplishing agency goals because the goals are so vague or progress toward them so difficult to achieve (much less measure) that there is no basis for persuasively claiming credit. But these executives always are vulnerable to criticisms. If that vulnerability can be reduced, if members of Congress, interest groups, and journalists cannot levy a plausible criticism against an agency, then these outsiders are deprived of an important means of asserting power over the agency. As a consequence its autonomy is increased. Avoiding learned vulnerabilities can become for a government executive the equivalent of earning a profit for a business executive. Each constitutes the bottom line.

Consequences of the Concern for Autonomy

The chief result of the concern for turf and autonomy is that it is extraordinarily difficult to coordinate the work of different agencies. (So important is this problem that a chapter will be devoted to it.) Business firms coordinate their actions by responding to market signals (prices); to the extent permitted by the antitrust laws they can also coordinate their actions by entering into explicit agreements (contracts) in which mutual material gain is the criterion for cooperation. They need not fear that such a contract will enable one firm to acquire the power to manage the internal affairs of the other. Government agencies, by contrast, view any interagency agreement as a threat to their autonomy.

Hence many agencies that must cooperate (or at least appear to cooperate) enter into agreements designed to protect each other from any loss of autonomy. The ground rules that govern the actions of the Joint Chiefs of Staff are a well-known example of this tendency to minimize threats to autonomy by signing mutual nonaggression pacts. The Joint Chiefs seem to operate by an informal rule of unanimity: No action will be taken regarding the definition of roles and missions if any service representative dissents, hence no action will be taken that threatens the role or mission (the turf) of any service.[33] Between 1955 and 1959, the Joint Chiefs recorded nearly three thousand decisions; in only twenty-three cases was a dissenting vote cast.[34] The passage of the Defense Reorganization Act of 1986 was an effort to alter this pattern by expanding the authority of the chairman of the Joint Chiefs so that he would be able to make the kinds of tough choices about roles and missions that the Joint Chiefs as a committee were reluctant to make. Whether the desired outcome is likely to occur is a matter on which observers are divided.

The concern for autonomy also leads government agencies to resist being regulated by other agencies. The Office of Federal Contract Compliance Programs (OFCC), part of the Department of Labor, supervises the efforts of federal agencies to insure that contractors doing business with the government are in compliance with laws and executive orders bearing on civil rights and affirmative-action hiring programs. The OFCC is supposed to make certain, for example, that the Defense Department adequately monitors the hiring practices of defense contractors. When Patricia Rachal studied the OFCC it was clear that hardly anybody thought it was achieving its goal. Its problem was clear: the OFCC did not control any resources—budgets or personnel—valued by DOD.[35] By contrast, when the federal government imposes a regulation on a private contractor it can threaten the resources of the firm either by withholding a contract or contract payment or by taking the firm to court.

Housing inspectors in Boston respond to tenant complaints about unsafe or unsanitary housing conditions. When Pietro Nivola studied that agency in the mid-1970s, he found a puzzle: though the housing inspectors cited both private and public landlords for housing code violations, the citations issued to private landlords resulted in corrective action more frequently and speedily than similar citations issued to the city's chief public landlord, the Boston Housing Authority.[36] The answer to the puzzle can be guessed readily—the housing inspectors were willing to press cases against private landlords and had resources (court orders) that they could invoke against recalcitrant landlords, but they were reluctant to press cases against another city agency and in any event had almost no power over that agency.

Electric utilities are increasingly expected to practice various forms of energy conservation (such as offering incentives to customers to cut their demand for electricity) and to explore the potential of various renewable or soft energy sources (such as solar, wind, and geothermal power). A study comparing three privately owned with three publicly owned utilities located in the same states and serving similar markets revealed that by any measure the private utilities were much more energetic in pursuing conservation and alternative-energy programs than were public utilities.[37] State regulatory agencies controlled resources valued by private utilities but not by public ones; the agencies could set the electric rates and determine the allowed rate of return (roughly, the profit) of investor-owned firms, but could not do the same with the municipally owned utilities.

A similar conclusion was reached in a study of the Tennessee Valley Authority. When the Environmental Protection Agency began ordering electric utilities to reduce the amount of certain pollutants they were emitting from their smokestacks, the TVA, a government-owned corporation, resisted implementing the rules longer and more successfully than did private utilities such as Pacific Gas & Electric Company.[38] In time the TVA changed, but the reason for the change illustrates the problem that one government agency has in controlling the behavior of another. The President of the United States happened to take a personal interest in the problem and decided to appoint pro-environmental directors to the TVA board. A key senator threatened to block a bill that the TVA urgently wanted passed. But most important of all, the courts held that the TVA could be sued. A coalition of various citizen groups as well as the attorneys general of two states filed suit against the TVA, charging it with failing to comply with environmental rules. In the consent decree that ended the suit the TVA promised to change its ways.[39]

The resistance of the TVA to complying with the Clean Air Act was the product of the agency's sense of mission: the primacy of efficient power production. This mission was an expression of the professional ethos of the power engineers that dominated the TVA (see chapters 4 and 5). The ability to make that resistance effective for so long was the result of the agency having acquired a high degree of autonomy. The ending of that resistance occurred because of factors that most government agencies never have to cope with—the direct personal intervention of the president and the threat of a law suit. Indeed, it is far from clear what authority the courts have, if any, when one federal agency seeks to sue another.

The magnitude of the problem is suggested by 1987 data indicating that federal facilities were less frequently in compliance with EPA guidelines than were private facilities. For example, at a site near Denver, Colorado, there were millions of gallons of various toxic chemicals. Two organizations were responsible, the Shell Oil Company and the Rocky Mountain Arsenal of the Department of Defense, both of which used the site. In 1983 the Justice Department took Shell Oil to court to recover the costs of cleaning up Shell's share of the mess. But no equivalent proceeding was begun against the Defense Department, partly because one agency is reluctant to pick a fight with another and partly because lawyers disagree as to what legal recourse, if any, a government has against another agency.[40]

Conclusions

The supposedly imperialistic character of government agencies is a vast oversimplification. Autonomy is valued at least as much as resources, because autonomy determines the degree to which it is costly to acquire and use resources. High autonomy means the agency has a supportive constituency base and a coherent set of tasks that can provide the basis for a strong and widely shared sense of mission. If autonomy can reasonably be assured, then the agency of course will seek more resources or an enlarged jurisdiction.

But that is a big "if." As the variety of government activities has increased, the opportunities for any agency to have an uncontested jurisdiction and a wholly supportive constituency have shrunk. Turf problems were not major problems when the only important federal agencies were the Post Office, the Pension Bureau, the army, and the Customs Service. Turf problems are large, and largely insoluble, when the government has within it dozens of agencies that make foreign policy, scores that make or affect economic policy, and countless ones that regulate business activity and enforce criminal laws.

This may explain what John Wanat found in his study of the patterns of growth in various federal agencies between 1952 and 1966. It turns out that after allowing for inflation many agencies did not grow at all.* Those that did grow were disproportionately research agencies.[41] Many research agencies (one thinks of the National Institutes of Health) have a very supportive constituency (who would oppose finding a cure for cancer?); an undisputed jurisdiction (there are no other agencies doing this job); and a coherent sense of mission (the research interests of professional scientists). Under these circumstances agency pressures for growth are likely to be strong because they are not costly. Of course, whether the agency's desire for growth actually results in growth will depend on many things beyond its control, including prevailing economic and budgetary conditions.

Very few federal agencies have the advantages of a cancer research institute. Most must struggle for both autonomy and resources. How that struggle is managed by agency executives is the subject of the next chapter.

*Obviously, some agencies must have grown; otherwise, government expenditures in 1966 would have equaled those in 1952. The growth was primarily in the military and in entitlements.

CHAPTER 11

Strategies

YOU LEARN VERY QUICKLY that you do not go down in history as a good or bad Secretary in terms of how well you ran the place. . . ."[1] In these words, Michael Blumenthal summarized the difference between his experience as secretary of the treasury, where good administration was not rewarded, and as chief executive officer of the Bendix Corporation, where it was.

Both government and business executives are responsible for maintaining their organizations. At first blush, it would seem easier to maintain a public agency than a private firm. After all, every year some fifty or sixty thousand businesses file for bankruptcy; no government agency ever does.[2] Government bureaucracies are not immortal; when Herbert Kaufman looked at the fate of 175 federal agencies that existed in 1923, he found that 15 percent no longer existed by 1973.[3] But if not immortal they are certainly hardy: It is a reasonable guess that 85 percent of all business firms extant in 1923 were not still alive half a century later. Moreover, many of the twenty-seven federal agencies that disappeared had their functions and most of their personnel absorbed into other agencies. They did not so much die as undergo reincarnation.

But these statistics can be misleading. There are two reasons why organizational maintenance is harder in the public than the private sector. First, maintenance means not merely survival but prosperity; and prosperity in turn means acquiring both autonomy and resources. As we saw in the last chapter the autonomy of most agencies is sharply limited, and so a federal executive spends much of his or her time fending off challenges from rival agencies, coping with criticism from the media and interest groups, and trying to win or retain presidential and congressional support. The chief executive officer of Bendix Corporation also must cope with competitors and find resources, but unlike the secretary of the treasury, he is able to do so in ways that do not give either competitors or resource holders much of a say in how his organization is run. Bendix obtains from resource holders commitments (i.e., promises to deliver capital, labor, and materials); the Treasury Department acquires from Congress and the White House a set of *contingencies* (i.e., conditional and changing agreements to provide support in exchange for a say in how the resources will be used). What this means is best expressed by former Secretary of State George Shultz: "It's never over." Nothing is ever settled; debates over what many agencies should do and how they should do it are continuous, and so the maintenance of support for the agency is a never-ending, time-consuming process of negotiating and then renegotiating a set of agreements with stakeholders who are always changing their minds.

Second, government executives face a different set of personal incentives than do private executives. The head of a business firm is judged and rewarded on the basis of the firm's earnings—the bottom line. The head of a public agency is judged and rewarded on the basis of the *appearance* of success, when success can mean reputation, influence, charm, the absence of criticism, personal ideology, or victory in policy debates. Sometimes, of course, success means achieving the agency's goals, as when NASA landed a man on the moon, the armed forces won World War II, or the Social Security Administration gets benefit checks out on time. But as previous chapters should make clear, many agencies have goals so vague, controversial, or difficult to achieve that progress toward their realization is hard to assess. Moreover, the rewards for public executives are not wholly, or even primarily, tangible; just as important are the intangible ones, egoistic or ideological considerations such as popularity, a reputation for power, or identification with a cause. Michael Blumenthal put it bluntly: In Washington, "you can be successful if you appear to be successful . . . appearance is as important as reality."[4]

These two factors taken together mean that maintaining the *executive* is not the same as maintaining the *organization*. We are familiar with secretaries of state who devote a lot of time to shuttle diplomacy and hardly any time to running the State Department. Whatever the worth of these diplomatic missions, their eager pursuit leaves no doubt that the reputation of the secretary of state has little to do with his management of the Department of State.

Kinds of Executives

There are two kinds of government executives (and several complicated combinations of the two). Political executives are appointed by the president, governor, or mayor in order to satisfy the elected official's political needs; career executives are appointed from within an agency (or brought in from a comparable agency elsewhere) because it is required by law or because there are no overriding political needs that must be served. In the federal government there are approximately seven hundred political executives (classified from Level I down to Level V in the "executive schedule") and over five thousand career executives who occupy the so-called supergrade positions (GS-16 through GS-18 of the civil service, or "general schedule"). The line between the two types is not clear; of late, some supergrade civil service positions have been filled by political appointees (these are called Noncareer Executive Assignments, or NEAs) and some executive schedule posts have been filled by careerists.[5]

The chief executive of most federal agencies, bureaus, and departments is a political appointee. There are some important exceptions, however: By tradition, the head of the Bureau of Prisons, the Weather Service, the Forest Service, and the Bureau of Standards as well as the chiefs of staff of the four military services have usually been careerists promoted from within. Local police departments typically are headed by career officers, not outside civilians, though many police chiefs get their posts because of their political support for the mayor. A rough but useful test of the status of an executive is length of service; political appointees tend to be in office for brief periods (in federal government it has averaged about two years or less)[6] while career executives usually serve much longer.

It is a common mistake to assume that a president or governor appoints the head of a department or bureau with a view to achieving certain policy goals. Sometimes that happens, but more often the president (or governor or mayor) has no clear idea of what policy his appointee will pursue. Agency executives are selected in order to serve the political needs of the president, and these may or may not involve policy considerations. Some are appointed to reward campaign workers, others to find places for defeated members of Congress, still others to satisfy the demands of interest groups. Sometimes the agency head is picked because he or she is thought to be an expert on the subject, but many times the president has no real idea of the content or policy implications of this expertise. As Hugh Heclo has written:

> [T]he selection process deemphasizes operational goals, making an appointee's journey through the Washington minefields into something like a random walk. If he is not entirely sure of what is expected of him, it is not surprising; in many cases neither are his selectors, many of whom are more interested in the process of getting their way than in the executive's eventual output.[7]

In the early 1970s, President Gerald Ford spoke out forcefully about the "overzealous" and "nit-picking" regulations being issued by the Occupational Safety and Health Administration, but the person he picked to head it, Morton Corn, was even more zealous than his predecessor. Why the gap between rhetoric and reality? Because Ford deferred to his secretary of labor, John Dunlop, in choosing the head of OSHA, and Dunlop's concerns were different from those of the president. By contrast, Ford's successor, Jimmy Carter, took a personal interest in the OSHA appointment and selected Eula Bingham, whom he knew would be, as he wished, a zealous regulator.[8]

Because presidents often pick agency heads as much to maintain the presidency as to maintain the various agencies, and because every agency head discovers that he or she is enmeshed in an enormously complex and restrictive set of constraints on executive action, the relationship between appointer and appointee typically ranges somewhere between benign neglect and active hostility. To the appointer the agency head will have "gone native"—sold out to the bureaucrats and interest groups. To the appointee the president and his chief aides will have "gone south"—forgotten their promise to support the agency head in his or her fights with Congress and the press.

A career agency head is not immune from these political relationships but is less affected by them precisely because the president (or other appointing authority) has decided that the costs of having the agency appear to be under his control exceed the benefits of that control. A mayor, for example, in appointing a new police chief to take over a department wracked with controversy and charges of political favoritism may promise to keep "hands off" and allow the agency to be run by a "professional" without interference. Ever since allegations that the White House was using the director of the FBI, L. Patrick Gray, to help it cover up the Watergate scandal, presidents have gone to considerable lengths to appear to leave the FBI alone, an appearance strengthened by a law passed after the Gray episode that gives the FBI director a ten-year term.

Scandal is not the only reason for leaving an agency in the hands of a careerist. The maintenance of some agencies depends so crucially on their appearing professional and nonpolitical that it would be foolhardy for an elected official to compromise that appearance. The National Bureau of Standards and the Weather Service are examples. Even agencies about which political disagreement is appropriate nonetheless may have built a reputation as an elite service that would be risky to tamper with. The Army Corps of Engineers, the Bureau of Prisons, and the Forest Service are examples.

Career executives also may emerge for reasons having little to do with the competence or ethos of the agency. Government employees, especially at the local level, will use their political influence with city councils and state legislatures to capture their agencies so that promotions from within are all but required by law. For example, it is virtually impossible to appoint as police chief of Los Angeles anyone other than a ranking member of the Los Angeles Police Department. Though outsiders may apply for the post, the civil service rules that determine the points awarded to each applicant in the competitive examinations give an almost insuperable advantage to an insider.

Types of Agencies and Types of Executives

To people of a reformist bent the idea of having nonpartisan experts run government agencies always has been appealing. Business executives and other outside observers often lament the fact that the "best people" are not in charge in government. In fact many of the best federal agencies have been managed for long periods by nonpolitical careerists (the Corps of Engineers, the Forest Service, the Bureau of Prisons, and the Social Security Administration are obvious examples). But to draw from these facts the conclusion that all agencies would be best run by experts or careerists is to ignore the differences among agencies and, in a single agency, the needs it has at different stages in its evolution.

If a career foreign service officer were to be secretary of state, then he or she in all probability would be so insulated from the political process in the White House as to render the secretary an ineffectual voice in making foreign policy and to relegate the department to the status of an elaborate mail room. As it is, even some political secretaries of state—William Rogers, secretary under President Nixon, comes to mind—have been left dangling on the remote periphery of policy making. The State Department is an example of what I have called (in chapter 8) a coping agency. Coping agencies rarely can develop the sense of mission and the external support necessary for their management to be left in career hands. These organizations can point to neither unambiguous accomplishments nor visible activity; as a result, they are likely to be enmeshed in controversy about their goals and engulfed in suspicion about their means.

Careerists have the best chance of being successful executives in production agencies—those in which both the work done and the outcomes produced are observable. Provided the goals command wide political support (as they do with the retirement program of the Social Security Administration and as they once did with NASA and the New York Port Authority), then a career executive has an opportunity to create or maintain an organization that operates efficiently and without scandal. Political superiors can readily assess the accomplishments of the organization and if they like what they see they can easily accept (and even insist upon) having this efficient machine headed by a nonpartisan professional. Such organizations often are applauded for their "businesslike" qualities; the praise is not misplaced, for in fact these agencies in principle are amenable to being managed in businesslike ways. Of course some production agencies such as the Postal Service never manage to acquire any consensus about their goals (is it more important to deliver the mail cheaply or quickly?) and so the opportunities for nonpolitical careerists to succeed are diminished. The Postal Service has labored mightily to install business-style management with some success, but given the political demands on it, success always will be partial.

Craft agencies also lend themselves to careerist leadership. Though the work of the operators is hard to observe the results are not. If the results are politically popular and if the work of the operators can be glamorized, political superiors are inclined to accept careerist leadership. The Army Corps of Engineers is led by career army officers, to the general satisfaction of almost everybody. Though there are disputes about some of its tasks hardly anyone suggests that things would be better if the corps were headed by a political appointee. The Forest Service has been able to retain (not without some difficulty) its status as an elite service under careerist leadership. Until recently, hospitals have been run by physicians; they were the experts. (When hospital costs began to soar the public decided that expertise was not enough, and so outside, nonmedical executives were brought in to run things.) The FBI under J. Edgar Hoover seemed to produce results (Dillinger was shot, Nazi saboteurs were caught, kidnappers and bank robbers feared the "G-Men"); no one was quite certain how FBI agents did it (in truth, they had a lot of help from other people) but that they did it at all was good enough, at least until what they did was itself controversial (such as investigating radical organizations at a time when the political elites no longer feared radicals). Then demands arose for the FBI to be placed under outside (that is, political) control, and this was done.

Career leadership may be especially easy to sustain in craft organizations that have developed an aura of mystery and romance. Career executives have managed to rise to the top of the Forest Service in part because forest rangers wear uniforms, are thought to lead lonely and rugged lives in distant places, and symbolize their work in the person of Smokey the Bear wearing a ranger hat. The absolute code of silence Hoover imposed on FBI agents when it came to talking about their work (except for official press releases) enhanced the aura of mysterious competence surrounding the bureau. Doctors in hospitals wear white coats, speak the incomprehensible language of medicine, and write prescriptions in an indecipherable script. For many people all this adds to rather than detracts from the confidence they have in professional management.

Procedural organizations, like coping ones, are hard for careerists to maintain because outsiders cannot easily observe and evaluate their outcomes. But outsiders can observe their work and therefore can insist that this work conform to the rules and constraints dear to whatever groups take an interest in the matter. No one knows whether prisons reduce or increase the crime rate or leave it unchanged, but everyone notices a prison riot or escape and everyone has an opinion as to whether the daily life of the inmates should be made better or worse. No one knows whether the United States Army in peacetime is actually ready to fight and win a given war, but anyone can find out if women are passed over for promotion, recruits harshly treated during basic training, or procurement contracts improperly awarded. Maintaining a prison system or a peacetime army requires political skills of a very high order. Some career executives may possess them and even win the top job, but their getting and holding that job depends less on their technical knowledge than on their ability to find political support, cope with critics, and negotiate a resolution of controversies.

Executives who do not understand what kind of organization they are maintaining (or worse, forget that they must *maintain*, not merely manage it) are in for tough sledding. Many police chiefs promoted from within mistakenly think that since professional competence got them the job, professional competence alone will enable them to keep the job. Such chiefs will emphasize vigorous law enforcement and the rational allocation of personnel but may neglect the community groups demanding that the police provide "inefficient" foot patrol or attend to such "non-police" matters as graffiti. Effective career chiefs are those who quickly learn how to cope with these political aspects of organizational maintenance.

The Key Strategy: Finding a Constituency

Thirteen successful government executives are described in a 1987 book on "entrepreneurs in government."[9] They include the well-known (Robert McNamara and Hyman Rickover) and the not-so-well-known (Austin Tobin and Nancy Hanks); the flamboyantly public (Gifford Pinchot and David Lilienthal) and the barely visible (Elmer Staats); people with a business background (James Forrestal and Marriner Eccles); people whose whole lives have been in the public arena (Wilbur Cohen and Robert Ball); and people who have been in and out of government with great regularity (James Webb).

The authors of these profiles asked what it was that made these people effective executives of their agencies. Certain personal qualities, especially an enormous capacity for work and (often) an obsession with the goals they wished to attain, were apparent in many. Beyond that their temperaments differed: Some, such as Lilienthal, head of the TVA, loved to be in the public eye and spoke out frequently; others, such as Nancy Hanks, head of the National Endowment for the Arts, were uncomfortable in public forums. Some, such as James Forrestal, first secretary of defense, managed by consensus and committee; others, such as Robert McNamara, a later secretary of defense, had little use for committees and loved to make personal decisions. Some, such as Austin Tobin, executive director of the New York Port Authority, built broad coalitions among affected interests; while others, such as Marriner Eccles, chairman of the Federal Reserve Board, had little flair and no taste for bargaining. Some, such as Robert Ball, administrator of Social Security, were pleasant and congenial personalities; but others, such as Hyman Rickover, head of the nuclear submarine program, were legendary curmudgeons. But all had one thing in common: They found or maintained the support of key external constituencies.[10] Sometimes the only constituency was Congress; this was the case for Elmer Staats, longtime head of the General Accounting Office (GAO). Sometimes it was the president, and often the president alone; this was the case with Robert McNamara at a time when he was taking on the military brass and had only the support of President Kennedy to fall back on. It was also the case with Gifford Pinchot when he used his friendship with President Theodore Roosevelt to defeat the Interior Department in a struggle over control of the national forests and with Marriner Eccles when President Franklin Roosevelt helped him survive some bruising battles with Congress and other cabinet officials. Often the constituency consisted of a broad array of interest groups, as when Nancy Hanks got most of the traditionally warring art and cultural factions to rally around the National Endowment for the Arts, or when Austin Tobin got the New York business community to support (and even to pretend to devise) his plans for expanding the role of the Port Authority. And sometimes the constituency was the public at large: Americans cheered the "underdog," Hyman Rickover, in his struggle against navy admirals who wanted him to retire and they watched breathlessly as astronauts were launched into space by a NASA headed by James Webb.

Webb could have spoken for all the others when he described the role of a government executive this way:

> The environment is not something apart from the endeavor; it is not just something in which the endeavor operates and which it needs to adjust; it is an integral part of the endeavor itself. . . . The total [executive] job encompasses external as well as internal elements, and success is as dependent on effectiveness in the one as in the other.[11]

Just how important is the environment was something Webb himself learned the hard way. After the Apollo program put a man on the moon NASA looked for a new program with which to maintain itself. There emerged no popular consensus as to what, if any, the next space mission would be; President Johnson, who had given Webb unequivocal backing, was preoccupied with the war in Vietnam and no longer in possession of the political capital Webb needed; the air force was pressing forward with its own space program in competition with NASA.[12] Some critics believe that NASA turned to the space shuttle program as a way of keeping itself in the public eye even though the shuttle itself was an inefficient and dangerous way to put payloads into orbit.[13]

James Forrestal also learned how quickly a constituency can disappear. He had been brilliantly successful as undersecretary of the navy during World War II, reorganizing the Navy Department to facilitate the production and procurement of immense fleets of ships and an endless stream of supplies. He was often in conflict with admirals and some members of Congress, but the wartime crisis assured him breathing room because he was delivering on his promises and thus the president was willing to back him. After the war Forrestal became secretary of the navy and began planning for peace and for the threatening possibility of military unification. This is something President Truman wanted and Forrestal did not; thus, the secretary was often in the position of publicly disagreeing with his boss. When the new Defense Department was created, Truman made Forrestal its first head—a mistake for both parties, since Truman was not prepared to give Forrestal, his critic, the full support that Forrestal, in trying to build a new organization, so desperately needed. In the end, the job overwhelmed the man, and he took his own life.[14]

Many years ago Norton Long put the executive's need for a constituency as well as it can be phrased:

> There is no more forlorn spectacle in the administrative world than an agency and a program possessed of statutory life, armed with executive orders, sustained in the courts, yet stricken with paralysis and deprived of power, an object of contempt to its enemies and of despair to its friends. The lifeblood of administration is power. Its attainment, maintenance, increase, dissipation, and loss are subjects the practitioner and student can ill afford to neglect.[15]

The principal source of power is a constituency. This plain fact repeated by generations of students of public administration still seems lost on those people (business executives, in particular) who upon taking a high-level job in Washington complain about the amount of time they must spend attending to the demands and needs of outside groups. All this time spent currying favor and placating critics, they argue, is time taken away from the real work of the agency, which is to "do the job." No. The real work of the government executive *is* to curry favor and placate critics. Skilled executives can do this without currying or placating in any demeaning or dishonest way, but the currying and the placating must be done, one way or another.

It is not only outsiders who find this distasteful; so do members of the executive's own agency. Graham Allison once observed that while executives are oriented to the power aspects of their situation, operators are oriented to the feasibility aspects of it.[16] The executive wants to cope with uncertainty by finding allies at any reasonable price; the operators want to cope with it by getting a clear commitment of support from above. The price executives pay for allies is often to impose complications and further uncertainties on operators. For example, police officers see themselves as coping with the harsh reality of the street; what they want from the chief is to be backed up, period. Police chiefs see themselves as trying to keep their organization out of political trouble; what they want from allies is support that they know will be temporary and resources that they know will be given conditionally. The price for this support and these resources will be to investigate and punish certain police officers for certain misdeeds, or to reassign officers from one job to another, or to embrace some newfangled scheme for ending crime and drug abuse. As was said earlier, two cultures develop in a police department: that of the street cop and that of the management cop. People sharing the former often distrust those embracing the latter because they have "sold out."

The external, constituency-oriented posture of most government executives explains why as Michael Blumenthal put it "appearance is as important as reality."[17] Though an executive's relations with some constituencies will be judged in hard dollars-and-cents terms (Did he deliver the grant or subsidy? Did he allow the tax break?), most relations with most groups will involve intangible matters (Did she pass the litmus test? Is she in the president's inner circle? Is she a clever speaker?). Reputation—for influence, style, and access—is a key part of the relationship between executive and constituency.[18]

Blumenthal spells out what maintaining the right appearance means in practical terms: Don't appear to be on the losing side in a struggle to influence the president's position (you will be seen as lacking in power). Don't appear to change your mind (you will be accused of inconsistency). Don't use certain code words (you will upset an interest group). Don't make mistakes (you will be thought incompetent). And don't try to do everything (when you fail at some task you will appear incompetent).

Maintenance and Policy

The short tenure and small rewards of much public service mean that for many political executives the chance to influence policy is a major incentive for taking a government job. In some states and cities, of course, the incentives are much greater because of the opportunities to deliver jobs and contracts to friends and supporters. At one time these incentives existed for federal executives as well, but that is much less true today.

Executives who want to influence policy but who define "policy" largely in terms of what outside constituencies want (or will not denounce) are in an awkward position—more awkward than they sometimes realize. To change their agency, these officials need to understand its workings, know its people, and appreciate its constraints. But the external, constituency-serving orientation of such executives, combined with their short tenure in office, reduce the time and energy they can devote to this learning process. As a result, the policy changes they make are likely to be ill-considered and inadequately managed. Even the Social Security Administration, an agency with a tradition of strong and well-informed leaders, seriously underestimated the difficulty of implementing the Supplemental Security Income (SSI) program in the early 1970s. Top executives were busy assuring Congress and the White House that the SSA could do the job of identifying three million aged, blind, or disabled persons, verifying their eligibility for SSI benefits, and hiring fifteen thousand new employees to service these beneficiaries; meanwhile, the working-level managers were approaching a state of panic, for they knew that the agency was in deep trouble. It could not possibly train the people and install the computer systems fast enough to meet the deadlines. Martha Derthick concluded her study of this episode with language that could describe executive-agency relations in many bureaus:

> It is impossible not to be struck by the differences between the view from the top, reflected in the serene pride that valuable social ends are about to be served, and the mounting panic and frustration in the field offices as unreadiness for the concrete task becomes all too clear.[19]

Nevertheless, political executives can change policy. They need not be either the captives of their agencies or the tools of congressional overseers.

The heads of OSHA appointed by Carter and Ford tried to reduce the "nit-picking" safety rules while pressing ahead to develop health rules. The heads of OSHA appointed by Reagan tried to cut back both kinds of regulations and to get the agency's inspectors to adopt a more flexible, less adversarial approach to enforcement.[20] But neither of these emphases produced wholesale changes in the agency's behavior because both required the executive to communicate complex, subtle directives to many distant employees. How do you instruct an inspector in the field to be less "nit-picking" or more "flexible"? The answer is, not very easily. Large organizations that lack operational goals only can be managed by indirection—by setting a tone at the top, promoting some kinds of people, getting rid of others. The executive sends out signals; but signals, like rumors in a college dormitory, quickly get lost or distorted.

In his insightful account of public managers at work, Philip Heymann analyzes two efforts to impart a new direction to the Federal Trade Commission: one, largely successful, led by Caspar Weinberger and Miles Kirkpatrick; and another, much less successful, led by Michael Pertschuk.[21] In 1969 the FTC was an agency under siege, simultaneously criticized by Ralph Nader and a commission of the American Bar Association. Both critics agreed that the FTC was attending to trivial rather than to important examples of unfair competition, and doing that badly. It spent more money checking up on the labeling of textiles and furs than on investigating monopolies. About the only constituency the FTC had was a small number of congressmen who cared mostly about placing friends in patronage positions at the commission.

Weinberger was expected by the president who appointed him, Richard Nixon, to change that. But to what ends? What exactly should the FTC do? On that the president had little to say; with a war in Vietnam, the future of the FTC was hardly uppermost in his mind. Weinberger (and later Kirkpatrick) looked for a strategy. To a political executive a good strategy is one that identifies a set of tasks that are both feasible and supportable—activities the organization has the capacity to engage in and that will elicit the backing of important constituencies. A good place to begin was to emphasize deceptive national advertising. No one could publicly defend deception. Investigating such cases was neither difficult nor expensive, and vigor in this area would attract the support of newly vocal consumer groups. To redefine tasks in this way required getting rid of certain veteran staffers and bringing in some energetic lawyers. This was done. Soon the FTC was displaying a newfound energy and enthusiasm, attacking questionable claims made by Wonder Bread, Bufferin, Excedrin, and Listerine. Companies found guilty of deceptive practices were required to run corrective ads.

When Michael Pertschuk became chairman in 1977 he brought to the FTC the zeal and convictions of a dedicated member of the consumer movement. He sought to expand even more the reach of the FTC by taking full advantage of new legal tools, in particular a 1975 law that authorized the FTC to issue and enforce industry-wide rules defining fair business practice. (Previously the FTC could only issue orders directed at single firms.) Pertschuk's Republican predecessors had initiated a number of such rule-making proceedings, but these came to fruition during his tenure and it was he who expanded on these initiatives by starting action against the producers of television advertising aimed at children ("kid-vids"), especially in connection with Saturday morning cartoon shows.

There were two things wrong with Pertschuk's more ambitious strategy. First, the FTC staff was divided over the merits of trying to regulate whole industries as opposed to attacking the misconduct of individual firms. As explained in chapter 4, lawyers tended to favor the case-by-case approach while economists favored the broader, "structural" approach. Second, the strategy aroused the opposition of broad segments of the business community. It was hard for a company to win much political sympathy if it were shown to be running a deceptive ad; it was a lot easier for entire industries to get such sympathy when without any clear showing of wrongdoing they were made the object of broad, new regulations. To make matters worse, many of these industries involved small businesses that were active in every congressional district: used-car dealers, funeral parlors, drugstores, vocational schools, gasoline stations, and opticians. Pertschuk may have thought that used-car dealers and undertakers had a lot of critics; he was about to discover that they also had a lot of friends. Congress cut the ground out from under him by slashing his budget, blocking his kid-vid rules, and restricting his rule-making powers. With President Reagan's accession to power in 1980, Pertschuk was replaced.

When Ronald Reagan became president, the FTC changed again. His transition team, headed by James C. Miller III, produced a report calling for FTC policies to be evaluated chiefly according to the criteria of economic efficiency—that is, by their effect on the functioning of the economy and the long-term welfare of consumers—and not simply according to legal criteria (the law in any event was vague). To Miller and his associates, this meant encouraging competitive market forces to work. Miller became chairman of the FTC and set about implementing the report's recommendations in the face of congressional hostility.

The need to maintain constituency support is a universal, but the degree to which it will restrict an executive's freedom of action depends on the political environment of the agency. When that environment involves client politics (see chapter 5), the freedom is very little. When it involves interest-group politics, it is greater but still constrained. When it involves entrepreneurial politics it is greater yet. The FTC was changed at a time when its environment was changing. The rising consumer movement made it possible for the FTC to break its clientlike relations with a patronage-oriented faction in Congress. The initial alliance it forged with consumerist entrepreneurs over the issue of deceptive advertising was not very costly, but when it broadened that alliance by moving aggressively into industrywide rule makings, it found that the rising tide of consumerism had washed up onto the beach some angry fishes—small businesses and their congressional allies who proceeded to redefine the FTC's environment by embedding the agency in the pull and haul of interest-group politics.

There was nothing inevitable about any of this. Nixon could have appointed to the FTC someone other than Weinberger who would have made less sweeping changes in the agency's personnel and mission. Pertschuk could have made a different assessment of the political limits on his freedom of action, thereby avoiding the hostile congressional reaction. Reagan need not have chosen Miller or backed his commitment to free-market economics. Why did Weinberger, Pertschuk, and Miller behave as they did? Answering that question requires a biographer, not an organizational theorist. Within limits, executives have choices.

Kinds of Strategies

Executives have choices because unlike many operators they play weakly defined roles. They are less bound by daily routines and peer expectations and are less dominated by situational and technological imperatives. Moreover, their (usually) short tenure in office means that many of their rewards come from outside the agency—their image in the press, their standing with the president, and their reputation among allies in the issue networks and interest groups that oversee the agency. Michael Pertschuk's aggressive stance at the FTC was rational if, as may have been the case, he assigned a higher value to his reputation among consumerists than to his standing in Congress. Personality is likely to explain more of the actions of executives than of operators. But differences among executive strategies are not simply a matter of personality. Circumstances and temperament interact to determine strategy. No better example can be found than the career of Caspar Weinberger in the Nixon and Reagan administrations. As chairman of the FTC he was a forceful decision maker determined to reshape the culture of his agency; as head of the Office of Management and Budget and then as secretary of Health, Education, and Welfare he was a relentless budget-cutter; and finally as secretary of defense he was a tireless fundraiser and program advocate.

There are many styles of executive action; it would be pointless to try to list all or to pretend that each type was wholly different from every other. Four types will be illustrated here: the advocate, the decision maker, the budget-cutter, and the negotiator. Many economists think that only the first style exists: if bigger is always better, executives will always try to maximize their budgets. In chapter 10 I tried to cast some doubt on that premise. It is often but not always true.

ADVOCATES

When President Reagan made Caspar Weinberger the secretary of defense, people who had seen him at work in OMB and HEW expected him to be a cold-eyed, cost-conscious program manager. Conservatives were aghast at the prospect of a budget-cutter, known in his OMB days as "Cap the Knife," taking over at the Pentagon. In 1972 Weinberger had defended the sharp decline in defense spending ordered by President Nixon and predicted that in the years ahead "we can . . . maintain a continued relatively level expenditure in the defense area."[22] Just as unsettling to the defense hawks were the people Weinberger brought with him—a number of "liberal" deputies from his days with the FTC and HEW.

The hawks were wrong. Within a year Weinberger had agreed to a large, across-the-board increase in defense spending. He backed the B-1 bomber, a project that as OMB chief he had tried to scuttle. He relentlessly supported the defense build-up against critics in and out of the administration. Meanwhile, he allowed the Defense Department to be managed by others on a decentralized basis that left intact the autonomy of the military services with respect to missions and procurement priorities.

The trait that Weinberger displayed in all his government posts was a deep loyalty to the program of the president who appointed him. One journalist described it this way: "His 'modus operandi' has stayed exactly the same: Get the brief. Set a course right away. Be tough with the opposition. Never waver. Make the President look good."[23] Since Weinberger was also a highly intelligent, invariably polite person, his lawyer-like advocacy of his "client's" case was usually quite effective.[24] In time, support for the build-up evaporated in Congress and became equivocal in the White House; with an uncertain client and personal problems to attend to, Weinberger resigned.

James Schlesinger was also something of an advocate at DOD, but for different reasons and in a different style. His commitment to a stronger defense flowed less from a desire to serve the president's policies than from a detailed analysis of the nation's defense posture. Weinberger was a lawyer, Schlesinger an economist. Moreover, the defense goals of Schlesinger's president, Gerald Ford, were not as cast in concrete as were those of Weinberger's. Where Weinberger saw himself as carrying out his president's desires (desires that Weinberger personally shared), Schlesinger undertook the job of persuading his president of what his desires ought to be. Schlesinger the analyst not only convinced himself and Ford that the Nixon defense cuts had gone too far and that rebuilding was necessary; he liked to make the decisions about the details of that rebuilding that Weinberger the advocate delegated to others. The price Schlesinger paid for his outspoken, intellectual, and sometimes abrasive style was the alienation of key members of Congress and of the White House staff. President Ford fired Schlesinger after a little over two years of Pentagon service.[25]

Advocates are not found only at the Pentagon. From 1961 through 1969, Wilbur Cohen served, in succession, as assistant secretary, undersecretary, and secretary of Health, Education, and Welfare. Even as a mere assistant secretary Cohen was the dominant figure in the department, owing in large measure to his lifelong commitment to the growth and extension of social welfare programs, especially Social Security and Medicare. In and out of government Cohen tirelessly argued for building a welfare state, American style. For twenty years he was a key official in the Social Security Administration; during the brief periods he was out of office he served as a professor at the University of Michigan where he wrote and lectured about "unmet needs." Chief among these needs in Cohen's view was medical insurance. As assistant secretary of HEW he was the chief spokesman on Capitol Hill for what became, in 1965, the Medicare program. When he became undersecretary of HEW in 1965 and then secretary in 1968, he continued to play the role of what Theodore Marmor calls a "program loyalist," working to assure that his policies were adequately funded and defended.

There was another role Cohen could have played at HEW. He could have tried to manage the department, reorganize its many bureaus, cut its rising costs, or decentralize its far-flung operations. These definitions of the job of HEW executive in fact were embraced at various times during the 1960s and 1970s by John Gardner, Robert Finch, Elliott Richardson, Caspar Weinberger, David Mathews, and Joseph Califano. But managing HEW was a daunting task, as these other secretaries discovered. HEW, like DOD today, was not so much an agency as a vast conglomerate of quasi-independent agencies, some with vague or contradictory goals, several headed by powerful individuals strongly backed by professional associations, and the largest administering budgets over which by law the secretary has virtually no control. (These are the "entitlement programs," such as Social Security and Medicare.) Moreover, much of what HEW attempts to do is done neither directly nor on its own, but indirectly through state and local governments and with the aid of private organizations such as health-care insurance companies.[26]

No secretary has ever really "managed" HEW (or Health and Human Services, as it is now called). Those who have tried found it a frustrating experience. Elliott Richardson told me not long after he stepped down as HEW secretary that the experience taught him to admire Fidel Castro's ability to assemble a vast throng of people in a city plaza, where they would stand listening to a four-hour speech and then go off and do whatever their leader said. Richardson wanted to give a "Castro speech" to HEW's employees, but of course neither he nor anyone else can do that and even if he could, the employees would not change their behavior. Wilbur Cohen's strategy, to be a fundraiser and policy advocate, suited both his own temperament and convictions as well as the constraints on the job.

DECISION MAKERS

As secretary of defense, Robert McNamara was a decision maker. He believed that the defense budget should not be set on the basis of the political preferences of the president nor the logrolling tendencies of the services but rather on the basis of what it would cost to have the "correct" mix of troops and weapons to achieve the stated goals of defense policy. McNamara explicitly rejected the executive role of maintaining the organization by adjudicating among service interests and explicitly embraced the role of leader, the person who probes for problems, gathers data, and acts decisively to solve the problems.[27]

There is no question that McNamara made a difference: Between 1961 and 1965, the share of the defense budget spent on strategic weapons (i.e., bombers and missiles) fell from 27 to 12 percent; the air force and the navy were ordered (over their objections) to develop for joint use the TFX (F-111) fighter; and the Pentagon supply system was reorganized. But the methods McNamara used—"rational," "quantitative" analyses—did not lend themselves to developing and leading a land army and in the eyes of many critics proved worse than useless when it came to using that army in Vietnam.[28]

John Gardner was a decision maker while secretary of HEW. His favorite decision tool was reorganization. He was not alone in this. During the 1960s, 270 federal offices were created, 109 were abolished, 61 were transferred, and 109 had their names changed. From 1953 to 1970 the Office of Education was reorganized six times and the Food and Drug Administration eight times.[29] Some of this reorganizing was a necessary adjustment to new legislation but much of it reflected the efforts of various secretaries to increase their power at the expense of the power of the bureau chiefs. Gardner, secretary from 1965 to 1968, had an additional reason for reorganizing: he believed, according to George Greenberg, that change, by challenging people, energized them.[30] Before coming to HEW Gardner had written books about the importance of "excellence" in societies and personalities and the need to stimulate people to higher accomplishments.[31] Many of his reorganizations, especially in the health field, had the opposite effect—they left some of his subordinates confused and demoralized and freed others to continue with business as usual.[32]

Joseph Califano, HEW secretary in the first part of the Carter administration, was also a decision maker. Like Gardner he reorganized, but unlike Gardner the reorganizations were not designed to stimulate creativity but rather to empower the secretary. He held the reins of power tightly and insisted on making key decisions personally.[33] Like his political mentor, Lyndon Johnson, Califano believed in an activist government and in activist leadership. And like Johnson he expected his subordinates to be on instant call and to serve unfailingly the political and media needs of their chief. Unlike many cabinet secretaries who are forced to accept whatever deputies the political staff of the White House sends over, Califano got his own people appointed before the Carter White House had settled in. Califano succeeded in making the decisions and putting his imprint on departmental policies—an (ill-fated) hospital cost-control plan, an anti-smoking campaign, and a response to the demands of the handicapped. It was a dazzling trapeze act without a safety net by an executive who insisted on being a leader, not merely a broker. There was an obvious risk; he might fall. Fall he did. Carter fired him.

The decision makers who succeed are those who manage to combine a clear vision of what they want the agency to do with the ability to communicate that vision effectively and to motivate the key civil servants to act on it. William Kristol called it "strategic governance."[34] He illustrated his argument with three Reagan appointees—William Bennett, chairman of the National Endowment for the Humanities (NEH) and later secretary of education and drug "czar"; James C. Miller III, chairman of the Federal Trade Commission; and Thomas Pauken, director of ACTION. Each was a success, where success means getting the bureaucracy to work effectively toward the executive's goals.

Bennett shifted the NEH away from funding what Kristol called "the shallowest and trendiest sorts of projects" toward supporting programs in the humanities and liberal arts as traditionally defined. Miller ended Pertschuk's emphasis at the FTC on kid-vid and got the commission to work on attacking restrictions (especially those created by government) on economic competition. Pauken converted ACTION from supporting what he regarded as New Left community-organizing projects to backing volunteer and self-help programs. Kristol contrasted these organizational successes with the failure of Anne Burford to redirect the Environmental Protection Agency (EPA). Burford knew she was supposed to change things but did not have a clear view of what direction the change was supposed to take, except that it should be vaguely "pro-business." As a consequence she was reduced to trying to "beat something with nothing"—defeat civil-service and interest group proposals by slowing down action, picking the least antibusiness proposals, and weakening the EPA's enforcement staff.

Kristol, himself a senior official in the Reagan administration's Department of Education, remarks that these successful examples of conservative executive strategies were carried out by individuals who felt they lacked any clear guidance or strong support from the White House. Conservatives who wish to change their agencies often have a harder time finding or creating a supportive constituency because most agency constituents are groups with a stake in the expansion of the agency. But the absence of a constituency need not always be fatal, as the case of budget-cutters makes clear.

BUDGET-CUTTERS

An executive who wishes to cut his or her agency's level of spending or otherwise force a retrenchment in agency activities may lack an organized constituency but possesses one great advantage: Congress has less influence on an agency that wants to shrink than on one that seeks to grow.

Caspar Weinberger tried to be a budget-cutter at HEW; Louis Johnson and Melvin Laird were budget-cutters at the Defense Department. Laird's case is especially instructive. When President Nixon made it clear that American involvement in the war in Vietnam was going to end and military spending would have to be cut, he turned to an experienced member of Congress to become secretary of defense. After Democratic Senator Henry Jackson declined the invitation, Republican Representative Melvin Laird took the job.

According to Richard Stubbing, a former defense budget analyst, Laird brought several valuable traits to the unenviable task of making an agency shrink—excellent personal relationships with members of Congress, carefully honed negotiating skills, a readiness to grant mission autonomy to the military services, and "an uncanny ability to mask his personal position on any issue."[35] He devoted endless hours to talking with people, restoring by his personal touch the goodwill between Defense civilians and military brass that had been destroyed during the McNamara years. As a result he was able to reduce the Pentagon's budget to a level even lower (in real terms) than it had been before the escalation of the Vietnam War. He minimized constituency pressure (in this case, admirals and generals privately going to Congress to plead their cases) by a combination of his personal standing with members of Congress and his willingness to let the brass make whatever weapons and personnel decisions they wanted within the confines of a strict budget ceiling. And then before things could turn sour he resigned after four years on the job. One admiring defense analyst summed it up this way: "He [Laird] achieved all his desired objectives and no one ever laid a glove on him."[36]

Many domestic programs have far more vigilant and politically influential constituency groups than do the armed forces. But even some of these can have their budgets cut, as Irene S. Rubin explains in her book, *Shrinking the Federal Government.*[37] She describes efforts during the Reagan years to cut spending in five federal agencies: the Bureau of Health Planning, the Employment and Training Administration (ETA), the Community Planning and Development Program (CPD), the Urban Mass Transportation Administration (UMTA), and the Office of Personnel Management (OPM). She found that both executive skill and constituency pressure made a difference.

Political executives committed to the Reagan philosophy were put in place in all five agencies and they proceeded to centralize decision making in their offices. Most accepted the White House mandate to cut expenditures, although two successfully resisted certain cuts. And contrary to what some critics of the civil service would predict, "there was little, if any, footdragging by career officials in the implementation of policy."[38] Some career officials quit because they disliked the new policies; a union tried to block a cut in personnel; and in one agency some employees complained to the department inspector general about alleged wrongdoing by political executives. But in general the civil servants followed orders.

Cuts were most effectively resisted in the case of those agencies that had strong clientele groups. Cities and private interests that benefited from urban development and mass transit grants were able to mobilize congressional allies to block some of the cuts in the CPD and UMTA; by contrast, OPM and the Bureau of Health Planning had no clientele group and ETA had alienated its own, and so these cuts stood.[39] Retrenchment is not costless. Political capital must be expended and sometimes the effect on employee morale is devastating. But contrary to the view of those who believe government agencies inevitably grow, cuts can be made.

NEGOTIATORS

Many if not most political executives are not preoccupied with raising or cutting budgets or with making mission-altering decisions. Instead they, like most private executives, seek to maintain their organizations by negotiating with various internal and external constituencies to reduce stress and uncertainty, enhance organizational health, and cope with a few critical problems. When John Dunlop was secretary of labor in the Ford administration he told an interviewer what many other political executives learn: a large government agency is like a "vast glacier" that can be neither melted nor redirected, but only "hacked at."

What Dunlop decided to hack at were two maintenance issues and three policy problems. The maintenance issues involved rebuilding support for the Department of Labor among two key constituencies, labor and business, and reducing the control over the department exercised by the staff of the Senate Labor Committee. Labor support had been weakened during the Nixon administration; restoring it required renewing departmental relations with AFL-CIO president George Meaney. Business support had rarely existed; instead, the department and industry typically were in an adversarial relationship. To change that Dunlop appointed a Republican business leader as undersecretary, put him in charge of departmental management, and created a business advisory council from which

Dunlop solicited opinions on labor issues. Senate committee control to some degree was inevitable, but Dunlop's detailed knowledge of labor-management relations (he had taught the subject at Harvard and had years of experience as a mediator) gave him an advantage in coping with congressional pressures not enjoyed by many less experienced cabinet officers.

The key policy problems involved the management of the Occupational Safety and Health Administration (OSHA), the implementation of a new pension law, and finding a solution to a business-labor quarrel over a bill that would allow unions to picket an entire construction site if any single contractor on that site was the object of a strike.

OSHA was a bone of contention between labor (that thought it too timid) and business (that thought it too intrusive and unreasonable); President Ford often complained about it. Dunlop tried to satisfy labor by helping arrange the appointment of a vigorous head of OSHA and to satisfy business by supporting a bill that would require OSHA to give on-site advice to firms in advance of citing them for violations (the bill failed). The new pension law, passed in 1974, created federal standards for private pension plans. It was a long, immensely complex statute that gave administrative responsibility to the Department of Justice as well as to the Department of Labor. Dunlop soon found himself in endless conferences trying to clarify the law's intent, approve regulations that would implement it, and settle the jurisdictional dispute between Justice and Labor. The common-site picketing law was passed by Congress over business objections after more than two decades of labor lobbying. Dunlop thought he had received private assurances from President Ford that he would sign the bill, but intense political pressure (including business threats to back Ronald Reagan's challenge to Ford in the 1976 presidential primaries) led Ford to veto it. Feeling that his credibility with labor was at an end, Dunlop resigned.

Dunlop was a savvy negotiator whose Washington career was typical of what most political executives experience: it was short, selective, and pressure-laden. Dunlop could take on only a few of the tasks that many outsiders might think a cabinet secretary who was really running his department would worry about. He did little about the Job Corps (that was supposed to be training the hard-core unemployed), the Employment and Training Administration, the Wage and Hour Division, or the Office of Federal Contracts Compliance (leading some feminist groups to complain that he was not interested in civil rights). Dunlop acknowledged that all of these bureaus had problems and needed help, but he had only so much time and political capital. He used almost the same words as Secretary of the Treasury Blumenthal: "You have to decide where to put your energies."[40]

Conclusions

Executives rarely put those energies into administrative matters because they tend to be judged not by whether their agency is well-run but by whether the policies with which they are identified seem to succeed or fail. Dunlop was judged by the fate of the common-site picketing bill, Blumenthal by the movement of interest rates and the value of the dollar. There are few rewards for being known as a good manager. Thus, to repeat the point with which this chapter began, in politics the maintenance of the *executive* is different from the maintenance of the *organization*. Under these circumstances what is surprising is that top government executives spend any time at all on managing their departments.

A few gifted political executives are able to fuse the maintenance of their own position with that of their organization's. Because of their exceptional talents combined with their good fortune in holding office at a time when their political environment is unusually malleable, these individuals manage to make that environment so supportive that in effect it becomes a universal constituency. Hyman Rickover, J. Edgar Hoover, and Robert Moses (the master highway builder of New York) were able to achieve this feat by means set forth in Eugene Lewis's book on public entrepreneurship.[41] Their ability to acquire autonomy for their agencies has few parallels: they fashioned around themselves a kind of "apolitical shield"[42] that enabled them to advance their programs while running their agencies.

The executives that not only maintain their organizations but transform them do more than merely acquire constituency support; they project a compelling vision of the tasks, culture, and importance of their agencies. The greatest executives infuse their organizations with value and convince others that this value is not merely useful to the bureau but essential to the polity.

CHAPTER 12

Innovation

ON AT LEAST FOUR OCCASIONS during the forty years following the end of World War II the United States Army made major changes in its war-fighting doctrine. The first of these, completed in 1958, involved redesigning the structure of its combat divisions. The traditional structure developed during the war in Europe deployed 17,460 troops organized into three regiments (or brigades); each regiment in turn was organized into battalions. The division had a large number of vehicles (tanks and trucks) and its own antiaircraft forces. Organized in this way, a division could bring centrally controlled, massive firepower to bear on the enemy.

The new structure, called the "pentomic" division, was very different. It was smaller (13,748 men) and organized into five battle groups rather than three regiments; there were no battalion commanders. The number of vehicles was reduced and the division was stripped of its own antiaircraft artillery. The new form was designed to facilitate the decentralized and dispersed defense of an area by semiautonomous units that could fight more or less independently of each other. The avowed rationale for the reorganization and the tactical doctrine on which it was based was that the introduction of atomic weapons into the battlefield made the old structure outmoded; a massed force defending a defined geographic area would be a sitting duck for a nuclear attack. Skeptics who think that armies always prepare for the last war were confounded by the speed with which the army converted all fifteen of its divisions into the new pentomic form.

Within a few years, however, army leaders had become dissatisfied with the pentomic structure. A shortage of communications equipment made controlling the new-style division difficult under the best of circumstances and almost impossible in practice. The cutback in vehicles made it hard to deploy the battle groups. And so in the early 1960s a new doctrine was approved: the Reorganization Objectives Army Division (ROAD). ROAD restored the earlier emphasis on mechanization and the earlier structure of three brigades as opposed to five battle groups.

In the early 1970s the army altered its doctrine once again. The problem addressed but not solved by the pentomic division still existed: How can one defend against a much larger, more heavily armed force? And new problems had become evident. Many officers had become demoralized by the Vietnam War and by the tendency for generals hovering overhead in helicopters to issue commands to infantrymen slogging through the forests below. The Arab-Israeli war of 1973 revealed the destructive power of precision weapons such as antitank and antiaircraft missiles. The new doctrine, called Active Defense, tried to address these issues by doctrinal rather than by structural change. The new doctrine instructed army commanders to give increased emphasis to defense (traditionally the army had always taught the superiority of offensive maneuvers) and encouraged commanders to rely on rapid mobility to engage attacking forces. Moreover, the doctrine specified in considerable detail what each command level was supposed to do.

Active Defense proved to be as controversial as the pentomic division. The new defensive doctrine required a degree of coordination that proved hard to achieve in training and that might prove impossible to attain in battle. Moreover, many military and civilian critics felt that the doctrine was based on unrealistic assumptions about Soviet military tactics. If the Soviets did not rely on the massive armored attacks that they employed in World War II but instead used flexible, probing attacks, then the thin, mobile defense defined by the new American doctrine might be overwhelmed. And so a fourth round of change began.

The result was a new doctrine called AirLand Battle, promulgated in a new field manual issued in the early 1980s. AirLand Battle restored the emphasis on offensive tactics by calling on American forces to respond to an attack by making counterstrikes deep behind the enemy's lines. This philosophy of the deep attack was aimed at disrupting the ability of Soviet forces to reinforce their first-wave forces. For it to work the army would need to have the ability to find and destroy enemy tanks while they were still miles behind the fighting front, and that in turn meant that highly sophisticated radars, computers, and missiles would have to be acquired. Until the new equipment could be produced, the doctrine would require an unprecedented level of cooperation between the army and the air force. Under these circumstances it is likely that more doctrinal and organizational changes will appear.

At one level, the history of the United States Army since World War II provides little support for the common view that bureaucracies never change. At the level of doctrine, and to some degree of organization, there has been little *but* change since 1945. And the modern period is not unique in this regard. Russell Weigley, in his history of the army, recounts many examples of reorganization as the size and mission of the army altered.[1]

But at a deeper level, very little changed. As Kevin Sheehan makes clear in his study of these four army doctrinal innovations, the army limited its innovations to thinking about better ways to counter a Soviet invasion of Western Europe. Every alteration in doctrine and structure was based on the assumption that the war for which the army should prepare itself was a conventional war on the plains of Germany. But during this period there was no such war. Instead the army found itself fighting in Korea, Vietnam, the Dominican Republic, and Grenada, and threatened with the prospect of having to fight in the Middle East and Central America. None of these *actual* or *likely* wars produced the same degree of rethinking and experimentation that was induced by the *possibility* of a war in Europe.[2] As a result, changes in the army were essentially limited to trying to find ways to take advantage of new technological developments in the kind of weaponry that either it or its adversary might employ in Bavaria.[3]

Before 1930, the United States Marine Corps was a small service that in peacetime guarded the brigs on navy ships and the doors to U.S. embassies and in wartime occupied various Central American nations for brief periods while Washington politicians tried to figure out what to do with places they liked to call "banana republics." The marines had indeed fought "from the halls of Montezuma to the shores of Tripoli," but there was little in the history of these backwater wars that would have led an outsider to predict the extraordinary change that the corps was about to undergo. By 1940 it had been utterly transformed, from a conventional naval infantry force into one able to wage amphibious warfare against bitterly defended Pacific islands. J. F. C. Fuller was later to write that these amphibious operations were "the most far reaching tactical innovation of the war."[4]

To understand the magnitude of the change one has to understand the difference between occupying Nicaragua in 1912 and occupying Iwo Jima in 1945. In the first case a few companies of marines stepped off ships tied up to serviceable docks, occupied the capital against little or no resistance, and raised the flag. In the second case several divisions of marines stormed a fiercely defended beach, launched carefully coordinated air and artillery strikes against dug-in Japanese troops, and waged hand-to-hand combat for weeks. As Steven Rosen notes in his illuminating history of this transformation, the hazards that had to be overcome were as much moral as they were technical: creating an organization that could train and equip men who were able and willing to wade ashore in the teeth of murderous fire without the advantage of surprise or concealment.[5] To support them one had to design and acquire specialized landing craft and create a Marine Air Corps. There were many navy and marine officers who did not believe it could be done and who opposed the effort.

There were good arguments made as early as 1905 for having such a force. If the navy were to operate in the Pacific it would have to have forward bases. It could not assume that in wartime those necessary bases would be available for hire; therefore a force would have to be created that could seize them. But between 1905 and the early 1930s nothing happened to induce the corps to abandon its existing set of tasks and adopt a new and different one. Given the oft-remarked inertia of organizations there is every reason to have expected that when war broke out against Japan the marines would have been utterly unprepared to conduct the kind of amphibious warfare that in retrospect proved to have been essential to victory.

The explanations Rosen gives for the change in the corps do not provide us with any simple or neat theory of innovation generally. But they have the advantage of being true. A few intellectual leaders within the corps made the argument for change. They found support from a key executive, Marine Commandant John Russell. The executive in turn created two important assets for the advocates of the new mission—a degree of organizational autonomy (in the form of the newly organized Fleet Marine Force) and a set of incentives (in the form of new opportunities for promotions). With energetic young officers protected by a top executive and mobilized by an attractive career path things began to happen—training manuals were written, exercises conducted, and equipment designed. By 1933–34 the corps was on its way to being transformed; by 1941, when the war began, it was ready to put its new doctrine to the test.[6]

Innovation and Tasks

We ought not to be surprised that organizations resist innovation. They are supposed to resist it. The reason an organization is created is in large part to replace the uncertain expectations and haphazard activities of voluntary endeavors with the stability and routine of organized relationships. The standard operating procedure (SOP) is not the enemy of organization; it is the essence of organization.[7] Stability and routine are especially important in government agencies where demands for equity (or at least the appearance of equity) are easily enforced. When, as in the United States, constituency groups can rather easily demand explanations for why case B was not treated in the same way as case A, there naturally will be a strong tendency to avoid any course of action that might set a controversial precedent. Thus the well-known bureaucratic adage: "Never do anything for the first time." Resistance to innovation is all the stronger when the members of the organization are endowed with a strong sense of mission that enjoys substantial support from political superiors who supply money and authority to the agency.

For the purposes of this discussion what I mean by innovation is not any new program or technology, but only those that involve the performance of new tasks or a significant alteration in the way in which existing tasks are performed. Organizations will readily accept (or at least not bitterly resist) inventions that facilitate the performance of existing tasks in a way consistent with existing managerial arrangements. Armies did not resist substituting trucks for horse-drawn carts. It is striking, however, how many technical inventions whose value seems self-evident to an outsider are resisted to varying degrees because their use changes operator tasks and managerial controls. When breech-loading rifles and machine guns became available, they dramatically increased the firepower of armies. But the improved firepower forced commanders either to disperse their infantry on the battlefield or to hide them in trenches and bunkers. The former response required decentralizing the command system, the latter permitted command to remain centralized. As we saw in chapter 2, the Prussian (and later German) army was more prepared to adopt the decentralized approach than the French or British. World War II vindicated the German response.[8]

This bias toward maintaining existing task definitions often leads bureaucracies to adopt new technologies without understanding their significance. The tank made its appearance in World War I. Armies did not ignore this machine, they purchased it in large numbers—but as a more efficient way of performing a traditional task, that of cavalry scouting. The true innovation occurred when some armies (but not most) saw that the tank was not a mechanical horse but the means for a wholly new way of conducting battles. In Europe, the Germans first saw this and created the Panzer division and the *blitzkrieg* doctrine. Similarly, many navies purchased airplanes before World War II but most viewed them simply as an improved means of reconnaissance. Thus, the first naval planes were launched by catapults from battleships in order to extend the vision of the battleship's captain. The organizational innovation occurred when aviation was recognized as a new form of naval warfare and the aircraft were massed on carriers deployed in fast-moving task forces.

Changes that are consistent with existing task definitions will be accepted; those that require a redefinition of those tasks will be resisted. This fact helps us understand the changes in the United States Army's doctrine after World War II. Successfully waging land warfare in Europe in 1944–45 was the great accomplishment of the army and the source of the rank and reputation of most of its leaders. The American government's commitment to NATO entailed a promise to maintain an army in Germany. That commitment in turn guaranteed to the army a share of the military budget. Moreover, that commitment offered a role for all branches of the army—infantry, armor, artillery, and aviation. The Eurocentric focus of the army thus satisfied several organizational needs for money, political backing, the continuation of tasks and roles defined by the battles of World War II, and for minimizing conflict among the service branches. By contrast, anyone who proposed changing the structure or doctrine of the army to meet the needs of low-intensity or mid-intensity warfare in Central America, the Middle East, or Southeast Asia would threaten many of these organizational needs: Unable to point to any political commitment equivalent to the NATO membership, he or she would have to sell the ideas to generals who for the most part had not achieved their positions by fighting unconventional wars in Third World nations, and would have to make hard choices among the branches—there is little need for big tanks in the Honduran jungles or for heavy artillery in the streets of Grenada.

The organizational bias in favor of changes consistent with existing tasks and constituencies makes all the more remarkable the success of young marine officers in creating the Fleet Marine Force (and the equally remarkable success of naval aviators in creating the carrier task force). Later we shall take a closer look at how such unlikely, rare victories are won.

The tendency to resist innovations that alter tasks is not limited to the military or even to government agencies. Take the computer. Its use spread quickly in some firms and was resisted in others. Without a close understanding of the core tasks of these organizations it is impossible to explain why some bought early and others late. When the core task was writing, filing, or calculating, the computer was seen as faster and more efficient, and so it was adopted. It was an improvement rather than an innovation (as the word is used here). For example, department stores were quick to acquire computers to make their accounting programs more efficient, but slow to make extensive use of computers for inventory control. The reason, as Harvey Sapolsky has shown, is that inventory control touches on the core task in a department store, that of the buyer: the person in charge of a line of goods (sportswear, budget dresses, men's furnishings) who in exchange for a share of the profits takes responsibility for buying, displaying, and selling that line. The use of a computer to manage inventory threatened to alter the role of buyer by taking decisions (over what and how much to buy) out of the hands of the buyer, who traditionally was a nearly autonomous businessperson, and placing them in the hands of central managers and staff officers.[9] In time the computer advocates won out and the power of the buyers was diminished.

Understanding that it is the way core tasks are defined that determines how a proposed change will be received helps put into perspective the frequent claim that government agencies, especially military ones, are excessively wedded to new technology. James Fallows has made this charge about military procurement, as has Ralph Lapp.[10] Charles Wolf, Jr., advances this argument in his otherwise excellent study of the criteria one should employ in choosing between markets and governments as ways of delivering services.[11] He claims that to a bureaucracy, "new and complex is better." That is true only when the new, sophisticated bit of technology is consistent with existing tasks. (The air force always wants the best new airplane even when an unsophisticated plane might do better, as when it resisted the use of slow, propeller-driven planes to serve as gunships in Vietnam.) But if the new technology requires a redefinition of core tasks it will be resisted, as Paul Stockton has shown in his study of how the American military has approached the development of new strategic weaponry.[12]

Schools are an especially revealing case of the circumstances under which innovation occurs and endures. In their review of educational "reforms" undertaken during the last fifty years, Michael Kirst and Gail Meister note that certain changes were readily accepted and have lasted: vocational education, drivers' education, remedial reading courses, health education, the use of teacher aides, school lunch programs, guidance counseling, the installation of movable desks, and special classes for students with limited English or with learning problems. By contrast, other changes either never took hold or lasted but a short time: team teaching, individualized instruction, programmed instruction with teaching machines, the "new math" curriculum, and using broadcast television in the classrooms.[13]

The reader who has understood why the military accepts or resists certain changes should have no trouble in explaining why public schools have accepted or resisted certain changes. Educational changes have endured when they have not altered the core tasks of the classroom teacher and have faltered or disappeared when they have required a major change in those core tasks. Schools have accepted changes that were "add-ons," especially if they were accompanied by increased levels of funding and had the backing of influential constituencies. Classroom teachers did not have to change what they were doing when a school decided to add a drivers' education course, hire a guidance counselor, serve school lunches, or set up new classes to help pupils with reading or learning difficulties. They did have to change what they were doing when they were told to teach math in a new way, teach together with another instructor, use computers, or provide individualized instruction.[14]

True innovation—that is, redefining core tasks—may be especially difficult in schools because teaching cannot be observed easily nor its effects readily measured. It was for these reasons that in chapter 8 schools are referred to as coping organizations. But some aspects of the work of the classroom teacher can be monitored, and when strong constituencies wish to alter that aspect of teaching they can succeed. For example, the imposition on schools of procedures for defining and enforcing certain student rights (having to do with such matters as discipline) was relatively successful, not because teachers welcomed the change (they often resisted it) but because strong outside groups insisted on it and compliance with it could be monitored.

Government agencies change all the time, but the most common changes are add-ons: a new program is added on to existing tasks without changing the core tasks or altering the organizational culture. The State Department accepted the job of improving security in American embassies by adding on a unit designed to do this; as we saw in chapter 6, the add-on did not significantly change the way foreign service officers behaved (and thus did not do much to improve embassy security). The old Federal Bureau of Narcotics, when it was reorganized into the Bureau of Narcotics and Dangerous Drugs, added to its core tasks (arresting heroin traffickers) the new task of controlling the distribution of legal but abusable drugs (such as amphetamines). But instead of altering the daily work of narcotics agents, the new tasks were given to a new subunit staffed by new personnel. The organization's culture remained that of the narcotics agent; the new task (often referred to derisively as controlling "kiddie drugs") was left to employees who were assigned a lower status and (for a long time) minimal promotion opportunities.[15] When President John F. Kennedy called for an improvement in the army's ability to fight guerrilla wars, the task was given (reluctantly) to a new "special forces" unit that, owing to strong leadership and presidential support, acquired its own sense of mission but that for many years was treated as a peripheral (and trivial) activity in the army as a whole.

Real innovations are those that alter core tasks; most changes add to or alter peripheral tasks. These peripheral changes often are a response to a demand in the agency's environment. Many observers have noted that most educational changes (they always seem to be called "reforms" without regard to whether in fact they make things better) were forced on the schools by the political system. Many important changes in the military also were reactions to political demands: Some key air force generals were at first reluctant to develop the intercontinental missile;[16] the navy for a long time was unsure about the desirability of a submarine-launched missile program;[17] the army bowed to presidential demands for a counterinsurgency unit. Outside forces—academic scientists, industrial engineers, civilian theorists, members of Congress, and presidential aides—all helped induce the military to embrace programs that initially seemed irrelevant to (or at odds with) their core tasks.

Sometimes entrepreneurs within an agency bring about the peripheral changes. In many cases their success depends on their ability to persuade others that the changes *are* peripheral and threaten no core interests. Despite the myths about General Billy Mitchell shaming the navy into acknowledging the military potential of the airplane, the navy had taken a keen interest in aviation from the very first.[18] At issue was the role the airplane was to play. The organizational culture of the navy—the black-shoe, battleship navy—was very much inclined to view the airplane as a scout. The first chief of the Bureau of Aeronautics, Rear Admiral William Moffett, took pains not to contradict this view. As a former battleship commander he had the credentials that line naval officers would respect. He endorsed the idea of the airplane as a scout for the battleship, suggesting only that this scouting function might be served more efficiently if the planes were on aircraft carriers that would accompany the battleship. But quietly, if not secretly, Moffett was promoting the idea of naval aviation as a separate striking force operating independently of battleships. He did this in confidential memos, by getting contracts for high-speed carriers approved, and by intervening in the promotion process to insure that a lot of aviators rose in rank. (By 1926 there were already four admirals, two captains, and sixty-three commanders who were aviators.[19]) So successful was he that a full year before Pearl Harbor ten fast carriers were under construction.

Had it not been for Pearl Harbor, however, the carrier task force might never have become the core of the surface navy. But after December 7, 1941, there was no alternative; five American battleships were sunk or put out of action. To fight a war in the Pacific it now would be carriers or nothing.[20]

Peripheral changes often can be easily reversed. This helps explain an otherwise puzzling aspect of arms-control negotiations. When President Reagan was negotiating a treaty with the Soviet Union calling for a reduction in intermediate-range nuclear forces (INF) in Europe, the Soviets demanded that all ground-launched cruise missiles (GLCM) be banned from Europe. These missiles are extremely accurate, low-flying, guided weapons that can carry either conventional or nuclear warheads. It is almost impossible to tell the difference between a nuclear and a non-nuclear GLCM. Many strategists believe that non-nuclear GLCMs are vital to the defense of Europe, since they offer a way of counterattacking against Soviet headquarters units and massed armor well behind the front line, all without risking the lives of American pilots. But when the Joint Chiefs of Staff were asked their views on GLCMs they indicated they were not opposed to a treaty provision banning them. Why did the brass surrender a weapon the politicians had spent so much time persuading the Europeans to accept? The answer, I conjecture, is that GLCMs were not seen by any military service as part of its core mission—they were neither aircraft to the air force, ships to the navy, nor tanks to the army.

Executives and Innovation

Whether changes are core or peripheral, externally imposed or internally generated, understanding why they occur at all requires one to understand the behavior of the agency executive. As persons responsible for maintaining the organization it is executives who identify the external pressures to which the agency must react. As individuals who must balance competing interests inside the agency it is they who must decide whether to protect or to ignore managers who wish to promote changes. Almost every important study of bureaucratic innovation points to the great importance of executives in explaining change.[21] For example, Jerald Hage and Robert Dewar studied changes that occurred in sixteen social welfare agencies in a midwestern city and found that the beliefs of the top executives were better predictors of the change than any structural features of the organizations.[22] If John Russell had not been commandant of the Marine Corps or William Moffett had not been chief of the Bureau of Aeronautics, the Fleet Marine Force and carrier-based naval aviation would not have emerged when and as they did.

It is for this reason, I think, that little progress has been made in developing theories of innovation. Not only do innovations differ so greatly in character that trying to find one theory to explain them all is like trying to find one medical theory to explain all diseases, but innovations are so heavily dependent on executive interests and beliefs as to make the chance appearance of a change-oriented personality enormously important in explaining change. It is not easy to build a useful social science theory out of "chance appearances."

In this regard the study of innovation in government agencies is not very different from its study in business firms. In a purely competitive marketplace there would never be any entrepreneurship because anybody producing a better product would immediately attract competitors who would drive the price down (and thus the entrepreneur's profits), possibly to the point where the entrepreneur's earnings from his or her new venture would be zero. Yet new firms and new products are created. The people who create them are willing to run greater than ordinary risks. Predicting who they will be is not easy; so far it has turned out to be impossible.

Executives are important but also can be perverse. Innovation is not inevitably good; there are at least as many bad changes as good. And government agencies are especially vulnerable to bad changes because, absent a market that would impose a fitness test on any organizational change, a changed public bureaucracy can persist in doing the wrong thing for years. The Ford Motor Company should not have made the Edsel, but if the government had owned Ford it would still be making Edsels.

Government executives are particularly prone to adopt one kind of often ill-advised change—those that appear to enhance their own power. Again, the military is rich with examples. The advent of first the telegraph, then the telephone, the radio, computers, and finally the helicopter gave to military commanders an increasing ability to receive and transmit orders and in the case of the helicopter to look down directly onto the battlefield. But as Martin Creveld has shown in his penetrating look at the role of command in war, improvements in communications tend to be used by high-level commanders to reduce the initiative and discretion of lower-level commanders, often with disastrous results. Creveld is quite blunt about the matter: "those armies have been most successful which did not turn their troops into automatons, did not attempt to control everything from the top, and allowed subordinate commanders considerable latitude."[23] The examples that support his conclusion include the Roman legions, Napoleon's marshals, Moltke's army commanders, Ludendorff's storm detachments in 1914, and Guederian's panzer corps in 1940.

Uncertainty, as Jonathan Bendor has written, is to organizations what original sin is to individuals—they are born into it.[24] Government organizations are steeped in uncertainty because it is so hard to know what might produce success or even what constitutes success. Executives and higher-level managers have an understandable urge to reduce that uncertainty. They also have a less understandable belief that more information means less uncertainty. That may be true if what they obtain by sophisticated communications and computation equipment is actually information—that is, a full, accurate, and properly nuanced body of knowledge about important matters. Often what they get is instead a torrent of incomplete facts, opinions, guesses, and self-serving statements about distant events.

The reason is not simply the limitations in information-gathering and -transmitting processes. It is also that the very creation of such processes alters the incentives operating on subordinates. These include the following:

1. If higher authority can be sent a message about a decision, then higher authority will be sent a message asking it to make the decision.
2. If higher authority can hear a lot, then higher authority will be told what it wants to hear.
3. Since processing information requires the creation of specialized bureaus, then these units will demand more and more information as a way of justifying their existence.

A good example of all of these incentives at work can be found in the consequences for some armies of the invention of the railroad and the telegraph. Now troop movement could be centrally planned (only headquarters could coordinate all the complex railroad timetables). Now army commanders could spend more time communicating with headquarters (because the telegraph and telephone lines running to the rear were likely to be intact) than with the troops at the front (where communication lines were often broken). As a result, commanders found it easier to yield to the temptation to adopt a headquarters perspective on the battle (which often was hopelessly distorted) than to take a fighting-front view of the battle. The reliance on railroads and telegraphs enhanced the power of engineering units at headquarters; soon the direction of the war itself came to be seen as an engineering matter only.[25] Creveld quotes an Austrian officer who wrote in 1861 that as a result of better communications a commander now "has two enemies to defeat, one in front and another in the rear."[26]

This makes the German army of 1940 all the more remarkable; it embraced those technologies (the tank, the dive bomber, the radio) that enhanced its war-fighting powers but did not use the radio and the telephone to shift discretion upward, at least on the French front in May 1940. But then Hitler and his generals decided to run the rest of the war from Berlin. Given their goals it was not a wise decision.

It is not simply that some innovations are perverse; it is also the case that any top-down change is risky. When government executives are the source of a change, they are likely to overestimate its benefits and underestimate its costs. This is true not only because executives lack the detailed and specialized knowledge possessed by operators and lower-level managers, but also because of the incentives operating on the executives. Often they are drawn from outside the agency to serve for a brief period. Their rewards come not from the agency but from what outsiders (peers, the media, Congress) think of them. A "go-getter" who "makes a difference" and does not "go native" usually wins more praise than someone who is cautious and slow-moving.

Studies of local government officials confirm this. R. O. Carlson was interested in explaining why some school systems attempt to be more innovative than others.[27] One important reason is the way in which school executives are recruited. Those brought in from outside the system proposed more changes than those who were promoted from within. The reason seems clear: the outsiders got many of their rewards from professional peers elsewhere in the country, whereas the insiders (who had spent their whole lives in the system they now administered) got their rewards from the job itself. The outsiders often were chosen because of the high opinion other outsiders had of them, and even if they failed in their new job they might expect to go on to even better jobs elsewhere, provided only that they failed for the right reason—that is, failed while striving to attain some goal that was approved of by their profession. For such executives, nothing succeeds like failure.

The same pattern has been observed among city managers. The more professional their orientation (that is, the more they had work and educational experiences outside the city now employing them), the more likely they were to take such controversial steps as fluoridating the city's water supply by administrative action[28] or hiring a change-oriented, "legalistic" chief of police.[29]

Sometimes being bold about top-down innovations is desirable, since operators not only have detailed knowledge, they have cultural and mission-oriented biases. Had they been listened to, battleship admirals might well have blocked the creation of a carrier navy until it was too late. Closing down hideously abusive juvenile reformatories might never have occurred if strong-willed executives had not imposed these changes.[30] Only an FBI director as strong as Clarence Kelley was able to override the objections of middle-level managers and shift the thrust of FBI investigative work away from minor auto theft cases and toward major criminal conspiracies.[31]

Moreover, there are kinds of innovations that almost no subordinate will support. If an executive sees that an agency ought to be abolished, he or she is not likely to find many supporters among the rank and file, even though in this case *how* it is abolished or drastically reduced in size ought to be guided by the knowledge that only operators possess. (One of the many deficiencies of the social-science study of innovation is that so little of it focuses on ending an organization, possibly because to many social scientists "innovativeness" is a characteristic of persons who are sensitive and progressive whereas "abolition" is the work of those who are mean-spirited and reactionary.)

When should executives defer to subordinates and when should they overrule them? If this were a book about how to run an agency, the answer would be: "It all depends. Use good judgment." Not very helpful comments. Moreover, the organizational arrangements that encourage members to propose an innovation often are different from those that make it easy to implement one, once proposed. An agency that wants its managers and operators to suggest new ways of doing their tasks will be open, collegial, and supportive; an agency that wishes to implement an innovation over the opposition of some of its members often needs to concentrate power in the hands of the boss sufficient to permit him or her to ignore (or even dismiss) opponents.

The FBI under J. Edgar Hoover was not exactly a graduate-school seminar; agents who made suggestions for new ways of doing things ran the risk of finding their next duty assignment in Butte, Montana. But if a suggestion caught the fancy of Hoover, there was no doubt that it would be implemented. By contrast, managing a state university *is* like presiding over an endless seminar that generates torrents of ideas, any one of which has almost no chance of being adopted because no one has the authority to carry it out. Most government agencies are somewhere in between the old FBI and a state university, but in terms of the internal diffusion of authority they are probably closer to the university than to the FBI.

However authority is distributed, the executive who wishes to make changes has to create incentives for subordinates to think about, propose, and help refine such changes, and this means convincing them that if they join the innovative efforts of a (usually) short-term executive, their careers will not be blighted if the innovation fails or the executive departs before it is implemented. Admiral Moffett did this in the navy; so did Commandant Russell in the Marine Corps and Clarence Kelley in the FBI.

To implement a proposed change often requires either creating a specialized subunit that will take on the new tasks (such as the Bureau of Aeronautics in the navy) or if the task cannot be confined to a subunit, retraining or replacing subordinates who oppose the change. Caspar Weinberger did this at the Federal Trade Commission where, in order to instill a new sense of vigor and commitment to consumer protection, he replaced eighteen of the thirty-one top staff members and about two hundred of the nearly six hundred staff attorneys.[32] Weinberger and his successors as FTC chairman brought in new people specially recruited because they supported a new way of defining the agency's core tasks (namely, to attack deceptive advertising and monopolistic structures rather than to prosecute small-scale price-fixing cases). At the FBI, Kelley and his successor, William Webster, were able to implement many changes because the retirement laws made it attractive for many FBI veterans to leave the bureau at age fifty, thereby creating many vacancies in middle management into which younger agents could be appointed who shared the executives' goals.

None of this implies that agency members always oppose innovations and therefore must be bypassed, dismissed, or re-educated. The reaction of operators to a proposed change will be governed by the incentives to which they respond; in government agencies that are limited in their ability to use money as a reward, one important set of incentives is that derived from the way tasks are defined. Tasks that are familiar, easy, professionally rewarded, or well adapted to the circumstances in which operators find themselves will be preferred because performing them is less costly than undertaking tasks that are new, difficult, or professionally unrewarded or that place the operator in conflict with his or her environment.

The Federal Trade Commission not only changed when Weinberger and other chairmen replaced many of its key members, but it continued to change because of the incentives operating on the new members. Many of them were recruited from the ranks of "Chicago School" economists and lawyers (see chapter 4); their own predispositions and their prospects for later academic recognition were served by pressing internally for actions consistent with the free-market approach advocated by James Miller and other leaders.

Sometimes an agency is given, by law or the preferences of the founding executive, a set of tasks that are less rewarding (or more costly) than an alternative available to the operators. In this case, the operators *will* press for change, or at least not resist it.

A good example, noted by Jerry Mashaw and David Harfst, is the transformation that occurred in the National Highway Traffic Safety Administration (NHTSA). We have already seen (chapter 4) how the professional orientation of the engineers led NHTSA to emphasize redesigning the automobile over improving the driver. But there are two ways of redesigning the car: one is to promulgate rules that specify in advance how a car should be built; the other is to recall cars proven to have a design defect. Initially (from 1966 to about 1974), NHTSA adopted the rule-promulgation approach. But promulgating rules is a costly task: the rules are complex documents that must survive elaborate review processes within the agency and close scrutiny by the courts.* Recalling defective cars, by contrast, is much easier; a car is marketed, defects appear, evidence is gathered to substantiate the existence of the defect, and the manufacturer is ordered to recall and repair the defect. As Mashaw and Harfst put it, NHTSA changed because of the nature of its tasks: "adopting rules is difficult; recalling 'defective' automobiles is easy."[33]

The longer an agency exists the more likely that its core tasks will be defined in ways that minimize the costs to the operators performing them, and thus in ways that maximize the costs of changing them. The most dramatic and revealing stories of bureaucratic innovation are therefore found in organizations—the navy, the Marine Corps, the FBI—that have acquired settled habits and comfortable routines. Innovation in these cases requires an exercise of judgment, personal skill, and misdirection, qualities that are rare among government executives. And so innovation is rare.

*NHTSA lost six of the twelve rule-making cases that the courts decided on the merits; by contrast, it suffered only one defeat in litigation from an auto recall order. Jerry L. Mashaw and David L. Harfst, "Regulation and Legal Culture: The Case of Motor Vehicle Safety," *Yale Journal of Regulation* 4 (1987): 273–74.

PART V

CONTEXT

CHAPTER 13

Congress

NO POLITICIAN ever lost votes by denouncing the bureaucracy. Jimmy Carter and Gerald Ford could agree on little else during their 1976 presidential contest than that "the bureaucracy" was a mess. Senator Edward M. Kennedy rarely has passed up a chance to attack the Food and Drug Administration for the way it endangers public health by "rushing" new drugs into the market. Members of the House of Representatives were outraged at the Federal Trade Commission's proposal to restrict television advertisements aimed at children and regulate used-car dealers and funeral parlors. When the National Highway Traffic Safety Administration ordered auto manufacturers to install seat belts that had to be fastened before the car could be started, the public and Congress erupted in anger. Senator Malcolm Wallop ran for office by towing an outdoor portable toilet around his state of Wyoming, ridiculing the officials of the Occupational Safety and Health Administration who, he charged, had ordered ranchers to use them for their field hands. The public schools are raked over the coals regularly by legislators furious at educators' apparent unwillingness to do more to increase pupil achievement and reduce school-yard violence. There is scarcely a city council member in the country who has not at one time or another denounced the local police department for being slow to respond to citizen calls for help. If ever the weapons procurement system used by the Pentagon has been praised by a member of Congress, history has failed to record the fact. These and countless other horror stories readily come to mind as evidence that in this country we confront a "runaway bureaucracy" indifferent to the wishes of its political superiors.

People angry about an out-of-control bureaucracy might be equally angry at the many scholars who argue that far from being runaway, government agencies in this country are under the control of the very legislators who so regularly denounce them. Virtually every political scientist who has studied the matter agrees that Congress possesses, in Herbert Kaufman's words, an "awesome arsenal" of weapons that it can use against agencies: legislation, appropriations, hearings, investigations, personal interventions, and "friendly advice" that is ignored at an executive's peril.[1] After closely studying six bureau* chiefs in Washington, Kaufman described their daily behavior in language that might just as easily be used to portray business executives worrying about fickle stockholders in an era of corporate takeovers:

> The chiefs were constantly looking over their shoulders . . . at the elements of the legislative establishment relevant to their agencies—taking stock of moods and attitudes, estimating reactions to contemplated decisions and actions, trying to prevent misunderstandings and avoidable conflicts, and planning responses when storm warnings appeared on the horizon. Not that cues and signals from Capitol Hill had to be ferreted out; the denizens of the Hill were not shy about issuing suggestions, requests, demands, directives, and pronouncements.[2]

But what does congressional control mean? One or more of three things: First, Congress controls the major day-to-day activities of an agency. Congress is the "principal," the agency is its "agent." If this is true it must mean that there are no other significant sources of influence. Second, Congress has the ability and inclination to intervene when it learns that an agency is sinning by omission or commission. But an agency would not sin if it were wholly the agent of Congress; thus this meaning of control presupposes that other forces—the president, the courts, interest groups, or the bureaucrats themselves—have influence on the agency independent of Congress. Third, Congress creates and maintains the structural conditions within which an agency operates.

The first kind of control can be likened to that which is supposed to operate between corporate executives and their boards of directors. The second can be compared to fire fighting; when an alarm goes off signaling that an agency may be violating some congressional interest, members of Congress rush in to put out the fire.[3] The third might be described as architectural; the life of an agency is constrained by its need to live within a certain space, move along prescribed corridors, and operate specified appliances.

Congress certainly is the architect of the bureaucracy. Most of the constraints described in chapter 7 were created and are sustained by Congress and its committees. For Congress to complain of agency red tape is

*The six bureaus were the Animal and Plant Health Inspection Service, Customs Service, Food and Drug Administration, Forest Service, Internal Revenue Service, and Social Security Administration.

akin to an architect complaining of a home owner who finds it necessary to walk up five flights of steps before he can get from his bedroom to the bathroom. And Congress—more accurately, its committees and subcommittees—are certainly fire fighters. They do not hesitate to use their powers of authorization, appropriation, investigation, and confirmation to call to task bureaus that depart from committee preferences. But in fighting bureaucratic fires members of Congress must compete with other political forces, some of whom are busy pouring gasoline on the flames. How successful Congress will be in using its power will depend not only on how resolute it is but also, as we shall see, on the tasks the agency is performing and the political environment in which it is embedded.

But Congress is almost never a "principal" that can give unchallenged direction to its "agent," the bureaucracy. (Some scholars trained in economics have tried to portray it in this way, but they are wrong. Readers who want to understand what this academic controversy is about can look at the appendix to this chapter.)

When members of Congress complain that an agency is "unresponsive" to Congress or is a "runaway bureaucracy," they are being disingenuous. No agency is free to ignore the views of *Congress*. An agency may, however, defer to the views of one *part* of Congress (say, one committee) instead of another, or balance the competing demands of the White House with those of some parts of Congress in ways that other parts may not like. The bureaucracy cannot evade political control nor sustain for long the view that there is a realm of "administration" that is immune from "politics." But it can maneuver among its many political masters in ways that displease some of them and can define its tasks for internal reasons and not simply in response to external demands.

The question we wish to answer in this chapter is not how powerful is Congress, but under what circumstances are the resources available to Congress likely to be most effective in shaping agency behavior? The answer requires us first to examine those resources and the steps Congress has taken to weaken their power to alter bureaucratic behavior; second, to understand how its political environment has led Congress to "micromanage" the bureaucracy in a somewhat different way than it once did; and finally to see how the tasks of each agency and the environment in which those tasks are performed affect the ability of Congress to determine agency outcomes.

The Means for Exercising Congressional Influence

Congress is extraordinarily powerful when compared to the parliaments of many European democracies. Though a parliament can select the prime minister, often it can do little more: the British House of Commons, for example, cannot without the permission of the prime minister amend a bill, alter a budget, conduct a hearing, or render a service. More exactly, it can do some of these things over the objection of the prime minister, but in doing so brings down the government and forces a new election. Incumbent politicians look forward to new elections with about the same enthusiasm that children look forward to visiting the dentist.

Senator Daniel Patrick Moynihan was scarcely exaggerating when he said that the United States is the only democratic government with a legislative branch. But that branch and the committees that comprise it do not speak with one voice, and neither Congress nor its committees have the means for exercising complete control over all bureaucratic agencies under all circumstances.

Congress can determine the number of employees an agency will have, but it cannot (excepting those few top posts that are subject to Senate confirmation) determine who those employees will be nor can it force employees it does not like to resign. By passing the civil service laws it has lost the power to choose or replace individual bureaucrats. Congress also has surrendered some of its power to control various regulatory agencies. If it wanted only to insure that these regulators served congressional desires it would make it easy to remove those who disobeyed. But many regulatory tasks have been handed over to commissions comprised of people appointed for long terms who cannot be removed except for cause (presumably, by the difficult method of impeachment). Congress would often like to keep the supply of money abundant and the rate of interest low, but in designing the agency with the most influence over these matters—the Federal Reserve Board—it gave to its members terms of fourteen years. Federal Trade Commission members serve for seven years; members of the Federal Communications Commission, Federal Deposit Insurance Corporation, Federal Energy Regulatory Commission, Interstate Commerce Commission, National Labor Relations Board, Securities and Exchange Commission, and Tennessee Valley Authority (among others) all serve for fixed terms ranging from five to nine years.

Congress can decide how much money a bureau may spend on personnel, but it cannot determine the pay of individual agency members. By setting bureaucratic pay on the basis of government-wide pay schedules pegged to the rank of employees it has forgone the opportunity to create different pay scales for different agencies, or for particular persons within a given agency.

Congress can fix the total expenditures of an agency and the amount that can be spent on particular projects within an agency's purview, but in many important cases it has left the determination of year-to-year changes in expenditures to a mathematical formula—the "cost-of-living adjustment," or COLA. For a long time Congress decided every two years (usually, just before an election) how big a Social Security check retired people would receive, but in 1972 it abandoned this method (and all its opportunities for claiming credit with constituents) in favor of a system whereby benefits automatically increased with changes in the cost of living.[4]

Some scholars assume that in their single-minded desire to get reelected members of Congress always seek to manipulate the bureaucracy in order to enhance their prospects for reelection. They would do well to ponder the lengths to which Congress has gone to weaken many of the powers that would permit it to exercise such control. Murray Horn has reminded us that once the patronage system worked to empower politicians; its replacement, the civil service system, works to protect bureaucrats.[5] Why did Congress surrender this power? In large part because wielding it was costly; voters grew increasingly restive about stories of politicians buying and selling offices and their patronage appointees using these offices to line their pockets.[6] And also in part because reforming this process was useful; presidents who wanted to tilt the bureaucracy in a particular ideological direction (Franklin Roosevelt was the leading example) could give patronage appointments to their followers and then insure their perpetuation in office by extending civil-service protections to them.[7] There is evidence that President Reagan promoted into policy-making posts career civil servants who were broadly sympathetic to his goals.[8]

Much the same arguments explain why Congress has given many regulatory commissioners long terms and freedom from routine dismissal and required that they be from both political parties. Creating an agency to regulate a segment of the economy was made easier by evidence that precautions had been taken to keep the regulation from being "too political," which is to say too much under the day-to-day control of Congress or the president. Moreover, long terms and barriers to removal made it easier for the legislative coalition that created the agency to protect it from having its membership changed by some future political coalition. In short, politicians have had good reasons to tie their own hands. But once tied, they cannot easily be untied.

Tying one's hands also seemed to be good politics in the case of certain indexed or automatic expenditures. Republicans did not like the fact that the Democrats (who usually controlled Congress) were always getting the credit for increasing Social Security benefits. The only politically feasible way to end this advantage was to make such increases automatic. Indexing also had another advantage to fiscal conservatives: it would keep benefit increases in line with the cost of living and thus prevent bidding wars among members of Congress eager to portray themselves as the "senior citizen's best friend." And so the biggest part of the budget of the biggest (in dollars spent) agency in Washington was put on automatic pilot.[9] Once on, it could not easily be taken off except by new, politically costly legislation. Congress had weakened its own powers.

Civil service, fixed terms for commissioners, and indexed spending increases are all examples of the fact that, as Murray Horn has shown, Congress's desire to please constituents is not always consistent with its efforts to manipulate bureaucracies. Sometimes legislators believe that it makes more sense to appear to be taking a hands-off position. The long-term consequence of the adoption of these and other self-denying ordinances is that Congress has reduced some of its influence over the bureaucracy. But it has not suffered greatly from this reduction; the overwhelming majority of all incumbent representatives, and most incumbent senators, easily win reelection.

Let us be clear: though it has forsworn the use of certain powers, Congress retains enormous influence over the bureaucracy. But the kind of influence it now wields differs from the kind it once had, to a degree. When Woodrow Wilson wrote *Congressional Government* in 1884 he was able to describe the committees of the House as "the ministers, and the titular ministers only confidential clerks."[10] Scarcely any employees were hired, ships built, cannon emplaced, duties levied, or offices opened save by the direct and specific authorization of the relevant congressional committee. There was little sentiment in Congress for selecting bureaucrats except as they pleased their representatives and worked for their reelection. The notion that pensions to the veterans of the Union army should be set by an automatic formula rather than by the deliberate and election-serving vote of the whole Congress was an idea that would have been regarded as ludicrous on its face.

Congress has changed since the days of Woodrow Wilson. Power is still to be found in the committees (and subcommittees), but the instruments of that power have been modified. The Senate retains the right to confirm presidential appointments and the Congress as a whole the right to investigate executive-branch conduct; appropriations and tax bills are still filled with benefits and loopholes for the advantage of important constituency interests. But the detailed regulation of bureaucratic conduct to some degree has given way to the multiplication of legislated constraints on that behavior. Where Congress once said, "open this fort" or "close this shipyard," it now says, "subject the opening of forts or the closing of shipyards to environmental impact statements." Where Congress once unabashedly directed the War Department to give a weapons contract to the Jedediah Jones Cannon Foundry, it now directs the Defense Department to insure that the contract is awarded to an American firm that tenders the lowest bid, employs the correct mix of women and minorities, makes provisions to aid the handicapped, gives subcontracts to a suitable number of small businesses, is in compliance with the regulations of the Environmental Protection Agency and Occupational Safety and Health Administration, and is not currently under indictment for contract fraud. To insure that these and other constraints are observed, Congress further directs the Pentagon to employ an army of contract officers and contract auditors and to publish its procurement policies in a book of immense length, excruciating detail, and soporific prose.

The change in control methods is illustrated by how members of Congress have protected military bases located in their states and districts. For many years Congress itself decided where bases should be. Not surprisingly, few were ever closed. During World War II, twelve million men and women were called to duty and so there was an enormous increase in the number of these bases; at the end of the war, many of them quickly became obsolete as the military shrank to two million uniformed members. But to close an unneeded base, the secretary of defense would have to wage war with the affected member of Congress, winning rarely and then only after paying a high cost in lost political backing on the Hill. Secretary Robert McNamara was able to close ninety-five bases in 1965 after a bruising fight with individual members of Congress and a presidential veto of a bill requiring congressional approval of such closings. Then in 1976 Congress devised a generalized constraint to replace individualized pressure: it passed a bill forbidding the Pentagon to close a domestic military base without first filing an environmental impact statement, the findings of which could be challenged in court. During the eleven years the law was in effect, not a single major base was closed and several new ones were opened despite the fact that almost every secretary of defense wanted some of them closed.

Then in 1988 Congress passed a bill that created an independent commission and authorized it to choose the bases that would be closed, subject to the right of the secretary of defense and Congress to accept or reject the list in its entirety. Congress cannot pick and choose among the bases to be shut down. Scholars who believe that Congress seeks to use the bureaucracy to enhance the reelection prospects of its members may have some difficulty explaining why those members would consider giving to an outside board the power to eliminate the jobs provided by military bases located in their districts.

The New Micromanagement

Congress is commonly criticized for "micromanaging" government agencies; it does, and always has. Because of its right to authorize programs, appropriate funds, confirm presidential appointees, and conduct investigations, Congress can convert any bureaucratic decision into a policy choice. As political scientists never fail to remind their students on the first day of class, in this country there is no clear distinction between policy and administration.

What is new—and what is obscured by scholarly writings about bureaucracies being the "agent" of Congress—is that the form of this micromanagement seems to have changed. As the preceding examples suggest, Congress is somewhat less likely today than formerly to make administrative decisions and more likely to enforce congressional constraints on how those decisions are made. Congressional micromanagement increasingly takes the form of devising elaborate, detailed rules instead of demanding particular favors for particular people.

There are many reasons for this change. Overt favor-seeking is now riskier; the press and political opponents find it easier than ever to make political capital out of anything that smacks of "influence-peddling." The decentralization of Congress and the weakening of the seniority system has encouraged individual representatives and senators to become policy entrepreneurs, using their powers as chairmen of committees or subcommittees (*half* of all Democrats in the House are chairmen of something) to advance pet causes or call attention to themselves.

This decentralized entrepreneurship occurred at the same time that the scope of government activity dramatically increased. The increase activated so many interests that there are now far more lobbyists in Washington pressing Congress to "do something" than ever before. As a consequence, congressional influence over the bureaucracy is now driven as much or more by the demands of national interest groups as by those of localized constituencies. *Geographical* representation is carried out by making particularistic demands and participating in pork-barrel legislation; *nationalized* representation is exercised by formulating rules that define in general terms the constraints on agency discretion. Both kinds of representation occur, but what is striking is that nationalized representation now rivals geographical representation in importance. This can be seen in the relative decline of pure pork-barrel politics. As we have noted, whereas federal jobs, contracts, projects, and benefits were once passed out almost exclusively by members of Congress on a particularistic, case-by-case basis, today they are more likely to be allocated by rule and formula. Those rules often are written and the formulas designed by the leaders of national interest groups.

Ironically, the rules often fail to please their authors. The controversy surrounding the enactment of legislation creating new forms of business regulation has led both proponents and opponents of these policies to insist on structural and procedural arrangements designed to insure that neither side's enemies would be able to prevail. The result, as Terry Moe has shown in his study of the Consumer Product Safety Commission, the Occupational Safety and Health Administration, and the Environmental Protection Agency, has been the creation of bureaucratic organizations that cannot function effectively. As he puts it, "Opposing groups are dedicated to crippling the bureaucracy and gaining control over its decisions, and they will pressure for fragmented authority, labyrinthine procedures, mechanisms of political intervention, and other structures that subvert the bureaucracy's performance and open it up to attack."[11]

Finally, the greater numbers and enlarged powers of committee staffs have led to the use of staff-written committee or subcommittee reports as "guidance" for the bureaucracy. Without ever passing a law or even approving a report, Congress can now instruct government agencies as to how it wants money spent or laws interpreted. Some members of the executive branch have objected to this practice, but so far to little avail.[12]

For a while, until the Supreme Court struck it down, Congress asserted the right to veto certain executive actions.* Even after the Court acted, Congress continued to pass bills that contained provisions that looked much like the legislative veto that was now supposedly unconstitutional.

This transformation of Congress has not eliminated favor-seeking but it has made possible much greater policy activism. Congress is not a passive institution that upon hearing a constituent sound the alarm rushes to aid him or her. It now patrols the policy activities of the bureaucracy with great attention to detail and abundant information sources.[13] That it does not always dominate the bureaucracy reflects the fact that other institutions—in particular the White House, the courts, and the interest groups—also have gained in power and knowledge.

The signs of this change to rule-oriented rather than benefit-oriented micromanagement are abundant. Before 1960, as Arthur Maass has shown, federal programs usually were authorized by Congress without limit of time. Such detailed controls over programs that Congress wanted to impose for the most part had to be done in annual appropriations bills. But appropriations committees are not comprised of congressional policy entrepreneurs; they tend to be made up of less visible members with an interest in economy and constituent benefits. Beginning in 1961, all expenditures for weapons systems had to be authorized annually, a change that greatly enlarged the powers of the House and Senate armed services committees. Thereafter Congress began to require annual rather than open-ended authorizations for just about everything the Defense Department does, including research and development, personnel levels, operations and maintenance, and ammunition.[14] Soon other departments fell under annual authorizations, including State, Justice, Energy, Transpor-

*The legislative veto was declared unconstitutional by the Supreme Court in *Immigration and Naturalization Service* v. *Chadha,* 103 S. Ct. 2764 (1983). At the time, over two hundred statutes contained provisions for a legislative veto in one form or another. In general, they required that a proposed executive-branch action be laid before Congress which could veto it if within a stated number of days one or both houses (or sometimes a congressional committee) passed a resolution disapproving it. Since such a resolution was not presented to the president for his signature, it violated the requirement in Article I of the Constitution that any action that was essentially legislative must be presented to the president for it to have effect.

tation, Housing and Urban Development, the Environmental Protection Agency, the Central Intelligence Agency, and many others.

More frequent authorizations meant more chances to devise and impose rules and policy guidance on agencies. That in turn has meant a more crowded legislative calendar and a reduction in administrative discretion. This is most evident in the case of the Defense Department. In Congress there are now 29 committees and 55 subcommittees that in one way or another oversee defense activities. In 1984 they held 441 hearings.[15] Whereas in 1977 the House debated the defense authorization bill for three days and considered no amendments, in 1986 it debated it for thirteen days and considered 148 amendments. A comparable change occurred in the Senate.[16] In 1970 the Congress requested of the Pentagon 36 reports; in 1985 it requested 1,172.[17]

Tasks and Environments

The extent to which congressional control of administration will amount to congressional dominance of the administrative agency will depend on the tasks the agency is doing and the political environment in which it is placed.

TASKS

Congress dominates much of the work of the Social Security Administration. SSA executives would bristle at the suggestion that they are dominated by Congress, but their irritation reflects not the facts but the unfortunate connotations that the word "dominate" has acquired. It implies interference, manipulation, and subservience, and the SSA would rightly resent the notion that this proud organization is servile to or manipulated by anybody. But lest any agency manager think that legislative domination broadly defined is not present, let that person try to decide unilaterally what the size of a retirement benefit shall be or who shall receive it. Congress dominates the SSA with respect to retirement programs because it fully and effectively specifies what the SSA shall do. It can make that specification because the goals of the SSA are entirely operational: its work is readily observable; its outputs are easily and fully measurable. In the language of chapter 8, this is known as a "production agency." But Congress is less successful in dominating SSA with respect to the disability program because those goals are not operational; in this respect, SSA is a procedural agency.

Legislatures ordinarily do not dominate the work of public schoolteachers or police patrol officers for the same reason that school superintendents or police chiefs cannot readily manage the work of their subordinates: They cannot observe the tasks being carried out, unambiguously assess their effect on the organizations' goals, or even state those goals in clear and precise language. Schoolteachers and patrol officers are part of coping agencies. To be sure, there are circumstances in which legislative dominance is possible: If the school or police department is corrupt (that is, if it uses its powers for unlawful personal gain) or devoted to serving a politician with votes and financial kickbacks, then it is under political dominance. Some schools and police forces have operated on this principle. But to the extent they are truly teachers or patrol officers—that is, individuals motivated to achieve the (admittedly vague) goals of enhancing learning and preserving the public order—it is very hard to make them the tools of legislators or of anyone else. Of course, a legislature can pretend to dominate such organizations by insisting that they add on certain new tasks, but that is a far cry from determining how the core tasks of the organizations are performed.

Efforts to assert legislative control become interesting and problematic in the case of craft or procedural agencies. Congress may judge an army by whether it wins a battle or the Corps of Engineers by whether it builds a dam, but it will have a most difficult time trying to specify in any meaningful way how to fight the battle or build the dam. Sometimes it tries, foolishly. Congress tried to tell President Lincoln how to fight the Civil War, but beyond inflating the reputation of certain generals and debasing others it did not accomplish much. A city council may judge police detectives by whether they solve a murder, but they will not have much success in trying to tell them how to conduct a murder investigation. These craft agencies resist legislative domination up to a point: Their goals are set and resources controlled by the legislature, but their tasks are defined by factors over which legislators have only imperfect control.

In peacetime the military may expect a great deal of unsolicited advice from Congress on how it is organized and equipped. The Marine Corps had to change the way it trained recruits when Congress decided that the training was too abusive. But Congress has no way of knowing whether the old or the "reformed" recruit training methods produce the best marines. The Food and Drug Administration is harassed regularly by Congress for either rushing risky new drugs into the market or withholding beneficial new drugs from sick people. Its procedures for evaluating these drugs will be intensively examined and criticized. But Congress is at a loss to answer the critical question: How much of a risk shall the FDA run for a given (likely) benefit? These are procedural agencies, vulnerable to any politician who wants to tell them how to do their job but deriving little help from them in evaluating how well the job is done.

Regulatory agencies like the FDA tend to be craft or procedural agencies and thus present a complex oversight problem. Many of them were given broad grants of power, in many cases because Congress could not reasonably choose a clear legislative standard. It could not decide in advance what constituted a "safe" drug, a "reasonable hazard," a "combination in restraint of trade," a "crashworthy automobile," or an "integrated school," and so it left these matters to "experts."* Later on when it tried to specify exact and rigid standards it found itself caught on the horns of a dilemma: The more binding the standard, the less freedom the agency had in trading off less attainment of that standard in favor of more attainment of some other standard. As we shall see in chapter 18, the Environmental Protection Agency was held to so rigid a standard of pollution reduction that it could not take into account the cost (in money spent or jobs lost) of attaining that standard.

Broad delegations of authority are inevitable if government is to intervene widely in society, but such delegations make congressional control difficult. Jeremy Rabkin has carefully traced how three federal agencies—the Office for Civil Rights, the Food and Drug Administration, and the Occupational Safety and Health Administration—imbued their vague statutory authority with concrete meaning; how, in the language of this book, they defined their tasks. It was the Office for Civil Rights, not Congress, that decided to investigate complaints of sex discrimination in high-school sports programs; it was the FDA, not Congress, that made restrictions on the introduction of new drugs more difficult here than in any other nation; it was OSHA, not Congress, that imposed tough restrictions on worker exposure to certain chemicals.[18] In this process of task definition the agencies have been encouraged (or even directed) by the courts to move in these directions, a matter to be considered in chapter 15. Congress has not objected to these changes, but that is not a sign that

*Some scholars have argued that legislatures delegate their powers to administrative agencies not to allow those agencies to use judgment but to permit the legislatures to avoid blame—they let bureaucrats make decisions so that bureaucrats and not legislators will have to take the heat when people dislike the regulations. See Morris Fiorina, "Legislative Choice of Regulatory Forms: Legal Process or Administrative Process?" *Public Choice* 39 (1982): 33–36; Matthew McCubbins and T. Page, "A Theory of Congressional Delegation," in M. McCubbins and T. Sullivan, eds., *Congress: Structure and Policy* (Cambridge: Cambridge University Press, 1987). But as Murray Horn has pointed out, there are some problems with this theory. First, it assumes that affected interest groups will be deceived by the stratagem and fail to notice that the legislators created the process now working to the interest groups' disadvantage. It would be especially hard to deceive them in this way if, as McCubbins and others argue, Congress in fact dominates the day-to-day decision making of the agencies. Second, shifting blame only would be possible in nations such as the United States where lines of bureaucratic authority are vague; it would not be possible in parliamentary regimes where the prime minister, the cabinet, and the governing party are held popularly accountable for everything the bureaucracy does. Yet in such countries—Great Britain, France, and Canada—we find the same pattern of broad delegation as we find here. (Horn, "Political Economy of Public Administration," 119–20.)

Congress approves of them, much less that by using its oversight powers it has required them; it is a sign only of two facts: Congress often cannot decide what it wants, and anyone wishing to force Congress to decide what it wants discovers that a few key congressional supporters of the agency can block any clarifying or amendatory legislation even from getting out of committee.[19]

OSHA is an example of this. In the health protection aspect of its work it is a procedural agency because no one can easily define a healthy worker or assess the long-term effect of OSHA regulations on worker health. Thus it is hardly surprising that the original law, passed in 1970, did not supply the agency with very exact goals. But as Graham Wilson has noted, the law did convey a tone: "Be tough." One provision instructed OSHA to insure, "to the maximum extent feasible" that "no employee" would "suffer impairment of health or functional capacity" even if exposed to a hazard "for the period of his working life."[20] Once the agency started to act tough, Congress had second thoughts. But it never amended the key phrases in its original statute. The goals remained the same. What changed were the means. After scores of investigations (there were over one hundred oversight hearings between 1973 and 1976 and over thirty between 1977 and 1981[21]) Congress passed a series of riders to appropriations bills that required OSHA to pay for advisory services for employers, to avoid inspecting farms or penalizing employers with fewer than ten employees, and to defer to state safety and health agencies. Confronting a procedural agency, Congress tried to control it by controlling its procedures. Is this congressional dominance? It is certainly congressional influence, but it is not dominance, for other actors, notably the health and safety professionals hired by the agency, were providing OSHA with their own definitions of its tasks. Had this not occurred Congress would have had no reason to invent a complex set of constraints to impose on these professionals.

The same limited effect of congressional efforts to control procedural or craft organizations is evident in the case of the FTC. Congress was effective in getting the FTC to back down on issuing certain industry-wide rules. It was less effective when the FTC, under the chairmanship of James Miller during the early 1980s, decided to apply an economic test to the cases it brought, allowing mergers that would increase market competition and attacking only those that would reduce it. Immediately, some members of Congress began calling the FTC a "rogue agency" pursuing "novel" economic theories.[22] Miller also sought to reduce FTC expenditures. If Congress "dominated" the FTC, it could have prevented these things. But it could not. Miller's economic philosophy became the FTC's philosophy, and the economists on the FTC staff began to dominate the lawyers. What Congress did was complain and seek to make *procedural* changes, such as stopping the closing of regional offices and appropriating more money than Miller had requested.

If carrying out the tasks of the FTC, FDA, OSHA, OCR, or any of a dozen other regulatory agencies would achieve specific, observable outcomes, the congressional dominance would be much easier. But then these would be production agencies, and so their entire system of management and governance would be very different. And if that were the case, then the president also would have greater opportunities to control the agencies, and so the stage would be set not for congressional dominance but for constitutional struggle.

ENVIRONMENT

The exercise of congressional power is shaped by the political environment of an agency as well as by its tasks. Congress dominates the SSA not only because its tasks are clear but because Congress speaks for the great majority of Americans who want their retirement benefits protected. A city council has trouble dominating a police department not only because its tasks are hard to manage but also because city councilors must balance the competing demands of rival groups with an interest in police activity: a neighborhood wanting more patrol officers at the expense of another neighborhood that also wants more; Mothers Against Drunk Driving seeking a crackdown on motorists over the objections of the American Civil Liberties Union; a civil rights organization demanding more black sergeants despite the claims of the Patrolmen's Benevolent Association that this constitutes reverse discrimination.

In chapter 5, agency environments were classified into four categories: majoritarian, entrepreneurial, clientelist, and interest group. Legislative dominance will be easier when an agency is part of a client environment than when it is embedded in an interest-group environment. In the first case, one discrete and relatively small interest stands to get the benefits of agency action while a large, diffuse majority will pay the costs. The client ordinarily will have little trouble in finding congressional allies and they (depending on the nature of the task) will have little trouble getting the agency to go along. Veterans usually do not find the House and Senate committees on veterans' affairs indifferent to their interests; as a consequence, the Department of Veterans Affairs rarely is indifferent to what these committees want. The Federal Maritime Administration is alert to the views of the House Committees on Merchant Marine and Fisheries or the subcommittee on merchant marine of the Senate Committee on Science, Commerce, and Transportation; one does not have to have a Ph.D. in political science to figure out that this alertness may have something to do with the special favor with which these committees view the maritime unions and the steamship companies.

As we have seen, Congress has harassed OSHA without fundamentally changing it. One reason already noted is the nature of some of its tasks: Nobody, including Congress, knows for certain whether OSHA in fact is improving worker health. With respect to health regulation OSHA is a procedural agency. But surely improving worker safety is relatively easy to assess. OSHA rules either do or do not lead to the use of devices that protect the eyes, extinguish fires, or keep fingers away from whirring blades. With respect to many safety matters OSHA could be regarded as a production agency. But the kind of congressional dominance that might be expected with respect to these clearer tasks is frustrated by the interest-group environment in which OSHA is embedded. Industry and labor unions quarrel incessantly about the desirability, feasibility, and cost of OSHA rules. Since OSHA's constituents are divided, Congress is divided: for every representative who wants tougher enforcement there is another representative who wants more lenient enforcement. As Graham Wilson observed, Congress's handling of the occupational safety and health issues has been "a classic example of the weakness of Congress as a policy-making institution": It could not resolve the dispute between business and labor except by allowing both sides to engage in some grandstanding.[23] Business supporters demanded that the agency be abolished while labor supporters demanded it be kept unchanged. No one was willing to amend the legislation to resolve the key issue: How should the benefits of worker protection be balanced against their costs? That would have been very hard to do, even in principle, but in practice it would have meant exposing oneself to the charge by labor supporters that one was "trying to put a price on human life."

Sometimes a policy entrepreneur manages to mobilize a legislative majority in favor of a course of action that is against the interests of a client group or that overrides a traditional interest-group conflict. Entrepreneurial politics tends to occur in brief, impassioned outbursts, but when they occur the legislature is able to overcome many of the political constraints that ordinarily impede legislative dominance. During the 1960s and early 1970s entrepreneurial politics resulted in the passage of legislation to regulate the automobile industry, tighten the regulation of pharmaceuticals, and create specific standards and timetables for reducing air and water pollution.[24] In 1975 the Magnuson-Moss Act empowered the FTC to promulgate industry-wide rules in addition to issuing traditional cease-and-desist orders against individual firms.

Entrepreneurial politics, whether it leads to the creation of a new agency or the redirection of an existing one, changes the political environment in which the bureaucracy operates. Zealous professionals rush to join the new or revitalized agency, old client groups are thrown on the defensive, and the president faces the choice of going with the flow or being branded an obstructionist. But entrepreneurial passions tend to be short-lived, and as they subside they leave behind a new constellation of interests that may or may not have a stake in pursuing the original legislative vision. The new recruits to the National Highway Traffic Safety Administration were eager to issue regulations governing the design of automobiles, but as time passed it became easier for them to order the recall of cars with safety defects than to solve the knotty and controversial problems associated with further rule making. Cleaning up the nation's air and water by a fixed date seemed a shining goal when the date first was picked, but as time passed and the cost in money and political opposition of cleaning the smog out of Los Angeles or the pollutants out of Lake Erie became known, the Environmental Protection Agency began talking of "tradeoffs" and "feasibility." Industry-wide rule making seemed like a good idea at the time to the Democratic senators who wrote the bill and to the Republican FTC chairmen who first administered it, but that was before used-car dealers and funeral directors had mobilized in opposition to the rules.

In these instances we can see the subtle and complex interplay between tasks and environment as they shape congressional opportunities for controlling the bureaucracy. Congress can dominate the industry-wide rule making efforts of the FTC. Such rules are clearly visible products *and* they arouse well-organized opposition. When in the grip of an entrepreneurial passion, Congress can require that such rules be issued; when the passion has quieted and industry objections are evident, they can require that such rules not be issued. By contrast, the cease-and-desist orders that the FTC traditionally has aimed at individual firms that are guilty of unfair or anticompetitive practices are hard to evaluate (the facts of a given case usually are complicated) and the economic consequences are hard to predict; moreover, the individual firm that is the target of such an order ordinarily has only a handful of friends, if any at all, on Capitol Hill. Congress is less likely to dominate these proceedings.

In sum, agencies with tasks that are easily designed and evaluated and that have strong majoritarian or client support are readily placed under legislative control; indeed, the control is so effortlessly achieved that often it is not recognized as dominance at all. Agencies with tasks that are hard to specify and difficult to evaluate and that are imbedded in conflict-ridden political environments can barely be controlled by legislatures at all, except by multiplying the procedural constraints that the agencies are supposed to observe. In between these extremes one finds a host of agencies that have either ambiguous outputs (procedural agencies) or invisible operations (craft agencies) that may or may not be subject to effective legislative control, depending on the shape of the political environment. When the work of the agency becomes the object of entrepreneurial politics there are episodic and often short-lived efforts at control; when the work of the agency has important distributional effects—benefiting some organized groups at the expense of others—there are continuous efforts at control that sometimes are paralyzed by the legislature's inability to decide on what distribution it wishes to achieve.*

Agency Response to Legislative Control

Though they do not use the awkward labels and cumbersome distinctions that I have employed, bureaucrats are keenly aware of the circumstances under which they must take into account legislative preferences. Being rational they respond to those circumstances by designing their relations with Congress in such a way as to satisfy those members who have an interest in the distributional effects of agency decisions. The bureaucracy is hardly the passive agent of its congressional overseer; like the wily man-servant in *The Marriage of Figaro*, it is constantly working to manipulate its master so as to achieve mutually profitable arrangements.

Douglas Arnold has calculated the extent of this accommodation in his analysis of the ways funds are obtained for water and sewer grants, model-cities programs, and military bases.[25] In at least two of these cases (water-sewer grants and military bases) the agencies involved are performing production tasks; in all three cases the results have strong distributional effects—some localities get the money, others do not. The bureaucrats implementing these programs do not merely react to this control, they anticipate and shape it.

They do so by extending the scope of their proposals so as to acquire support from key members of Congress. Whenever an agency sends up a budget request it makes certain that there will be projects in it that will serve the districts represented by the members of the appropriations sub-committees (as well as members of certain key legislative committees). The bureaucratic effort to build a supportive coalition on the Hill adds, Arnold estimates, somewhere between 10 and 30 percent to the cost of the programs.

A recent example of this process is the decision by former secretary of the navy John F. Lehman, Jr., to build support for his plan to increase the size of the navy by "homeporting"—that is, assigning new ships to a large number of local ports rather than concentrating them all in a few major naval bases. Key members of Congress, many of them critics of

*A comparable but not identical analysis of the amenability of government agencies to legislative control can be found in Lester M. Salamon and Gary L. Wamsley, "The Federal Bureaucracy: Responsiveness to Whom?" in Leroy N. Rieselbach, ed., *People vs. Government: The Responsiveness of American Institutions* (Bloomington, Ind.: Indiana University Press, 1975), 151–88.

military spending in other respects, worked diligently to help insure that a battleship and its escort vessels were homeported in their cities.[26]

Critics call this "pork barreling" and argue that it is wrong. One critic, President Jimmy Carter, tried to reduce it by vetoing a bill providing funds for a number of local water projects. What got cut instead was his political neck: He failed, and alienated Congress in the process. Despite its association with highway contractors and military facilities, pork is not limited to bridges, sewer systems, and naval bases. It includes public parks, wastesite cleanups, and university research projects. It benefits liberals as much as conservatives. This suggests that porking (as it is sometimes called) is not an aberration in American politics but a fundamental aspect of it. It is the logical and inevitable outcome of a system that requires legislators to serve local interests more than party interests and that endows Congress with independent power over the bureaucracy.

Porking in the broad sense of coalition-building is common, but in the narrow sense of directing specific funds to specific projects it is relatively uncommon. Arthur Maass has pointed out that contrary to what many people think, Congress ordinarily does not "name individual projects in the authorizing statutes [or] allocate funds to them in appropriations statutes."[27] Instead it sets standards and criteria for allocating funds among projects, leaving it to the executive branch to make the actual choices. Why does it do this? Because of its fear of being criticized for favoritism, and because assembling ad hoc majorities within Congress is made easier if every state and district sees in principle that it can qualify for a project.

When Congress is considering authorizing activities to achieve vague goals in the indefinite future, porking is less common. Under these circumstances the rational agency strategy is not to promise to deliver the goods but to be frank and forthcoming about the agency's activities. Members of Congress do not like being deceived,[28] and in a political system where keeping secrets is next to impossible, deception is eventually discovered. Legislative oversight of coping or procedural agencies—that is, agencies that can discuss their activities but cannot verify their achievements—consists in large measure of congressional committees inspecting those activities and their costs. To a cynic it is Parkinson's Law fulfilled: members of Congress debating whether an agency should close an office in Dallas but ignoring the work that goes on in that office. But the cynical view is only partly correct; what Congress is doing is not simply asserting localistic concerns over where offices should be established but also testing the competence and honesty of the agency managers by looking closely at cases (such as acquiring and operating an office) where competence and honesty can be evaluated by busy legislators. Experienced agency executives know this and thus work hard to maintain a good reputation.[29]

Members of Congress like bureaucrats who do things for their district, accomplish stated goals economically, or (if they lack information on these matters) behave in a forthcoming and frank manner in their dealings with Congress with respect to the use of resources and the treatment of citizens. (Sometimes members are extremely hard on bureaucrats they like; there is nothing personal in this, only the need to take sides in an interest-group quarrel over the agency's mission.) These considerations help us identify agency heads that have the easiest and the most difficult jobs in pleasing their overseers. The administrator of the Social Security Administration can explain that at least with respect to the retirement program she is accomplishing goals (they are known and measurable) and doing things in all congressional districts (there are thousands of local SSA offices); moreover, she has no need to conceal information. (The SSA's disability program is another matter; she cannot defend it on the basis of having attained clear goals but only on the basis of having exercised "reasonable" judgment about ambiguous and controversial criteria.) The secretary of state, by contrast, does nothing for any member's district, can rarely prove that progress is being made toward any important goal, and sometimes must be less than frank in order to safeguard delicate negotiations or preserve political options. Small wonder that secretaries of state spend so much time staying as far away from Washington as possible.

APPENDIX
"Congressional Dominance": A Closer Look

Barry R. Weingast and Mark J. Moran[30] noted the angry congressional reaction to what members described as the "runaway" FTC decision to regulate television advertising aimed at children, issue tough rules governing the used-car and undertaker businesses (among others), and break up the alleged monopoly power of the big cereal manufacturers and oil companies. Many academic observers accepted the politicians' explanation for the controversy: The FTC had used its wide discretion to make policy without regard to congressional preferences. This happened because Congress, though it has powerful weapons for controlling agency behavior, rarely uses them; congressional oversight of bureaucratic behavior is either perfunctory or episodic.

Weingast and Moran suggested a different interpretation, namely, that the FTC all along pursued the interests of the congressional oversight committees (the subcommittee on consumer affairs of the Senate Commerce Committee and the equivalent subcommittee of the House Committee on Energy and Commerce). During the early 1970s these committees wanted an activist, antibusiness FTC, and that is what they got. In the late 1970s these committees wanted a less activist, more probusiness FTC and (in time) this is what they got. The public fuss occurred because the FTC was unable to reverse its policy directions as quickly as the congressional committees wanted, and so for a year or so it got blasted as a "runaway" agency. But soon it was once again in full compliance with committee views.

To prove this claim, Weingast and Moran divided FTC cases into two kinds: "traditional" (or trivial) cases, such as those involving claims that a firm violated laws governing how fur, wool, and textiles should be labeled; and "activist" (or important) cases, such as those entailing the enforcement of the Truth-in-Lending or Fair Credit Reporting Act. They then showed that there was a statistical association between the frequency of these two kinds of cases and the liberalism of the members of the House and Senate oversight committees. In particular, as the oversight subcommittee members became more liberal (as measured by the scores they received from Americans for Democratic Action, a liberal interest group), the FTC commissioners began hearing more "activist" cases and fewer "traditional" ones. This happened during the late 1960s and early 1970s. As the oversight subcommittees (especially the one in the Senate) became less liberal, the FTC reduced the number of activist cases and increased the number of traditional ones. This occurred in the late 1970s as a result of an almost complete turnover in the membership of that subcommittee. The public furor and the attendant charges that the FTC was out of control were heard during the brief period that the agency was shifting gears.

This analysis has been criticized at length by others; only its central problems need be mentioned here. First, the data on which Weingast and Moran rely does not support their prediction that as Congress became more conservative in the late 1970s the FTC would shift toward more traditional, less activist cases.[31] Second, the congressional dominance theory would predict that the FTC would reject the free-market principles associated with the Chicago School of economics—especially those principles that tolerated mergers where no loss in consumer welfare could be proven—if the relevant congressional committees did not share those views. The committees did not have these views, and yet the FTC moved in precisely this direction during the Reagan administration.* The agency dropped its case against Kellogg and approved both the acquisition of Gulf by SoCal and the joint venture between General Motors and Toyota.[32] Third, and most important, Weingast and Moran did not test their explanations of FTC behavior against rival explanations.[33] These rival explanations can be summarized in four words: president, executives, staff, and courts. To show that Congress dominates an agency, it is not enough to show that its behavior changes as the attitudes of some members of Congress change; one also must show that changes in bureaucratic behavior cannot be more easily explained by the actions of the president, the agency executives he appoints, the staff that works at the agency, and the courts that hear complaints about what the agency has done. To read Weingast and Moran and other exponents of the congressional dominance theory, one would hardly know that these other actors existed.

A government agency may be thought of as an "agent," but it is an agent quite unlike any to be found in a corporation, for it serves not a single principal (such as a corporate board of directors) but many diverse principals. We already know (see chapter 12) that Caspar Weinberger and Miles Kirkpatrick replaced many of the FTC's key staff members and redirected its priorities away from investigating mislabeled fur products and toward challenging mergers and monopolies. We already know (see chapter 4) that economists define FTC tasks differently than do lawyers; the Weinberger-Kirkpatrick changes enhanced the power of the economists in the FTC. We will soon learn (chapter 15) that the federal courts affect agency behavior by the kinds of cases they are willing to hear; by the late 1960s, the courts were making it so hard for the FTC to win some of its traditional cases that it had just about stopped trying. Throughout the whole period, presidents varied in the amount and kind of attention they gave to the FTC. Presidents Roosevelt, Truman, Kennedy, and Johnson pretty much ignored it except as a source of patronage jobs they could pass out to the political allies of influential members of Congress. President Eisenhower took a different tack, appointing people to the FTC who would streamline the agency and make it more efficient. President Nixon, by contrast, decided to use the FTC as a way of appealing to consumer groups, and so he appointed first Weinberger and then Kirkpatrick to give it a new direction. President Carter was even more determined to make the FTC a vanguard agency in consumerism and so he appointed Michael Pertschuk. President Reagan changed the FTC's philosophical tone by appointing commis-

*When Robert Katzmann interviewed senior FTC officials in 1987–88, they were unanimous in saying that congressional policy directives (as opposed to procedural haggling over budget levels and the closing of regional offices) were unusual. One remarked that except for "bothersome congressional hearings" that "went nowhere," "we can do just about anything—or not do just about anything." Another said, "I cannot think of a single enforcement action dictated by Congress since I've been here." When a congressional committee investigated the FTC it was regarded by the agency's leaders as being largely for show: "After he [the committee chairman] satisfies his constituents . . . things go on exactly as before." (Robert Katzmann, interview notes, July 31, 1988.)

sioners such as James Miller III, who used the FTC to promote market competition rather than consumerist rule making. As Terry M. Moe has remarked, what is astonishing about the theorists of congressional dominance is that their analysis focuses almost entirely on *Congress* and scarcely at all on the agency that supposedly is doing Congress's bidding, with the result that "presidents, reorganizations, FTC chairmen and commissioners, agency structures and processes, internal disputes over policy—all these and more are ignored."[34]

And even if one focuses on Congress, it is a mistake to limit one's attention to only two legislative committees. Every federal agency is overseen by at least four committees (or subcommittees): the House and Senate committees that authorize the agency and shape the legislation it enforces and the House and Senate appropriations committees that determine the size of its staff and budget. It is common for there to be important conflicts among these committees. The House Energy and Commerce Committee, for example, has long attracted to its ranks representatives with a keen interest in consumer and environmental affairs; by contrast, the House Appropriations Committee traditionally has attracted to it representatives with an interest in economy and constituency service.[35] An agency head needs support from both kinds of committees, but he or she often gets inconsistent signals from them: "Do more!" is heard from the legislative committee, "Spend less!" from the appropriations committee.

CHAPTER 14

Presidents

ALMOST EVERY PRESIDENT in modern times has admitted to his advisors, if he has not shouted from the rooftops, that he rued the day a "disappointed office seeker" killed President Garfield, thereby energizing the civil-service reform movement. Presidents see much of the bureaucracy as their natural enemy and always are searching for ways to bring it to heel. Even though they can already make upward of four thousand appointments outside the merit system, many presidents would like to make even more. Those who do not want more appointments want better ones, and so they encourage the promotion into the top administrative ranks of senior civil servants who seem to be their ideological allies. And when they are not reaching for more numbers or searching for purer ideology, presidents reorganize agencies and create White House offices designed to oversee, coordinate, and (if necessary) do the work of the bureaucracy.

All this would seem quite strange to the British prime minister. Beyond her cabinet she makes perhaps a dozen "political" appointments to the bureaucracy and seems quite content with that. The British civil service is satirized, as in the popular television series *Yes, Minister*, but it is not confronted. In the mid-1940s, Labour prime ministers worried that the "Tory" civil service would undo their policies, but when that did not happen they stopped worrying and their successors spent little time trying to get "our kind of people" into top posts. Unlike the White House, Number 10 Downing Street is not filled with special assistants, special advisors, counselors, committees, and offices designed to ride herd on the bureaucracy.

Why the difference? In a word, the answer is the Constitution. That document makes the president and Congress rivals for control of the American administrative system. The rivalry leads to struggle and the struggle breeds frustration. Those agencies that Congress regards as unresponsive the president views as unaccountable; those bureaus that from Capitol Hill seem to be runaway rogues appear from the White House to be insolent sloths. In Great Britain, the prime minister and parliament are not rivals because the House of Commons has no significant power to supervise, investigate, intervene in, or even obtain answers from the bureaucracy. If the British civil service is indifferent to the wishes of the prime minister and her cabinet, that fact is best not advertised for it would only reflect discredit on the one person—the prime minister—with authority to oversee the bureaucracy.

Our Constitution instructs the president to "take care that the laws be faithfully executed"; the president reads this as meaning that government agencies should be accountable to him. But the Constitution also grants to Congress "all legislative powers"; Congress reads this as meaning that the agencies it has created ought to be responsive to their creator. In Great Britain, by contrast, accountability and responsiveness are one and the same thing, owed to one and the same person.

The notion that the president, as the chief executive officer of the United States, should administer and hold accountable to him executive branch agencies is a relatively recent one. Before 1921 there was not even an executive budget; before 1939, the Bureau of the Budget was located not in the White House but in the Treasury Department. Until well into the administration of Franklin Roosevelt there was no White House staff of any consequence; it is a measure of how ill-equipped the president was that the report of a commission FDR appointed to study the matter suggested the creation of a senior staff "not exceeding six in number."[1] Before 1921 bureaus and departments could and did submit their own bills directly to Congress without clearing them with the president; after 1921 this was prohibited with respect to appropriations bills and during the 1930s with respect to all other matters.

The changes that occurred during the Roosevelt administration were couched in the language of "improving efficiency" and "good management" but in fact were inspired by deeper political convictions. The goal was not simply to tidy up the machinery of government but to make the president the effective head of the government. And that in turn meant weakening the ability of Congress to deal directly with the various executive agencies. The plans for central budgeting, central legislative clearance, and central personnel management; the proposal to allow the president to reorganize and consolidate departments and bureaus; the suggestion that the many functions of the independent regulatory commissions be given over to agencies reporting, through the departments, to the president; all these were ideas based on the belief that the constitutional assignment of "the executive power" to the president was to be broadly interpreted and that the opportunities for Congress to share in the executive power were to be sharply limited.

Many of the recommendations of the President's Committee on Administrative Management were adopted, but the fundamental tension remained. Formally, all bureaus cleared their budgetary and legislative proposals with the White House; informally, Congress had no difficulty learning which bureau chiefs differed with the president on these matters. Formally, all agencies within the executive branch were subordinate to the president; informally, Congress, by virtue of its authority to authorize, appropriate, and investigate, had little difficulty in influencing at least the more visible activities and in shaping the more operational goals of these agencies.

As a result, bureaus are the agents of different and divided masters, and so their daily operation reflects the ongoing tensions between the White House and Capitol Hill. The resources each master has devised to enhance influence over the bureaucracy have grown since FDR's time, but every advance in the power of the president has been matched by a comparable advance in Congress. Senator Daniel Patrick Moynihan has called this the "Iron Law of Emulation"*: "Whenever any branch of the government acquires a new technique which enhances its power in relation to the other branches, that technique will soon be adopted by the other branches as well."[2]

President Roosevelt acquired a Bureau of the Budget, later converted by President Nixon into an even more powerful Office of Management and Budget (OMB). Congress responded by creating the General Accounting Office (GAO) so that it could make certain the agencies spent only what was appropriated; later, it created the Congressional Budget Office (CBO) so that it would have its own source of budgetary information independent of the president's. When it noticed that OMB was not only making up budgets but also altering management practices in the bureaucracy, Congress directed the GAO to study management and policy implementation as well as to audit the books. In 1962 the president formed the Office of Science and Technology to give him scientific advice; a decade or so later, Congress created the Office of Technology Assessment to give *it* such advice. The White House grew rapidly from its original six special assistants; Congress noticed this and set in motion arrangements that led to the proliferation of its own staff, increasing from just over fifteen hundred when FDR was in office to nearly fifteen thousand by the time Ronald Reagan took office.[3] (Members of Congress who complain about the cost of the presidential bureaucracy might well recall the price tag of their own: In 1978 Senator Claiborne Pell noted that the cost of running the United States Senate alone exceeded the national budgets of seventy-four nations.[4]) In 1947 the president acquired the Central Intelligence Agency; in time, Congress responded by creating the House and

*Quoting me as the source of the idea; the phrase was Moynihan's.

Senate Select Committees on Intelligence, the members and staffs of which by law are entitled to full and timely information on everything of consequence the CIA is doing. In 1963 the president added to the White House a Special Representative for Trade Negotiations; a decade later, the Senate Finance Committee created a subcommittee on international trade whose members are official advisors to the president's trade negotiators.

This process of organizational emulation may seem inevitable and even necessary, but it has a cost: The presidency and Congress, two institutions that once dealt with each other on a personal basis, now deal with each other on a bureaucratic basis. Presidents still meet with legislators face to face, but once that was almost the only way they conducted their mutual business. Today these direct meetings have been eclipsed in significance by the indirect contacts managed by staffers from the president's Office of Legislative Affairs dealing with other staffers on Capitol Hill; officials of OMB talking to officials of CBO; and White House press spokesmen trading punches in the media with House and Senate press spokesmen.

Caught in the middle, the bureaucracy watches all this with fear and loathing. It is one thing to serve two masters; it is another thing to serve masters who themselves have become vast bureaucratic organizations with their own cultures and maintenance needs. Whereas individuals deal with one another by making demands and offering deals, bureaucracies deal with one another by imposing constraints and manipulating information. The constraints on agency life described in chapter 7 reflect constituency demands filtered through White House and congressional bureaucracies. The old face-to-face wheeling and dealing may have had its disadvantages, such as cronyism and special favors, but the newer process of negotiating interagency treaties (called MOUs, or memoranda of understanding) and bargaining over procedural rules has its own disadvantages, one of which is paralysis.

The president brings to this struggle four main weapons: choosing people, altering procedures, reorganizing agencies, and coordinating activities.

People

A remarkable transfiguration occurs at the very moment a president administers the oath of office to cabinet secretaries or bureau chiefs. Just before the appointees place their hand on the Bible they are committed followers of the president's principles and policies. The oaths uttered, the hands are lifted from the Bible; almost immediately, the oath takers begin to experience a soul-changing conversion. Suddenly they see the world through the eyes of their agencies—their unmet needs, their unfulfilled agendas, their loyal and hard-working employees.

Presidential staffers who have watched this conversion do not attribute it to Biblical inspiration but to "marrying the natives," that is, embracing the views and supporting the programs of those whom they must lead. Surprisingly, not many presidents have made a determined effort to stop the marriage. The president usually does not know well more than a tiny fraction of the people he must appoint and is besieged by job seekers and friends of job seekers, all urging on him plausible but largely unknown names. The president will pay close attention to his immediate circle of White House advisors and to those in charge of principal cabinet departments—Defense, State, and Treasury—and to the CIA. Beyond that, he must depend on subordinates, party leaders, interest groups, and members of Congress for ideas. In addition to his own interests, which incline him toward the Big Issues, he confronts political incentives that reward him for appearing to do well on the Big Issues, such as the state of the economy, Soviet-American relations, and his reputation in the media. He is not likely to be inclined toward nor rewarded for fixing up the Park Service, redirecting the Securities and Exchange Commission, or improving the management of the Labor Department.

It is therefore to be expected that he will appoint people to these and similar agencies who have weak commitment, if any, to the president's philosophy despite what they profess, even assuming he has a philosophy about parks, securities transactions, or labor policy. Traditionally these posts were filled by people suggested by the interest groups that stood to benefit from the agencies' activities. But in recent years, ideology has begun to displace clientelism as the basis of many such appointments. Presidents Nixon, Carter, and Reagan tried to put a distinctive philosophical stamp on most if not all federal agencies. Nixon began a purge of the subcabinet (i.e., the undersecretaries and assistant secretaries of the major departments), filling it with followers whose loyalty had been tested by prior service on Nixon's White House staff.[5] Carter systematically appointed liberals to the posts vacated by outgoing conservatives.[6] Reagan took office determined to make effective use of his powers of appointment. He created a number of task forces to manage the transition, filling them wherever possible with true believers, many of whom went on to take the very jobs in the agencies they had been charged with studying. The White House Office of Presidential Personnel assembled a staff of one hundred to screen potential appointees for philosophy as well as competence and integrity. The president made political use of the Senior Executive Service (SES), removing certain career officials and replacing them, as he is entitled to do, with more partisan managers.[7] The Reagan administration had more success than almost any preceding administration in shaping the leadership of the bureaucracy,[8] but even so found that it had appointed many people who proved to be deficient in either conservatism or competence or both. For every successful appointment there was an unhappy surprise.

The Reagan administration was accused of appointing cabinet and subcabinet officials who had "a common hostility to the programs they were supposed to run."[9] To some extent that was true, but the reliance on ideology more than clientele connections as a basis for appointment was not invented by Reagan; Jimmy Carter was charged by his critics with appointing scores of left-leaning activists to subcabinet posts.[10]

It is not clear what difference all this makes. Ideology is not enough to change the direction of a government agency; skill and perseverance are equally important. As we saw in chapters 11 and 12, some executives have had the ability to redirect their agencies, some have not. Caspar Weinberger changed the FTC; Anne Burford failed to change the EPA. Michael Pertschuk tried to make the FTC the government overseer of whole industries and failed; James Miller tried to imbue the FTC with a distinctive economic philosophy and succeeded. James Watt's stormy tenure as secretary of the interior provided plenty of ammunition for his critics, but other than generating headlines (and aiding the fund-raising efforts of environmentalists), it is not clear how much he achieved. Henry Kissinger certainly brought a coherent world view and immense intelligence to his job as secretary of state, but his success as a secretary was directly proportional to his willingness to ignore the department he nominally headed. As Laurence H. Silberman, a former ambassador, tells the story, Kissinger dominated the State Department by centralizing all important decisions in his office, ignoring lower-level officials and even leaving them uninformed as to what he was doing.[11] Kissinger ably served two presidents, but he did not thereby place the Department of State under presidential control. Policy was under Henry Kissinger's control; the department was under nobody's control.

Management

Some presidents have tried to change policy by changing procedures. President Reagan, for example, started or accelerated programs designed to make the management of government agencies more efficient and the regulations issued by those agencies more cost effective. These involved creating a Cabinet Council on Management and Administration, a Task Force on Regulatory Relief, an Office of Regulatory Affairs on OMB, and the President's Private Sector Survey on Cost Control (popularly known after its chairman as the Grace Commission). In this he was following in the footsteps of Franklin Roosevelt (who created the President's Commission on Administrative Management), Harry Truman (who, with the support of Congress, created the Hoover Commission to study many of the same management issues studied by the PCAM), Dwight Eisenhower (who recreated the Hoover Commission to produce yet more studies), Richard Nixon (who created the Ash Commission to reexamine many of the issues studied by the PCAM and the Hoover Commission), and Jimmy Carter (who launched all manner of procedural changes dealing with budgeting, organization, and government regulation).

All of these enterprises essentially have produced the same findings: the government is poorly managed. If management were to improve, the president would need more effective staff assistance (to set policy and evaluate performance) and department heads would need more authority (to organize their agencies, hold subordinates accountable, and adopt businesslike management methods).[12] In principle, there is no conflict between proposals to enhance the president's powers to set policy and hold subordinates accountable and proposals to enhance the ability of department heads to manage their agencies with a minimum of constraints. Indeed, this view is a staple of business-school teaching: Top executives oversee operating divisions by authorizing budgets, collecting information, and allocating rewards; division chiefs use their budgets to achieve goals, report information on goal achievement, and await their rewards.

In political reality, there is a profound conflict between the two sets of proposals. Congress will not tolerate giving department heads or bureau chiefs independent authority to reorganize their agencies, select their own personnel, or acquire and dispose of assets. To do so would be to reduce, if not eliminate, Congress's ability to make these agencies responsive to its wishes. Quite the contrary; Congress has tended to proliferate, not curtail, constraints on agency management. On the other hand, from time to time Congress has been willing to enhance the staff resources of the presidency. It has been willing to do this especially when the ideological tendencies of Capitol Hill and the White House are broadly compatible, as they were when Roosevelt and Johnson (and to some extent Eisenhower and Carter) were president. But even when the two branches of government were under the control of rival parties, Congress up to a point has deferred to the constitutional position of the president and his demands for a White House organized as he thinks best.

The result of these political realities is that efforts to improve management have tended to enhance the powers of the president without enlarging the freedom of the department heads. One-half of the business-school teaching has been implemented: The president has gained marginally in his quest for a greater capacity to set administrative policy but the department heads and bureau chiefs have been neither made more directly accountable to the president nor equipped with the tools to manage their own domains. The net effect has not been the decentralization of administration under presidential supervision but the centralization in the White House of certain checks on agency discretion.

The choice of key management personnel is more directly under White House control than was once the case. The White House, via the OMB, now reviews proposed regulations issued by the agencies to see if, in its judgment, they achieve legitimate goals at minimum cost. The OMB plays a much more aggressive role in designing and enforcing presidential budget policy: whereas it once reviewed agency requests to see if they conformed to the president's program and the canons of administrative efficiency, it now (at least in the Reagan administration) sets policy by mandating reductions and redirections in spending plans. The National Security Council (NSC) has become a major force in generating, not merely evaluating, defense and intelligence policy.

This has been the view of the Comptroller General of the United States and of the National Academy of Public Administration. The latter suggested that the increase of White House control systems has produced a "managerial overburden" in which procedure overwhelmed substance.[13] That may be too harsh a judgment (whether you think regulatory review is a burdensome set of procedures or a desirable shift in substance depends largely on whether you approve of the way the regulations were changed), but its essence—that White House efforts at improving management tend to centralize management decision making—surely is on the mark.

This can have wholly unanticipated consequences for the president. He thinks that his staff has grasped the core of policy only to discover that in fact what they have grasped are the minutiae of operations or the details of procedure. After Robert Wood had been undersecretary of Housing and Urban Development in the Johnson administration he described the "curious inversion" that results when the White House tries to "do too much at the top" by making more and more decisions itself:

> Operational matters flow to the top—as central staffs become engrossed in subduing outlying bureaucracies—and policymaking emerges at the bottom. At the top minor problems squeeze out major ones, and individuals lower down the echelons who have the time for reflection and mischief-making take up issues of fundamental philosophical and political significance.[14]

Reorganization

Given the difficulty of changing policy by changing procedures and the incomplete control the president has over many important subordinates, it is hardly surprising that presidents have taken to reorganizations the way overweight people take to fad diets—and with about the same results.

A reorganization promises a painless way of making big changes: an offending agency is made subordinate to a friendlier agency, an uncooperative bureau chief suddenly becomes somebody else's deputy bureau chief, and programs that once worked at cross purposes now will work in happy unison. Or so the theory goes. Of course, not all reorganizations are intended to make a difference; some, such as the creation of the Department of Education or the Department of Veterans Affairs, were intended chiefly to satisfy campaign promises or to appease politically important interest groups. But many reorganizations in fact are designed to change what the bureaucracy does or how it does it. The success rate for these has not been high.

Reorganizations make a difference if they alter in an important way how resources flow to programs, how career rewards are distributed to people, or how tasks get defined. Occasionally these things happen. More often they do not.

In 1967 Frederick C. Mosher published a careful review of twelve government reorganizations at various levels of government. Those that were aimed at changing what the agency did were less successful than those aimed at solving some administrative problem; those imposed from outside the affected agency tended to be less successful than those generated from within it.[15]

Reorganizations imposed from the outside tend to reflect the very top-down view of bureaucracies against which this book has been railing. People at the top (the White House staff, a presidential commission) see two separate agencies performing apparently similar tasks; this is immediately labeled "wasteful duplication." Or they see a bureau whose activities are not coordinated with that of other bureaus in the same policy area; this shows the lack of "clear lines of accountability."

Whether or not the tasks are duplicative requires a close analysis of what agency operators actually do; whether the line of accountability should run to one cabinet secretary or another depends on which department offers the most congenial organizational culture for a given bureau. These are not matters easily determined by high-level commissions.

The history of efforts to reorganize the enforcement of drug laws reveals what can and cannot be expected from reorganizations. Beginning in the 1930s, the Federal Bureau of Narcotics (FBN) and the Customs Service, both located in the Treasury Department, struggled for authority to control the importation of drugs. In 1968 President Johnson issued an executive order that transferred FBN out of Treasury, changed its name to the Bureau of Narcotics and Dangerous Drugs (BNDD), and put it in the Justice Department. This new structure, as Patricia Rachal observed, "did nothing to alleviate the feuding; it simply made it interdepartmental rather than intradepartmental."[16] Then in 1973 President Nixon issued a reorganization plan that called for the creation of the Drug Enforcement

Administration (DEA), putting into it both the old BNDD and all of the narcotics agents who used to work for the Customs Service; DEA would be part of the Justice Department and made the "lead agency" for narcotics enforcement. To partially appease Customs some Immigration and Naturalization Service (INS) inspectors who formerly had worked at Justice were transferred to Customs.*

For a while this reorganization muted the feuding, but did not end it. The reason is simple: the turf battle reflected an underlying reality that no organizational scheme could overcome. The task of the Customs Service was to guard the U.S. borders in order to collect taxes due on imported merchandise and to prevent smuggling. In the course of this work it was inevitable that it would discover drugs. When it did, it would investigate to determine who the smugglers were. There was no way to take Customs out of the drug-enforcement business other than by dismantling it entirely, obviously an impractical idea. The goal of the DEA was "to enforce the drug laws," a vague statement that DEA members converted into clearly understood tasks, namely, to make undercover buys of narcotics and use this evidence to arrest middle- and upper-level dealers. Naturally this buy-and-bust tactic would be employed at or near the borders as well as in the big cities and would be directed against foreigners trying to import drugs as well as against Americans trying to distribute them. Inevitably DEA would investigate cases that Customs also was investigating, and so the two agencies came into conflict.

The several reorganizations did not alter the fundamental tasks, financial resources, or career rewards of the two bureaus. From time to time some skilled agency heads succeeded in negotiating better relations between the two rivals. Customs and DEA officers began to work at joint tasks, such as the El Paso Intelligence Center, and in the process became more comfortable with the idea of agency cooperation. But so long as the core tasks remained the same there would remain large gaps in drug-law enforcement. For example, DEA often found it hard to bring conspiracy charges against large underworld organizations because local DEA offices were reluctant to cooperate with each other and because proving conspiracy charges often required agents to spend long, tedious hours studying wiretap transcripts or telephone toll-charge records rather than making undercover buys and kicking in doors. Moreover, DEA was a relatively small agency with a modest budget.

*It might interest the reader to know that I was involved in both the 1968 and 1973 reorganizations. The 1968 change resulted from a recommendation of the White House Task Force on Crime (of which I was the chairman); the 1973 change occurred while I was chairman of the National Advisory Commission on Drug Abuse Control. I supported both reorganizations. In retrospect I believe that many of the participants, myself included, gave the issues less careful thought than they deserved.

In 1982 the Reagan administration reorganized drug enforcement once again, this time by placing DEA under the control of the FBI. The FBI director appointed the top DEA executives and determined the policies governing hiring, training, organization, and fiscal control. At first it produced a profound culture shock. DEA agents, accustomed to working in a highly decentralized organization, getting cash on short notice to make drug buys, and learning their jobs on the streets, suddenly found themselves part of an organization that emphasized centralized decision making, tight (and sometimes slow and stingy) control of cash, and elaborate formal training programs. DEA agents resisted the organizational marriage, complaining that the typical FBI agent wouldn't make a drug arrest for fear of spoiling his clean white shirt; many FBI agents barely could conceal their contempt for the casually dressed, fast-moving drug agents who seemingly operated out of control.

In time, tempers cooled and real changes occurred. FBI training programs began to produce, even in the eyes of DEA veterans, better quality agents. The FBI administrators in turn began to loosen their tight central controls in order to accommodate the realities of street-level enforcement. Promotion patterns changed so as to reward agents who participated in complex investigations that led to the prosecution of major drug conspiracies. At the local level, interagency committees were established to channel funds into promising investigations aimed at high-level dealers; the availability of the money enhanced agency cooperation in sharing information. The FBI's habits, experience, and technical equipment made it easier and more rewarding to use wiretaps for acquiring evidence. At the same time, the DEA's pool of drug informants remained a key resource that the FBI could not duplicate.

In sum, the 1968 and 1973 reorganization plans that moved boxes around on the government's organization chart had relatively little effect on drug-law enforcement, except to cause turmoil and confusion. Changing lines of accountability made little difference so long as organizations were allowed to define operating tasks as they saw fit and career incentives remained unchanged. The "semi-merger" of the FBI and DEA made a much bigger difference because it altered promotion lines, provided new resources, and led (after a period of resistance) to redefining somewhat the core tasks of both the FBI and DEA.

There are many other examples that tend toward the same conclusion. Taking the Army Air Force out of the army and changing it into the United States Air Force made a very great difference: an agency with a distinctive culture struggling to assert itself inside a department with a very different culture acquired autonomy, career lines, and budget appropriations.[17] By contrast, assembling a variety of agencies together into a Department of Health, Education, and Welfare made little difference: the component bureaus, each with its distinctive culture, professional outlook, and congressional supporters, continued for the most part to operate independently of each other and of HEW's central leadership.

Even a president who understands what a reorganization plan can and cannot accomplish in principle may still find it very hard to know what difference, if any, it will make in a particular case. The Federal Aviation Administration (FAA) is charged with regulating air traffic in the interests of safety. Well and good. But where should the FAA be located? From 1940 to 1958 it was part of the Department of Commerce; from 1958 to 1967 it was an independent agency, reporting (in theory) directly to the president; after 1967 it was part of the Department of Transportation; in 1988 Congress was considering a bill to make the FAA once again an independent agency. When it was independent, critics claimed that there was no way to "coordinate" air traffic safety with other transportation programs; when it was part of the Department of Commerce (and later the Department of Transportation), critics charged that air traffic safety was being "downgraded."[18] Should a president favor coordination at the cost of downgrading, or upgrade at the cost of autonomy? There is no obvious answer, especially since the FAA is embedded in a network of interest groups (airline companies, private-pilot associations, airplane manufacturers, and the air traffic controllers' association, among others) with divergent views as to what would be desirable.

Whatever the president decides, it will be Congress that has the final word. From 1939 to the mid-1970s, the president had the power to propose a reorganization plan that would take effect unless either house of Congress within sixty days passed a resolution objecting to the plan. Since the legislative veto is now unconstitutional, the reorganization-plan method is no longer available; a statute instead must be enacted. In debating such laws, Congress is exceptionally sensitive to the implications of any reorganization for its own internal allocation of power. Taking a bureau out of one department and putting it into another often means shifting oversight responsibility for that bureau from one committee (or subcommittee) to another. A willingness to surrender turf is as rare among members of Congress as it is among cabinet secretaries.

Coordination

In a phrase that every student of public administration has committed to memory, Harold Seidman described the quest for coordination as the "twentieth-century equivalent of the medieval search for the philosopher's stone." In words heavy with irony, he explained: "If only we can find the right formula for coordination, we can reconcile the irreconcilable, harmonize competing and wholly divergent interests, overcome irrationalities in our government structures, and make hard policy choices to which no one will dissent."[19]

Certainly this cynical assessment is amply supported by Basil Mott's detailed study of one common mechanism for achieving coordination, the interagency committee, in this case the Interdepartmental Health and Hospital Council (IHHC) of the State of New York.[20] Active for two decades, spanning three different governors, and strongly supported by its participants, the IHHC seemed a model of what could be achieved by way of coordinating executive-branch agencies with overlapping interests. Model it may have been, but hardly one of achievement. Mott concluded that the council did little to foster the integration of the mental health services provided by different departments, failed to coordinate the vocational and employment services available to the mentally ill, did not even examine the environmental health functions of the several departments serving on the council, and was unable to act on the health education programs offered by the state. "The Council was ineffective with respect to decision-making. It did not systematically examine problems in their broad implications or decide on means and ends for dealing with them. Although the Council's committees conducted many useful studies, such efforts . . . typically skirted sensitive and controversial issues."[21] The council was popular with its members, not in spite of these limitations but because of them. Its existence shielded the member agencies from other kinds of external threats (gubernatorial intervention, legislative control) while not altering essential working procedures.

Why this failure of a coordinating council to coordinate? The answer is that it operated on the basis of the Rule of Unanimity: No decision would be taken if any member disagreed. A necessary correlate of the Rule of Unanimity was the Rule of Triviality: If only unanimous decisions could be made, then no decision would be made on any controversial (that is, important) matter.[22] But why did the council adopt the Rule of Unanimity? Because any other rule would have threatened the autonomy of member agencies. If decisions would be made by majority vote, some agencies might form a coalition against the interests of other agencies. No agency head is willing to subordinate his or her organization to a procedure that allows other agencies to define its tasks or allocate its resources.

But Roger Porter reports a very different experience with the Economic Policy Board (EPB) that operated in the White House during the Ford administration. The EPB was quite successful in providing the president with consistent and timely advice on economic policy and in resolving disagreements among the cabinet secretaries represented on the board. Its success was not purchased at the price of tending only to trivial matters; it drafted the essential features of President Ford's 1975 tax-cut proposals, coordinated this government's position on grain sales to the Soviet Union, and was deeply involved in a complex international trade issue involving the importation of footwear.[23]

In many ways, the IHHC and the EPB were similar: each about the same size, each equipped with a small professional staff, and each holding meetings that faithfully were attended. But there were some key differences. First, the Economic Policy Board met daily, the Health Council met monthly. This meant that the EPB became a central, not a peripheral, activity in the lives of its members and a source of organizational loyalty in its own right. Second, the board met in the White House and reported directly to the president; the council met in its own quarters and was not an intimate part of the governor's group of political insiders. Third, the EPB seems to have been concerned chiefly with policy, not operations. Cabinet secretaries were asked to agree to courses of action, not to change the missions of their own organizations. The council, by contrast, seems to have been faulted by Mott chiefly for its failure to do things that would have required a redefinition of tasks and new ways of delivering services.

In my judgment the council is the more common form of coordinating mechanism; the board was the exception. The council exemplifies Seidman's metaphor: "Interagency committees are the crabgrass in the garden of government. Nobody wants them, but everyone has them. Committees seem to thrive on scorn and ridicule."[24] They are common because the problem of coordination is pervasive; they rarely are effective because a president or governor cannot give his or her personal and frequent attention to more than a handful of such entities and because few (including, I think, the EPB) can alter agency tasks.

The history of Franklin Roosevelt's efforts to coordinate the American government's management of the economy and of the procurement of military supplies during World War II can be read as a long experiment in finding a machine that would work. As told by Herman Somers in his book, *Presidential Agency*,[25] it is a story of one failed expedient after another until by luck or circumstance the right mechanism was created and put into the hands of the right man.

The War Resources Board, formed in 1939, was a "blue-ribbon commission": a group of distinguished civilians appointed to draft a war mobilization plan. It lasted but a few months and never issued a report. In its place came the National Defense Advisory Commission, another blue-ribbon commission; though legally powerless, it assumed the power to approve defense contracts and to advise the War Department on how to manage procurement. It gave some good advice, but its assumed powers proved inadequate to the task of getting the military to pay it much heed. It lasted a year. In its place FDR created the Office of Production Management, equipped with real power, but not enough, especially in view of the fact that the president regularly undercut its authority by creating rival offices and yielding to unhappy subordinates. Within a few months it too was gone, replaced by the Supply Priorities and Allocations Board. This was a clear step backward, for the board was little more than a committee of cabinet members and OPM holdovers. The president gave it little authority; as a result, it is hardly surprising that the board set few priorities and allocated even fewer supplies. Next came the War Production Board, created in 1942 under the chairmanship of Donald M. Nelson, an affable executive to whom FDR gave (under irate Senate prodding) a broad grant of real power. It had some success but in time came to be seen by other government agencies as a rival and, worse, one that could be ignored. Nelson had power but did not know what to do with it. He created "czars" to manage the manpower and rubber programs but then let them out from under his control. Every time an issue arose between the WPB and a military service, Nelson had to go to the White House for a decision. The following year, FDR replaced the WPB with the Office of War Mobilization (OWM). This time he got it right.

The OWM was a small adjudicatory body located in the White House and headed by a man who experience and reputation enabled him to assume, in fact if not in title, the post of assistant president. Jimmy Byrnes had been a congressman from South Carolina, a high-level executive branch official, and a justice of the Supreme Court. He was popular with Congress and loyal to the president. But most important of all, he knew how to create a coordinating organization.

To avoid the weakness of cabinet committees and commissions, OWM was a decision maker. To avoid the jealousy and rivalry inspired by the War Production Board, OWM ran no programs, created no czars, and had a minuscule budget. To avoid challenges to its authority, OWM was given a broad legal mandate by Congress and was located in the White House under arrangements that made it clear there would be no appealing its decisions to the president. To avoid meddling in the work of existing agencies, OWM was kept very small (it had only ten employees, five of whom were clerks). To avoid being seen as an entity that would redefine the tasks of agencies, it refused to produce any plans, contenting itself with refereeing disputes between agencies. Byrnes was an arbitrator, not a manager; OWM was a courtroom, not an agency. It worked.

The lessons of OWM or the Economic Policy Board, though occasionally rediscovered, rarely are remembered. Whenever a political crisis draws attention to the fact that authority in our government is widely shared, the cry is heard for a "czar" to "knock heads together" and "lead" the assault on AIDS, drug abuse, pollution, or defense procurement abuses.*

*A recent example was the suggestion by Sandra Panem that responsibility for managing a "novel health emergency" (she had in mind the AIDS epidemic) should be "centralized" in the hands of one federal official. See *The AIDS Bureaucracy* (Cambridge, Mass.: Harvard University Press, 1988), 137. The problem with this suggestion (in addition to the obvious

Our form of government, to say nothing of our political culture, does not lend itself to czars; even the unusually adroit organizational strategy designed by Jimmy Byrnes required wartime conditions for it to work.

Presidents, aware that coordination by committee rarely works unless they give it their personal attention, have been inclined in recent years to attempt to coordinate by central management. Sometimes it works, when the tasks lend themselves to central direction and the political costs are tolerable. Presidents Carter and Reagan established central mechanisms for reviewing proposed government regulations of business; they took heat from people in Congress who wanted more rather than less regulation, but in general they made their decisions stick.[26] The reason in large part is that the contents of a proposed regulation is a negotiable matter; an agency's lawyer proposes X, the president's lawyer counters with Y, they settle on Z. Regulatory review is difficult and time-consuming, but it does not require the impossible: central management of the ongoing operations of departments and bureaus.

The disappointments attendant on many reorganizations and the difficulties inherent in coordinating committees have encouraged presidents to expand the power of the White House staff to make decisions and even run programs. The costs of this are nowhere more apparent than in the Iran-Contra affair when someone decided that the staff of the National Security Council (NSC) should design and manage programs.

The NSC, created by the passage of the National Security Act of 1947, was intended to "advise the President with respect to the integration [i.e., the coordination] of domestic, foreign, and military policies relating to the national security."[27] Its statutory members are the president, the vice-president, the secretaries of state and defense, and certain lesser executives; other persons can be added by the president. The NSC is served by a staff under the direction of the national security advisor. Under President Eisenhower, the NSC staff performed the functions originally envisioned for the council: advising the president and attempting to coordinate the implementation of policies approved by the president.

Under Presidents Kennedy and Johnson, however, the NSC staff began to serve as a source of policies, not simply as the source of advice about the proposals of others. By the time of the Nixon administration, the NSC staff had grown to fifty professionals (and many support personnel), all under the direction of Henry Kissinger, a powerful advocate as well as

---

one that no single official can manage the complex research, treatment, and service-delivery systems found at all levels of government) is that a new organization created to handle the AIDS crisis will be ill-adapted to handle the next "novel health emergency." A new ailment will likely have an entirely different source, be spread through quite different mechanisms, and involve wholly new treatment methods, at which point someone will write a book attacking the "AIDS czar" for being "unresponsive" to the new problem.

policy analyst. The council itself had spawned a host of committees and subcommittees, all designed to coordinate policy implementation.

President Reagan initially sought to downgrade the national security advisor and his staff, but in time Reagan discovered what his predecessors had learned, namely, that imposing a presidential perspective on foreign and defense policy is no easy task, and that doing it effectively requires a strong NSC staff. The difficulty of getting the departments of defense and state as well as the CIA and the military to work together harmoniously toward presidential objectives is like untying the Gordian knot; even with a strong NSC staff, it is difficult and sometimes impossible. Though the NSC was created to "coordinate," presidents have found that it must do more than this; in particular, the NSC must help him define a presidential strategy for the conduct of foreign and military affairs. The president has both unique responsibilities and a unique perspective; his breadth of view is not likely to be shared by any single agency.

So far, so good. But it is only a small step from this conclusion to the far more sweeping and dangerous one that the easiest thing to do is not to untie but to cut the Gordian knot. The NSC staff not only would formulate a strategy, it would reduce the strategy to particular programs and carry them out. And so, by a process not yet fully understood, the staff acquired the power to both make and implement policy—in short, to become an operating agency.

The report of the President's Special Review Board (called the Tower Commission after its chairman) found that in 1985–86 key members of the NSC staff conceived the idea of selling arms to Iran in hopes that that country would use its influence with terrorist groups to release American hostages held in the Middle East, and then to use funds received from this sale to support the insurgents (the "Contras") fighting against the Marxist regime in Nicaragua.[28]

When all this became public, the result was a political disaster for the president. The Tower Commission Report makes quite clear what went wrong: When the NSC became an operational agency it ceased to be a policy evaluation agency, and thus there was no longer any systematic White House review of policy proposals. The NSC staff—the last stop on the path that a policy proposal follows on its way to the president's desk—became an advocate instead of a referee. As a result, risky, controversial ideas were given perfunctory review and some of them (the transfer of funds to the Contras, for example) were not reviewed by anybody, including the president.[29] Moreover, the NSC staff was a group of inexperienced amateurs trying to run operations that would have strained the most skilled CIA professionals. In short, a White House trying to bypass the bureaucracy (and Congress) and "do it ourselves" led to a White House shooting itself in the foot.

Our system of government makes policy coordination difficult, but like most governmental difficulties, the solution rarely is to be found in ignoring the system. In fact, there is something to be said (and Martin Landau has said it) on behalf of duplication and overlap. In some governmental systems as in many mechanical ones, redundancy is useful. Overlapping agencies, like back-up computers on the space shuttle, can detect errors; duplicating functions is not always wasteful, it can lead to more flexible responses and generate alternatives. The problem, of course, is to choose between good and bad redundancies, a matter on which scholars have made little progress.[30]

The Bureaucracy Responds

The bureaucracy is far from the helpless pawn of whatever control measures the president seeks to put in place. In this respect it welcomes the fact that it has two masters, for though it may prefer one that is benevolent and supportive, it prefers two if one turns out to be hostile or meddlesome.

Richard Pious has described very well what bureaucrats want from the president:

> Careerists want the president's support. They resent his campaign attacks on "bureaucracy" . . . They want him to recommend pay raises and defend the "merit" system. They expect him to promote careerists into the ranks of political executives, especially at the assistant secretary levels. . . . Above all, careerists expect the president to support their budget requests, grant them maximum autonomy in their operations, and protect the missions of their bureaus. In all these expectations they are usually disappointed.[31]

What do they do if they are disappointed? Fight back. How? By getting Congress to give them the money, the autonomy, and the missions that the White House has threatened.

Pious notes the several tactics available to an embattled agency to block what it regards as excessive presidential control. It can acquire a measure of formal autonomy, as did the Legal Services Division of the Office of Economic Opportunity. Comprised of liberal lawyers committed to using lawsuits as a way of altering the power position of the poor, it felt threatened so long as it was a division within an office subject to presidential control. So it got Congress to convert it into the Legal Services Corporation, headed by a governing board not subject to direct presidential control.* When President Reagan took office, determined to eliminate the agency, he discovered that Congress would not abolish it; when he tried to take control of it, he discovered that the Senate would not confirm many of his proposed nominees for the board.

Bureaus can also try to convince Congress to put into the authorizing legislation provisions that certain professional or career qualifications are required for senior positions (thus sharply reducing the president's ability to appoint his outsiders to key posts) or add to the appropriations bills provisions that assign funds to specific programs (thus reducing the president's power to shift funds among programs).[32] And of course bureaucrats can leak presidential proposals to friendly reporters and urge sympathetic interest groups to sue them in court to "force" agencies to do what they would like to do anyway.

What is surprising is not that bureaucrats sometimes can defy the president but that they support his programs as much as they do. The reason is rather simple: Hardened cynics will find it hard to believe, but bureaucrats want to do the right thing. The more skillful of Reagan's conservative appointees proved that: Though most bureaucrats were much more liberal than their political superiors and though there were pockets of resistance, in many agencies—the Office of Management and Budget, the Department of Education, the Justice Department, the Federal Trade Commission—the careerists served the policies of their ideologically distant chiefs.

Agencies differ in the extent to which they are amenable to presidential control. Those that have easily assessed outcomes—that is, production and craft agencies—are more readily brought under external control than those (such as procedural and coping organizations) that have uncertain or unknown outcomes. Of course, the very factors that make agencies more susceptible to presidential influence also make them more susceptible to congressional control.

Which political branch will dominate the work of a production or craft agency will depend in large part on the kinds of programs it manages. If the program affects all parts of the country the same way, then Congress will have less interest in its daily management than if the program affects different parts in different ways. When the Treasury Department tries to manage the dollar in international markets, it is engaging in an activity that has few distributional consequences, and so Congress is (usually) not very interested in its internal affairs. But when the Department of Housing and Urban Development funds housing projects in cities, it is doing something that confers a concrete benefit on some localities and not others, and so Congress takes a keen interest in how HUD makes those decisions. The Treasury Department (and other bureaucracies that have observable

*In 1971 President Nixon had vetoed a bill to do this, but by 1974, badly weakened by the Watergate scandal and facing the threat of impeachment, he signed a new bill effecting the change just two weeks before he resigned the presidency.

outcomes with few distributional effects) will be "presidential" agencies; HUD (and other bureaucracies that produce easily observed distributional effects) will be "congressional" agencies.*

Making the bureaucracy accountable to the president in any comprehensive or enduring way is impossible; making it alert to his preferences is possible in those cases where presidents put loyal and competent subordinates in charge of making decisions in presidential agencies. Not every president understands these distinctions, hence some do too little (ignoring the qualities of their appointees and failing to hold them accountable for their point decisions) and some too much (trying to manage agencies with complex, poorly understood tasks).

If presidents do what they reasonably can they will attempt less than the public expects. Since conforming to public expectations is the essence of presidential reelection campaigns, they have a strong incentive to attempt more than they can produce. This disposition is reinforced by the view from the White House: "Many miles and many layers of organizational hierarchy intervene between it and the performers of the tasks upon whom realization of [presidential] designs ultimately depend," writes Martha Derthick. Presidential plans, therefore, often "lack realism, refinement, concreteness, and subtlety. They are suffused with a false simplicity, the product both of faulty comprehension of applied tasks and the quest for order and uniformity that is associated with a central perspective."[34]

Central management of the bureaucracy, in all its important respects, is not possible. Dean Acheson, one of the wisest political executives of the twentieth century, put it this way: "One fact . . . is clear to anyone with experience in government: The springs of policy bubble up; they do not trickle down."[35]

*Douglas Yates has supplied a somewhat different way of distinguishing between presidential (or what he calls "Type A") and congressional (or "Type B") agencies. Our respective arguments overlap but are not quite identical.[33]

CHAPTER 15

Courts

ON NOVEMBER 25, 1837, Susan Decatur, the widow of the American naval hero, Commodore Steven Decatur, brought suit against Secretary of the Navy James K. Paulding, claiming that he had failed to pay her the pension to which she was entitled. Earlier that year Congress had passed a law providing pensions to the widows of officers who had died in naval service and on the same day had adopted a resolution specifically awarding a five-year pension to Mrs. Decatur. Secretary Paulding had paid Mrs. Decatur one pension but not the other. Mrs. Decatur argued that she was entitled to both. The court denied her claim and she appealed to the Supreme Court.

The Supreme Court refused even to consider the merits of her claim on the grounds that to do so would require the Court to tell an executive officer of the government how to do his job. More particularly, Chief Justice Roger Taney, speaking for the Court, said that the federal courts cannot "guide and control" the "judgment or discretion" such officers exercise in the performance of their duties. The courts can compel an officer to perform a "ministerial" act—that is, one clearly and precisely prescribed by law—but they cannot tell him how to perform an "executive" act, that is, one involving judgment or discretion. Even though Congress had passed two laws that on the face of it seemed to require giving Susan Decatur two pensions, the Court took the view that the secretary of the navy was entitled to choose whether to follow both or only one; after all, he was responsible for conserving the funds available for paying naval pensions. Thus he had discretion and thus the courts were powerless to tell him how to use it. "The interference of the Courts with the performance of the ordinary duties of the executive departments of government, would be productive of nothing but mischief."[1]

Over one hundred and thirty years later, a group of citizens sued Secretary of Transportation John Volpe to block the building of a highway through a public park in Memphis, Tennessee. Secretary Volpe thought he had the right to authorize this highway. The Federal-Aid Highway Act of 1968 allowed highways to be built through public parks if no "feasible and prudent" alternative route existed and if the secretary engaged in "all possible planning to minimize harm to the park." Given the distinction the Supreme Court had made earlier between "ministerial" and "discretionary" actions, one might have supposed Volpe was right. After all, such phrases as "feasible and prudent," "all possible planning," and "minimize harm" obviously were imprecise and allowed for—indeed, clearly called for—the exercise of judgment. Whether or not the highway through Overton Park was a good idea in this view was not the issue; what was at issue was whether the courts had the power to tell an executive officer how to use his discretion. But that is not the view the Supreme Court took: It rejected the claim that the law gave Secretary Volpe discretion to act as he wished and instead ordered the lower federal court to hold a hearing on the propriety of Volpe's decision, clearly implying that if he was unable to show that he had used proper discretion the highway would not be built.[2]

About the same time as the Overton Park decision, Kenneth Adams, a black student in Mississippi, sued Secretary of Health, Education, and Welfare Elliot Richardson and his subordinate, the director of the Office for Civil Rights (OCR), for failing to enforce the Civil Rights Act of 1964. Adams claimed that Title VI of that law forbade giving federal aid to any segregated public school. OCR was obliged to "effectuate the provisions of the act" by "issuing rules, regulations, or orders of general applicability" and it "*may*" (italics added) terminate federal grants to such schools or use "other means authorized by law." Cutting off funds—the ultimate power placed in the hands of OCR—was to be used as a last resort after the agency had determined that compliance could not be obtained by voluntary means and had given the offending school a chance to defend itself in a hearing. The law was silent on how long the OCR should wait after an order was issued and voluntary compliance sought before federal funds actually were cut off. In short, one way of reading the law was that it imposed on obligation on the OCR but left to the agency's discretion the manner and timing of the actions designed to carry out that obligation. But that was not how the federal court saw matters. It found for Adams and began a process, still going on in 1989, under which it reviewed and controlled almost every aspect of the work of OCR.[3] And the Court did not limit its attention to the matter raised by Adams. It added to the case the claims raised by the Mexican-American Legal Defense and Education Fund, the Women's Equity Action League, and the National Federation of the Blind. In effect, a federal agency was placed in receivership, much as if it were a bankrupt business.[4]

Obviously something had changed. A Court that turned a deaf ear to Susan Decatur was all ears to the people worried about Overton Park and to Kenneth Adams and his many associates.

In 1923, Mrs. Harriet Frothingham, a citizen of Massachusetts, sued Secretary of the Treasury Andrew Mellon to prevent the implementation of the Maternity Act. Under this law federal funds would be given to states that followed certain procedures designed to improve maternal and infant health. She argued that the Maternity Act was not authorized by the Constitution and that the federal government had no right using her tax money to pay for an unconstitutional program. The Supreme Court rejected her claim, not because it thought the Maternity Act was constitutional but because Harriet Frothingham was not entitled to bring suit. It was not enough to be a taxpayer; she would have to show that she had sustained "some direct injury" as a result of enforcing this statute. Being merely one among millions of taxpayers created at best an interest that was "minute and indeterminable." Spending money under the Maternity Act would have an effect on her future tax bill that was "so remote, fluctuating and uncertain" as to afford no basis for asking a court for help.[5]

Fifty years later, five law students living in the Washington, D.C., area brought suit against the Interstate Commerce Commission. The ICC had allowed railroad companies to increase the rates they charged for shipping freight by 25 percent. The students said that they liked to hike and camp and argued that the higher freight rates might make hiking and camping less attractive. Their reasoning went as follows: Higher freight rates might discourage people from shipping scrap paper and metal that could be recycled; if less were shipped, less would be recycled; if less were recycled, then there would be more litter in parks and more trees would be cut down to make paper and more mines dug to find metal; if this happened, the hiking would be less pleasant. One might suppose that a Court unwilling to let Mrs. Frothingham, the taxpayer, sue the government was a Court unwilling to allow hikers to sue the government. If being a taxpayer created an interest that was "minute," "indeterminable," "remote," and "uncertain," then surely being a hiker worried about the environmental effect of shipping costs created an interest that was at least as remote and speculative as Mrs. Frothingham's. Not so. The Court, admitting that the students' line of reasoning was "attenuated," nonetheless decided that they had standing to sue the ICC.[6]

Obviously, something had changed.

What had changed were the federal courts. Once it was difficult to use the courts to alter the discretionary decisions of executive agencies; now it is relatively easy. Once it was difficult to argue that you have been directly affected by a federal decision; now it is relatively easy. These changes have greatly multiplied the constraints on government bureaus: to the fear of media attacks, the tension of presidential-congressional rivalry, and the pressure of constituency demands has been added the detailed oversight of the courts.

The two changes illustrated by these cases have to do with the meaning of "policy" and the nature of "standing." When Susan Decatur was trying to get her second pension, the courts drew a sharp line between "rights" and "policy." "Rights" were relatively few, albeit of constitutional importance: the right to life, liberty, and property. Courts adjudicated rights. "Policy," on the other hand, was a course of action decided on by the "political" branches of government, the president and Congress, and insofar as it did not violate any clear constitutional or legal rights possessed by individuals, a policy could be almost anything the president and Congress wanted it to be. Policy necessarily involves discretion, the right to choose among alternative courses of action. Even the tiny amount of discretion claimed by Secretary Paulding (the right to decide whether Congress meant for Mrs. Decatur to have one or two pensions) was enough to shut the door to any court interference.[7] If the door were not kept shut, the courts reasoned, everybody would fight out every issue of policy before a judge; anybody who lost in Congress would try again in the nearest federal court. Moreover, if the courts became too officious, many judges feared they would be accused of acting undemocratically.

By the time Secretary Volpe sought to build a highway in Memphis, the courts had abandoned any sharp distinction between law and policy and thus were prepared to insist that he use his discretion in certain ways. The Court was not quite ready to tell him whether to build a highway but it certainly was ready to require him to conduct certain studies, assemble certain data, and compile a lengthy record showing that he had used his discretion "properly."

The doctrine of "standing" refers to a federal court rule that requires a person who enters court to first show that he or she has a personal interest in the controversy and that this interest involves some right that is being threatened by government action. For a long time being a mere taxpayer was not enough, because having to pay taxes did not create a direct or personal interest in an issue different from that of any other taxpayer. But in time the courts began to give standing to taxpayers if they showed that the government action violated an important constitutional provision. In 1968, for example, the Supreme Court gave standing to taxpayers who argued that the federal aid to education program violated the constitutional requirement that church and state be kept separate.[8] Just five years after this the Court decided that the five law students had standing; apparently the quality of the environment (no matter how remote or speculative the threat to it) was as important to the judges as the Bill of Rights.

The SCRAP case, as it came to be called, was the high-water mark of the broad definition of standing; the Supreme Court has since retreated a bit. It has denied standing to a man who claimed that as a taxpayer he had a right to know the budget of the Central Intelligence Agency,[9] to a group of persons who complained that a city zoning ordinance tended to exclude low-income people,[10] and to an organization that favored the separation of church and state and so were opposed to the transfer of government property to a religious college.[11]

Despite these ups and downs the trend is clear: The courts, on their own initiative, today are far more willing to allow people to challenge government decisions, even those involving a substantial amount of executive discretion, than was once the case. Congress has contributed to this change by the laws it has enacted. When it passed the Clean Air Act it specifically allowed citizens to sue the Environmental Protection Agency (EPA) for "failing to perform any act or duty under this act which is not discretionary." Several other regulatory laws passed in the 1970s contained similar provisions.[12]

These laws retain the form of the old jurisprudence. They speak of "nondiscretionary" duties. But the courts' willingness to broaden the definition of what is "nondiscretionary" has meant that the new laws have taken on a meaning far different from anything Secretary of the Navy Paulding would have recognized. For example, a federal court allowed the Sierra Club to sue the EPA. That in itself had few precedents, for the Sierra Club by the old rules governing standing would have had a hard time proving that *it* had been directly and adversely affected by whatever decisions the EPA was making. But the court went further; despite the language of the Clean Air Act authorizing suits for failing to perform "nondiscretionary" duties, the court decided that the EPA should perform certain *discretionary* tasks—namely, designing a program to prevent any significant deterioration in the quality of the air in places that were already meeting the air standards specified in the statute.[13] Richard Stewart, in his masterful review of the changes in administrative law in this country, concludes that it was the courts, not Congress, that made the decisive difference—changing a political discussion of policy and discretion into a legal discussion of rights and procedures.[14]

These changes in the relationship of federal agencies to the courts have had their counterparts at the state and local level. Police and fire departments have had their recruitment and promotion policies challenged in court. Prisons in at least thirty states (as of 1986) were under court orders to reduce populations, improve facilities, and alter procedures. Public schools in dozens of states have been, and in some cases still are, under court supervision designed to increase racial integration. But court intervention in school management is not limited to giving effect to the constitutional ban on segregation. Between 1858 and 1980, schools in California were the object of 811 law suits, only nine of which involved desegregation; almost all the rest pertained to school administration, teacher selection, textbook adoptions, and the content of various educational programs. Over two hundred such cases were filed in just the ten years between 1969 and 1979.[15]

The causes of increased court control over local and federal bureaucracies are somewhat different, but the effects are the same: The constituencies to which administrators must be attentive and the constraints that they must observe have multiplied dramatically. When Robert C. Wood was superintendent of schools in Boston in the 1970s, his department was obliged to obey the contents of more than two hundred court orders ranging "from major efforts at planning to the repair and maintenance of classrooms." When Wood asked his staff attorney whether they were in compliance with all these orders, the lawyer shrugged his shoulders and said, "Who knows—it's hard enough to count the orders, let alone read them."[16]

The Effects on Agency Management

"Who knows?" also would be a good answer to the question, "What difference has all this court intervention made in agency management?" There have been countless essays on whether the courts should intervene as they do but scarcely any that describe what systematic (as opposed to particular) changes in bureaucratic life this intervention has produced.

COST

The one difference that everyone acknowledges is cost: Intensive court intervention immeasurably increases the time and money it takes to reach a decision. Agency heads that face the prospect of frequent legal challenge become even more risk averse than they already are, and thus institute rule-making procedures that are far more complex than anything required by the Administrative Procedure Act. That law allows the courts to overturn any agency decision that is "arbitrary, capricious, an abuse of discretion, or otherwise not in accord with law."[17] In practice the courts have insisted that the decision not only be nonarbitrary and free of caprice but that it be supported by "substantial evidence" set forth in a written record. Something like this is what the Supreme Court wanted from Secretary of Transportation Volpe before he built his road in Memphis: a full record of all the evidence and factors he took into consideration in reaching his decision.

Only one of the twenty-four health standards issued by the Occupational Safety and Health Administration (OSHA) was not challenged in the courts as of 1985.[18] The OSHA administrator, like any of us, decided it is better to be safe than sorry, and so before OSHA issues a formal rule it conducts courtlike hearings before a qualified hearing examiner, with provisions for cross-examinations. A complete transcript of the proceedings is kept. Since industry often has an interest in avoiding a new regulation it has an interest in protracting these proceedings as long as possible. The combined effect of the judicialization of the agency and the interests of the constituents can be measured in time and volume. It takes OSHA an average of four years to devise a new health standard. The record is commensurately long: in the case of a proposed new standard for cotton dust it included 105,000 pages of testimony in addition to uncounted pages of documents.[19]

Judicializing agency procedures not only takes time and money, it often makes agency heads reluctant to change. Jeremy Rabkin argues that "contemporary administrative law reinforces . . . administrative tendencies to inertia and passivity."[20] The more one has to explain and justify the less one is likely to do. If the cost of issuing a regulation increases, fewer regulations will be issued, especially those that embody novel ideas or approaches.

Delay may confer some benefits. Forced to compile so elaborate a record, OSHA often does a better, or at least more thorough, analysis of the proposed regulations.[21] This poses an interesting tradeoff: Procedural delays lead to more analysis and presumably better standards, but these same delays inevitably lead to fewer standards. What gain in quality is worth the lack of quantity? People will disagree about this, but the courts are not obliged to discuss it. Probably the tradeoff was not important when a court objected to the fact that OSHA had not shown on the record why it had selected a certain standard for the number of lavatories that should be provided for every one hundred workers; a delay in this regard surely did not cause any worker to experience a major health hazard. But when a federal court invalidated an emergency standard governing the use of dry-cleaning chemicals because all of the details were not in the record it was a different matter. The court was not required to ask itself whether workers in dry-cleaning plants were being harmed by the delay in issuing the standard.[22]

The costs of the judicialization of agency discretion are not limited to the internal management of the organization. When two organized groups know that it will be the court, not the agency, that has the final say on the issue that divides them, the two parties have no incentive to negotiate a settlement with the agency. Thus, the head of EPA usually has little chance of getting industry and environmentalists to accept a compromise regarding some proposed air-quality standard. Instead, the two rivals have every incentive to use the EPA hearing to stake out their opposed positions in order to create a record that then can be used to sway the court when the agency is sued by whichever party lost the first round. (Over 80 percent of the three hundred or so regulations EPA issues each year wind up in the courts.[23]) The tendency to be combative rather than cooperative before the agency is furthered by the fact that environmental groups rely on their visible and dramatic conflicts with industry as a way to raise funds from their supporters.*

POWER

Court procedures, like any political arrangements, tend to give more power to some and less to others. Access to the courts is expensive and requires legal skills; thus, as courts become more important to bureaucracies, lawyers become more important in bureaucracies. The management of the EPA often has been dominated by lawyers, much to the disgust of many engineers and scientists, because the key output of that agency, a regulation, is framed in a political environment that makes it more important to withstand legal attack than to withstand scientific scrutiny.[24] In the EPA the allies of the lawyers are the public-health specialists who strongly believe that health is too important a matter to be weighed in the balance against economic cost or engineering feasibility.[25]

Lawyers do not have free rein inside EPA and to some extent must rely on scientists and other professionals for assistance. But not all bureaucracies have a wide variety of professional specialists able to balance competing views of the public good. In 1971 a court held that as a matter of right the Pennsylvania schools must offer special education to retarded children.[26] The court decision was followed three years later by a federal law that confirmed and extended this obligation. The result, according to David Kirp and Donald Jensen, has been to empower lawyers, not children. Though new programs were begun and some children were helped, the core tasks of the public school were not altered but simply embedded in a system of "due process" whereby parents were supposed to use formal hearings to make claims about what their children needed. Parents hired lawyers to represent their children and school systems hired lawyers to defend their practices. The result was a system of courtlike confrontations with formal records and procedural motions. The parents who benefited from this were middle-class people who were willing and able to take the

*In the mid-1980s EPA tried to reduce the adversarial nature of their relations with business and environmentalists by encouraging both parties to negotiate regulations that each could accept. This process of regulatory negotiation (or "regneg," as bureaucrats call it) led to some successes, such as a proposed standard for wood-burning stoves that was agreed to by all parties. But the incentives to engage in regneg are weak, not only for the reasons already given but because a successful regneg requires a small number of participants and a proposal that raises only a limited number of issues. Such circumstances are relatively uncommon. See Rochelle L. Stanfield, "Resolving Disputes," *National Journal* (Nov. 15, 1986): 2764–68. See also Philip J. Harter, "Negotiating Regulations," *Georgetown Law Journal* 71 (1982): 2.

time and trouble to work the system; most were families who planned to take their children out of the public schools and wanted public money to pay for private schooling. Lower-class families were less likely to use this forbidding system.[27]

When the Urban Mass Transportation Administration was trying to decide how to implement a new law that prohibited discrimination against handicapped persons in programs (such as urban mass transit) that received federal aid, it might have left matters in the hands of its engineers and planners. These professionals would have designed guidelines for building, for example, new subway stations in ways that permitted handicapped persons to enter them. Instead the UMTA turned the question over to its lawyers who proceeded to devise sweeping regulations that required existing stations to be made accessible. There were two reasons for letting lawyers rather than engineers decide this important matter. First, lawyers in UMTA and elsewhere urged the Senate Subcommittee on the Handicapped to require the federal government to issue the more sweeping regulations (all done without the knowledge of the relevant cabinet secretaries). Lawyers persuaded other lawyers to empower lawyers. Second, the government was facing lawsuits brought by organizations representing the handicapped. The regulations written would have to satisfy these external constituencies. Lawyers were necessary to settle demands raised by other lawyers. The chief counsel at UMTA was quite candid about her motives: The "regulations were developed for litigation and political reasons, and say what they must in order to satisfy those concerns."[28]

Court intervention may sometimes empower professions other than that of lawyers. Lawyers gain to the extent procedural requirements become complex, but other specialists gain to the extent the courts tend to favor one substantive outcome over another. Economists increased their strength in the Federal Trade Commission (FTC) in the 1980s not only because economists such as James Miller came to head it but also because certain federal judges came to believe that antitrust cases should be judged on the basis of their likely contribution to economic efficiency and consumer welfare. (Some of these judges were appointed by President Reagan and drawn from the ranks of law school professors who had acquired a professional knowledge of economic theory.) As the courts became reluctant to uphold the FTC in cases charging violations of the Robinson-Patman Act, prosecutions under that act declined. As the courts became skeptical of the argument that big corporations were inherently less desirable than small ones, the FTC became less likely to bring cases that asserted the proposition that big was bad.

When federal judge Frank Johnson ordered a massive revamping of the mental hospitals of Alabama, he did not impose a wholly unwelcome order on a bitterly resistant bureaucracy. As Phillip J. Cooper shows in his careful analysis of the case, there were some mental health professionals in the Alabama system who wanted change and looked to the judge for support. Some top administrators with a therapeutic orientation wanted to see major changes made in the state system. But some superintendents of particular hospitals, struggling to cope with their custodial responsibilities, were leery of change. Judge Johnson gave the state ample time to propose and voluntarily implement various reforms; only after years had passed with little accomplished did the judge place the system in the hands of a court-appointed receiver.[29]

What determines which professional group gains power? The answer is the preferences of the judges, and those preferences tend to favor professional experts as opposed to professional managers. Nathan Glazer, reflecting on judicial intervention in schools, prisons, and hospitals, notes that "such proceedings give great weight to *theoretical knowledge* as against *practical or clinical knowledge*. [The experts who testify] have generally never taught children, guarded prisoners, cared for the retarded, dealt with welfare patients."[30] When judges look at schools, the environment, and prisons, they tend to see vulnerable people in difficult circumstances. Since no one can know the exact effects of those circumstances, experts are asked to make predictions based on theoretical, often imperfect knowledge. Once the effects are asserted, protections are afforded in the form of rights, and lawyers comprise the profession that specializes in defining rights.

That it is judicial preference that leads to this differential empowerment can be seen by a mental experiment: If you interpret the facts differently, you are led to adopt different remedies. For example, one might see schools as organizations attempting to educate children and conclude that educators need more power and students need fewer rights. Which remedy you, the judge, are likely to select depends on how you think the world works and that in part depends on whose opinions you are prepared to believe.

The new definition of standing clearly displays judicial preference. Merely being a taxpayer worried about high taxes generally is insufficient to acquire standing to sue the government. But being a taxpayer worried about the First Amendment prohibition on the "establishment of religion" does give you standing. And so, as Jeremy Rabkin notes, the American Civil Liberties Union may enter court to fight government spending that touches on First Amendment guarantees, but the National Taxpayers' Union may not enter court to contest government spending that touches on non-First Amendment guarantees.[31]

POLICY

It is obvious that judicial intervention often determines the policies adopted by agencies. It is to change policy that people go to court and judges make decisions. But what is less obvious is that the policies adopted as a consequence of court intervention may not always be the best ones, *even from the point of view of the persons bringing the suit.* All political action has unintended consequences; the kind of political action practiced by judges is no exception.

Consider the problem of enforcing air quality standards. There are thousands of factories and power plants that emit pollutants into the atmosphere scattered across fifty states. When Congress passed the Clean Air Act in 1970, it gave to the EPA the task of setting air quality standards adequate to protect public health and to the states the job of devising "state implementation plans," or SIPs, that would achieve the goals set in the national air quality standards. If the EPA judged a state plan to be inadequate it was required to produce a plan of its own for that state. The requirements stated in an SIP are enforceable in court. This arrangement—national goals, state implementation—is a common feature of federalism in the United States.

Almost every state plan contained a provision allowing some official to exempt from control any source of pollution if forcing that source to comply with the plan would cause "undue hardship" without an offsetting public benefit.[32] These exemptions came to be known as "variances." A lobbying group, the National Resources Defense Council (NRDC), took one look at the variance procedure and decided that it was a gigantic loophole that would enable businesses to go on polluting the atmosphere. To close the loophole, the NRDC sued the EPA, asking federal appeals court judges in six circuits to order the EPA to disapprove any state plan that had a variance procedure.[33] The NRDC and most of the judges hearing the cases assumed that emission limitations in the state plans were good and that polluters would not conform to these limitations if they thought they could get a variance. As Shep Melnick shows in his careful analysis of this and several other instances of court control of the EPA, the judges were wrong on both counts.[34]

The state plans often contained unrealistic, ill-considered, or hopelessly ambiguous emission limitations. Moreover, many polluters easily could escape punishment when they failed to conform even to reasonable limitations; they hardly needed a variance to defeat the efforts of small, often poorly staffed state enforcement agencies. To reduce pollution effectively, industry had to be induced to conform to realistic rules. This required protracted, case-by-case negotiations in which the state would modify limitations that were vague or unrealistic and offer exemptions, or variances, to industries that needed more time to comply. In these negotiations it was to the states' advantage to have both a stick and a carrot: The stick would be a tough rule, the carrot would be the prospect of an exemption from this limitation *if* the polluter was ready to make a good-faith effort to reduce the pollution. In addition, unforeseen crises such as the Arab oil embargo of 1973 made the use of variances essential: when oil low in certain pollutants (such as sulfur) became scarce and expensive, it seemed to make sense to allow many industries to use cheaper or more abundant fuels that contained more sulfur.

When the courts stepped into this extraordinarily complex, decentralized, rapidly changing enforcement environment, they did it with all the finesse and grace of a two-ton rhinoceros. The first, second, and eighth circuit courts ordered the EPA not to allow the states to grant variances that would result in postponing industry compliance with the air quality standards. (To complicate matters, the ninth circuit court allowed the use of variances.)[35] The courts and the NRDC thought they had closed a loophole; in fact they had gutted an incentive. The states, irritated by the EPA order complying with the court rulings, reduced their enforcement efforts, substituted informal for formal procedures, and refused to cooperate with much of the EPA's program. To the states, the federal government had displayed a head-in-the-clouds ignorance of the complexity and variety of local pollution problems and had taken out of the states' hands a vital incentive that could be used to induce industry compliance with the clean-air program. In short, a series of court decisions intended to toughen the enforcement of anti-pollution laws in fact weakened it.[36] In 1975, the Supreme Court overruled the circuit courts and upheld the use of variances, at least for certain purposes, but by then the damage had been done.[37]

The variance case shows how courts are often ill-equipped to evaluate and control government administration that relies on incentives rather than on rules and on informal rather than formal procedures. Other cases show a different problem: Even when a court requires the adoption of a desirable policy, it sometimes does so in a way that ignores the opportunity costs of pursuing that policy. More plainly, if an agency must implement Policy A at any cost (because failure to do so would put it in contempt of court) then it must cut back on the implementation of Policies B, C, and D. This problem of priorities could be minimized if Congress increased an agency's budget every time a court ordered the agency to do something, but Congress rarely does so, even when it approves of the new policy.

Consider the policy of preventing any significant deterioration in the quality of air in places where the air quality already is above federal standards. The Clean Air Act was silent on this matter. It called for setting national air standards but said next to nothing about what, if anything, should be done about pollution in areas that already met those standards. William Ruckelshaus, the first administrator of EPA, thought his agency's primary mission was to clean up the air where it was dirtiest—in and around big cities. Areas that met clean air standards tended to be rural states; spending scarce time and money worrying about air that was already clean was to him a bad idea. As he put it, EPA's job is to protect "people, not prairie dogs."[38] Judge John H. Pratt of the federal district court for the District of Columbia saw things differently. In 1972 he ordered the EPA to disapprove any state plan that would permit the "significant deterioration" of air quality anywhere in the state.[39] There were some good policy arguments for this decision. Environmentalists worried that electric utilities would build their new generating plants in the desert and rural areas to escape the costs and regulations that made it difficult to build them in urban areas. The states were divided on this matter: some wanted to keep their air pristine pure, others were willing to accept less-than-pristine air in exchange for economic growth. But whatever the policy arguments for or against the new program, there were virtually no *legal* arguments for it. The law was silent. The legislative history of the law was all but silent. But Judge Pratt decided that a phrase in the preface to the Clean Air Act could be used to justify the new policy, and it was so ordered.

Many people think the new policy is a good idea. They may be correct. But it threw EPA into turmoil. It had to design and implement a major new program without any substantial new resources. It had to decide what "significant deterioration" meant (Judge Pratt did not define the term) and then how to achieve it (Judge Pratt did not tell them). Solving these problems meant that the EPA had less time and money to spend on getting major polluters in areas with manifestly dirty air to reduce their pollution. And the new policy gave cities that had a lot of big polluters a weapon they could use to hang onto these factories and the jobs and taxes they created: "Stay here," they would say, "and continue in business as usual, because the EPA's policy against significant deterioration means you can't move to another region of the country."[40]

OSHA offers another example of a well-intentioned court decision having unintended and unwanted consequences. The groups that use the courts to control OSHA rule making have an understandable bias; they want strict, not lenient, standards, and they worry more about newly discovered hazards than about old, widely used ones. Both tendencies are easily explained: In order to mobilize supporters and raise money, public-interest organizations must show they are demanding tough rules governing highly publicized dangers. But if a court accepts this view and converts it into policy it could well lead OSHA to stop working on modest standards for old hazards, standards that if put into effect would save far more lives than strict standards for new hazards, especially since the enforcement of strict standards is likely to be blocked or at least postponed by law suits brought by industry.

Jeremy Rabkin has shown this to be more than a hypothetical possibility. In 1983 Public Citizen, a Ralph Nader organization, sued to require OSHA to adopt a tough new standard on ethylene oxide.[41] The judge ordered quick action. Quick (by bureaucratic standards) action was forthcoming; a new ethylene oxide standard was issued within a year. But meanwhile work lagged on a new asbestos standard. Rabkin quotes sources suggesting that the ethylene oxide standard might save three to five lives a year whereas the (delayed) asbestos standard might save seventy-five lives a year. Moreover, there are many old hazards that (as of late 1987) had no standard at all despite the fact that they may cause hundreds of cancer cases a year.[42] Management involves choices; forcing management to make new choices effects all other choices it makes.

The case of Kenneth Adams recounted early in this chapter illustrates the point. The court order forced the Office for Civil Rights to take action on a great many cases of racial discrimination in southern schools and it made the agency more sensitive to complaints alleging discrimination. Well and good. But when OCR focuses on individual complaints it has fewer resources to launch investigations of its own. Individual complaints often involve a handful of people; OCR investigations often affect hundreds if not thousands of people. Meeting court-ordered demands to respond to individual complaints may produce fewer benefits than initiating broader investigations. Moreover, the benefits from answering complaints may go to individuals with access to lawyers, such as middle-income feminists, at the expense of people without access to lawyers, such as poor immigrants.[43]

This discussion of the unintended and unwanted policy effects of court intervention in agency management may leave the impression that all such interventions are a bad idea. That is not the conclusion I wish the reader to draw. The court is a vitally important forum in which individuals can assert fundamental rights and seek appropriate remedies, even (especially!) against administrative agencies. The courts began the process of school desegregation, put a stop to some bestial practices in prisons and mental hospitals, and have enabled thousands of people to get benefits to which they were entitled or ended abuses they were suffering. Without courts and lawyers skilled at using them some of these conditions might be far more common today. But like all human institutions, courts are not universal problem solvers competent to manage any difficulty or resolve any dispute. There are certain things courts are good at and some things they are not so good at; the cases discussed in the preceding paragraphs are illustrations of the latter. Now we want to ask more generally what these things are.

Judges versus Bureaucrats

Judges and bureaucrats see the world differently, partly because of their different backgrounds but mostly because of the tasks they perform and the organizations in which they operate.

Judges see two or more parties arguing about their rights, rights defended by reference to legal principles. The judges learn the facts chiefly from presentations made in a courtroom under rules of evidence; though judges learn a lot off the bench—by reading studies, talking with colleagues, and consulting their own philosophies—the facts on which they base their findings are supposed to be those that have been taken into evidence. After judges decide whose claims are correct they fashion remedies, judicial orders or rules intended to enforce a right or redress a wrong. If an order is addressed to a government agency, it specifies the goals the agency must serve and the criteria its actions must meet in order to give effect to the remedy.

Bureaucrats see the world rather differently: They see a loosely coordinated group of people performing a variety of tasks under a complex array of constraints and with uneven degrees of political support. Agency heads often have difficulty learning exactly what these people are doing and frequently have vague and changing standards by which to evaluate those actions that they can observe. The managers of an agency are keenly aware that they spend rather little time making decisions and quite a lot gathering information, going to meetings, persuading colleagues, replying to critics, and generally trying to keep a complicated process moving. They are well aware that it is unrealistic to expect that their subordinates will be able to follow subtle or complex directives; often, "management" at best will involve little more than trying to instill a general sense of mission coupled with detailed instructions on the myriad procedural rules that define how an agency is to function.

When a judge imposes an order on an agency, its effect will be easiest to predict when the agency is performing a relatively simple task, the outcome of which is readily observable. This is most often the case in what I call production agencies and to a lesser extent, in craft agencies. It is not likely to be the case in procedural or coping agencies.

Court orders are written rules; before issuing them the judges should ask themselves whether there is any evidence that the agency under review has been effectively governed in the past by written rules. Some aspects of police departments, public schools, and regulatory agencies can be defined by a written rule, but other parts, often the core tasks of the agency, cannot be so defined. If what a police officer, schoolteacher, or business regulator does is not already determined by written instructions, new written instructions are not likely to change what they do in accordance with the author's intentions.

In sum, a court, like a president, is best able to achieve the effect it intends when it issues a clear rule of conduct and when compliance is relatively easy to monitor. It is easier to tell a school to stop excluding blacks than to tell a school how to improve the educational achievements of blacks. It is easier to tell a prison to stop torturing inmates than to tell a prison to rehabilitate them. It is easier to tell the EPA to set an air quality standard than it is to tell it how best to secure compliance with that standard. But increasingly judges do not do this; in Jerry Mashaw's phrase, they have developed a "range of techniques for intruding without deciding."[44]

When Judge Jack Weinstein sought to desegregate the Mark Twain Junior High School located in the Coney Island section of Brooklyn, he had a choice: supervise a large number of local agencies as they sought to eliminate racial separation in the area, or instruct the school to conform to a clear rule that was attractive to the local families. The first option involved getting the public housing projects to attract both white and black tenants, inducing the police department to enhance the security of whites who might be willing to move into the area, and arranging a busing program that would bring white pupils into the school. The second option involved ordering the school system to produce a "magnet school" that would voluntarily enroll both white and black pupils. Judge Weinstein chose the second option, over the objections of many of the people who brought the suit. According to Robert Katzmann, who has analyzed the judge's decision, the second option worked because it took into account the organizational realities of the agencies. It minimized the need to coordinate the activities of many agencies, to alter the self-defined missions of these agencies, or to find new resources for them. Instead, one agency—the local school board—was asked to carry out a task it had itself proposed in a way that would enhance its own sense of mission and under circumstances that would make success relatively easy to measure: Either a racially mixed group of pupils would apply for admission or they would not.[45] It worked; the new school was inundated with applicants.

Judges often are criticized for their institutional inability to play an effective policy-making role.[46] There is much truth in these criticisms but some exaggeration as well. Shep Melnick's account of the role of judges in shaping clean air policy does not give support to the view that the judges are unable to find and master complex technical information. The judges were well-informed on the mysteries of air quality standards, the technology of smokestack scrubbers, and the amounts of sulfur in eastern and western coal. Nor are all judges indifferent to the economic implications of alternative policies. What judges are unaware of are not the technical facts but the organizational ones.[47]

Judges see bureaucrats at a distance and through the lenses of conventional stereotypes. From a distance, a government agency is a machine designed to achieve a goal. The judge's job is to start the machine, change the goal, or both. But surely it long since has become obvious to the reader that bureaucracies only rarely are machines and when they are they operate as much by inertia as by the conscious attainment of goals. Judges who know this distant view to be wrong "correct" it by seeing the agency through one or the other of two sets of lenses. Through one set the agency is the "captive" of the interests with which it works; through the other set it is the "rogue elephant" of misguided zealots.[48] The task of the judge is to "free" the agency from its captors or "rein in" its zealots.

Some agencies are, indeed, the captives—more accurately, the clients—of certain interests (see chapter 5) but not all; not even most. Some agencies do reflect the zeal of their members or of a profession that accounts for a large part of its members (see chapters 4 and 6) but not many; in fact, very few.

Government agencies are at least as complex and hard to understand as an exotic and distant native culture that a traveler has entered for the first time. If judges are to become serious about guiding agencies they will have to become serious about understanding agency cultures. For often it is not the substance of what judges seek to achieve that is the problem but the context in which they seek it and the spirit in which they express it.

This becomes abundantly clear when one traces the history of one judge's attempt to "reform" the Texas prison system. John DiIulio tells the story with a sympathetic eye toward much of what the judge wanted to achieve: in particular, an end to a system whereby the control of inmates to some degree had been given over to a group of "trusted" inmates called building tenders. Though once a small and useful part of the system of prison governance, by a process of administrative neglect the building tenders had become a large and dangerous part of the system, degenerating into little more than a racket in which tough inmates used force and intimidation to secure privileges for themselves. After court inquiries and proceedings that lasted nine years, Judge William Wayne Justice issued a 248-page order requiring scores of changes in almost every aspect of the Texas prison system.[49] Despite the fact that an appeals court struck down some of his orders and cautioned him to go slow on others, Judge Justice's assertion of control over the system remained intact. It was, of course, bitterly resisted by the system's administrators. In the battle, the system was very nearly destroyed. Babies were thrown out with the bath water in wholesale numbers.[50]

The judge did not content himself with ordering an end to identifiable abuses ("making a choice"), he ordered massive changes in the procedures by which the prisons were governed ("managing a process"). Those procedures are described here in chapter 2 and in greater detail in DiIulio's own book.[51] Apart from certain abuses that had crept in just before the judge heard the case, the system of prison governance in fact had produced a safe, decent, law-abiding set of institutions. The prison administrators had instilled a sense of mission in their subordinates, held them accountable for their work, and motivated them to take the work seriously. Prisoners were neither abused by the guards nor (until the building tender system got out of hand) by other prisoners. What needed to be changed was clear, *if* the judge had a good understanding of how prisons work.

But of course few judges are likely to have such an understanding of prisons, any more than they are likely to know much about schools, police departments, welfare agencies, or regulatory commissions. At one time when judges deferred to administrators, drew a careful distinction between policy and law, and denied standing to people with only remote interests in the decisions of the government, this ignorance was not a problem. The new administrative law has made it a problem. If they wish to help manage agencies, judges will have to learn about agencies and their management. This cannot be done from afar or from books. Even this book.

CHAPTER 16

National Differences

WHEN health and safety inspectors enter factories in Sweden and the United States, they come to enforce pretty much the same set of rules. They look for ladders that are unsafe, floors that are slippery, guardrails that are missing, and fumes that are toxic. Many of the standards developed by the two countries to govern these matters are not merely similar, they are identical.[1]

But what the inspectors do in these factories is very different. The American inspectors, all employees of the Occupational Safety and Health Administration (OSHA), tend to "go by the book"—if they see a violation of the rules they write up a formal citation. If the violation is serious, a fine is mandatory and the inspector does not hesitate to levy it. Even if the violation is not serious, the inspector may impose a fine. If the employer does not correct the violation within a specified number of days, further penalties may be assessed. The OSHA inspectors believe that this is the way it must be: When Steven Kelman interviewed them they said that most employers would ignore any violations unless they were penalized. "Teeth are the only way to impress management," one inspector said; without the power to impose penalties employers would "laugh at you when you came into the plant," another remarked.[2] Most American inspectors did not take into account the economic condition of the firm; whether or not it could afford the cost of correcting violations wasn't their concern.[3] OSHA managers reinforced these attitudes with a lengthy field manual that prescribed in great detail every step in a workplace inspection; with the compilation of data on every aspect of the inspection; and by using these figures to compare the productivity of their inspectors (being "productive" meant making a lot of inspections and issuing a lot of violations). The inspectors were keenly aware of their bosses looking over their shoulders.[4]

In Sweden, the inspectors for the ASV (the *Arbetarskyddsverket*, or Worker Protection Board) are expected to use their discretion and not go by the book. There is scarcely any book to go by; the procedures they are supposed to follow are outlined in general language in a six-page pamphlet. Often they arrive at a factory only after giving the employer advance notice; while there, they spend much of their time advising the employer on how to improve conditions. If there are violations of the rules, the inspector typically makes oral recommendations; only occasionally will he or she issue a written notice. Fines are not automatic; they are levied only after persistent failure to correct the violation.[5] If a firm complains that it cannot afford to make the changes, Swedish inspectors are much more likely than Americans to give the firm more time. Moreover, the Swedes have an optimistic view of employer behavior: When Kelman spoke to them they felt most owners were law-abiding and so sanctions were not of crucial importance.[6] The ASV managers gathered far fewer statistics about their inspectors than did their OSHA counterparts and made little use of the few they did collect.[7]

Kelman summarized the differences between these two agencies, each with essentially the same goal, as follows:

> American inspections are designed more as formal searches for violations of regulations; Swedish inspections are designed more as informal, personal missions to give advice and information, establish friendship ties between inspector and inspected, and promote local labor-management cooperation.[8]

As far as Kelman could tell, the informal and cooperative Swedish system produced a level of compliance with safety and health rules that was as high or higher than that achieved by the formal and punitive American system.[9]

Such striking differences in bureaucratic behavior are not limited to Sweden or to industrial safety. Graham Wilson has shown that British regulation of the industrial workplace has much more in common with Sweden than it does with the United States: Whereas OSHA is ready and willing to file complaints and levy fines, its counterpart in Great Britain, the Factory Inspectorate, is averse to prosecution and like the ASV tends to give assistance rather than enforce regulations.[10] David Vogel found that regulations designed to reduce air and water pollution were administered in a more flexible, informal, and cooperative manner in Great Britain than they were in the United States.[11] A study of how four nations regulate pesticides, food additives, and industrial chemicals concluded that in Great Britain, France, and West Germany the administrative system afforded the bureaucrats more discretion than was enjoyed by their American counterparts and encouraged them to use informal procedures in formulating and enforcing rules.[12] Environmental protection legislation is implemented in Japan by "administrative guidance" rather than by legal enforcement, with considerable flexibility shown in accommodating the needs of particular industries and localities.[13]

There was no clear relationship between how each nation managed its regulatory process and the laws it enforced or the results it achieved; the consensual European administrative practices essentially served the same goals and produced the same outcomes as the adversarial American practices. How can we explain why similar bureaucracies with identical goals behave so differently in different nations? There are two possibilities: politics and culture.

Politics

The nations that enforce their regulatory policies in a consensual (that is, flexible, nonpunitive, or accommodationist) manner have parliamentary regimes; the nation that enforces its policies in an adversarial (that is, rigid, punitive, or legalistic) manner* has a presidential regime. That this should be the case is puzzling in view of the widespread belief that in the United States business has privileges and influence denied to firms in those nations such as Sweden, which have a much larger public sector, many more nationalized industries, and a more egalitarian income distribution.[14]

The puzzle disappears when we realize what political incentives are created by the way in which political authority is organized. A parliamentary regime concentrates almost all political authority in the hands of a prime minister and cabinet chosen from the majority party (or from a majority coalition of several parties) in the legislature. It is only a slight exaggeration to say that what Prime Minister Margaret Thatcher wants she gets. So long as she has a majority in the House of Commons her proposals become law; if that majority ever deserts her, Commons will be dissolved and a new election held. Between elections the legislature can defy her leadership only at the risk of committing political suicide, that

*By saying that the United States has an adversarial enforcement system I do not mean to imply that it implements its regulatory policies in as stern or uncompromising a manner as the most dedicated advocates of those policies would prefer, nor that it does so wholly without fear or favoritism. I mean only that *in comparison with parliamentary democracies* it is more likely to rely on legal sanctions and less likely to grant enforcement operators wide discretion.

is, being told to face the voters. Parliament has little authority to intervene in the conduct of bureaucratic affairs; its members can ask questions of the political heads of these agencies, but ordinarily it cannot obtain information that the agencies wish to conceal or direct their discretion in ways that they oppose, nor can it investigate their conduct over the objections of the prime minister. The courts do not constitute an important check on the exercise of bureaucratic discretion. Though British courts have become somewhat more activist in recent years, it remains the case that no citizen has much hope of getting a judge to tell a government official what policies to adopt or what procedures to follow. Unless the bureaucracy has directly affronted one of the traditional liberties of a British subject, it has little to fear from the courts. It is almost unthinkable that a British judge should give orders to British air-quality regulators that remotely resemble the orders federal judges routinely have given to the Environmental Protection Agency in this country.

Matters are more complicated in other European democracies. Where, as in Italy or West Germany, the prime minister's party has no absolute majority in parliament, he or she can govern only with the support of a coalition of several parties. These coalitions, especially in Italy, often are unstable. Should one party leave the coalition, a new prime minister may take office even without new elections. In France, a directly elected president exists alongside the conventional parliamentary system, leading to the possibility that the president and the prime minister may be of different parties, as happened in the early 1980s. Moreover, special French courts exist to hear citizen complaints against the bureaucracy that have no counterpart in Great Britain. Sweden has a special constitutional officer, the "ombudsman," or people's representative, who like the French administrative courts will respond to citizens who believe they have been mistreated by the bureaucracy.

But these complexities do not alter fundamentally the central fact of a parliamentary democracy, that political authority over both making and implementing policy is concentrated in one set of hands, those of the executive. Neither the French administrative courts nor the Swedish ombudsmen permit citizens to shape policy; at best, they remedy individual grievances about bureaucrats who clearly have overstepped their legal authority. But when that authority is granted in sweeping language, as it often is, there is no boundary to be overstepped.

If authority is concentrated, the incentives to organize politically (other than to contest elections) are weakened. If a group is unable to persuade the majority party to embrace its programs, it has no recourse but to wait for the next election in hopes that a different majority will assume office. It cannot expect to make an end run around the prime minister's decision by getting a legislative committee to do informally (through the conduct of investigations, the exercise of committee "guidance," or the requirement for committee "clearance") what formally the legislature as a whole would not do. It cannot demand that the executive in charge of the program be a person approved by or drawn from the ranks of the group; the direction of programs will be in the hands of career bureaucrats who owe little or nothing to outside interests. It cannot anticipate that a friendly judge will review an agency's decisions to insure that wherever the statutory language is vague they will conform to the "intent" of the legislature as manifested in obscure reports written by like-minded staff members of some congressional committee; judges in parliamentary regimes ordinarily will not substitute their views for those of appointed officials. It cannot assume that the media will embarrass bureaucrats who have acted contrary to the group's interests with real and imagined misdeeds; bureaucrats in parliamentary regimes find it relatively easy to keep things secret from the press.

If a potential group cannot entertain these hopes or make these demands it has little incentive to organize and express them. Of course, there are well-organized interest groups in Europe as there are in the United States, but abroad these groups typically take the form of peak associations—large, nationwide assemblages of workers, employers, or professionals. They are large and national because they must concentrate their resources on influencing the key policy decisions of a few national leaders.[15] A small organization consisting of a handful of activists, a foundation grant, and a catchy name is less likely to appear (or, if it appears, to be successful) in Europe than in the United States because there are far fewer points in the political system abroad at which such a group could gain access and wield influence.

These institutional arrangements contribute to the adversarial nature of bureaucratic politics in this country. All policies are continuously contested. The legislative coalition that enacted a new program will be quickly supplanted by another coalition that influences the implementation of that policy. No sooner had Senator Hubert Humphrey promised Congress that the Civil Rights Act of 1964 did not contemplate the cutting off of federal aid as its principal enforcement device than civil rights groups were pressing a federal judge to order the Office for Civil Rights to do exactly that.[16] No sooner had Congress passed an Occupational Safety and Health Act authorizing OSHA to use coercive measures than industry was lobbying members of Congress to insure that OSHA followed a conciliatory strategy; and no sooner had this lobbying begun than labor went to court to make certain that OSHA took a tough line.[17]

Policy making in Europe is like a prizefight: Two contenders, having earned the right to enter the ring, square off against each other for a prescribed number of rounds; when one fighter knocks the other one out, he is declared the winner and the fight is over. Policy making in the United States is more like a barroom brawl: Anybody can join in, the combatants fight all comers and sometimes change sides, no referee is in charge, and the fight lasts not for a fixed number of rounds but indefinitely or until everybody drops from exhaustion. To repeat former Secretary of State George Shultz's remark, "it's never over."

Under these circumstances a prudent bureaucrat will realize that any effort to keep agency proceedings secret, informal, and flexible will entail heavy political costs. Matters can be kept secret only if there are a few key participants (say, one peak business association and one nationwide labor union) who are aware that they must work with the bureaucracy because there is no one else to whom they can appeal its decisions. If there are many participants and easily available appeals, trying to keep anything secret can be portrayed as a "cover-up." Implementation can be informal and flexible only if the interests involved have an incentive to accept the agency's actions, and they will have that incentive only if they do not think they can get a better deal elsewhere—in court, the press, Congress, or the streets. No agency head relishes the idea of being called in the media a "lackey" of some special interest, being hauled into court to explain why he or she failed to follow every detail of the prescribed procedure, or being grilled by a congressional committee as to why he or she interpreted a vague statutory provision in a way that favored "special interests" rather than the "public interest" or that allowed Company A to take more time in complying with an order than was given to Company B.

The political base of an American agency is often insecure; the coalition supporting it is frequently weak, short-lived, or shot through with internal contradictions. Under these circumstances a bureaucrat who may wish to adopt informal and flexible procedures first must establish authority so that flexibility will not be construed as a sign of weakness or evidence of a sell-out. Ronald Brickman and his colleagues, authors of an important cross-national study of chemical regulation, came to the same conclusion:

> The fragmentation of political authority leaves U.S. administrators in a peculiarly vulnerable position. They are confronted with contradictory statutory mandates. . . . These must often be implemented under the critical eye of other government institutions, and in full view of warring private interests. . . . Unable to strike bargains in private, American regulatory agencies are forced to seek refuge in "objectivity," adopting formal methodologies for rationalizing their every action.[18]

It makes sense then for the bureaucracy to take a tough line: Insist that everything be on the public record, insist that everything be done "by the book," insist that "everybody be treated the same," and insist that the full force of the law fall on every violator.

That acting this way is less risky does not mean that every agency will act this way. The political environment of some agencies involves client politics—a cozy, low-visibility relationship between a private interest and its like-minded government bureau. Or a strong-willed (and unusually lucky) president may succeed in getting an agency head to act other than as his or her immediate political interests require. But the institutional incentives to adopt a formalistic and adversarial mode in managing agency-interest relations are very strong (and, as the next section will suggest, are getting stronger all the time) and so we should not be surprised to discover that on the whole American regulatory agencies behave very differently from their European counterparts.

Graham Wilson compares a regulatory agency to a classroom: "A teacher whose authority is assured may be able to adopt a more friendly and relaxed approach than a teacher whose authority seems highly uncertain."[19] In Europe, regulators tend to have a more secure base of authority than they do here. Thus, left-leaning, "antibusiness" regimes abroad actually may have friendlier and more accommodative relationships with business than do conservative, "probusiness" regimes in this country.

Culture

But politics cannot be the whole story. The American political system based on the separation of powers is essentially the same today as it was thirty or forty years ago; however, regulatory agencies at that time were given far greater discretionary authority than is the case today. The British political system based on prime ministerial rule is not very different today from what it was a century ago; but then, in the early years of factory inspections, employers not only complained bitterly about the hostile behavior of the inspectors, they occasionally assaulted them as they made their rounds.[20]

The political costs attached to secret administrative proceedings make secrecy difficult to maintain; there is, as Edward Shils pointed out many years ago, a populist streak in the American character that provides ample ammunition for any politician eager to attack a "cover-up."[21] For decades, the British quietly have accepted a level of governmental secrecy that would have led to rebellion in the United States. It is inconceivable that the United States would ever adopt an Official Secrets Act comparable in scope and severity to that which long has been on the books in Great Britain.

The ability of the courts to intervene in American administration is based on their power of judicial review (that is, on their right to declare executive and legislative acts unconstitutional) and on such laws as the

Administrative Procedure Act, but the present-day scope of judicial activism could not be predicted simply from knowing its constitutional or statutory foundation. As we saw in chapter 15, the federal courts for many years maintained rules of standing and deferred to administrative discretion in such a way as to make judges relatively modest influences on federal administrative agencies. Today those rules and that deference are a thing of the past and so judges, because of decisions they have chosen to make, are major players in bureaucratic politics.

Finally, there are many government bureaucracies in the United States that display in their everyday routines a degree of informality and flexibility that seems to belie the findings about regulatory agencies. No one who has spent even a few hours in a representative French and American schoolroom could fail to observe the looser, less directive, more individualized atmosphere of the American public school. The level of discipline in the American armed services is less than that in many European armies.* British sailors are more deferential to their officers on merchant ships than are American sailors.[22] The group-based decision-making style of Japanese managers has been contrasted with the individualistic style of American executives so often as to have become a cliché, but it is true.[23]

Michel Crozier has provided us with an insightful look at two French government agencies performing routine clerical and manufacturing tasks. Though he made no explicit comparisons with similar American agencies, the picture he painted of the French agencies left little doubt that their managerial atmosphere was quite different from what one encounters here. In France, the organizational culture was rigidly formal, with little informal communication, few work-based voluntary associations, heavy reliance on written rules and procedures, and elaborate (though often resentful) deference to the outward trappings of status and rank. The easy give-and-take among workers at different hierarchical levels so typical of the daily life of most American bureaucracies was conspicuously absent in the French system.[24]

In short, the way in which a bureaucracy operates cannot be explained simply by knowing its tasks and the economic and political incentives that it confronts. Culture makes a difference.

Chapter 6 discussed organizational culture; here we are discussing national culture. In both cases culture is defined as a set of patterned and enduring ways of acting, passed on from one generation to the next. A national culture consists of those patterned and enduring ways of acting characteristic of a society or a significant part of that society. Culture is to a group what personality is to an individual, a disposition that leads people to respond differently to the same stimuli. Though every traveler

*Apparently, even in the marines. See the comparisons between training and discipline in the U.S. Marines and in various European elite military formations in Daniel da Cruz, *Boot* (New York: St. Martin's Press, 1987), 282ff.

is immediately aware of how differently the British or the Japanese or the Swedes respond to meeting a stranger, addressing a clerk, or joining a group, there is no systematic, well-established account of these differences. As with most important things in life, we are aware of more than we can explain. But it is possible to list a few major cultural factors that from the available research seem to influence how people behave in formal organizations.*

DEFERENCE VERSUS SELF-ASSERTIVENESS

In some societies the right of government officials to make decisions is taken for granted. People may disagree about the substance of the decision but they do not question the authority behind it. As a consequence they defer to officials who act for the government. Police officers have authority by virtue of their badges, teachers by virtue of their positions, bureaucrats by virtue of the laws that authorize their offices. In other societies the right of government officials to make decisions frequently is challenged. People usually are disposed to accept a governmental decision but they are always ready to question the right of a police officer to stop them, a teacher to control them, or a bureaucrat to decide a matter of importance to them. The formal signs of authority—badges, uniforms, laws, regulations—do not produce in the citizenry a habitual deference to the persons who display those signs.

Steven Kelman contrasts the deferential Swedish political culture with the self-assertive or adversarial American political culture to explain why the Swedish ASV is able to rely on informal, consensual methods not only for enforcing health and safety rules but also for writing them.[25] Modern Sweden, like many northern European nations, emerged from a long history during which power was centralized in the hands of a king or an aristocracy; for centuries, a wide, unbridgeable gulf separated the rulers from the ruled. Deference to authority was obtained by a combination of coercion and awe: the king's power was enhanced by his grandeur. When Swedes replaced the king with a parliament and the aristocracy with a bureaucracy, they did not replace deference with self-assertiveness. The democractic Swedish state was in every sense a *state*, that is, a supreme institution that was expected to rule and was accustomed to ruling. The deference once accorded an absolute monarch was now given to a set of elected and appointed officials. The fact that Sweden, beginning shortly

*There is very little systematic, quantitative research that analyzes cultural differences in the beliefs of bureaucrats and almost none that discusses how those different beliefs affect behavior. One interesting comparative study of international differences in work-related values among several thousand members of a large, multinational corporation is Geert Hofstede, *Culture's Consequences* (Beverly Hills, Calif.: Sage Publications, 1980). There are certain parallels between Hofstede's description of "power distance," "uncertainty avoidance," and "individualism" and my account of deference, formalism, and individualism.

after the advent of parliamentary democracy, was ruled by the same political party, the Social Democrats, for nearly a half century and that this party put in place policies that transformed Swedish society made it easy for people to transfer their deferential habits to the new state.

This interpretation of Swedish political culture is not unique to Kelman; studies by Thomas Anton, Donald Hancock, and Sten Johansson have come to much the same conclusion.[26] The consequences of this culture for Swedish politics are clear: Swedes accord government officials high status, do not participate (except by voting) in many political associations, and believe that experts and specialists are best qualified to make governmental decisions. Given these attitudes it is hardly surprising to find that industrial health and safety regulations were not hammered out in the legislature after long, bitter fights between contending interests but rather were written by a series of small committees consisting of experts drawn from government, business, and labor who met privately, resolved their differences by discussion, and did not have to confront any challenges in the legislature. Nor is it surprising to learn that in enforcing these regulations the Swedish ASV relied heavily on the exchange of expert advice among like-minded people in government, a particular firm, and its associated labor union. Experts—people with professional training—are an important influence on American bureaucracies, but they seem to be the dominant influence on Swedish ones.

American political culture hardly could be described as deferential. Americans value expertise but they do not defer to it; an expert who takes an unpopular position or acts contrary to the self-interest of an individual or a group will be treated as roughly as any other adversary. Americans admire their form of government but do not admire or accord high status to the officials who work for it.* Americans always entertain the suspicion that the government is doing something mischievous behind their backs and greet with outrage any indication that important decisions were made in a way that excluded any affected interest, no matter how marginal. Americans define their relationship with government in terms of rights and claims and are prepared to hire lawyers or complain to the newspapers at the slightest hint that a right has been violated or a claim ignored.

A deferential political culture is not unique to Sweden; elements of it can be found in all Scandinavian nations, in Germany, and in Great Britain. Steven L. Elkin, who had learned in this country that urban development decisions are the result of an intensely political process involving much conflict, aroused publics, and weak planners, was not prepared for what he found when he studied the same subject in London, where major new projects were undertaken with scarcely any public notice, much less

*More precisely, they tend to revere the presidency but not the president; they dislike Congress and "the bureaucracy" though usually they have a good opinion of their own representatives and report that their experience with a given bureaucrat was satisfactory.

participation. Large tracts were cleared and new developments begun on the unchallenged authority of town planners employed by the London County Council. The reason was clear: Such decisions, though they affected the lives, property, and incomes of thousands of people, were made in London by officials who were effectively insulated from community pressures. There seemed to be general agreement that the job of the government was to govern; there was little doubt as to who should make the decisions (appointed officials), how they should be made ("rationally"), or even what they should be. If American city planners had moved to London they would have thought they had died and gone to heaven.[27]

An adversarial political culture is not unique to the United States, but it is in the United States that the political institutions—the separation of powers, judicial review, and federalism—allow it full expression and reinforce its central features. Everywhere, of course, institutions and the incentives they create interact with culture and the habits it fosters. American political culture and institutions are remarkably congruent, however, so much so that it is hard to imagine parliamentary institutions being transplanted here.

FORMALITY VERSUS INFORMALITY

In France, and no doubt in many other countries as well, the members of an organization deal with one another formally; that is to say, impersonally, at arm's length, and with close attention to rank and titles. Though two workers may become friends they do not form cliques or voluntary associations that cut across hierarchical lines or carry over to life outside the workplace.

Crozier attributes this to the influence of French cultural traits that place great emphasis on the formal equality of individuals and impart a strong desire to see the exercise of power constrained by formal rules rather than by consultation or organizational checks and balances.[28] At each level in a bureaucratic hierarchy authority is absolute; the limits on the exercise of that absolute authority are the written rules and prescribed procedures that the holder of authority must obey. The informal give-and-take of an American workplace is less common in France; by the same token, French citizens are far less likely than Americans to join or be active in voluntary associations. The employees of the two agencies he studied were prepared to obey the rules but not submit to the rulers; submission, cooperation, or informality would threaten the autonomy of each individual.

Crozier follows Alexis de Tocqueville in locating the source of these attitudes in the experiences of the French peasantry under the old monarchy. France was ruled from the center—that is, from Paris—by a succession of kings eager to consolidate their power and to extract from the people tax monies with which to finance the nation's endless wars. Taxes were collected in a way that gave to every taxpayer a powerful incentive to spy upon his neighbors and notify the tax collector whenever he saw any increase in their wealth.[29] Local self-government existed in name only; nothing of consequence could happen unless at the direction or with the approval of the king's ministers in Paris.[30] Where meaningful local government does not exist the people will have little incentive or opportunity for forming local associations to voice their grievances or press their claims; there is no one at hand who can hear the grievance or grant the claim. There were no assemblages in which peasants might learn to work with one another or become acquainted with officers and aristocrats. The French political system split French society into "small, isolated, self-regarding groups."[31]

When the French Revolution swept away the monarchy and discredited the aristocracy it left behind a mass of people who sought to use their new powers to guarantee by law and constitution the formal equality of all citizens. A French Assembly replaced the king; then Napoleon replaced the Assembly; then a bewildering succession of emperors and new assemblies replaced the old ones. But throughout it all Paris never lost its grip over the countryside nor its insatiable appetite for tax monies with which to finance the army and the bureaucracy. Under these circumstances it is hardly surprising that the French people had little reason to trust one another, let alone their government. Power existed; that was a fact. Power was centralized; that had been decreed by history. Now power had to be checked, but the only check with which the French had any experience was that embodied in laws and rules. Crozier argues that this legacy of legalism and formalism has shaped the conduct of French government agencies right down to the present.

The United States followed a different path. There was scarcely any central government before, during, or for long after the Revolution; survival depended not on the benevolence of some lord but on the individual farmer's capacity for work and cooperation. Cooperation was encouraged not only by the need to subdue the wilderness but by the policy of self-government on which the Protestant churches were founded. This tradition of political and religious self-government was so strong that it nearly prevented the ratification of the Constitution, and even that document created a government of limited and circumscribed powers. The founders knew very well the views of the citizens and did not for a moment consider relying on legal rules and formal rights as the chief guarantee of individual liberty; in the words of James Madison these were but "parchment barriers"[32] that without "auxiliary precautions"[33] would not prevent the exercise of absolute power. The additional precautions were, of course, the separation of powers and the system of checks and balances. These devices insured that officials would negotiate with one another because without a negotiated policy there would be no policy at all. Consultation, participation, and informal arrangements all were part of the general scheme of government and, before that, of the daily life of Americans in their towns and villages. Small wonder that they should be part of the ongoing administration of the agencies spawned by that government.

As with deference, so also with formalism: What culture may have begun, institutions keep intact. The informality of Americans is a fact of their daily life. (Is there any other nation where everybody, including waiters and flight attendants, is so insistent on addressing people by their first names?) This informality animates our governing institutions but in turn is reinvigorated by them.

GROUPS VERSUS INDIVIDUALS

The importance of consultation to American bureaucrats is great, but it pales into insignificance compared to its place in the lives of Japanese bureaucrats. This is puzzling because Japanese administration is far more hierarchical than its American counterpart. In this country, officials of different ranks meet frequently and address one another by their first names rather than by their titles. Such informality would be shocking to a Japanese; dealing with hierarchical unequals as if they were social equals simply is not done. The "formal status of every member, in relation to other members in the hierarchy, is defined in the most meticulous and particularistic manner."[34]

Within a given hierarchical level, however, Japanese management takes the form of group decision making in which individual differences are minimized and individual assertions of leadership or claims of credit are discouraged. The group emphasis is evident, as Gregory Noble notes, even in the physical arrangements. Where an American administrative unit usually will consist of a large office for the head and separate offices down the hall for each of his or her subordinates, a comparable Japanese unit will consist of a chief whose subordinates sit in the same room with him, their desks arranged in a semicircle.[35] Organizational charts in the United States often contain the names of each official; in Japan, many of the boxes have no names in them. American police officers wear badges with individual identification numbers and sometimes personal nameplates as well; Japanese officers wear no badges, numbers, or nameplates.[36] Americans leave their offices and go home when they have finished their individual tasks; Japanese linger in their offices until all members of the group have finished their duties and when they finally leave, it is often to go to a bar where they relax and drink together.

The importance of the group is heightened by the way new employees are socialized on the job. Individual job descriptions are vague or even nonexistent. Training emphasizes character-building and group loyalty as much or more than technical knowledge.[37] When a group must make a decision, individual argumentation and personal clashes are avoided in favor of indirect suggestion and protracted exploration.[38] The emphasis is on harmony and consensus, even at the cost of speed and decisiveness.

Lewis Austin explored these values in his probing interviews of Japanese and American elites. Though the sample was small, the differences were striking. Whereas the Americans attached the greatest importance to individualism, equality, and competition, the Japanese assigned greater weight to hierarchy, group solidarity, and harmony. The Americans described a good leader as someone who was decisive, knowledgeable, and willing to delegate; the Japanese described him as someone who was sincere, warm, and willing to listen.[39]

When group-centered decision making is linked with rigid hierarchical distinctions the problem of coordination can become acute. The loyalty to one's work group can impede communication with someone else's group; the need to achieve unanimity in one office before acting can get in the way of negotiating an agreement with another office. Chalmers Johnson, a perceptive student of Japanese politics, describes the problem this way: "[T]he most difficult coordinating task in the Japanese policy-making process is among ministries and agencies themselves; once an interministerial agreement has been reached, the chores of taking the proposal or bill through the party, cabinet, and Diet stages are relatively less onerous."[40]

The reason why dealing with party politicians is easier than coordinating with fellow bureaucrats is that in Japan the bureaucracy *is* the government. The bureaucracy drafts the laws, determines the budget, has a near monopoly on the relevant information, enjoys great esteem, recruits the most talented graduates of the best universities, and has remained virtually intact (despite wars, military occupation, and constitutional change) for over a century.[41] Only one party has governed Japan since 1955; its leaders have had much the same view as the bureaucracy. Moreover, Japan, like Sweden, is a nation governed by the principle that the state is supreme and expert knowledge is decisive. The bureaucracy embodies the traditional understanding of what governance is all about, and so it is the central institution of the regime rather than, as in the United States, a necessary but unwelcome contrivance that exists in order to implement the decisions of others.

The power of the bureaucracy may have structural or political explanations, but its manner of operating clearly has cultural roots. The importance of the group is not an administrative invention, much less one that can be exported; it is the institutional embodiment of a pervasive communalism in Japanese life, a communalism that can be found in the family, the schools, and the neighborhood.[42]

IMPERSONAL VERSUS PERSONAL

Most nations of Latin America have a government bureaucracy at least as large and complex as anything found in Sweden or France; most also intervene in their economies—by regulation, licensing, and subsidy—at least as much as did England in its most mercantilist phase. But unlike the administrative systems of these European countries, most Latin American bureaucracies do not embody the tradition of the rule of law, the expert application of general rules to particular cases, or the impersonal conduct of public affairs.

Almost every scholar who has written about Latin American government stresses the patrimonial nature of administrative rule. The Spanish colonies in the New World were treated as the personal property of the monarch; the advent of independence replaced distant kings with local presidents, but many of the presidents maintained the feudal view that they were the patrons and the people their clients.[43] "Not only is politics concentrated in the office and person of the president, but it is by presidential favors and patronage that contracts are determined, different clientele are served, and wealth, privilege, and social position parceled out. The president is *the* national *patron*, replacing the local landowners and men on horseback of the past."[44] Lower-level officials are selected on the basis of their loyalty to the chief or his political faction. Though nepotism is not as widespread as is sometimes alleged, recruitment on the basis of personal friendship and political sympathies is.[45]

The administrative system is centralized as well as paternalistic. Though a few Latin nations such as Argentina, Brazil, Mexico, and Venezuela have in theory a federal regime with important powers left in local hands, in reality the central government either is wholly dominant or it reserves (and exercises) the right to intervene in local affairs whenever it chooses.[46]

Patrimonial or personalistic rule embedded in a centralized state has at least three consequences. First, all power is lodged at the top so that even the most routine decisions and minor memoranda must be referred to the head of the agency. As a result, communication is slow and difficult, decisions are delayed and often ill-informed.[47] Second, when power is both concentrated and used at the pleasure of the leader, the incentives for corruption are very large. The corruption can take the form of lower-ranking officials accepting bribes from people who wish to short-circuit the official procedures or high-ranking officials using their great powers to line their own pockets.[48] Third, to facilitate central control over a rapidly growing bureaucracy and to reduce the degree of corruption, Latin governments have relied on formal rules and increasingly complex laws and procedures. Every official is enmeshed in a web of regulations, many either ambiguous or contradictory. This legalism amounts to what one scholar called the "code fetish."[49]

American bureaucrats weary from the effort of coping with a tangle of procedural constraints might feel their spirits lift (even if their burdens do not lighten) by contemplating the vastly greater procedural morass in which their Latin American counterparts find themselves, made all the more frustrating because it does not serve its goals. Multiplying rules neither enhances central control nor eliminates corruption. What it does instead is revealed by anecdotes such as this: "In Brazil a patient citizen waited ten years for a tax refund, only to see inflation reduce it to virtually nothing. When he offered to donate the pittance to the government, a bureaucrat begged him to keep the money in order to avoid another prolonged procedure."[50] The Guatemalan bureaucracy consists of "executives seated behind mounds of petitions, memos, and requests for rulings; besieged by clients, friends and subordinates begging assistance or opinions; and occasionally and hastily scanning a report that is probably largely fictitious and almost inevitably devoid of critical analysis."[51]

To cope with the cumbersome, rule-bound, and overcentralized government bureaucracy, many Latin nations have created autonomous government corporations and independent agencies to which are given tasks that the central bureaucracy has shown itself unable to perform. Some produce steel or oil; others set prices and wages; still others distribute water, run schools, or administer social security. Some have become models of efficiency and integrity; others merely have increased the administrative confusion in which the government is immersed. But all contribute to the enormous power of the state. We expect the government to dominate the economy in Marxist Cuba or Nicaragua, but the dominance is nearly as great in Brazil, Colombia, or Mexico. For example, Howard Wiarda and Harvey Kline estimate that the Brazilian government either by itself or through public corporations generates 55 to 60 percent of that country's gross national product.[52]

The United States has had its share of patrimonial rule in urban political machines, corrupt county courthouses, and overcentralized Washington bureaucracies. It has responded to these problems by attempting to use formal procedures and legal constraints to convert patrimonial rule into impersonal rule, but with a difference: In the United States, the state is limited (it produces only about 11 percent of the gross national product) and it is decentralized (state and local governments play large roles and exercise substantial powers).

Statist and Non-statist Regimes

The limited scope and constrained powers of the American government are its most important features. By European standards it is not truly a "state"—that is, a sovereign body whose authority penetrates all aspects of the nation and brings each part of that nation within its reach.[53] In this country sovereignty belongs in theory to the people and in practice to no one; to the extent that it exists at all it is shared by national and state governments. What someone once said of the British House of Commons—that it could do anything except change a man into a woman—can be said of no institution in this country.

State-centered regimes are executive-centered regimes, and executive-centered regimes are dominated by their bureaucracies. Despite their many important differences, the governments of France, Japan, Sweden, Brazil, and Mexico are alike in making the administrative apparatus the center of official action. The bureaucracy, with relatively few checks from either the legislature or the judiciary, drafts laws, issues regulations, allocates funds, and guides policy. Since no single institution can manage affairs unaided, the bureaucracy enlists or commands the help of private interests—corporations, labor unions, and professional groups. These join together comfortably or warily to propose policies and implement laws. There is an easy interchange of ideas and people between the public and private sectors, so easy an interchange that it is hard to draw any clear line between them. Senior government bureaucrats not only deal routinely and privately with their corporate counterparts, they join the corporate world as top executives upon retiring from government service (the Japanese call it "descending from heaven").

Political scientists have begun to describe such states as corporatist, meaning nations in which the major segments of society (especially industry and labor) are represented directly in the state as bodies entitled to participate in making laws and carrying them out.[54] In the United States business and labor among all other segments of society form interest groups or lobbies to press claims on the government; in corporatist states these interests need not press anything, for they are, informally if not formally, part of the government. The formulation and implementation of industrial safety policies in Sweden with which this chapter began is an example of corporatism in action.

Cultural and constitutional factors produce important differences in state-centered regimes and in how their bureaucracies function. In Japan and northern Europe the statist governments might be called rationalistic: They embody the values of deference, impersonal rule, and administrative discretion. In the state-centered regimes of Latin America the governments reflect the values of an adversary culture, personal rule, and procedural formalism.

In the first case the bureaucracy tends to operate on universalistic principles (the expert application of neutral rules), to recruit its members on the basis of achievement criteria (skills acquired by education and training), and to serve collective interests (the state, society, and the ruling party). In the second case the bureaucracy tends to operate on particularistic principles (give each person what he deserves), to recruit its members on the basis of ascriptive criteria (hire people with the "correct" social, familial, or political connections), and to serve personal interests (those of the president, the junta, or the minister).

Of course these sweeping distinctions oversimplify reality, ignore important exceptions (there is corruption even in Sweden!), and neglect trends that are moving once-different nations toward greater similarity. To do justice to these matters would require a book on comparative government. But simple as they may be, they highlight what is distinctive about the bureaucracy of the United States. It serves a weak state (though one that is growing stronger); it copes with an adversarial rather than a deferential culture; it has found its exercise of discretion falling under suspicion and so has tried to constrain that discretion by formal procedures and elaborate rules; it is staffed by individualistic rather than group-oriented workers; and it has taken steps to reduce personal and patrimonial rule in favor of impersonal and rationalistic standards.

In doing so, the American bureaucracy has been afflicted with many problems, some common to all bureaucracies and some unique to our own. We turn next to an analysis of those problems.

PART VI

CHANGE

CHAPTER 17

Problems

ON THE MORNING OF MAY 22, 1986, Donald Trump, the New York real estate developer, called one of his executives, Anthony Gliedman, into his office. They discussed the inability of the City of New York, despite six years of effort and the expenditure of nearly $13 million, to rebuild the ice-skating rink in Central Park. On May 28 Trump offered to take over the rink reconstruction, promising to do the job in less than six months. A week later Mayor Edward Koch accepted the offer and shortly thereafter the city appropriated $3 million on the understanding that Trump would have to pay for any cost overruns out of his own pocket. On October 28, the renovation was complete, over a month ahead of schedule and about $750,000 under budget. Two weeks later, skaters were using it.[1]

For many readers it is obvious that private enterprise is more efficient than are public bureaucracies, and so they would file this story away as simply another illustration of what everyone already knows. But for other readers it is not so obvious what this story means; to them, business is greedy and unless watched like a hawk will fob off shoddy or overpriced goods on the American public, as when it sells the government $435 hammers and $3,000 coffeepots. Trump may have done a good job in this instance, but perhaps there is something about skating rinks or New York City government that gave him a comparative advantage; in any event, no larger lessons should be drawn from it.

Some lessons can be drawn, however, if one looks closely at the incentives and constraints facing Trump and the Department of Parks and Recreation. It becomes apparent that there is not one "bureaucracy problem" but several, and the solution to each in some degree is incompatible with the solution to every other.[2] First there is the problem of accountability—getting agencies to serve agreed-upon goals. Second there is the problem of equity—treating all citizens fairly, which usually means treating them alike on the basis of clear rules known in advance. Third there is the problem of responsiveness—reacting reasonably to the special needs and circumstances of particular people. Fourth there is the problem of efficiency—obtaining the greatest output for a given level of resources. Finally there is the problem of fiscal integrity—assuring that public funds are spent prudently for public purposes. Donald Trump and Mayor Koch were situated differently with respect to most of these matters.

Accountability

The Mayor wanted the old skating rink refurbished, but he also wanted to minimize the cost of the fuel needed to operate the rink (the first effort to rebuild it occurred right after the Arab oil embargo and the attendant increase in energy prices). Trying to achieve both goals led city hall to select a new refrigeration system that as it turned out would not work properly. Trump came on the scene when only one goal dominated: get the rink rebuilt. He felt free to select the most reliable refrigeration system without worrying too much about energy costs.

Equity

The Parks and Recreation Department was required by law to give every contractor an equal chance to do the job. This meant it had to put every part of the job out to bid and to accept the lowest without much regard to the reputation or prior performance of the lowest bidder. Moreover, state law forbade city agencies from hiring a general contractor and letting him select the subcontractors; in fact, the law forbade the city from even discussing the project in advance with a general contractor who might later bid on it—that would have been collusion. Trump, by contrast, was free to locate the rink builder with the best reputation and give him the job.

Fiscal Integrity

To reduce the chance of corruption or sweetheart deals the law required Parks and Recreation to furnish complete, detailed plans to every contractor bidding on the job; any changes after that would require renegotiating the contract. No such law constrained Trump; he was free to give incomplete plans to his chosen contractor, hold him accountable for building a satisfactory rink, but allow him to work out the details as he went along.

Efficiency

When the Parks and Recreation Department spent over six years and $13 million and still could not reopen the rink, there was public criticism but no city official lost money. When Trump accepted a contract to do it; any cost overruns or delays would have come out of his pocket and any savings could have gone into his pocket (in this case, Trump agreed not to take a profit on the job).

Gliedman summarized the differences neatly: "The problem with government is that government can't say, 'yes' . . . there is nobody in government that can do that. There are fifteen or twenty people who have to agree. Government has to be slower. It has to safeguard the process."[3]

Inefficiency

The government can't say "yes." In other words, the government is constrained. Where do the constraints come from? From us.

Herbert Kaufman has explained red tape as being of our own making: "Every restraint and requirement originates in somebody's demand for it."[4] Applied to the Central Park skating rink Kaufman's insight reminds us that civil-service reformers demanded that no city official benefit personally from building a project; that contractors demanded that all be given an equal chance to bid on every job; and that fiscal watchdogs demanded that all contract specifications be as detailed as possible. For each demand a procedure was established; viewed from the outside, those procedures are called red tape. To enforce each procedure a manager was appointed; those managers are called bureaucrats. No organized group demanded that all skating rinks be rebuilt as quickly as possible, no procedure existed to enforce that demand, and no manager was appointed to enforce it. The political process can more easily enforce compliance with constraints than the attainment of goals.

When we denounce bureaucracy for being inefficient we are saying something that is half true. Efficiency is a ratio of valued resources used to valued outputs produced. The smaller that ratio the more efficient the production. If the valued output is a rebuilt skating rink, then whatever process uses the fewest dollars or the least time to produce a satisfactory rink is the most efficient process. By this test Trump was more efficient than the Parks and Recreation Department.

But that is too narrow a view of the matter. The economic definition of efficiency (efficiency in the small, so to speak) assumes that there is only one valued output, the new rink. But government has many valued outputs, including a reputation for integrity, the confidence of the people, and the support of important interest groups. When we complain about skating rinks not being built on time we speak as if all we cared about were skating rinks. But when we complain that contracts were awarded without competitive bidding or in a way that allowed bureaucrats to line their pockets we acknowledge that we care about many things besides skating rinks; we care about the contextual goals—the constraints—that we want government to observe. A government that is slow to build rinks but is honest and accountable in its actions and properly responsive to worthy constituencies may be a very efficient government, *if* we measure efficiency in the large by taking into account *all* of the valued outputs.

Calling a government agency efficient when it is slow, cumbersome, and costly may seem perverse. But that is only because we lack any objective way for deciding how much money or time should be devoted to maintaining honest behavior, producing a fair allocation of benefits, and generating popular support as well as to achieving the main goal of the project. If we could measure these things, and if we agreed as to their value, then we would be in a position to judge the true efficiency of a government agency and decide when it is taking too much time or spending too much money achieving all that we expect of it. But we cannot measure these things nor do we agree about their relative importance, and so government always will appear to be inefficient compared to organizations that have fewer goals.

Put simply, the only way to decide whether an agency is truly inefficient is to decide which of the constraints affecting its action ought to be ignored or discounted. In fact that is what most debates about agency behavior are all about. In fighting crime are the police handcuffed? In educating children are teachers tied down by rules? In launching a space shuttle are we too concerned with safety? In building a dam do we worry excessively about endangered species? In running the Postal Service is it important to have many post offices close to where people live? In the case of the skating rink, was the requirement of competitive bidding for each contract on the basis of detailed specifications a reasonable one? Probably not. But if it were abandoned, the gain (the swifter completion of the rink) would have to be balanced against the costs (complaints from contractors who might lose business and the chance of collusion and corruption in some future projects).

Even allowing for all of these constraints, government agencies may still be inefficient. Indeed, given the fact that bureaucrats cannot (for the most part) benefit monetarily from their agencies' achievements, it would be surprising if they were not inefficient. Efficiency, in the large or the small, doesn't pay.

But some critics of government believe that inefficiency is obvious and vast. Many people remember the 1984 claim of the Grace Commission (officially, the President's Private Sector Survey on Cost Control) that it had identified over $400 billion in savings that could be made if only the federal government were managed properly.[5] Though the commission did not say so, many people inferred that careless bureaucrats were wasting that amount of money. But hardly anybody remembers the study issued jointly by the General Accounting Office and the Congressional Budget Office in February 1984, one month after the Grace Commission report.[6]

The GAO and CBO reviewed those Grace recommendations that accounted for about 90 percent of the projected savings, and after eliminating double-counting and recommendations for which no savings could be estimated, and other problems, concluded that the true savings would be less than one-third the claimed amount.[7]

Of course, $100 billion is still a lot of money. But wait. It turns out that about 60 percent of this would require not management improvements but policy changes: for example, taxing welfare benefits, ending certain direct loan programs, adopting new rules to restrict Medicare benefits, restricting eligibility for retirement among federal civilian workers and military personnel, and selling the power produced by government-owned hydroelectric plants at the full market price.

That still leaves roughly $40 billion in management savings. But most of this would require either a new congressional policy (for example, hiring more Internal Revenue Service agents to collect delinquent taxes), some unspecified increase in "worker productivity," or buying more services from private suppliers. Setting aside the desirable goal of increasing productivity (for which no procedures were identified), it turns out that almost all of the projected savings would require Congress to alter the goals and constraints of public agencies. If there is a lot of waste (and it is not clear why the failure to tax welfare benefits or to hire more IRS agents should be called waste), it is congressionally directed waste.

Military procurement, of course, is the biggest source of stories about waste, fraud, and mismanagement. There cannot be a reader of this book who has not heard about the navy paying $435 for a hammer or the air force paying $3,000 for a coffeepot, and nobody, I suspect, believes Defense Department estimates of the cost of a new airplane or missile. If ever one needed evidence that bureaucracy is inefficient, the Pentagon supplies it.

Well, yes. But what kind of inefficiency? And why does it occur? To answer these questions one must approach the problem just as we approached the problem of fixing up a skating rink in New York City: We want to understand why the bureaucrats, all of whom are rational and most of whom want to go a good job, behave as they do.

To begin, let us forget about $435 hammers. They never existed. A member of Congress who did not understand (or did not want to understand) government accounting rules created a public stir. The $3,000 coffeepot existed, but it is not clear that it was overpriced.* But that does

*This is what happened: The navy ordered a package of maintenance equipment. One of the items was an inexpensive hammer; some of the others were very expensive test devices. Under the accounting rules then in effect, the supplier was allowed to allocate overhead costs in equal percentages to each item. This was simpler than trying to figure out how much overhead should be attributed to each individual item (in which case the difficult-to-make items would, of course, have accounted for more of the overhead than the easy-to-make ones such as a hammer). As a result, the bill showed the hammer as costing several hundred dollars in "overhead," for a total of $435. When a sailor unpacked the box, he found

not mean there are no problems; in fact, the real problems are far more costly and intractable than inflated price tags on hammers and coffeemakers. They include sticking too long with new weapons of dubious value, taking forever to acquire even good weapons, and not inducing contractors to increase their efficiency. What follows is not a complete explanation of military procurement problems; it is only an analysis of the contribution bureaucratic systems make to those problems.

When the military buys a new weapons system—a bomber, submarine, or tank—it sets in motion a procurement bureaucracy comprised of two key actors, the military program manager and the civilian contract officer, who must cope with the contractor, the Pentagon hierarchy, and Congress. To understand how they behave we must understand how their tasks get defined, what incentives they have, and what constraints they face.

TASKS

The person nominally in charge of buying a major new weapon is the program manager, typically an army or air force colonel or a navy captain. Officially, his job is to design and oversee the acquisition strategy by establishing specifications and schedules and identifying problems and tradeoffs. Unofficially, his task is somewhat different. For one thing he does not have the authority to make many important decisions; those are referred upward to his military superiors, to Defense Department civilians, and to Congress. For another, the program he oversees must constantly be sold and resold to the people who control the resources (mostly, the key congressional committees). And finally, he is surrounded by inspectors and auditors looking for any evidence of waste, fraud, or abuse and by the advocates of all manner of special interests (contractors' representatives, proponents of small and minority business utilization, and so on). As the Packard Commission observed, the program manager, "far from being the manager of the program . . . is merely one of the participants who can influence it."[8]

Under these circumstances the actual task of the program manager tends to be defined as selling the program and staying out of trouble. Harvard Business School professor J. Ronald Fox, who has devoted much of his life to studying and participating in weapons procurement, found that a program manager must spend 30 to 50 percent of his time defending his program inside DOD and to Congress.[9] It is entirely rational for him

---

this bill and, not understanding the equal-allocation formula, called his congressman. A myth was born. See James Fairhall, "The Case for the $435 Hammer," *Washington Monthly* (January 1987): 47–52. The "coffeepot" did cost about $3,000, but it was purchased to make coffee for the more than three hundred soldiers who would be carried on a C-5A transport. Commercial airlines often pay that much for coffeemakers on their jumbo jets. See J. Ronald Fox, *The Defense Management Challenge* (Boston: Harvard Business School Press, 1988), 31.

to do this, for a study by the General Accounting Office showed that weapons programs with effective advocates survived (including some that should have been terminated) and systems without such advocates were more likely to be ended (even some that should have been completed).[10] Just as with the New York City skating rink, in the Pentagon there is no one who can say "yes" and make it stick. The only way to keep winning the support of the countless people who must say "yes" over and over again is to forge ahead at full speed, spending money at a rate high enough to prevent it from being taken away.[11]

The program manager's own background and experience reinforce this definition of his task. He is a military officer, which means he cares deeply about having the best possible airplane, tank, or submarine. In recommending any tradeoffs between cost and performance, his natural inclination is to favor performance over savings. After all, someday he may have to fly in that airplane or sail on that ship. This often leads to what is commonly called "goldplating": seeking the best possible, most sophisticated weapon and making frequent changes in the contract specifications in order to incorporate new features. The program manager, of course, does not make these decisions, but he is an integral part of a user-dominated process that does make them.

The civilian counterpart to the program manager is the contracting officer. What is clear is that he or she, and not the program manager, is the only person legally authorized to sign the contract. In addition, the contracting officer administers the contract and prepares a report on contractor performance. Everything else is unclear. In principle, contracting officers are supposed to be involved in every step of the acquisition process, from issuing an invitation to bid on the contract through the completion of the project. In practice, as Ronald Fox observes, contracting officers often play only a small role in designing the acquisition strategy or in altering the contracts (this tends to be dominated by the program manager) and must share their authority over enforcing the terms of the contract with a small army of auditors and advocates.[12]

What dominates the task of the contract officer are the rules, the more than 1,200 pages of the Federal Acquisition Regulation and Defense Acquisition Regulation in addition to the countless other pages in DOD directives and congressional authorization legislation and the unwritten "guidance" that arrives with every visit to a defense plant where a contracting officer works. Contract officers are there to enforce constraints, and those constraints have grown exponentially in recent years.

INCENTIVES

In theory, military program managers are supposed to win promotions if they have done a good job supervising weapons procurement. In fact, promotions to the rank of general or admiral usually have been made on the basis of their reputation as combat officers and experience as military leaders. According to Fox, being a program manager is often not a useful ticket to get punched if you want to rise to the highest ranks.[13] In 1985, for example, 94 percent of the lieutenant colonels who had commanded a battalion were promoted by the army to the rank of colonel; the promotion rate for lieutenant colonels without that experience was only half as great.[14] The armed services now claim that they do promote procurement officers at a reasonable rate, but Fox, as well as many officers, remain skeptical.[15] The perceived message is clear: Traditional military specialties are a surer route to the top than experience as a program manager.

Reinforcing this bias against acquisition experience is the generalist ethos of the armed services—good officers can do any job; well-rounded officers have done many jobs. As a result, the typical program manager has a brief tenure in a procurement job. In 1986, the GAO found that the average program manager spent twenty-seven months on the job, and many spent less than two years.[16] By contrast, it takes between eleven and twenty years to procure a major new weapons system, from concept to deployment.[17] This means that during the acquisition of a new aircraft or missile, the identity of the program will change five or ten times.

In 1987, the services, under congressional prodding, established career paths for acquisition officers so that they could rise in rank while continuing to develop experience in procurement tasks. It is not yet clear how significant this change will be. If it encourages talented officers to invest ten or twenty years in mastering procurement policies it will be a major gain, one that will enable program managers from DOD to deal more effectively with experienced industry executives and encourage officers to make tough decisions rather than just keeping the program alive.

Civilian contract officers do have a distinct career path, but as yet not one that produces in them much sense of professional pride or organizational mission. Of the more than twenty thousand civilian contract administrators less than half have a college degree and the great majority are in the lower civil-service grades (GS-5 to GS-12).[18] Even the most senior contract officers rarely earn (in 1988) more than $50,000 a year, less than half or even one-third of what their industry counterparts earn. Moreover, all are aware that they work in offices where the top posts usually are held by military officers; in civil-service jargon, the "head room" available for promotions is quite limited.

Of course, low pay has not prevented the development of a strong sense of mission in other government agencies (see chapter 6). But in those organizations training and indoctrination are intensive. In the Defense Contract Adminstration Service they are not. In 1984, the DOD inspector general reported that two-thirds of the senior contract officers had not received the prescribed training.[19]

The best evidence of the weakness of civilian incentives is the high turnover rate. Fox quotes a former commander of the military acquisition program as saying that "good people are leaving in droves" because "there is much less psychic income today" that would make up for the relatively low monetary income.[20] The Packard Commission surveyed civilian procurement personnel and found that over half would leave their jobs if offered comparable jobs elsewhere in the federal government or in private industry.[21]

In short, the incentives facing procurement officials do not reward people for maximizing efficiency. Military officers are rewarded for keeping programs alive and are encouraged to move on to other assignments; civilian personnel have weak inducements to apply a complex array of inconsistent constraints to contract administration.

CONSTRAINTS

These constraints are not designed to produce efficiency but to reduce costs, avoid waste, fraud, and abuse, achieve a variety of social goals, and maintain the productive capacity of key contractors.

Reducing costs is not the same thing as increasing efficiency. If too little money is spent, the rate of production may be inefficient and the managerial flexibility necessary to cope with unforeseen circumstances may be absent. Congress typically appropriates money one year at a time. If Congress wishes to cut its spending or if DOD is ordered to slash its budget requests, the easiest thing to do is to reduce the number of aircraft, ships, or missiles being purchased in a given year without reducing the total amount purchased. This stretch-out has the effect of increasing the cost of each individual weapon as manufacturers forgo the economies that come from large-scale production.* As Fox observes (but as many critics fail to understand), the typical weapons program in any given year is not overfunded, it is *under*funded.[22] Recognizing that, the Packard Commission called for adopting a two-year budget cycle.

Reducing costs and eliminating fraud are not the same as increasing efficiency. There no doubt are excessive costs and there may be fraud in military procurement, but eliminating them makes procurement more efficient only if the costs of eliminating the waste and fraud exceed the savings thereby realized. To my knowledge no one has systematically compared the cost of all the inspectors, rules, and auditors with the savings they have achieved to see if all the checking and reviewing is worth it.

*The evidence is clear that stretch-outs increase unit costs. A Rand study found unit-cost increases in virtually every case of a reduced rate of acquisition and the CSIS found that changes in quantity were responsible for the largest fraction of cost increases in weapons systems. See Michael Rich and Edmund Dews, *Improving the Military Acquisition Process*, Report R-3373-AF/RC (Santa Monica, Calif.: Rand, 1986), 28; and Center for International and Strategic Studies, *U.S. Defense Acquisition: A Process in Trouble* (Washington, D.C.: Georgetown University Press, 1987), 35.

Some anecdotal evidence suggests that the checking does not always pay for itself. In one case the army was required to spend $5,400 to obtain fully competitive bids for spare parts that cost $11,000. In exchange for the $5,400 and the 160 days it took to get the bids, the army saved $100.[23] In short, there is an optimal level of "waste" in any organization, public or private: It is that level below which further savings are worth less than the cost of producing them.*

The weapons procurement system must serve a number of "social" goals mandated by Congress. It must support small business, provide opportunities for minority-owned businesses, buy American-made products whenever possible, rehabilitate prisoners, provide employment for the handicapped, protect the environment, and maintain "prevailing" wage rates (see chapter 7). One could lower the cost of procurement by eliminating some or all of the social goals the process is obliged to honor; that would produce increases in efficiency, narrowly defined. But what interest group is ready to sacrifice its most cherished goal in the name of efficiency? And if none will volunteer, how does one create a congressional majority to compel the sacrifice?

Weapons procurement also is designed to maintain the productive capacity of the major weapons builders. There is no true market in the manufacture of missiles, military aircraft, and naval vessels because typically there is only one buyer (the government) and no alternative uses for the production lines established to supply this buyer.† Northrop, Lockheed, Grumman, McDonnell Douglas, the Bath Iron Works, Martin Marietta—these firms and others like them would not exist, or would exist in very different form, if they did not have a continuous flow of military contracts. As a result, each new weapons system becomes a do-or-die proposition for the executives of these firms. Even if the Pentagon cared nothing about their economic well-being it would have to care about the productive capacity that they represent, for if it were ever lost or much diminished the armed services would have nowhere else to turn when the need arose for a new airplane or ship. And if by chance the Pentagon did not care, Congress would; no member believes he or she was elected to preside over the demise of a major employer.

This constraint produces what some scholars have called the "follow-on imperative": the need to give a new contract to each major supplier as work on an old contract winds down.[24] If one understands this it is

*With one qualification: You may wish to spend more eliminating fraud than you save in order to deter would-be perpetrators of fraud. This is akin to an insurance company spending $50,000 to investigate a fradulent claim for $25,000—it sends a message to other policyholders not to submit fraudulent claims.

†There are, of course, opportunities for sales to foreign governments, but those sales are closely regulated by the U.S. government.

not necessary to imagine some sinister "military-industrial complex" conspiring to keep new weapons flowing. The armed services want them because they believe, rightly, that their task is to defend the nation against real though hard to define threats; the contractors want them because they believe, rightly, that the nation cannot afford to dismantle its productive capacity; Congress wants them because its members believe, rightly, that they are elected to maintain the prosperity of their states and districts.

When these beliefs encounter the reality of limited resources and the need to make budget choices, almost everyone has an incentive to overstate the benefits and understate the costs of a new weapons system. To do otherwise—to give a cautious estimate of what the weapon will achieve and a candid view of what it will cost—is to invite rejection. And none of the key actors in the process believe they can afford rejection.

THE BOTTOM LINE

The incentives and constraints that confront the military procurement bureaucracy push its members to overstate benefits, understate costs, make frequent and detailed changes in specifications, and enforce a bewildering array of rules designed to minimize criticism and stay out of trouble. There are hardly any incentives pushing officials to leave details to manufacturers or delegate authority to strong program managers whose career prospects will depend on their ability to produce good weapons at a reasonable cost.

In view of all this, what is surprising is that the system works as well as it does. In fact, it works better than most people suppose. The Rand Corporation has been studying military procurement for over thirty years. A summary of its findings suggests some encouraging news, most of it ignored amidst the headlines about hammers and coffeepots. There has been steady improvement in the performance of the system. Between the early 1960s and the mid-1980s, cost overruns, schedule slippages, and performance shortfalls have all decreased.[25] Cost overruns of military programs on the average are now no greater than they are for the civil programs of the government such as highway and water projects and public buildings. Moreover, there is evidence that for all its faults the American system seems to work as well or better than that in many European nations.[26]

Improvements can be made but they do not require bright new ideas, more regulations, or the reshuffling of boxes on the organizational chart. The necessary ideas exist in abundance, the top-down reorganizations have been tried without much effect, and the system is drowning in regulations. What is needed are changes in the incentives facing the key members. But as we shall see in the next chapter, the conventional response has always been "regulate and reorganize."

Arbitrary Rule

Inefficiency is not the only bureaucratic problem nor is it even the most important. A perfectly efficient agency could be a monstrous one, swiftly denying us our liberties, economically inflicting injustices, and competently expropriating our wealth. People complain about bureaucracy as often because it is unfair or unreasonable as because it is slow or cumbersome.

Arbitrary rule refers to officials acting without legal authority, or with that authority in a way that offends our sense of justice. Justice means, first, that we require the government to treat people equally on the basis of clear rules known in advance: If Becky and Bob both are driving sixty miles per hour in a thirty-mile-per-hour zone and the police give a ticket to Bob, we believe they also should give a ticket to Becky. Second, we believe that justice obliges the government to take into account the special needs and circumstances of individuals: If Becky is speeding because she is on her way to the hospital to give birth to a child and Bob is speeding for the fun of it, we may feel that the police should ticket Bob but not Becky. Justice in the first sense means fairness, in the second it means responsiveness. Obviously, fairness and responsiveness often are in conflict.

The checks and balances of the American constitutional system reflect our desire to reduce the arbitrariness of official rule. That desire is based squarely on the premise that inefficiency is a small price to pay for freedom and responsiveness. Congressional oversight, judicial review, interest-group participation, media investigations, and formalized procedures all are intended to check administrative discretion. It is not hyperbole to say that the constitutional order is animated by the desire to make the government "inefficient."

This creates two great tradeoffs. First, adding constraints reduces the efficiency with which the main goal of an agency can be attained but increases the chances that the agency will act in a nonarbitrary manner. Efficient police departments would seek out criminals without reading them their rights, allowing them to call their attorneys, or releasing them in response to a writ of habeas corpus. An efficient building department would issue construction permits on demand without insisting that the applicant first show that the proposed building meets fire, safety, sanitation, geological, and earthquake standards.

The second great tradeoff is between nonarbitrary governance defined as treating people equally and such governance defined as treating each case on its merits. We want the government to be both fair and responsive, but the more rules we impose to insure fairness (that is, to treat all people alike) the harder we make it for the government to be responsive (that is, to take into account the special needs and circumstances of a particular case).

The way our government manages these tradeoffs reflects both our political culture as well as the rivalries of our governing institutions. Both tend toward the same end: We define claims as rights, impose general rules to insure equal treatment, lament (but do nothing about) the resulting inefficiencies, and respond to revelations about unresponsiveness by adopting new rules intended to guarantee that special circumstances will be handled with special care (rarely bothering to reconcile the rules that require responsiveness with those that require equality). And we do all this out of the best of motives: a desire to be both just and benevolent. Justice inclines us to treat people equally, benevolence to treat them differently; both inclinations are expressed in rules, though in fact only justice can be. It is this futile desire to have a rule for every circumstance that led Herbert Kaufman to explain "how compassion spawns red tape."[27]

DISCRETION AT THE STREET LEVEL

We worry most about arbitrary rule at the hands of those street-level bureaucracies that deal with us as individuals rather than as organized groups and that touch the more intimate aspects of our lives: police, schools, prisons, housing inspectors, mental hospitals, welfare offices, and the like. That worry is natural; in these settings we feel helpless and The State seems omnipotent. We want these bureaucracies to treat us fairly but we also want them to be responsive to our particular needs. The proper reconciliation of these competing desires requires a careful understanding of the tasks of these organizations.

There are at least two questions that must be answered: What constitutes in any specific organization the exercise of arbitrary or unjust power? Under what circumstances will the elaboration of rules reduce at an acceptable cost the unjust use of power? Police officers act unjustly when they arrest people without cause. "Equality before the law" is the bedrock principle of our criminal justice system, however imperfectly it may be realized. And so we create rules defining when people can be arrested.

But making an arrest is different for police patrol officers than for FBI agents. When the former go to the scene of a fight they are trying to restore order and ascertain who started the fight and who wielded the knife. An arrest, if any, is often the culmination of a long, subtle, low-visibility process of interviewing victims, observing people, and questioning suspects, all done on the street in the absence of a supervisor and all based on making inferences from incomplete and disputed assertions. The essence of this process is judgment: deciding whose conduct, demeanor, and appearance make it likely that he has committed a crime. In assessing those traits officers are required not to "treat all people alike" but to treat them very differently. They cannot do their jobs unless they know that young people are more likely to commit assaults than old, males more likely than females, and acquaintances more likely than strangers. These are only probabilities, but they are important ones. It is very difficult to specify by rule in advance who should be stopped, questioned, or searched. When such rules are specified, as they are when officers are told the circumstances under which they can stop, question, and search people, inevitably the rules will be cumbersome, incomplete, and even inconsistent. Some officers determined to do their jobs will evade the rules; others, determined to stay out of trouble, will use the rules as an excuse for doing as little as possible; and still others will give vent to their frustration in trying to comprehend the rules. In many other democratic nations the law defining a legitimate arrest is not very different from that in the United States, but there are far fewer rules defining what an officer may do short of (or in anticipation of) an arrest. We extend rules further back down the chain of inference and discretion than do our counterparts abroad.

FBI agents are in very different circumstances. They are detectives, not patrol officers; they "solve crimes" rather than "handle situations" or "maintain order." Except in special circumstances they do not intervene in barroom or bedroom quarrels. They usually come to the scene of a crime some time after it occurred; when they are ready to make an arrest they almost always are able to obtain an arrest warrant. A warrant means that in the opinion of a third party—a judge—the rules governing an arrest have been satisfied. Because their tasks are different from those of patrol officers, FBI agents complain much less about the restrictive nature of rules and are less frequently accused of making arbitrary or unjustified arrests.[28]

Prison administrators differ in their understanding of arbitrary rule. For over twenty years the Texas Department of Corrections ran its prisons by issuing to every officer and inmate a slim, simple book of rules that were enforced to the letter.[29] By contrast, the Michigan Department of Corrections had three fat volumes of rules governing every aspect of prison life, from personal property (six single-spaced pages) to prisoner organization. But the rules were not consistently enforced, nor were they intended to be so enforced: The rulebook told officers that "there is no requirement that every rule violation" be punished.[30]

John DiIulio explained the reasons for the differences. The Texas officials believed that the overriding imperative of prison life was to insure order and maintain security; to that end the rules had to specify inmate conduct, be few and simple (otherwise they could not be communicated and enforced), and be rigidly applied (otherwise inmates would think they could ignore them). If order were assured, programs and services then could be supplied. The Michigan officials, by contrast, believed that the overriding imperative of prison life was to encourage inmates to take responsibility for their own behavior; to that end the rules had to specify inmate rights, be many and complex (for rights could not briefly be summarized), and be flexibly enforced (because a rule should never stand in the way of achieving the right result). If inmate self-rule were achieved, order would follow automatically. In Texas "arbitrary rule" meant the inconsistent or unfair enforcement of regulations; in Michigan it meant the failure to encourage inmate self-governance. DiIulio's evidence suggests that the Texas officials were right and the Michigan officials wrong. Until the system deteriorated, Texas inmates were treated justly (that is, they were not abused either by the guards or by other inmates) whereas the Michigan prisoners often were treated unjustly (they were abused by other inmates if not by the guards).

Police patrol officers are members of coping organizations: their discretion is not easily limited by imposing rules.[31] An excessive reliance on rules can lead to shirking or to subversion. To solve the problem of arbitrariness one must rely on effective management, especially on the part of first-line supervisors—sergeants and lieutenants. FBI agents are members of craft organizations: Their outputs are relatively easy to assess, and so they can be held accountable for those outcomes even though their daily routine is hard to observe or control. Rules can be used to limit discretion *if* they are linked to the definition of a good outcome. Prison guards are members of procedural organizations: What they do is observable but the results (at least in terms of the long-run behavior of ex-inmates) are not. Managers therefore are powerfully tempted to design procedures (rules) that reflect a theory of human behavior, ignoring (as in the case of Michigan) the evident short-run costs of applying that theory in the untested belief that long-run benefits would follow.

DISCRETION AT THE HEADQUARTERS LEVEL

Interest groups also complain about arbitrariness, especially when they deal with regulatory agencies that have either no clear rules (and so the groups do not know whether policies in effect today will be in effect tomorrow) or rules so clear and demanding that there is no freedom to adjust their activities to conform to economic or technological imperatives.

The exercise of discretion by regulatory agencies does not occur because their activities are invisible or their clients are powerless but because these agencies and their legislative supporters have certain beliefs about what constitutes good policy. For many decades after the invention of the regulatory agency, Progressives believed that good decisions were the result of empowering neutral experts to decide cases on the basis of scientifically determined facts and widely shared principles.[32] No one took it amiss that these "principles" often were so vague as to lack any meaning at all. The Federal Communications Commission (FCC) was directed to issue broadcast licenses as the "public interest, convenience, and necessity" shall require. A similar "standard" was to govern the awarding of licenses to airline companies by the now-defunct Civil Aeronautics Board (CAB). The Antitrust Division of the Justice Department was charged with enforcing the Sherman Act that made "combinations in restraint of trade" illegal.

What the statute left vague "experts" were to imbue with meaning. But expert opinion changes and some experts in fact are politicians who bow to the influence of organized interests or ideologues who embrace the enthusiasms of zealous factions. The result was an invitation for interests to seek particular results in the absence of universal standards.

One might suppose that the agencies, noticing the turmoil caused by having to decide hard cases on the basis of vacuous standards, would try to formulate and state clear policies that would supply to their clients the guidance that the legislature was unwilling to provide; but no. For the most part regulatory agencies with ambiguous statutes did not clarify their policies. I conjecture that this is because the agencies realized what Michel Crozier has stated: Uncertainty is power.[33] If one party needs something from another and cannot predict how that second party will behave, the second party has power over the first. In the extreme case we will do almost anything to please a madman with life-or-death power over us because we cannot predict which behavior will produce what reaction.

The FCC is not a madman, but it has realized that a broadcaster uncertain as to how the FCC would react to a controversial broadcast often would cancel the program rather than risk offending the agency. And this would happen despite the clear statutory provision that forbade the FCC from controlling the contents of programs.[34] The FCC had life-or-death power over a broadcaster because every few years it could decide whether its license to broadcast would be renewed. If it left the broadcaster in doubt as to what went into the renewal decision (which is to say, if it did not write down any clear, comprehensive policies), the broadcaster's worries would lead it to conform to even the most subtle hints and cues from the FCC or its staff.

Do not suppose that regulators were unaware of the power that flowed from ambiguity. Abe Fortas, later to be a justice of the Supreme Court, wrote in 1937 about how the Securities and Exchange Commission ought to behave:

> Unless the administrator has effective bargaining power, little can be expected. He must have sanctions or desired favors which he can trade for changes in [business] practices. . . . He may be asked to exercise his discretion, for example, to accelerate the effective date of registration [of a new security]. Then, if the need is sufficiently urgent, a trade may be consummated. In return for the favor of the

> administrator, the registrant may amend his practices in accordance with the administrator's conception of justice and equity.[35]

If you find nothing wrong with the SEC bargaining with firms trying to sell stock, reread this quotation, substituting the word "police officer" for "administrator," "citizen" for "registrant," and "right to hold a protest meeting" for "effective date of registration."

In the next chapter we shall look at how regulatory agencies and Congress have changed their views as to the value of administrative discretion, just as legislators and courts have changed their views as to the value of police discretion. Common to both is a fear of arbitrary rule and an inclination to substitute rules for discretion. But we have already seen in the case of the police and prisons that it is not easy to know the circumstances under which rules will improve matters or what kinds of rules will achieve what effects. In chapter 18 we will find confirmation for what we have already seen in chapter 16 and elsewhere: In this country, we have a profound bias toward solving problems by adopting rules.

Conclusions

Neither inefficiency nor arbitrariness is easily defined and measured. Inefficiency in the small, that is, the excessive use of resources to achieve the main goal of an agency, is probably commonplace; but inefficiency in the large—the excessive use of resources to achieve all the goals, including the constraints—may not be so common. To evaluate the efficiency of a government agency one first must judge the value of the constraints under which it operates; to improve its efficiency one must decide which constraints one is willing to sacrifice. The best way to think about this is to ask whether we would be willing to have the same product or service delivered by a private firm. That is the subject of chapter 19.

If we decide that the constraints are important then we should be clear-eyed about the costs of retaining them. Those costs arise chiefly from the fact that most bureaucrats will be more strongly influenced by constraints than by goals. Constraints apply early in the process: You know from day one what will get you into trouble. Goals apply late in the process (if then): You must wait to see if the goal is achieved, assuming (a big assumption) that you can state the goal or confirm its achievement. Constraints are strongly enforced by attentive interest groups and their allies in Congress, the White House, the courts, and the media; goal attainment is weakly enforced because an agency head can always point to factors beyond one's control that prevented success. Constraints dissipate managerial authority;

every constraint is represented in the organization by someone who can say no. Goals, if they exist and can be attained, are the basis for increasing managerial authority; a clear and attainable goal provides an opportunity for one person to say yes.

Bureaucracies will differ in their vulnerability to the tradeoff between goal attainment and constraint observance. Production organizations, having clear and attainable goals, are more easily evaluated from the standpoint of economic efficiency and thus the cost of any given constraint is more easily assessed. Coping and procedural organizations are impossible to evaluate in terms of economic efficiency and so the cost of a constraint is hard to assess. Craft organizations are a mixed case; because their outputs are observable, we know if they are attaining their goal, but because their work is hard to observe we may think mistakenly that we can alter those work procedures without paying a cost in goal attainment.

The Social Security Administration and the Postal Service are not hard to judge in efficiency terms, though the latter presents a more difficult case than the former because we want the USPS to serve a number of partially inconsistent purposes. The State Department and public schools are impossible to evaluate in efficiency terms, and so we regularly pile on more constraints without any sense that we are paying a price. Police detectives or the Army Corps of Engineers can be evaluated, but only after the fact—the crook is caught, the bridge completed—but we are at somewhat of a loss to know what alteration in procedures would have what effect on these outcomes. Prisons can be evaluated in terms of the resources they consume and the complaints they engender, but ordinarily we have little information as to whether changes in resources or complaints have any effect on such objectives as security, rehabilitation, or deterrence.

Arbitrariness means acting without legal authority, or with such authority in ways that treat like cases in an unlike manner or unlike cases in a similar manner. Deciding what constitutes a "like case" is the heart of the problem. Prisons require rules, but what ends should the rules serve—custody? Security? Self-governance? Rehabilitation? Regulatory agencies formulate rules, but under what circumstances can those rules be clear and comprehensive as opposed to vague and partial? The next chapter will not answer all these questions, but it will suggest how Americans have tried to use rules, as well as the problems with rule-oriented bureaucracy.

CHAPTER 18

Rules

ON FEBRUARY 8, 1967, Robert H. Weaver, the secretary of the Department of Housing and Urban Development, announced that henceforth persons applying for apartments in federally financed public housing projects would be given such apartments on a first-come, first-serve basis. Weaver, who is black, issued the new rule in response to the criticism of civil-rights organizations (including a group he once headed) that the local managers of these projects practiced or condoned segregation.

Under the old rules the city agencies that ran these projects gave to individual project managers great discretion to pick their tenants. The effect of that discretion, combined with the preferences of the tenants, was that projects tended to be all-white or all-black. In Boston, for example, there were twenty-five public housing projects built for low-income tenants. Thirteen of these were more than 96 percent white, two were entirely black, and the rest were predominately of one race or the other. These differences could not be explained entirely by neighborhood considerations. The Mission Hill project was 100 percent white; across the street from it, the Mission Hill Extension project was 80 percent black.[1]

Weaver's order became known as the "1-2-3 Rule." It worked this way: All housing applicants would be ranked in numerical order based on the date they applied for housing, their need for housing, and the size of their families. When a vacancy became available it would be offered to the family at the top of the list. If there were more than one vacancy the one offered first would be drawn from the project with the most vacancies. If the family turned it down it would be offered another, and then a third. If all three vacancies were rejected the family would go to the bottom of the list and the next family in line would receive the offer.[2] The Weaver order was an effort, typical of many in government, to prevent the arbitrary use of discretion by replacing discretion with a rule.

Eight years later a group of tenants sued the Boston Housing Authority (BHA). In his findings, the Housing Court judge determined that public housing in Boston still was being allocated in a way that perpetuated racial segregation, a view confirmed by a 1976 report of the Department of Housing and Urban Development.[3] What had gone wrong? How could a discriminatory pattern of tenant assignment persist for so long after the BHA had implemented, albeit reluctantly, a clear federal rule that on its face did not allow race to be taken into account in choosing tenants?

The answer, supplied by the research of Jon Pynoos[4] and Jeffrey M. Prottas,[5] suggests the limit to rules as a means for controlling the discretion of bureaucrats. First, the 1-2-3 Rule combined three criteria: date, need, and family size. To rank applicants by these criteria someone had to decide how to measure "need" and then how much weight to give to need as opposed to family size or date of application. The evaluation of need inevitably was subjective. Moreover, the neediest familes almost by definition were those who had been on the waiting list for the least time. For example, a family living on the street because its home had burned down the night before clearly is going to be regarded as needier than one whose home is livable but who may have been on the waiting list for many months. Second, the rules were inconsistent with the incentives facing the applicants. Applicants wanted to live in the "nicest" projects, but these usually had few vacancies. The worst projects, those with the most crime, litter, and graffiti, had the most vacancies. Applicants would rather turn down a bad project, even if it meant going to the bottom of the list. Since the bad projects often were all-black, this meant that hardly any families, especially any white families, were willing to move in, and so they tended to remain all-black. Third, the rules were inconsistent with the incentives facing the project managers. Managers were exposed to pressure from the tenants in the buildings they operated to keep out the "bad element"—drug users, prostitutes, families with noisy children—and to attract the "good element," such as retired couples and the elderly. The managers bent to these pressures by various stratagems such as concealing the existence of vacancies from the central office or finding ways to veto the applications of certain tenants.[6]

Rules and Discretion

Max Weber said that the great virtue of bureaucracy—indeed, perhaps its defining characteristic—was that it was an institutional method for applying general rules to specific cases, thereby making the actions of government fair and predictable.[7] Weber's belief in the superiority of rule-based governance has been echoed by Theodore J. Lowi, who has criticized the exercise of administrative discretion in the modern American state on the grounds that it leads to the domination of the state by interest groups, thereby weakening popular control and creating new structures of privilege.[8] To restore democratic accountability he called for replacing discretionary authority with what he termed "juridical democracy": governance based on clear legislative standards for bureaucratic action or, failing that, on clear rules formulated by the bureaucracies themselves.[9] When rules are clear, governance is better. Lawrence Friedman has argued that welfare and public housing programs are especially suitable for governance by rule because they involve the simple allocation of resources on an equitable basis.[10]

The faith in the power of rules to prevent or correct the failings of government is ancient and deeply rooted. Aristotle said that "to seek for justice is to seek for a neutral authority; and law is a neutral authority."[11] This view was adopted by Elizabethan jurists such as Sir Edward Coke as a way of defending the rights of Parliament against the claims of the king.[12] John Locke thought the essence of freedom in a political society was to have "a standing rule to live by, common to every one of that society . . . and not to be subject to the inconstant, uncertain, arbitrary will of another man."[13] The Constitution of the United States is suffused with such Lockean sentiments, as when it speaks of the "equal protection of the laws."

These sentiments were less favorably received on the Continent. The French Revolution, unlike the American one, was not animated by a desire for limited government but for one based on popular sovereignty. Americans distrusted everyone who wielded power and sought to prevent the abuse of power by surrounding its holders with constitutional checks and subjecting its exercise to the rule of law. The French revolutionaries and their many successors were not afraid of power, they simply distrusted those persons—the king and his court—who then exercised it. Hardly anyone in France, or later in Sweden, wanted *limited* government; they wanted *popular* government. If the people ruled, they should rule fully; thus, the discretionary authority once possessed by the monarchy should be transferred intact into their hands. As we saw in chapter 16, these views continue to operate and help to explain why European administration is less rule-bound than its American counterpart.

On occasion, Americans have temporarily abandoned their fear of discretion and their insistence on rules. During the New Deal a number of regulatory agencies—the Securities and Exchange Commission, the National Labor Relations Board, the Federal Communications Commission—were endowed with great powers and vague standards. But in time we have returned to our natural posture, insisting that the powers of any new agencies carefully be circumscribed by law (as they were with the Environmental Protection Agency) and that the powers of existing agencies be if not precisely defined then at least judicially reviewable. But the love of rules has obscured the question of the circumstances under which rules will work. Clearly, an apparently simple rule did not solve the problems of the Boston Housing Authority.

As we saw, the first-come, first-served rule had several defects. Those defects suggest some of the properties a workable and fair rule should have. First, a good rule should treat equals equally. The BHA rule attempted to allocate dissimilar things among dissimilar claimants. Not all apartments were the same: They varied in size, amenity, and, above all, location. Not all clients were the same: Some were law-abiding, some lawless; some were orderly, some disorderly. Second, an effective rule will specify the tradeoffs to be made among the criteria governing the application of the rule. The BHA rule did not do this and in fact could not have done it. Need and time on the waiting list often were in conflict and there was no nonarbitrary way to resolve the conflict. Third, a workable rule will be consistent with the incentives operating on the administrators and on at least some of the clients. Neither the BHA clients nor its managers had many incentives to conform to the rules. The clients wanted to move into "nice" housing; very few wanted to integrate housing, whatever the cost in amenity. The managers wanted to get "nice" clients; very few wanted problem families. We want rules to be clear, but the BHA rule only seemed to be clear.

Rules and Tasks

When the work and the outcomes of a government agency are observable and unambiguous some but not all of the conditions for management by rule are present. I have called such bureaus production agencies (see chapter 9). Processing claims for old-age and survivors' insurance in the Social Security Administration (SSA) is subject to very detailed rules. These rules seem to work well. This happens not only because the work (processing claims) and the outcomes (who gets how much money) are easily observed, but also because the rules meet or come very close to meeting the tests described in the preceding section: They refer to comparable cases (people of a defined age and marital status), they do not involve difficult tradeoffs (unless the Social Security Trust Fund runs out of money, everybody who meets certain tests gets money), and they conform to the natural incentives of the agency members (the service ethos of the SSA leads its employees to want to give money to every eligible person).

SSA also manages the disability insurance program. This makes the use of rules a bit more complicated because the definition of a disabled person is much more ambiguous than that of an elderly or retired one. In Jerry Mashaw's excellent book on SSA management of the disability program he concluded that despite the ambiguity the program works reasonably well. One reason is that every disabled person in entitled to benefits whatever his or her financial need; thus the definition of "disabled," although vague, does not have to be traded off against an even vaguer definition of need. Moreover, the lack of clarity in the rules defining disability is made up for by the working environment of the operators. The examiners who review claims for disability payments work elbow-to-elbow with their peers and supervisors. The claims are all in writing, there is no need to make snap judgments, and the decisions are reviewable by quality assurance inspectors. Dissatisfied claimants can appeal the decisions to administrative law judges.[14] Out of this deliberate process there has emerged a kind of common law of disability, a set of precedents that reflects pooled experience and shared judgments.*

The use of rules becomes more difficult in local welfare offices. These agencies administer the federal Aid to Families with Dependent Children program that, until it was changed in 1988, authorized the states to pay money to needy women who had children but no husbands and were otherwise fit but unemployable parents. It is very hard to make clear rules on these matters. What is a "fit"or an "employable" parent? How much does a given woman "need"? Some countries such as Great Britain do not try to solve these problems by rule; instead they empower welfare workers to make a judgment about each case and to use their discretion in approving payments.[15]

In the United States, we use rules—up to a point. Since many of the rules are inevitably vague, the welfare workers who administer them have a significant amount of discretion. An intake worker could use that discretion to deny benefits to women on grounds of fitness or employability. But in fact they rarely do. Joel Handler, who studied welfare administration in Wisconsin in the 1960s, described how welfare workers used the rules they were given: In essence they focused on what was measurable. In each of the six counties investigated by Handler, the questions asked of applicants chiefly involved assessing the women's financial resources.[16] The rule that was enforced was the means test: "Are your resources sufficiently inadequate as to justify your participation in this program?" If the applicant passed the means test the rest of the interview was about

*Mashaw may have spoken too soon. When President Reagan decided that SSA was too generous in granting disability claims, the inherent uncertainty in how that task should be defined was exposed, with unhappy consequences for agency morale and effectiveness. The SSA's "common law" on disability claims was overturned; in the effort to adapt to a new, tougher policy line, the organization was beset with conflict and confusion. (*New York Times*, January 8, 1989.)

her budget—how much money she needed and for what. In only a minority of the cases were any questions asked about employability, marriage plans, or child-care practices. Though the federal government once tried by a law passed in 1962 to get welfare workers to deliver "social services" to their clients, the workers did not deliver them.

Welfare workers could get in trouble for allowing ineligible clients to get on the welfare rolls. But only *financial* ineligibility was easily determined, and so the rules governing money were the rules that were enforced. The workers had little incentive to find out how the clients led their lives and even less to tell them how they ought to lead those lives.

If rules are such an imperfect guide to action even in welfare and housing agencies (where according to Friedman their application was supposed to be straightforward), it is not hard to imagine how much more imperfect their use will be in coping, procedural, or craft agencies. Consider police patrol officers. We expect them to prevent disorderly conduct, but it is virtually impossible to define disorderly (or orderly) conduct.[17] Behavior that is frightening to an old woman or nerve-wracking to a diamond-cutter is fun to a teenager or necessary to a garbage collector. Because we cannot produce a clear rule by which to guide the police control of disorderly conduct does not mean that the police should do nothing about disorder. But what they will do always will be a matter of dispute.

Or consider the "rules" contained in the Education for All Handicapped Children Act passed by Congress in 1975. It required each state to guarantee by a certain date a free and appropriate education for all handicapped children between the ages of three and twenty-one. That goal, however laudable, strained the capacity of every state's educational system. But if tight timetables and scarce resources were the only problems the law would not have raised any fundamental administrative problems. What made matters worse was that the law did not leave the selection of means to local authorities; instead it required the schools to develop for each eligible child an Individualized Education Program, or IEP, that specified short-term and annual instructional goals as well as the services that were to be supplied to attain those goals. Each IEP was to be developed jointly by a team comprised of the child's teacher and parents together with specialists in education for the handicapped and others "as necessary." If a parent disagreed with the IEP, he or she was afforded a due-process hearing.[18] Here, a bureaucracy—the public school—the work and outputs of which can barely be observed (much less measured) was obliged to follow a rule that called for the education of every handicapped child (but not every normal one) on the basis of an individual plan that could be shaped and enforced by going to court.

Rules, like ideas, have consequences. When there is a mismatch between legal rules and bureaucratic realities, the rules get subverted. The subversion in this case took two forms. First, teachers struggling to find the time and energy for their daily tasks would not refer potentially eligible children to the special-education program. And when they did refer them they often made the decision on the basis not of which child most needed special education but of which child was giving the teacher the most trouble in the classroom. Second, some parents but not others took advantage of their due-process rights. Most observers agree that competent, middle-class parents were more effective at using the legal system than less competent, lower-class parents.[19]

Because of the law, more is being done today for handicapped children than was once the case, but how it is being done cannot readily be inferred from the IEP rules. If some critics are right the insistence on defining education by means of formal, legally enforceable rules has led to substituting paperwork and procedure for services and results.[20] This should not be surprising. A rule is a general statement prescribing how a class of behaviors should be conducted. Using a general statement to produce an individualized result is almost a contradiction in terms. We tailor behavior in accordance with individual circumstances precisely in those cases when the circumstances defy classification by rule.

The bureaucratic behaviors that most easily can be defined by rule tend to be those that are frequent, similar, and patterned—those that are routine. SSA easily applied rules in advance to its retirement benefits; with somewhat more difficulty it began to develop rules for disability claims. By contrast, the National Labor Relations Board (NLRB) has few rules. "Neither the fulminations of commentators nor the prodding of courts," Mashaw writes, "has convinced it that any of its vague adjudicatory doctrines can bear particularization or objectification in regulatory form."[21] The Federal Communications Commission (FCC) for a long time resisted demands that it formulate into clear rules the standards it would use for awarding broadcast licenses. The NLRB and the FCC saw themselves as quasi-judicial bodies that decided each unique case on its individual merits. In fact, many NLRB and FCC policies probably could have been reduced to rule. The FCC did this when it finally announced what it had long practiced: that broadcast licenses routinely would be renewed absent some showing that they should not be. Commissions, like courts, resist routinization, perhaps because they delve so deeply into the matters before them that they see differences where others see similarities.

Rules and Impermissible Outcomes

Even where bureaucratic behavior is not so routinized that it can be conveniently prescribed by rule, we insist on rules when there is a significant risk of an impermissible outcome. There is no reason in principle why we could not repeal the laws against homicide and create in their stead a Commission on Life Enhancement and Preservation (CLEP) that would hear complaints about persons who had killed other persons. It would consider evidence about the character of the deceased: Was he lazy or dutiful, decent or disorderly, likable or hateful? On the basis of this evaluation of the lost life and relying on the professional judgment of its staff, the CLEP would decide whether the life lost was worth losing and, if not, whether the person who took it was justified in doing so. By thus decriminalizing homicide, we surely would experience a reduction in the number of events officially labeled murders since the CLEP would undoubtedly conclude that many who had been killed richly deserved their fate.

Most of us would not vote for such a proposal because we attach so high a value to human life that we are unwilling to trust anyone, especially any bureaucrat employed by CLEP, to decide who should die and who should live. We hold this view despite our belief that there are probably some (perhaps many) that the world would be better off without. In short, the risk of error—in this case, wrongly deciding that a worthy life had been a worthless one—is so great that we allow no discretion to the government. If a person who kills another is to escape punishment, it must be for particular excusing conditions (for example, self-defense) and not because of a government-assessed valuation of the lost life.

The laws of this country have multiplied beyond measure the number of outcomes that are deemed impermissible. From 1938 to 1958, the Food and Drug Administration (FDA) had the authority to prevent the sale or distribution of any drug unless it was shown by "adequate tests" to be safe. In 1958 new legislation was passed that directed it to bar from sale or distribution any food additive, food color, or drug administered to food animals if "it is found to induce cancer when ingested by man or animal."[22] This was the so-called Delaney Amendment, named after the New York congressman who sponsored it.

Ignoring for the moment certain exceptions, the Delaney Amendment implied that we should swallow nothing that might cause cancer in the kinds of laboratory animals on which scientists test foods. In principle, this meant that the FDA was hostage to progress in analytical chemistry: As scientists improved their ability to detect cancer-causing chemicals, the FDA would be obliged to ban those chemicals (and the foods they contained) from the supermarket shelves. Cancer was a risk, the FDA was told, that it was impermissible to run, whatever the costs. Thus it was to enforce the rule, "no cancer."

But when the FDA in 1979 used this rule to ban saccharin, the artificial sweetener used in such products as "Sweet 'n Low," it suddenly discovered that Congress did not mean what it had said—at least in this case. "All hell broke loose," recalled one representative.[23] Consumers wanted to use saccharin in order to lose weight, even if scientists had discovered that in very high dosages it induced bladder cancer in laboratory animals. Faced with this popular revolt, Congress swiftly passed a law delaying (and ultimately prohibiting) the FDA ban on saccharin.[24] But Congress did not review the Delaney Amendment: It stood as a rule that could not (with certain minor exceptions) be traded off against any other rule.*

All along the FDA has recognized that it could not guarantee that a food had *no* tendency to produce cancer; some scientist somewhere was likely to discover that a food additive increased a person's lifetime risk of getting cancer by one in a billion. But the FDA has not had much success in finding a politically viable rule of reason by which to balance risks and benefits. At one stage the agency proposed that it be allowed to approve things fed to food-producing animals if chemists could not detect in the food thus produced any residue that increased a person's lifetime risk of cancer by more than one in a million.[25] But the rule was never made final. Throughout the 1970s and 1980s the FDA was caught between consumerist organizations that insisted on banning any food additive unless they could be shown to present zero risk and industry groups that wanted additives allowed if the risk was minimal. In the Carter years it leaned toward the zero-risk view, in the Reagan years toward the *de minimis* view, but in all years it has been under heavy congressional pressure to apply the Delaney Amendment absolutely. Cancer is a source of public fear and thus of political pressure, more potent than any other consideration, except obesity.

Harvey Sapolsky has generalized this problem to most health issues. Our political system is extremely sensitive to new calamities, real and imagined. The media thrive on stories of deaths and disasters; lobbying organizations, struggling to attract members and defeat opponents, have every incentive to exaggerate. As a result, government agencies are regularly being given new Absolute Rules That Must Not Be Broken. In 1983 the secretary of Health and Human Services announced that AIDS was now the federal government's "number one health priority." Ignored in her statement was the fact, Sapolsky observed, that "the same priority designation had been only recently used by the department to describe the unfinished efforts to control cigarette smoking, drunk driving, drug abuse, and teenage pregnancy."[26] To be sure, all of these are important problems, but by making each simultaneously the Most Important Problem, government agencies are induced to lurch from one crash program to another.

*Ironically, an earlier FDA ban on another artificial sweetener, cyclamate, stood even though subsequent tests consistently have shown that cyclamate does not produce cancer. See Linda C. Cummings, "The Political Reality of Artificial Sweeteners," in Harvey M. Sapolsky, ed., *Consuming Fears: The Politics of Product Risks* (New York: Basic Books, 1986), 128.

Environmental protection laws are replete with examples of rules intended to guarantee results that in fact have guaranteed frustration. The Water Pollution Control Act of 1972 asserted that *all* effluents entering the nation's rivers and streams were to be eliminated by 1985. The Clean Air Act specified that emissions of carbon monoxide and hydrocarbons were to be reduced by 90 percent between 1970 and 1975. But as Shep Melnick has suggested, these rules, because they did not permit the Environmental Protection Agency to take into account cost and feasibility, led to industry demands that Congress relax the deadlines, which in turn led to environmentalist charges that Congress and the EPA had "sold out" to industry.[27] The central issue—how can we best protect the environment?—gets lost in charges and countercharges about "over-zealous" or "craven" bureaucrats.

The United States relies on rules to control the exercise of official judgment to a greater extent than any other industrialized democracy. The reason, I think, has little to do with the kinds of bureaucrats we have and everything to do with the political environment in which those bureaucrats must work. If we wish to complain about how rule-ridden our government agencies seem to be, we should direct those complaints not to the agencies but to the Congress, the courts, and the organized interests that make effective use of Congress and the courts.

Rules: Gains and Losses

The difficulty of striking a reasonable balance between rules and discretion is an age-old problem for which there is no "objective" solution any more than there is to the tension between other competing human values such as freedom and order, love and discipline, or change and stability. At best we can sensitize ourselves to the gains and losses associated with governance by rule rather than by discretion.

Rules, if they are clear, induce agencies to produce certain observable outcomes: nursing homes must have fire sprinklers, hotels must have smoke alarms, dairy products may not contain polychlorinated biphenyls (PCBs), automobiles must be equipped with crashworthy bumpers and steering wheels. But rules often cannot induce organizations to improve hard-to-observe processes. A nursing home may be safer because it has certain equipment installed, but it will not be well run unless it has competent head nurses.[28] Eugene Bardach and Robert Kagan make this point by comparing public and private factory inspections. An inspector from OSHA charged with enforcing rules will evaluate the physical aspects of a factory: the ventilation, guardrails, and safety devices. By contrast, an inspector from an insurance company charged with assessing the insurability of the firm will evaluate the attitude and policies of management: its safety consciousness.[29] The difference in approaches is important because, if John Mendeloff is correct, "most workplace injuries are not caused by violations of standards [i.e., rules], and even fewer are caused by violations that inspectors can detect."[30]

Rules create offices, procedures, and claims inside an organization that can protect precarious values. An automobile company is required to comply with OSHA rules. If the only effect of the rules were the company's fear of inspectors, not much would happen. But to cope with the inspectors the company will hire its own industrial safety experts, and these in turn will establish procedures and generate pressures that alter the company's behavior even when it is not being inspected.[31] At the same time, rules generate paperwork and alter human relationships in ways that can reduce the ability of the organization to achieve its goals and its incentives to cooperate with those who enforce the rules. To verify that military aircraft are built according to government specifications, hundreds of pounds of forms must be filled out that document each operation on each aircraft; these forms, one set for every individual airplane, must be stored for twenty years. Nurses must record every step in medical treatments. Personnel officers must document the grounds for every hiring and promotional decision. Teachers must fill out sign-in sheets, absence slips, attendance records, textbook requests, lesson plans, student evaluations, questionnaires, ethnic and language surveys, free-lunch applications, time cards, field-trip requests, special-needs assessments, and parental conference reports.[32] Rarely does anybody read these forms. They are, after all, what Bardach and Kagan call a "declaration of innocence"; no aircraft company, charge nurse, personnel officer, or schoolteacher will use these forms to admit their wrongdoing, and so no government inspector will read them. The rules and the forms contribute to the adversarial relationship that so often characterizes the relationship between regulator and regulatee.[33]

Rules specify minimum standards that must be met. This is a clear gain when an organization, public or private, is performing below the minimum. But minimum standards often become maximum standards. Alvin Gouldner first noticed this in his study of a private firm, the General Gypsum Company (a pseudonym). Suppose workers were expected to "get the day's job done." Some would work less than eight hours, some much longer. Now suppose that a rule is announced—"everybody will work eight hours"—and a device (the time clock) is installed to enforce it. Laggards would now work eight hours but zealots would stop working more than eight.[34] Bardach and Kagan observed this in the case of OSHA rules: At one time, a company would improve ventilating or lighting systems when workers or union leaders complained about these matters; later, the company would make no changes unless required by OSHA rules.[35]

To decide whether the gains from imposing a rule outweigh the costs you must carefully judge the particular circumstances of a given organization. In other words, no rule can be promulgated that tells you when promulgating rules is a good idea. But at least the tensions highlighted in this section should make you aware that rules have risks and teach you to be sensitive to the fact that the American political system is biased toward solving bureaucratic problems by issuing rules. Given that bias, people who worry about the costs of rules usually will not be heard very clearly in the hubbub of concern about an unmet need or a bureaucratic failure.

Talented, strongly motivated people usually will find ways of making even rule-ridden systems work. This is especially the case when complying with the rules is seen as a mere formality; a form to be filled out, a box to be checked, a file to be kept. Teachers, nurses, police officers, and housing project managers can find ways of getting the job done—if they want to.

The managerial problem arises from two facts: First, talented, strongly motivated workers are a minority in any organization. People who can cope with rules will be outnumbered by people who hide behind them. A study of fifty-eight enforcement officials in forty-three municipal regulatory agencies found that those workers with the least training and talent were the ones most likely to take a legalistic view of their agency's rules and to apply them mechanistically without regard to their overriding purpose.[36] Much the same thing was observed by William K. Muir in his study of patrol officers in a big-city police department. The "good cops" were "street-corner politicians" who controlled their beats in the common interest by selectively enforcing the rules, sometimes letting off people for behavior for which others were arrested. The not-so-good cops were those who either retreated from the confusion and dangers of the street altogether or mechanically applied every rule as the law required.[37] No one knows what proportion of the police use rules instead of either abusing them or hiding behind them but it is probably not large.

Second, whatever behavior will get an agency executive in trouble will get a manager in trouble; whatever gets a manager in trouble will get an operator in trouble. Or put another way: Agency executives have a strong incentive to enforce on their subordinates those rules the violation of which create external political difficulties for the executive. This means that even talented and motivated operators will not be free to violate rules that threaten their agency, even if the rule itself is silly. Many agency executives do not understand this. They are eager to deflect or mollify critics of their agencies. In their eagerness they suppose that announcing a rule designed to forbid whatever behavior led to the criticism actually will work. Their immediate subordinates, remote from field pressures (and perhaps eager to ingratiate themselves with the executive) will assure their bosses that the new rule will solve the problem. But unless the rule actually redefines the core tasks of the operators in a meaningful and feasible way, or significantly alters the incentives those operators value, the rule will be seen as just one more constraint on getting the job done (or, more graphically, as "just another piece of chicken———t").

CHAPTER 19

Markets

TRY TO THINK of a government activity that has never been done or is not now being done by a private firm operating in a more or less competitive market. It's not easy. Everybody knows that businesses as well as governments have collected trash, swept streets, operated buses, managed hospitals, and run schools. Some of us are aware that private security firms have more employees than do municipal police departments. Americans who have traveled abroad know that in many foreign nations the governments own and operate the airline companies, telephone systems, electric utilities, and television stations, services that here are provided in large part by private enterprises. A few of us are aware that in some states businesses are running prisons. The historically-minded among us will recall that at one time private banks issued their own money and nations going to war hired mercenary armies.

But there are many more less obvious examples. Fire-fighting once was done almost exclusively by private firms in this country and still is done that way in many places in Denmark. (For-profit fire departments have staged a modest comeback here: One company now operates fifty fire departments in five states.[1]) Private weather forecasters compete with the National Weather Service. Businesses have been hired to manage Medicare insurance claims, train the unemployed, man naval vessels, and supply inspectors for the agency that verifies Soviet compliance with the treaty banning intermediate-range nuclear weapons. Once parcels were delivered to our homes almost entirely by the U.S. Postal Service; now that function has been largely taken over by private carriers such as UPS. We have national parks and forests run by the Park Service and the Forest Service, but we also have privately owned and managed parks and some environmentalists believe that more private ownership would improve things.[2] In some states, people pressing legal claims are making use of what in effect are private courts: judges and arbitrators hired to settle law suits.

These cases and others like them are cited in the rising debate over privatization—that is, over whether government services are better supplied by private organizations than by public agencies. That debate is not the same as the argument over whether government should play a large or small role in our lives or take from us a lot or a little in taxes. We could have a small, minimalist government dear to the heart of the strictest libertarian that nevertheless conducted its business entirely through public bureaucracies. Conversely we could have a large, activist government with great powers and vast revenues that hired private firms to exercise those powers and dispense those funds. Though many advocates of privatization are conservatives, that is not always the case. Many leftist regimes, including the People's Republic of China, are experimenting with the substitution of private suppliers for public ones. The reason is obvious: they are seeking for ways to overcome the problems of bureaucracy.

E. S. Savas, one of the most dedicated proponents of privatization, puts it this way: "The essence of collective action . . . consists of making decisions and raising money."[3] Implementing the decisions or spending the money do not necessarily require collective action. Economic theory has shed a great deal of light on what kinds of decisions governments must make. It has made it clear, for example, that government (that is, an institution wielding coercive powers) must compel us to pay for national defense or clean air because the market will not supply these things. The reason is simple: Since everybody will benefit from national defense or clean air if anyone in particular benefits, no one has any incentive to pay for these things voluntarily. We all would be free riders because none of us feasibly could be excluded from these benefits if he or she refused to pay.*

But economic theory (or any other theory) gives us little guidance as to how government should carry out its responsibilities. Once a decision has been made to have national defense or clean air, what organizational arrangements best will deliver these things? Should weapons be built in government arsenals or by private contractors? Should clean air standards be enforced by government agencies issuing directives or by private parties suing one another?

The difficulty is to decide what we mean by "best." Economists evaluate enterprises, whether public or private, by the efficiency criterion, that is, obtaining the most output for a given level of resources. But as we have

*For a more elaborate discussion of these matters, see Vincent Ostrom and Elinor Ostrom, "Public Goods and Public Choices," in E. S. Savas, ed., *Alternatives for Delivering Public Services* (Boulder, Colo.: Westview Press, 1977), 7–49, especially the useful typology at p. 12.

seen in chapter 17, the output of government always is complex and often controversial. If an agency has multiple or vague objectives, it is not easy to tell whether those goals are being attained efficiently, or being attained at all. Moreover, government programs often have distributional effects; some people are helped or hurt more than others. Business decisions also have such effects, but economists deal with this on the basis of willingness to pay: If some people get bigger cars or fancier food it is because they are willing to pay more. Government programs, funded by coerced payments (that is, tax revenues), usually are expected to benefit all people in a given category "equally" or "fairly" (though what constitutes equality or fairness is very much a matter of dispute). Reinforcing this demand for equity is a political system that gives one vote to each person and one district to each legislator, thereby inclining everyone to ask "why not me?" whenever a government benefit comes into view. The currency of the marketplace may be wealth, which is divided unequally, but the currency of politics is votes, which are distributed equally.

We also expect government agencies to be accountable in a way that firms are not. When we send our child to a private school, we may complain to the headmaster if things go badly and we may become active in some school programs, but we do not expect to be given the right to hire and fire the headmaster or to determine by voting the content of the curriculum. If our complaints go unanswered, we take our child out of the school and send him or her to another. But when we send our child to a public school, we expect, especially in the United States, to have some voice, however marginal, in setting policy, selecting the management, allocating the budget, and above all making the rules. We justify our assertion of citizenship rights partly because the public enterprise is funded with money taken from us by force and partly because government services often are a monopoly such that there is no competitor to whom we can turn. Some people worry that the private delivery of publicly sanctioned services will reduce the extent to which government is accountable to the people and thus reduce the extent to which we are citizens, not merely customers.

Finally, people believe that certain government undertakings are endowed with indefeasible authority: There are certain commands that only the state ought to issue. Perhaps this is because we believe that whatever is done "in the name of the people" should be done in a way that reflects the core values of the people. For example, we could hire firms to perform the functions of prosecutor, judge, and executioner in a murder case. The government would establish the law against murder and the rules of evidence and would provide the funds to pay for the trial and punishment; but arguing the case, deciding on the verdict, and carrying out the execution would be in the hands of Universal Justice, Inc. Many people would be troubled by this way of doing things, feeling that anything so solemn as pronouncing on guilt or imposing a dreadful sentence should be done by the direct and sworn representatives of the people.

In short, there are at least four standards against which to measure alternative arrangements for supplying some publicly funded service: efficiency, equity, accountability, and authority. Given that the government has decided to do something, will a public agency or a private firm do it in the least costly, fairest, and most responsive way? And how important is it that the entity performing the service partake directly of the authority of the state?

These standards are not entirely independent. Take efficiency, for example: It is possible that people working for a government agency could be paid less than those working for a business firm because government employment provides a satisfaction (the status of public office or the ethic of public service) absent from private employment. As a result, private managers might demand higher salaries than public ones to make up for the lessened opportunity to enact their personal views. By the same token, many police officers believe that private security guards (whom they describe as "rent-a-cops") are less willing than sworn officers to run risks and face down attackers precisely because they are not sworn, that is, pledged to uphold the law whatever the danger. If these conjectures are correct then there is an interaction between the "publicness" of an organization (its having the authority of the state) and its efficiency. The truth of these conjectures remains uncertain; it may turn out that money motivates behavior much better than the ethic of public service.

Efficiency

If the preceding chapters have made nothing else clear, they should have persuaded the reader that government bureaus are less likely than private agencies to operate efficiently, at least with respect to the main goal of the organization. There are three reasons for this. First, government executives are less able than their private counterparts to *define* an efficient course of action. The public officials must serve a variety of contextual goals as well as their main or active goal and they are given little guidance as to what might constitute an acceptable tradeoff among these goals. Second, public executives have weaker incentives than do private executives to *find* an efficient course of action. The former have no property rights in the agency; they are not, in the language of economists, "residual claimants" who can put into their own pockets the savings achieved by greater efficiency.[4] Third, public executives have less authority than private ones to *impose* an efficient course of action. Legislatures usually refuse to give to agency managers the power to hire and fire or to raise and allocate funds. Therefore, when it is important that executives have the ability, authority, and incentive to act efficiently, government agencies will not perform as well as their private counterparts.

With few exceptions the evidence overwhelmingly supports these predictions. In 1982, economist Thomas Borcherding and his colleagues summarized fifty empirical studies that compared public with private provision of various services in several nations. They concluded that in forty of the fifty cases private supply was more efficient than public supply; in three cases the public agency was less costly than its private counterpart; in the rest of the cases there was either no difference or the results were ambiguous.[5] In 1987, E. S. Savas could add new studies to the list without changing the results.[6] For example: There are at least fourteen studies comparing public and private trash collection in the United States, Canada, Switzerland, and Japan; in eleven of the cases, private collection was more efficient; in only one case was municipal collection cheaper (in two instances there was no difference).[7] The cost of water,[8] street cleaning,[9] ship maintenance,[10] housing construction,[11] school bus operation,[12] and railroad track repair[13] were all lower when done by private firms rather than by government agencies.

The advantages of private provision were not limited to organizations supplying a physical service. Randy Ross reviewed several studies comparing public and private mental health hospitals. Much of the research failed to control for the characteristics of the patients or the quality of the services, but one study that did[14] found that the cost per day for a stay in a public institution in Wisconsin was much higher than that for similar private hospitals in that state.[15] The Comptroller General in a report to the Senate Finance Committee found that for-profit day-care centers cost less per child than not-for-profit (including governmental) ones.[16]

David G. Davies has compared the efficiency of the state-owned Trans Australian Airlines (TAA) with that of the privately-owned Ansett Australian Airlines. Despite the fact that both are tightly regulated by the government, charge the same fares, pay essentially the same wages, and are allowed to compete only with respect to minor amenities, Ansett is more efficient (that is, uses fewer employees to transport a given amount of freight or number of passengers) than TAA.[17]

In Denmark, almost half the population receives fire protection from a private firm, Falck. When Ole P. Kristensen at the Danish Institute of Political Science compared the two suppliers he found that the cost per capita for government fire departments was nearly three times greater than that for Falck, the private company.[18]

There are two important exceptions to the greater efficiency of private suppliers: hospitals and electric utilities. At least two studies have found that proprietary (that is, investor-owned) hospitals charged more and had higher costs (per admission or per patient day) than did voluntary (that is, private but non-profit) or government-owned hospitals.[19] These comparisons are difficult to make because different hospitals may serve different kinds of patients or provide different quality services, matters that are not adequately addressed in most of the studies that have been done so far. One effort to deal with quality differences compared hospitals solely with respect to one kind of high-tech service, nuclear medicine, a procedure that uses radio isotopes to diagnose and treat illnesses. Confining the comparison to this specific (and one supposes, relatively homogeneous) medical service, proprietary hospitals operate more efficiently than either voluntary or government hospitals.[20]

Most studies find that publicly-owned utilities produce a kilowatt hour of electricity for less money than do investor-owned utilities.[21] It is not clear why this should be so, if in fact it is so. The comparison is hard to make because most government-owned utilities are relatively small,* pay no taxes, and buy much of their power wholesale from private generators. Moreover, government utilities invest less heavily in conservation and alternative energy sources than do private utilities serving comparable communities.[22] If it is true that government utilities charge less, even after allowing for the many special aspects of their situation, it may be because the governmental bodies (e.g., city councils) to which they are responsible demand low rates and use the existence of nearby private utilities as a yardstick against which to measure municipal performance.

The greater efficiency of private suppliers of most public services seems to be chiefly the result of three factors: lower labor costs, more effective management, and greater competition. The most extensive comparisons are with respect to solid-waste collection. The study of New York City by E. S. Savas is a good example. There a public agency (the Department of Sanitation) collected rubbish from residences while various private cartage firms collected it from commercial establishments. The clients of the two organizations were somewhat different, but the differences tended to cancel each other out. The average residential pickup was smaller than the average commercial one (thus allowing the cartage firm to get more trash per stop), but the residential pickup was made at the curbside whereas the commercial one was made from on the premises (thus allowing the Department of Sanitation to spend less time at each stop). Both the direct and the indirect labor costs were much lower for the private firm than for the public department.[23]

The study by Barbara Stevens of eight municipal services came to similar though not identical conclusions. The contractors she studied did not pay their workers a lower wage than did the cities, but they did use their

*The average government-owned utility serves about fifteen thousand people, whereas the typical investor-owned utility serves around one million.

manpower more economically. Firms were more likely to use part-time rather than full-time workers, to give workers shorter vacations, and to pay smaller pension benefits. In addition, she found that the private firms were more likely than municipal agencies to have an incentive system for their managers that rewarded productivity increases and to give their managers the right to fire subordinates.[24]

For private supply to be more efficient, competition is essential. If a government agency awards a long-term contract to a single firm to supply a given service on a monopoly basis it should not expect the firm to be much more efficient than its own bureaucracy. The firm must feel that it faces a real risk of being supplanted by a rival. Failure to recognize this has led to bad experiences with giving exclusive, long-term contracts to bus companies to provide public transit.[25] One of the barriers to improving efficiency in the procurement of major weapons systems is that while there is fierce competition in the design of a new weapon there is little competition in its production. Many defense contractors do not operate in a truly competitive market.[26]

Even government agencies under certain circumstances may benefit from competition. In California, the so-called Lakewood Plan allows municipalities to choose between producing government services themselves with their own bureaus or buying those services from a county agency. For example, the Los Angeles County Sheriff provides law-enforcement services to roughly half the cities in the county.[27] The sheriff has an incentive to price his services competitively and manage them efficiently; otherwise, a client city may elect to organize its own police department. Stephen Mehay and Rodolfo Gonzalez measured the effect of this quasi-market by examining the costs of law enforcement in California counties that did and did not make extensive use of the Lakewood Plan. They found that after allowing for differences in population, crime rates, and other social factors the operating expenditures (per capita) of a sheriff's department were lower in counties where contracting was common.[28]

Whether law enforcement was better or worse as a result of the contracting-out process is unclear. Mehay[29] doubts that the Lakewood Plan has improved the service. The analytical problem arises from the difficulty of evaluating a sheriff's output. Patrol work occurs in what I have called a coping organization—neither the work nor the achievements of its members are easily observed or assessed. Because of this the contracts that California cities wrote with the sheriffs who served them specified only the inputs (how many officers and patrol cars they would get) and not the outputs (what level of crime or order they hoped to get). But merely because outputs cannot be defined by either a contract or a scholar does not mean that the contracting system is useless; the cities entering into the contracts evaluated the services they received in the same way that students evaluate their teachers: They formed impressions, made judgments, and hoped for the best. The key to any plan that contracts out for public services is not that the problem of evaluating those services thereby is made easier, but that once an evaluation is made, however subjective or impressionistic it may be, the government issuing the contract is free to select a different contractor.

In short, the competitive delivery of public services may improve satisfaction even when the service being delivered cannot be measured, so long as there are alternative suppliers among which the citizens or their government are able to choose. Matters are no different in the private sector. We cannot easily evaluate, much less measure, the quality of private schools or colleges, but we can reward (with our tuition payments and financial contributions) those that seem to be "better," for whatever reason. The effort by government agencies to acquire and maintain autonomy (see chapter 10) has the effect of blocking this opportunity for choice.

Equity

Unlike the case with efficiency there are no clear theoretical grounds on which to make predictions about whether government bureaus or private firms will be fairer in distributing outputs and acquiring inputs. Some readers will be shocked by even this modest statement, because to them government inherently is fairer than firms. But it is not clear why they should take this view. A private firm seeks a profit. If because of the prejudices of its management it fails to sell its service to some people willing to pay for it or it refuses to hire people able to work for it, it is incurring costs that will reduce that profit. Racism is not free.[30] At one time, the mores—and even the laws—of many states led firms to discriminate with respect to both customers and employees, but those same mores and laws also led government agencies to practice discrimination. The United States Armed Forces did not begin to integrate blacks into their ranks until the Second World War, and even then change was slow. If blacks, women, and other groups have had to use lawsuits and protest tactics to get access to private jobs, they have had to use these same methods to get access to public schools, police departments, and fire departments. Moreover, as we shall see in the next section, there is some evidence that it is easier for the government to induce (by law or regulation) private firms to hire employees in a nondiscriminatory manner than it is for government to get its own agencies to do this. Government bureaus are extremely sensitive to political demands that they treat equal cases equally, but these demands are based on political definitions of what constitutes equality. At one time the government of the United States defined blacks as unequal to whites, and today many other nations define one ethnic, tribal, or religious group as more equal than others and thus more entitled to offices and benefits.

Even at a time when explicit racism is no longer government policy, what constitutes fair treatment is still politically determined. As we saw in chapter 7, the procurement regulations of the United States government require that special consideration (not only fair treatment, but *special* treatment) be given to small businesses, minority-owned businesses, and American-owned businesses. Though the beneficiaries of such consideration probably think it only fair, those denied that consideration probably think it quite unfair.

Charles Wolf, Jr., at Rand, in his thoughtful assessment of the equity issue, reminds us that government empowers some people to make decisions for other people. That power can be used for good or for ill as the people wielding it are inclined.[31] The economic market distributes goods and services on the basis of willingness to pay; the political market distributes them on the basis of law and influence. Which system produces the fairest outcome is not always obvious.

Suppose we wish to distribute gasoline. If we sell it at the market price and that price suddenly rises, poor people (for whom the marginal dollar is very dear) will cut back on their driving more than rich people (for whom the marginal dollar is less dear). You may think this unfair. But compared to what? The alternative is to distribute gasoline at less than the market price by rationing it. It can be rationed by issuing people ration coupons that entitle everybody to the same amount (this was done during World War II) or by putting a ceiling on gasoline prices, thereby leading people to form long lines at those few stations that have gasoline (this was done during the oil embargo in the early 1970s). Both alternatives to the market benefit some people more than others. Rationing benefits people who do not need much gas and harms those who need a lot, and creates opportunities for politically influential persons to acquire (by bribes or favors) extra ration coupons. Long lines benefit people with either a great deal of leisure time, private information about which stations have fuel, or a willingness to use threats and force to get to the head of the line. Money may be unequally distributed, but so too are needs, influence, leisure, and aggressiveness.

For most people the key equity problem arises when an important service is made available on the basis of user charges to people with unequal incomes. But this in itself is not an argument for the government production of the service. It is at best an argument for government action to correct the income inequality, by redistributing income through the tax system or by issuing income supplements (in the form of vouchers) that make it possible for poor persons to buy more of the service than they would otherwise.

Vouchers are widely used to enhance the ability of people to acquire public services. One out of every twelve Americans uses food stamps (a voucher) to help pay for groceries at a cost of nearly $11 billion a year.[32] Under the G.I. Bill, millions of veterans of the Second World War and the Korean conflict received vouchers with which to purchase a college education. In theory the government could have run these programs by establishing government-operated food warehouses or government-run universities; instead they allowed private supermarkets to distribute the food and private as well as public colleges to provide the education.

Some people may regard Medicare and Medicaid benefits as voucher plans also. It is true that the recipients of these benefits are free to select their own doctors or hospitals and are not obliged to get medical care from a single, government-run facility. But as Gary Bridge and others have noted, these medical programs are not true vouchers because they do not supply the beneficiary with strong incentives to shop around. The prices doctors and hospitals charge are fixed and the patient cannot keep any savings he or she may realize by finding the least costly health care. Food stamps, by contrast, do provide such an incentive: If you pay $1.50 for an item that costs $2.00 at another store, you have saved 50 cents that you can use to buy something else.[33]

Vouchers solve the equity problem in distributing public benefits if there are several competing suppliers of the service about which people are reasonably well-informed; in short, if there is a true market.

Perhaps the most important test of the extent to which vouchers might serve a public goal in an equitable way was the Experimental Housing Allowance Program begun in the early 1970s to find a better way of housing the poor. The traditional way had been to build government-owned-and-operated public housing projects into which poor people could move. A variant on this was to subsidize private contractors to build low-cost housing for the poor. Both required the government to design or oversee the design of the housing; neither gave the beneficiaries much choice about where to live. When it built the housing itself, the government spent far more money—25 percent more—than would a private builder of the same quality shelter.[34] Then some government agency had to serve as the landlord, managing buildings filled with poor people and bearing the stigma of a "poor person's project." Some of the problems that arose were described in the last chapter. When it subsidized private firms to build and operate the housing it found itself caught up in a political tug-of-war over which developer would get the subsidies and under what terms. Some of the developers who were willing to tolerate the complex rules and onerous conditions attendant on building government-sponsored projects turned out to be fast-buck operators who did poor work and overcharged for it. Mortgage lenders had no incentive to police the quality of the work because the government, by guaranteeing the repayment of loans, removed all risk.[35]

The experimental program took a different approach. It gave to poor families direct cash payments, calculated as follows: The housing allowance equaled the difference between the rental cost of adequate housing and one-fourth of the families' income. The average payment turned out to be roughly $75 per month. The families were free to live where they wished (provided they lived in units that met minimum standards) and free to spend more or less than 25 percent of their income on rent. If they spent more they paid the difference; if they spent less they kept the difference. The experiment (with some variations) was carried out in twelve different communities located in all parts of the country.

By most standards the experiment was a success.[36] The program reached genuinely poor families who participated at a higher rate than they had in the traditional public-housing programs; even so, fewer than half the eligible families joined. Though in some communities minority groups had difficulty in finding housing, by and large they were well-represented in the program. Contrary to the predictions of some skeptics the program did not result in an inflation in the cost of available housing. The rental units met minimum standards of decency—generally, the standards set by local building and housing codes—and where they did not the tenants saw to it that they were fixed up. Most important, the share of each family's income that went to housing fell sharply; before the program the median family was spending from one-third to one-half of its income on rent, whereas after joining the experiment it spent no more than one-quarter, and often much less. Most participants did not move from one neighborhood to another, but when they did it was from a worse to a better one.

Why then were some observers, especially in the Department of Housing and Urban Development (HUD), unhappy with the results? Because the program did not lead to a "dramatic revitalization of cities"[37] nor to a big improvement in the quality of housing in which poor people were living. HUD wanted poor people to move into better housing; poor people, by contrast, wanted to spend less money on housing. The poor got what they wanted; HUD did not. To the poor the main problem was not having enough money; when they got their housing allowance they decided to spend less of their income on housing. To HUD the main problem was that people were not living in "good enough" housing; it wanted the people who got the allowances to spend all of it, and more, on better housing.

Bernard J. Frieden summarized the issue in language that will come as no surprise to readers of this book:

> If the problem has changed, the search for solutions should not be held captive to HUD's traditional organizational mission. HUD should have a mission that encompasses a range of housing problems, and a capacity to use the right tool for each purpose. . . . The poor do not give housing *quality* the high priority that program administrators do.[38]

The housing allowance program revealed quite clearly a fundamental ambiguity in how we apply the fairness test to the private supply of public goods. Many of us not only want everybody to have a fair chance to participate, we also want them to participate in the "right way" by doing what we think is best for them. Many of us want the poor to rent better housing, which they probably would do if money were no object; but given the money they have, they would like to spend more of it on other things. The same issue arises when it is proposed that parents be given vouchers (or tuition tax credits) with which to buy schooling for their children. Many of us worry that they will spend on the "wrong sort" of schooling, that is, on parochial schools, or fundamentalist schools, or New Age schools, or whatever. There are ways of meeting the equity standard in the private supply of public services, but almost all of them require us to defer to the tastes of the clients, something that many of us are unwilling to do.

Accountability

The accountability problem is the mirror image of the consumer preference one: It arises when we are unwilling to confine our control over a firm supplying a service to the government's right to grant, withhold, or cancel the contract. It is most visible in defense contracting: No sooner have we told Lockheed or Northrop to build an airplane that will do certain things than we start telling them how to build it. But it is not limited to weapons systems; almost every large firm that has done business with the government complains of the amount of detail that is part of the contract and the intrusiveness of the scrutiny that is part of the audit. Governments are rule-oriented; they try to manage their own departments by multiplying rules, and so it is not surprising that they often manage private suppliers in the same way.

But we need not leave matters at what sounds to be merely another complaint about politics. The relationship of government to a firm can be seen in the same way as the relationship between a firm and the market. Oliver Williamson has explained that firms are created when the cost of coordinating behavior through market exchanges gets to be more than the cost of coordinating it administratively.[39] He calls these transaction costs: the costs of planning, negotiating, directing, and evaluating the activities necessary to produce something. They are in addition to the costs of actually producing the good or service. Transaction costs in economics are akin to friction in physics.[40] General Motors can try to assemble automobiles by contracting with other firms for each necessary part and assembly, or it can decide to buy raw materials and labor and assemble the cars in its own plant. How it assembles cars will depend on the transaction cost of each alternative. Obviously, GM has decided it is cheaper to oversee the assembly of cars in its own plants than to oversee assembly done by dozens of independent firms and workers. But most home builders have reached the opposite conclusion: It is cheaper to hire carpenters and plumbers and buy lumber and pipe as the need arises than to organize a firm that will build a house from scratch using all its own employees.

The idea of transaction costs has not been applied, so far as I know, to government activities. But I see no reason why it should not be. If we do apply it, we are led to ask interesting questions that we might ignore otherwise. For example: In this chapter we have seen many reasons for believing that government is well-advised to purchase its street cleaning, day care, air transportation, ship maintenance, refuse collection, and bus service from private firms and to allow firms to supply housing to poor people who are equipped with income supplements (i.e., vouchers). But why should it not also buy its diplomatic representation or military planning from firms? The answer, I think, is that it is cheaper to maintain control over these activities by having them done inside the government by government workers than to contract for these services from a private supplier. The National Security Council and the State Department are in charge (more or less!) of activities that involve continuous, subtle, and often ambiguous changes in direction. Diplomacy is a process of suggesting, testing, considering, and reconsidering proposals and counterproposals. It would be difficult if not impossible to write a contract that specified in advance what the firm (Diplomats, Inc.) should do in each case, in large part because the government itself does not know; its preferences are formed by the process of negotiation.

At some point along the continuum between the State Department and the Sanitation Department the costs of governance begin to exceed the costs of contracting. At that point, acquiring the service from the market begins to make sense. For city governments, one does not have to move very far along that continuum. La Mirada, California, a city of over forty thousand residents, has fewer than sixty employees; most of its activities are managed by contractors, some of which are county agencies but most of which are private firms that supply services ranging from refuse collection and park maintenance to counseling, employment development, and even probation.[41]

Keeping market suppliers accountable to government buyers requires effort, but probably less effort than keeping government suppliers accountable. It is easier for government to regulate private firms than public bureaucracies. When Washington decided to increase the proportion of female workers in shipyards, it obtained more compliance by far from private shipyards doing business with the government than from shipyards operated by the U.S. Navy.[42] When state regulatory agencies began urging electric utilities to encourage conservation among their customers and to develop alternative energy sources, investor-owned utilities did more than municipally-owned utilities serving comparable markets.[43] For many years the Environmental Protection Agency had more success in getting private power generators to reduce pollution than it had in getting the Tennessee Valley Authority to do so.[44] As we saw in chapter 10, agencies enjoy political protections denied to most firms.

The desire to keep *all* suppliers of public services "accountable" by the process of governance, rule making, and popular participation arises in part from a failure to think through the costs of such transactions. People will differ over where to draw the line, but once drawn in a particular case it ought to be drawn clearly.

Authority

Careful attention to transaction costs will not alone determine where that line should be drawn, however. As mentioned at the outset of this chapter, there are certain tasks that we expect government to perform, not because government is cheaper or more efficient, but because it alone embodies the public's authority. Certain tasks are sovereign tasks.

The issue most recently has arisen in connection with the private management of correctional institutions. Though newly discussed, the idea is an old one. At one time private prison farms were commonplace. They fell into disrepute because of corruption: The private wardens would pocket funds intended to feed and clothe their prisoners, supplying neglect and abuse where confinement and correction had been intended. But the replacement of private with public keepers was limited chiefly to adult facilities; for juveniles, private correctional programs continued to exist and even grew in number. Private organizations, both for-profit and not-for-profit, now operate countless halfway houses, youth shelters, and (supposedly) therapeutic programs. As far as one can tell, they do at least as well as their public counterparts.

Of late, adult jails and prisons once again are being operated by private firms such as the Corrections Corporation of America (CCA). (It offered, without success, to run the entire prison system of the state of Tennessee.) We have no good, independent studies of the efficiency of such enterprises, though preliminary data suggest that firms can run certain low-security prisons more cheaply than public agencies and still provide a level of amenity and decency comparable to and perhaps better than that supplied by many state agencies.[45]

Let us assume that privately-managed prisons are more efficient and provide more amenities than public ones. Under what circumstances should private prison guards be allowed to use force, including deadly force, in subduing unruly inmates? Should private wardens have the right, as do many public wardens, to send an inmate into solitary confinement or to control his release date as ways of maintaining order inside the walls? If a prisoner is condemned to death, do we care whether the penalty is carried out by a government official (e.g., the state-appointed warden) or by the private firm hired to run the maximum-security prison in which Death Row is located? However thoughtful people decide these matters, I doubt they will decide them on economic grounds.

The Case of Public Schooling

All the issues raised by the idea of privatization are raised with special force by the proposal that marketlike arrangements be introduced into public schooling.

The argument for an educational market is straightforward. Parents have a constitutional right to choose the school their child attends.[46] They can make that choice either by sending their children to a private rather than to a public school or by moving to a new neighborhood based on the quality of its public schools. But exercising that choice is very costly for poor parents, who lack the funds to pay private-school tuition or to purchase housing in the affluent neighborhoods that usually have the better public schools. (Some poor families are willing to make the great sacrifices necessary to take advantage of these opportunities.) As a result, the public schools in many neighborhoods provide a monopoly service.

Whenever any organization, public or private, has a monopoly it has weak incentives to offer services that match the preferences of its clients. Public-school systems attempt to overcome this by allowing their clients to participate in making school policy by voting for school-board members (in those places where they are elected) and joining parent-teacher or other advisory groups. This method of exercising control may work well in small systems where even a few votes or a modest amount of talking and campaigning can make a difference, but it is unlikely to be of much value in populous districts, especially when school-board members are appointed rather than elected and a large central bureaucracy oversees many local schools. Chester E. Finn, Jr., formerly assistant secretary for research and improvement in the U.S. Department of Education, described the big-city problem this way:

> Our school system today holds few incentives or rewards for entrepreneurship or risk-taking, for initiative or heterodoxy. Responsibility and authority are rarely joined. Most crucial management decisions are made far away from the workplace. Teachers are treated alike whether they are good or bad; in any case, their employer is the "school system" downtown, although their immediate supervisor is down the corridor. Success brings no prizes, failure no sanctions, mediocrity no response at all except intermittent alarms sounded by distant national commissions.[47]

To create more educational choices for parents and at the same time stimulate schools to improve their offerings, a growing number of observers have called for providing more choice—that is, for creating broader educational markets. One version of this involves allowing parents to select any public school as they now can select any private one (if they have the money). This is called open enrollment. Another version is to give vouchers to parents equal in value to the cost of educating their children in a typical public school and allow the parents to "spend" the voucher in any school, private or public, that they wish (provided all eligible schools meet minimum state standards). A variant on the voucher plan is the tuition tax credit that rebates to the parents the taxes they paid for public education should they elect to use private schools instead. In either variant the parents would be free to supplement the value of the voucher (or the tax credit) with their own funds.

To some people these are radical ideas; to much of the educational establishment they are heresies. In fact, most of these things are going on now. Take open enrollment, for example. In many small towns in Maine and Vermont, parents can send their children to any accredited school, public or private, and the town will pay that school a tuition grant equal to the state average for all school districts.[48] Some cities have open-enrollment plans as a way of achieving greater racial balance in the schools. In Cambridge, Massachusetts, every school is open to every child, provided that the net result meets state racial balancing goals.[49] Boston, among other cities, allows black parents to send their children to suburban schools of their choice.

In the Netherlands and Denmark, groups of like-minded parents may start a school and the government will pay for it provided that minimum standards are met. In Australia, parents can claim a tuition tax credit (that is, a deduction on their federal income tax) for the costs incurred in sending their children to private schools.[50]

The voucher plan was tried in the Alum Rock School District in San Jose, California. But what began as a test of the effect of giving vouchers to parents who would then be free to send their children to any school ended up a good deal less than this. Initially, no private schools were allowed to participate; later they were allowed in but only under very restrictive rules. To judge by what the parents thought of them, the Alum Rock schools were not doing a bad job, and so the parental demand for choice was weak. Not many children changed schools; hardly any elected to go to a private or alternative school. The evaluation suggested that children who took advantage of such choices as existed did not do better educationally than those who stayed where they were.[51] Even if the children did not change, however, the schools did. Authority within them was decentralized, teachers gained somewhat greater autonomy, and a few teachers organized their own "minischools" within the existing public schools.[52]

Whatever their effects on reading scores, educational markets are worrisome to many people on grounds of equity and accountability.

Equity

"Open-enrollment or voucher plans may encourage racial separation." While it is true that more well-off people than poor people now send their children to private schools, we do not know what the distribution would be if poor people had their purchasing power enhanced with vouchers. We do know that there is now *less* racial separateness in private than in public high schools.[53] Moreover, popular support for the use of vouchers is greater among blacks than among whites.[54]

Accountability

"Private schools will teach the wrong things, even if they meet minimum educational standards." Different critics have different views as to what the wrong things are, but the list probably includes teaching religion, secularism, political liberalism, political conservatism, social conformity, and countercultural values. In short, many of us do not trust parents to make choices for their children because we disagree with those parents. But of course the alternative is for one group to use the government to impose its preferences on another group. Up to a point that is proper (after all, the requirement that all children be schooled is the result of a political majority imposing its will on a minority that wants parents left free to decide whether their children go to school at all). Beyond such minimal requirements, however, it is not clear that the values currently taught in public schools (which hardly are neutral) always ought to be preferred to those that many parents hold dear.

We do not know the effect, on values, educational attainment, or operating efficiencies, of a true market in publicly-supported education in which there are strong incentives for parents to make choices and strong incentives for schools to adapt to those choices. We do know that many organizations speaking for public-school teachers and administrators are determined that we not find out.[55] As with all other kinds of market alternatives to bureaucratic management, only carefully done experiments will tell us what we need to know.

Conclusions

There are two fundamentally different ways of improving the delivery of a public service: rules and contracts. Rules pervade governmental agencies because the institutions constraining those agencies—courts, legislatures, executive staffs—usually find the formulation and imposition of a rule to be more rewarding. A rule can be drafted that describes a grievance, and thus it appears to be immediately responsive to the person or group bringing the grievance. Rules often need not be reconciled with one another, and therefore the political institutions employing them do not have to make painful choices among competing goals. Rule-imposing bodies do not routinely monitor the output of agencies or bear any of the costs of managing highly constrained organizations and so they need not solve problems of feasibility. Rules tend to heighten the (formal) authority of executives and managers and as a consequence these people often find them attractive.

Contracts—that is to say, agreements about the terms of an exchange—are less attractive to governments. A contract, unlike a set of rules, does not specify every procedure to be undertaken. The agreement may specify the desired outcome (the desk or truck being purchased), leaving the procedures employed to the discretion of the contractor, or it may specify the service to be rendered (streets to be patrolled, instruction to be provided), leaving the outcomes undetermined. The uncertainty inherent in contracting is unattractive to political actors who wish to see their interests—all of them—fully protected. A contract, being an agreement about an exchange, must reconcile at least certain major tradeoffs, between cost and quantity, for example, or between time and money. The contracting parties must bear the full cost of the agreement: The purchaser must pay for the good or service and the supplier must absorb the costs of supplying it. Contracts often leave substantial discretion in the hands of customers or lower-level operators.

Though there are many exceptions and qualifications to the contrasts I have drawn, taken as a whole they suggest why governments often prefer to solve problems by imposing rules rather than by letting contracts. This is especially the case for services that are at all controversial: The government is required to act as if all preferences can be accommodated simultaneously rather than to let markets allocate goods on the basis of the strength of individual preferences. As a result, the evidence for the superiority of contracts often falls on deaf ears.

Onc may think that contracting would work best for what I have called production and craft bureaus: that is, bureaus with observable, often measurable outputs. Contracting is easy to design and administer in these cases and the efficiency gains are easy to calculate. But efficiency gains may not be the most important gains. It certainly is desirable to save money wherever possible, but it is even more important to satisfy human wants. Important human needs often are dealt with by procedural and coping organizations. Schools and housing programs are good examples. If we made greater use of marketlike arrangements in these areas, we might find it very hard to know whether we have thereby made the program more efficient; to measure efficiency one first must be able to measure goal attainment, and we have only vague notions as to what constitutes an educated child or an adequate shelter. But we can learn rather easily whether we have satisfied people, for the essence of a market is the opportunity it affords clients to vote with their feet.

CHAPTER 20

Bureaucracy and the Public Interest

THE GERMAN ARMY beat the French army in 1940; the Texas prisons for many years did a better job than did the Michigan prisons; Carver High School in Atlanta became a better school under Norris Hogans. These successes were the result of skilled executives who correctly identified the critical tasks of their organizations, distributed authority in a way appropriate to those tasks, infused their subordinates with a sense of mission, and acquired sufficient autonomy to permit them to get on with the job. The critical tasks were different in each case, and so the organizations differed in culture and patterns of authority, but all three were alike in one sense: incentives, culture, and authority were combined in a way that suited the task at hand.

By now, nineteen chapters after these points were first made, the reader may find all this painfully obvious. If they are obvious to the reader, then surely they are obvious to government officials. Intellectually perhaps they are. But whatever lip service may be given to the lessons I have drawn from the agencies discussed in this book, the daily incentives operating in the political world encourage a very different course of action.

Armies

Though the leadership and initiative of field officers and noncoms is of critical importance, the Pentagon is filled with generals who want to control combat from headquarters or from helicopters, using radios to gather information and computers to process it. Though the skill of the infantryman almost always has been a key to military success, the U.S. Army traditionally has put its best people in specialized units (intelligence, engineering, communications), leaving the leftovers for the infantry.[1] Though it has fought wars since 1945 everywhere except in Europe, the army continues to devote most of its planning to big-tank battles on the West German plains.

Prisons

The success of George Beto in the Texas DOC was there for everyone to see, but many observers gave the most favorable attention to prison executives who seemed to voice the best intentions (rehabilitation, prisoner self-governance) rather than the best accomplishments (safe, decent facilities).

Schools

Especially in big cities, many administrators keep principals weak and teachers busy filling out reports, all with an eye toward minimizing complaints from parents, auditors, interest groups, and the press. Teachers individually grumble that they are treated as robots instead of professionals, but collectively they usually oppose any steps—vouchers, merit pay, open enrollment, strengthened principals—that in fact have given teachers a larger role in designing curricula and managing their classrooms. Norris Hogans received little help from the Atlanta school system; politically, extra resources had to go to all schools "equally" rather than disproportionately to those schools that were improving the most.

These generals, wardens, administrators, and teachers have not been behaving irrationally; rather, they have been responding to the incentives and constraints that they encounter on a daily basis. Those incentives include the need to manage situations over which they have little control on the basis of a poorly defined or nonexistent sense of mission and in the face of a complex array of constraints that seems always to grow, never to shrink. Outside groups—elected officials, interest groups, professional associations, the media—demand a voice in the running of these agencies and make that demand effective by imposing rules on the agencies and demanding that all these rules be enforced all of the time. Moreover, habitual patterns of action—the lessons of the past, the memories of earlier struggles, the expectations of one's co-workers—narrow the area within which new courses of action are sought.

Bureaucrats often complain of "legislative micromanagement," and indeed it exists. As we saw in chapter 13 with respect to the armed forces, there has been a dramatic increase in the number of hearings, reports, investigations, statutory amendments, and budgetary adjustments with which the Pentagon must deal.[2] But there also has been a sharp increase in presidential micromanagement. Herbert Kaufman notes that for a half century or more the White House has feared agency independence more than agency paralysis, and so it has multiplied the number of presidential staffers, central management offices, and requirements for higher-level reviews. Once you start along the path of congressional or White House control, the process acquires a momentum of its own. "As more constraints are imposed, rigidities fixing agencies in their established ways intensify. As a result, complaints that they do not respond to controls also intensify. Further controls, checkpoints, and clearances are therefore introduced."[3] Much the same story can be told with respect to the growing involvement of the courts in agency affairs.

With some conspicuous exceptions the result of this process has been to deflect the attention of agency executives away from how the tasks of their agencies get defined and toward the constraints that must be observed no matter what the tasks may be. Who then decides what tasks shall be performed? In a production agency with observable outputs and routinized work processes, the answer is relatively simple: The laws and regulations that created the agency also define its job. But in procedural, coping, and craft agencies, the answer seems to be nobody in particular and everybody in general. The operating-level workers define the tasks, occasionally by design, as in those cases where operator ideology makes a difference, but more commonly by accident, as in those instances where prior experiences, professional norms, situational and technological imperatives, and peer-group expectations shape the nature of the work.

From time to time a gifted executive appears at a politically propitious time and makes things happen differently. He or she creates a new institution that acquires a distinctive competence, a strong sense of mission, and an ability to achieve socially-valued goals. The Army Corps of Engineers, the Social Security Administration, the Marine Corps, the Forest Service, the FBI: For many years after they were created, and in many instances still today, these agencies, along with a few others that could be mentioned, were a kind of elite service that stood as a living refutation of the proposition that "all bureaucrats are dim-witted paper-shufflers." And these are only the federal examples; at the local level one can find many school systems and police departments that have acquired a praiseworthy organizational character.

But one must ask whether today one could create from scratch the Marine Corps, or the FBI, or the Forest Service; possibly, but probably not. Who would dare suggest that a new agency come into being with its own personnel system (and thus with fewer opportunities for civil servants to get tenure), with a single dominant mission (and thus with little organizational deference to the myriad other goals outsiders would want it to serve), and with an arduous training regime designed to instill *esprit de corps* (and thus with less regard for those niceties and conveniences that sedentary people believe to be important)? Or how optimistic should we be that today we could organize a Social Security Administration in a way that would bring to Washington men and women of exceptional talent? Might not many of those people decide today that they do not want to risk running afoul of the conflict-of-interest laws, that they have no stomach for close media and congressional scrutiny, and that they would not accept the federal pay levels pegged to the salaries of members of Congress fearful of raising their own compensation?

It would be a folly of historical romanticism to imagine that great agencies were created in a golden age that is destined never to return, but it would be shortsighted to deny that we have paid a price for having emphasized rules and constraints to the neglect of tasks and mission. At the end of her careful review of the problems the SSA has had in managing disability insurance and supplemental security income, Martha Derthick makes the same point this way: "If the agencies repeatedly fall short, one ought at least to consider the possibility that there is a systematic mismatch between what they are instructed to do and their capacity to do it."[4] In recent years, when Congress has been creating new programs and modifying old ones at a dizzying rate, often on the basis of perfunctory hearings (or, as with the Senate's consideration of the 1988 drug bill, no hearings at all), a government agency capable of responding adequately to these endless changes would have to be versatile and adaptable, "capable of devising new routines or altering old ones very quickly." These qualities, she concludes, "are rarely found in large formal organizations."[5] I would only add that government agencies are far less flexible than formal organizations generally.

Things are not made much better by our national tendency to engage in bureaucrat-bashing. One has to have some perspective on this. It is true that bureaucracies prefer the present to the future, the known to the unknown, and the dominant mission to rival missions; many agencies in fact are skeptical of things that were "NIH"—Not Invented Here. Every social grouping, whether a neighborhood, a nation, or an organization, acquires a culture; changing that culture is like moving a cemetery: it is always difficult and some believe it is sacrilegious. It is also true, as many conservatives argue, that the government tries to do things that it is incapable of doing well, just as it is true, as many liberals allege, that the government in fact does many things well enough. As Charles Wolf has argued, both markets and governments have their imperfections; many things we might want to do collectively require us to choose between unsatisfactory alternatives.[6]

A Few Modest Suggestions That May Make a Small Difference

To do better we have to deregulate the government.* If deregulation of a market makes sense because it liberates the entrepreneurial energies of its members, then it is possible that deregulating the public sector also may help energize it. The difference, of course, is that both the price system and the profit motive provide a discipline in markets that is absent in non-markets. Whether any useful substitutes for this discipline can be found for public-sector workers is not clear, though I will offer some suggestions. But even if we cannot expect the same results from deregulation in the two sectors we can agree at a minimum that detailed regulation, even of public employees, rarely is compatible with energy, pride in workmanship, and the exercise of initiative. The best evidence for this proposition, if any is needed, is that most people do not like working in an environment in which every action is second-guessed, every initiative viewed with suspicion, and every controversial decision denounced as malfeasance.

James Colvard, for many years a senior civilian manager in the navy, suggests that the government needs to emulate methods that work in the better parts of the private sector: "a bias toward action, small staffs, and a high level of delegation which is based on trust."[7] A panel of the National Academy of Public Administration (NAPA), consisting of sixteen senior government executives holding the rank of assistant secretary, issued a report making the same point:

> Over many years, government has become entwined in elaborate management control systems and the accretion of progressively more detailed administrative procedures. This development has not produced superior management. Instead, it has produced managerial overburden. . . . Procedures overwhelm substance. Organizations become discredited, along with their employees. . . . The critical elements of leadership in management appear to wither in the face of a preoccupation with process. The tools are endlessly "perfected"; the manager who is expected to use these tools believes himself to be ignored. . . . Management systems are not management. . . . The attitude of those who design and administer the rules . . . must be

*I first saw this phrase in an essay by Constance Horner, then director of the federal Office of Personnel Management: "Beyond Mr. Gradgrind: The Case for Deregulating the Public Sector," *Policy Review* 44 (Spring 1988): 34–38. It also appears in Gary C. Bryner, *Bureaucratic Discretion* (New York: Pergamon Press, 1987), 215.

reoriented from a "control mentality" to one of "how can I help get the mission of this agency accomplished."[8]

But how can government "delegate" and "trust" and still maintain accountability? If it is a mistake to foster an ethos that encourages every bureaucrat to "go by the book," is it not an equally serious problem to allow zealots to engage in "mission madness," charging off to implement their private versions of some ambiguous public goal? (Steven Emerson has written a useful account of mission madness in some highly secret military intelligence and covert-action agencies.[9]) Given everything we know about the bureaucratic desire for autonomy and the political rewards of rule making, is there any reason to suppose that anybody will find it in his or her interest to abandon the "control mentality" and adopt the "mission accomplishment" mentality?

Possibly not. But it may be worth thinking about what a modestly deregulated government might look like. It might look as it once did, when some of the better federal agencies were created. At the time the Corps of Engineers, the Forest Service, and the FBI were founded much of the federal government was awash in political patronage, petty cabals, and episodic corruption. Organizing an elite service in those days may have been easier than doing so today, when the problems are less patronage and corruption than they are officiousness and complexity. But the keys to organizational success have not changed. The agencies were started by strong leaders who were able to command personal loyalty, define and instill a clear and powerful sense of mission, attract talented workers who believed they were joining something special, and make exacting demands on subordinates.

Today there is not much chance to create a new agency; almost every agency one can imagine already has been created. Even so, the lessons one learns from changing agencies confirm what can be inferred from studying their founding.

First: Executives should understand the culture of their organizations—that is, what their subordinates believe constitute the core tasks of the agency—and the strengths and limitations of that culture. If members widely share and warmly endorse that culture the agency has a sense of mission. This permits the executive to economize on scarce incentives (people want to do certain tasks even when there are no special rewards for doing it); to state general objectives confident that subordinates will understand the appropriate ways of achieving them; and to delegate responsibility knowing that lower-level decisions probably will conform to higher-level expectations.

A good executive realizes that workers can make subtle, precise, and realistic judgments, but only if those judgments refer to a related, coherent set of behaviors. People cannot easily keep in mind many quite different things or strike reasonable balances among competing tasks. People want to know what is expected of them; they do not want to be told, in answer to this question, that "on the one hand this, but on the other hand that."

In defining a core mission and sorting out tasks that either fit or do not fit with this mission, executives must be aware of their many rivals for the right to define it. Operators with professional backgrounds will bring to the agency their skills but also their biases: Lawyers, economists, and engineers see the world in very different ways. You cannot hire them as if they were tools that in your skilled hands will perform exactly the task you set for them. Black and Decker may make tools like that, but Harvard and MIT do not. Worker peer groups also set expectations to which operators conform, especially when the operators work in a threatening, unpredictable, or confrontational environment. You may design the ideal patrol officer or schoolteacher, but unless you understand the demands made by the street and the classroom, your design will remain an artistic expression destined for the walls of some organizational museum.

These advantages of infusing an agency with a sense of mission are purchased at a price. An agency with a strong mission will give perfunctory attention, if any at all, to tasks that are not central to that mission. Diplomats in the State Department will have little interest in embassy security; intelligence officers in the CIA will not worry as much as they should about counterintelligence; narcotics agents in the DEA will minimize the importance of improper prescriptions written by physicians; power engineers in the TVA will not think as hard about environmental protection or conservation as about maximizing the efficiency of generating units; fighter pilots in the USAF will look at air transport as a homely stepchild; and navy admirals who earned their flag serving on aircraft carriers will not press zealously to expand the role of minesweepers.

If the organization must perform a diverse set of tasks, those tasks that are not part of the core mission will need special protection. This requires giving autonomy to the subordinate tasks subunit (for example, by providing for them a special organizational niche) and creating a career track so that talented people performing non-mission tasks can rise to high rank in the agency. No single organization, however, can perform well a wide variety of tasks; inevitably some will be neglected. In this case, the wise executive will arrange to devolve the slighted tasks onto another agency, or to a wholly new organization created for the purpose. Running multitask conglomerates is as risky in the public as in the private sector. There are limits to the number of different jobs managers can manage. Moreover, conglomerate agencies rarely can develop a sense of mission; the cost of trying to do everything is that few things are done well. The turf-conscious executive who stoutly refuses to surrender any tasks, no matter how neglected, to another agency is courting disaster; in time the failure of his or her agency to perform some orphan task will lead to a political or organizational crisis. Long ago the State Department should have got out of the business of building embassies. Diplomats are good at many things, but supervising carpenters and plumbers is not one of them. Let agencies whose mission is construction—the Army Corps of Engineers or the navy's Seabees—build buildings.

Second: Negotiate with one's political superiors to get some agreement as to which are the *essential* constraints that must be observed by your agency and which the marginal constraints. This, frankly, may be impossible. The decentralization of authority in Congress (and in some state legislatures) and the unreliability of most expressions of presidential or gubernatorial backing are such that in most cases you will discover, by experience if not by precept, that all constraints are essential all of the time. But perhaps with effort some maneuvering room may be won. A few agencies obtained the right to use more flexible, less cumbersome personnel systems modeled on the China Lake experiment, and Congress has the power to broaden those opportunities. Perhaps some enlightened member of Congress will be able to get statutory authority for the equivalent of China Lake with respect to procurement regulations. An executive is well advised to spend time showing that member how to do it.

Third: Match the distribution of authority and the control over resources to the tasks your organization is performing. In general, authority should be placed at the lowest level at which all essential elements of information are available. Bureaucracies will differ greatly in what level that may be. At one extreme are agencies such as the Internal Revenue Service or maximum-security prisons, in which uniformity of treatment and precision of control are so important as to make it necessary for there to be exacting, centrally determined rules for most tasks. At the other extreme are public schools, police departments, and armies, organizations in which operational uncertainties are so great that discretion must be given to (or if not given will be taken by) lower-level workers.

A good place in which to think through these matters is the area of weapons procurement. The overcentralization of design control is one of the many criticisms of such procurement on which all commentators seem agreed. Buying a new aircraft may be likened to remodeling one's home: You never know how much it will cost until you are done; you quickly find out that changing your mind midway through the work costs a lot of money; and you soon realize that decisions have to be made by people on the spot who can look at the pipes, wires, and joists. The Pentagon procures aircraft as if none of its members had ever built or remodeled a house. It does so because both it and its legislative superiors refuse to allow authority to flow down to the point where decisions rationally can be made.

The same analysis can be applied to public schools. As John Chubb and Terry Moe have shown, public and private schools differ in the locus of effective control.[10] At least in big cities, decisions in private schools that are made by headmasters or in Catholic schools that are made by small archdiocesan staffs are made in public schools by massive, cumbersome headquarters bureaucracies. Of course, there are perfectly understandable political reasons for this difference, but not very many good reasons for it. Many sympathetic critics of the public schools believe that the single most useful organizational change that could be made would be to have educational management decisions—on personnel, scheduling, and instructional matters—made at the school level.[11]

Fourth: Judge organizations by results. This book has made it clear that what constitutes a valued result in government usually is a matter of dispute. But even when fairly clear performance standards exist, legislatures and executives often ignore them with unhappy results. William E. Turcotte compared how two state governments oversaw their state liquor monopolies. The state that applied clear standards to its liquor bureaucrats produced significantly more profit and lower administrative costs than did the state with unclear or conflicting standards.[12]

Even when results are hard to assess more can be done than is often the case. If someone set out to evaluate the output of a private school, hospital, or security service, he or she would have at least as much trouble as would someone trying to measure the output of a public school, hospital, or police department. Governments are not the only institutions with ambiguous products.

There are two ways to cope with the problem in government One (discussed in the preceding chapter) is to supply the service or product in a marketlike environment. Shift the burden of evaluation off the shoulders of professional evaluators and onto the shoulders of clients and customers, and let the latter vote with their feet. The "client" in these cases can be individual citizens or government agencies; what is important is that the client be able to choose from among rival suppliers.

But some public services cannot be supplied, or are never going to be supplied, by a market. We can imagine allowing parents to choose among schools but we cannot imagine letting them choose (at least for most purposes) among police departments or armies. In that case one should adopt the second way of evaluating a public service: carry out a demonstration project or conduct a field experiment. (I will use the two ideas interchangeably, though some scholars distinguish between them.[13]) An experiment is a planned alteration in a state of affairs designed to measure the effect of the intervention. It involves asking the question, "if I change X, what will happen to Y, having first made certain that everything else stays the same?" It sounds easy, but it is not.

A good experiment (bad ones are worse than no experiment at all) requires that one do the following: First, identify a course of action to be tested; call it the treatment. A "treatment" can be a police tactic, a school curriculum, or a welfare program. Second, decide what impact the treatment is intended to have; call this the outcome. The outcome can be a crime rate, an achievement score, a work effort, a housing condition, or an income level. Third, give the treatment to one group (the experimental group) and withhold it from another (the control group). A group might be a police precinct, a class of students, the tenants in a housing project, or people who meet some eligibility requirement (say, having low incomes). It is quite important how the membership in these groups is determined. It should be done randomly; that is, all eligible precincts, schools, tenants, or people should be randomly sorted into experimental and control groups. Random assignment means that all the characteristics of the members of the experimental and control groups are likely to be identical. Fourth, assess the condition of each group before and after the treatment. The first assessment describes the baseline condition, the second the outcome condition. This outcome assessment should continue for some time after the end of the treatment, because experience has shown that many treatments seem to have a short-term effect that quickly disappears. Fifth, make certain that the evaluation is done by people other than those providing the treatment. People like to believe that their efforts are worthwhile, so much so that perhaps unwittingly they will gather data in ways that make it look like the treatment worked even when it did not.*

The object of all this is to find out what works. Using this method we have discovered that tripling the number of patrol cars on a beat does not lower the crime rate; that foot patrol reduces the fear of crime but not (ordinarily) its incidence; and that arresting spouse-beaters reduces (for a while) future assaults more than does counseling the assaulters.[14] We have learned that giving people an income supplement (akin to the negative income tax) reduces work effort and in some cases encourages families to break up.[15] We have learned that giving special job training and support to welfare mothers, ex-offenders, and school drop-outs produces sizable gains in the employment records of the welfare recipients but no gain for the ex-offenders and school drop-outs.[16] We have learned that a housing allowance program increases the welfare of poor families even though it does not improve the stock of housing.[17] We have learned that more flexible pay and classification systems greatly benefit the managers of navy research centers and improve the work atmosphere at the centers.[18]

There also have been many failed or flawed management experiments.

*Matters are, of course, a bit more complicated than this summary might suggest. There is a small library of books on evaluative research that go into these matters in more detail; a good place to begin is Richard P. Nathan, *Social Science in Government* (New York: Basic Books, 1988). On the political aspects of evaluation, see Henry J. Aaron, *Politics and the Professors* (Washington, D.C.: The Brookings Institution, 1978). On the technical side see Thomas D. Cook and Donald T. Campbell, *Quasi-Experimentation* (Chicago: Rand McNally, 1979). There is even a journal, *Evaluation Review*, specializing in these issues.

In the 1930s, Herbert Simon carried out what may have been the first serious such experiment when he tried to find out how to improve the performance of welfare workers in the California State Relief Administration. Though elegantly designed, the experimental changes proved so controversial and the political environment of the agency so unstable that it is not clear that any useful inferences can be drawn from the project.[19] The attempt to evaluate educational vouchers at Alum Rock was undercut by the political need to restrict participation by private schools (see chapter 19). There are countless other "studies" that are evaluations in name only; in reality they are self-congratulatory conclusions written by program administrators. The administrative world is a political world, not a scientific laboratory, and evaluators of administration must come to terms with that fact. Often there are no mutually acceptable terms. But where reasonable terms can be struck it is possible to learn more than untutored experience can tell us about what works.

Such dry and dusty research projects probably seem thin fare to people who want Big Answers to Big Questions such as "How can we curb rampant bureaucracy?" or "How can we unleash the creative talents of our dedicated public servants?" But public management is not an arena in which to find Big Answers; it is a world of settled institutions designed to allow imperfect people to use flawed procedures to cope with insoluble problems.

The fifth and final bit of advice flows directly from the limits on judging agencies by their results. All organizations seek the stability and comfort that comes from relying on standard operating procedures—"SOPs." When results are unknown or equivocal, bureaus will have no incentive to alter those SOPs so as better to achieve their goals, only an incentive to modify them to conform to externally imposed constraints. The SOPs will represent an internally defined equilibrium that reconciles the situational imperatives, professional norms, bureaucratic ideologies, peer-group expectations, and (if present) leadership demands unique to that agency. The only way to minimize the adverse effect of allowing human affairs to be managed by organizations driven by their autonomous SOPs is to keep the number, size, and authority of such organizations as small as possible. If none of the four preceding bits of advice work, the reader must confront the realization that there are no solutions for the bureaucracy problem that are not also "solutions" to the government problem. More precisely: All complex organizations display bureaucratic problems of confusion, red tape, and the avoidance of responsibility. Those problems are much greater in government bureaucracies because government itself is the institutionalization of confusion (arising out of the need to moderate competing demands); of red tape (arising out of the need to satisfy demands that cannot be moderated); and of avoided responsibility (arising out of the desire to retain power by minimizing criticism).

In short, you can have less bureaucracy only if you have less government. Many, if not most, of the difficulties we experience in dealing with government agencies arise from the agencies being part of a fragmented and open political system. If an agency is to have a sense of mission, if constraints are to be minimized, if authority is to be decentralized, if officials are to be judged on the basis of the outputs they produce rather than the inputs they consume, then legislators, judges, and lobbyists will have to act against their own interests. They will have to say "no" to influential constituents, forgo the opportunity to expand their own influence, and take seriously the task of judging the organizational feasibility as well as the political popularity of a proposed new program. It is hard to imagine this happening, partly because politicians and judges have no incentive to make it happen and partly because there are certain tasks a democratic government must undertake even if they cannot be performed efficiently. The greatest mistake citizens can make when they complain of "the bureaucracy" is to suppose that their frustrations arise simply out of management problems; they do not—they arise out of governance problems.

Bureaucracy and the American Regime

The central feature of the American constitutional system—the separation of powers—exacerbates many of these problems. The governments of the United States were not designed to be efficient or powerful, but to be tolerable and malleable. Those who devised these arrangements always assumed that the federal government would exercise few and limited powers. As long as that assumption was correct (which it was for a century and a half) the quality of public administration was not a serious problem except in the minds of those reformers (Woodrow Wilson was probably the first) who desired to rationalize government in order to rationalize society. The founders knew that the separation of powers would make it so difficult to start a new program or to create a new agency that it was hardly necessary to think about how those agencies would be administered. As a result, the Constitution is virtually silent on what kind of administration we should have. At least until the Civil War thrust the problem on us, scarcely anyone in the country would have known what you were talking about if you spoke of the "problem of administration."

Matters were very different in much of Europe. Kings and princes long had ruled; when their authority was captured by parliaments, the tradition of ruling was already well established. From the first the ministers of the parliamentary regimes thought about the problems of administration because in those countries there was something to administer. The centralization of executive authority in the hands of a prime minister and the exclusion (by and large) of parliament from much say in executive affairs facilitated the process of controlling the administrative agencies and bending them to some central will. The constitutions of many European states easily could have been written by a school of management.

Today, the United States at every level has big and active governments. Some people worry that a constitutional system well-designed to preserve liberty when governments were small is poorly designed to implement policy now that governments are large. The contrast between how the United States and the nations of Western Europe manage environmental and industrial regulation (described in chapter 16) is illuminating: Here the separation of powers insures, if not causes, clumsy and adversarial regulation; there the unification of powers permits, if not causes, smooth and consensual regulation.

I am not convinced that the choice is that simple, however. It would take another book to judge the advantages and disadvantages of the separation of powers. The balance sheet on both sides of the ledger would contain many more entries than those that derive from a discussion of public administration. But even confining our attention to administration, there is more to be said for the American system than many of its critics admit.

America has a paradoxical bureaucracy unlike that found in almost any other advanced nation. The paradox is the existence in one set of institutions of two qualities ordinarily quite separate: the multiplication of rules and the opportunity for access. We have a system laden with rules; elsewhere that is a sure sign that the bureaucracy is aloof from the people, distant from their concerns, and preoccupied with the power and privileges of the bureaucrats—an elaborate, grinding machine that can crush the spirit of any who dare oppose it. We also have a system suffused with participation: advisory boards, citizen groups, neighborhood councils, congressional investigators, crusading journalists, and lawyers serving writs; elsewhere this popular involvement would be taken as evidence that the administrative system is no system at all, but a bungling, jerry-built contraption wallowing in inefficiency and shot through with corruption and favoritism.

That these two traits, rules and openness, could coexist would have astonished Max Weber and continues to astonish (or elude) many contemporary students of the subject. Public bureaucracy in this country is neither as rational and predictable as Weber hoped nor as crushing and mechanistic as he feared. It is rule-bound without being overpowering, participatory without being corrupt. This paradox exists partly because of the character and mores of the American people: They are too informal, spontaneous, and other-directed to be either neutral arbiters or passionless Gradgrinds. And partly it exists because of the nature of the regime: Our constitutional system, and above all the exceptional power enjoyed by the legislative branch, makes it impossible for us to have anything like a government by appointed experts but easy for individual citizens to obtain redress from the abuses of power. Anyone who wishes it otherwise would have to produce a wholly different regime, and curing the mischiefs of bureaucracy seems an inadequate reason for that. Parliamentary regimes that supply more consistent direction to their bureaucracies also supply more bureaucracy to their citizens. The fragmented American regime may produce chaotic government, but the coherent European regimes produce bigger governments.

In the meantime we live in a country that despite its baffling array of rules and regulations and the insatiable desire of some people to use government to rationalize society still makes it possible to get drinkable water instantly, put through a telephone call in seconds, deliver a letter in a day, and obtain a passport in a week. Our Social Security checks arrive on time. Some state prisons, and most of the federal ones, are reasonably decent and humane institutions. The great majority of Americans, cursing all the while, pay their taxes. One can stand on the deck of an aircraft carrier during night flight operations and watch two thousand nineteen-year-old boys faultlessly operate one of the most complex organizational systems ever created. There are not many places where all this happens. It is astonishing it can be made to happen at all.

NOTES

Preface

1. See the opinion surveys summarized in Charles T. Goodsell, *The Case for Bureaucracy*, 2nd ed. (Chatham, N.J.: Chatham House, 1985), chap. 2; and Daniel Katz, Barbara A. Gutek, Robert L. Kahn, and Eugenia Barton, *Bureaucratic Encounters* (Ann Arbor, Mich.: Institute for Social Research of the University of Michigan, 1975).
2. James G. March and Herbert A. Simon, *Organizations* (New York: John Wiley & Sons, 1958), 5.

Chapter 1. Armies, Prisons, Schools

1. Alistair Horne, *To Lose a Battle: France 1940* (New York: Penguin Books, 1979), 233.
2. Martin van Creveld, *Fighting Power: German and U.S. Army Performance, 1939–1945* (Westport, Conn.: Greenwood Press, 1982), 5; Barry R. Posen, *The Sources of Military Doctrine: France, Britain, and Germany Between the World Wars* (Ithaca, N.Y.: Cornell University Press, 1984), 82–83, and sources cited therein.
3. Len Deighton, *Blitzkrieg: From the Rise of Hitler to the Fall of Dunkirk* (New York: Alfred A. Knopf, 1980), 172–73.
4. Ibid., 164–65; Posen, *Sources*, 84.
5. Deighton, *Blitzkrieg*, 175.
6. Horne, *To Lose*, 126.
7. For evidence discounting the importance of ideology see Edward A. Shils and Morris Janowitz, "Cohesion and Disintegration in the Wehrmacht in World War II," *Public Opinion Quarterly* 12 (1948): 280–315; Daniel Lerner, *Psychological Warfare Against Nazi Germany* (Cambridge, Mass.: MIT Press, 1971); Creveld, *Fighting Power*, 87. For a contrary argument, see Jürgen E. Förster, "The Dynamics of *Volksgemeinschaft*: The Effectiveness of the German Military Establishment in the Second World War," in Allan R. Millett and Williamson Murray, eds., *The Second World War*, vol. 3, *Military Effectiveness* (Boston: Allen & Unwin, 1988), 204–8.
8. Deighton, *Blitzkrieg*, 154.
9. Quoted in Horne, *To Lose*, 197.
10. Vivian Rowe, *The Great Wall of France* (London: Putnam, 1959).
11. John J. DiIulio, Jr., *Governing Prisons: A Comparative Study of Correctional Management* (New York: Free Press, 1987).
12. Calculated from ibid., tables 2.1–2.3, 54–56.
13. Bruce Jackson, *Law and Disorder: Criminal Justice in America* (Urbana, Ill.: University of Illinois Press, 1984), 240.
14. Joan Petersilia et al., *The Prison Experience of Career Criminals* (Santa Monica, Calif.: Rand, 1980), 16.
15. Ibid., xiv, 67.
16. Compare DiIulio, *Governing Prisons*, tables 2.2 and 2.3, 55–56.
17. Ibid., table 2.8, 60.

18. James W. Marquart and Ben M. Crouch, "Judicial Reform and Prisoner Control: The Impact of Estelle v. Ruiz on a Texas Penitentiary," paper delivered at the 1985 meeting of the Southern Sociological Society (cited in DiIulio, *Governing Prisons*, 62).

19. Jan M. Chaiken and Marcia R. Chaiken, *Varieties of Criminal Behavior* (Santa Monica, Calif.: Rand, 1982), 31.

20. DiIulio, *Governing Prisons*, 60–62, 157–79, and DiIulio, "True Penal Reform Can Save Money," *Wall Street Journal* (September 28, 1987).

21. Sara Lawrence Lightfoot, *The Good High School* (New York: Basic Books, 1983), chap. 1.

22. James S. Coleman et al., *Equality of Educational Opportunity*, 2 vols. (Washington, D.C.: United States Office of Education, 1966).

23. Eric A. Hanushek, "Throwing Money at Schools," *Journal of Policy Analysis and Management* 1 (1981): 19–41.

24. Michael Rutter et al., *Fifteen Thousand Hours: Secondary Schools and Their Effects on Children* (Cambridge, Mass.: Harvard University Press, 1979), chap. 6.

25. Frederick C. Mosher, *Governmental Reorganizations* (Indianapolis, Ind.: Bobbs-Merrill, 1967); Rufus E. Miles, "Considerations for a President Bent on Reorganization," *Public Administration Review* 37 (March-April 1977): 160; David S. Brown, "Reforming the Bureaucracy: Some Suggestions for the New President," *Public Administration Review* 37 (March-April 1977): 163–70; George D. Greenberg, "Reorganization Reconsidered: The U.S. Public Health Service," *Public Policy* 23 (1975): 483–86; Harold Seidman and Robert Gilmour, *Politics, Position, and Power: From the Positive to the Regulatory State*, 4th ed. (New York: Oxford University Press, 1986), 12–36.

26. Patricia Rachal, *Federal Narcotics Enforcement: Reorganization and Reform* (Boston, Mass.: Auburn House, 1982); and James Q. Wilson, *The Investigators: Managing FBI and Narcotic Agents* (New York: Basic Books, 1978), esp. chap. 1 and 183–91.

Chapter 2. Organization Matters

1. John E. English, A *Perspective on Infantry* (New York: Praeger, 1981), 67–70.

2. B. H. Liddell Hart, *The Future of Infantry* (London: Faber and Faber, 1933), 27.

3. Alistair Horne, *The Price of Glory* (New York: Penguin, 1964), 337, 342–44; English, *Perspective*, 24.

4. English, *Perspective*, 26.

5. Barry R. Posen, *The Sources of Military Doctrine* (Ithaca, N.Y.: Cornell University Press, 1984), 182–88.

6. English, *Perspective*, 24, 64; Len Deighton, *Blitzkrieg* (New York: Alfred A. Knopf, 1980), 143.

7. Martin van Creveld, *Fighting Power* (Westport, Conn.: Greenwood Press, 1982), 36.

8. General von Lossow, quoted in Creveld, *Fighting Power*, 36.

9. Creveld, *Fighting Power*, 62.

10. Ibid., 132, 137.

11. Quoted in ibid., 28–29 (emphasis in the original).

12. Ibid., 114.

13. Ibid., 115.

14. Edward A. Shils and Morris Janowitz, "Cohesion and Disintegration in the Wehrmacht in World War II," *Public Opinion Quarterly* 12 (1948): 280–315.

15. Creveld, *Fighting Power*, 45.

16. Ibid., 75–76.

17. Ibid., 163–64.

18. John J. DiIulio, Jr., *Governing Prisons* (New York: Free Press, 1987), 162.

19. Quoted in ibid., 162.

20. Quoted in ibid., 162–63.

21. Ibid., 169–70.

22. Quoted in ibid., 254.

23. Ibid., figure 3.1.

24. Ibid., 140.
25. Ruiz v. Estelle, 503 F. Supp. 1265 (1980).
26. DiIulio, *Governing Prisons,* 322–27.
27. Sara Lawrence Lightfoot, *The Good High School* (New York: Basic Books, 1983), chap. 1.
28. Gwendolyn J. Cooke, "Striving for Excellence Against the Odds: A Principal's Story," *Journal of Negro Education* 54 (1985): 366.
29. Kenneth Tewel, "The Best Child I Ever Had: An Examination of Sources of Influence on the Decision-Making of the Principals of Three Urban High Schools in Crisis," Ph.D. diss., Union for Experimenting Colleges and Universities, Cincinnati, Ohio (1985).
30. Robert E. Klitgaard, "Going Beyond the Mean in Educational Evaluation," *Public Policy* 23 (1975): 59–79.
31. James S. Coleman et al., *Equality of Educational Opportunity,* 2 vols. (Washington, D.C.: United States Office of Education, 1966); Christopher S. Jencks et al., *Inequality* (New York: Harper & Row, 1972).
32. J. S. Coleman, T. Hoffer, and S. Kilgore, *High School Achievement* (New York: Basic Books, 1982).
33. Ibid., chap. 6, esp 176–77.
34. Ibid., 178.
35. Michael Rutter et al., *Fifteen Thousand Hours* (Cambridge, Mass.: Harvard University Press, 1979).
36. Lawrence C. Stedman, "A New Look at the Effective Schools Literature," *Urban Education* 20 (1985): 305; S. C. Purkey and M. S. Smith, "Effective Schools: A Review," *Elementary School Journal* 83 (1983): 427–52.
37. Stedman, "New Look."
38. Herbert A. Simon, *Administrative Behavior,* 3d ed. (New York: Free Press, 1976), xvi.
39. Ibid.
40. Chester I. Barnard, *The Functions of the Executive* (Cambridge, Mass.: Harvard University Press, 1968), 72 (first published in 1938).
41. Edward C. Banfield, "Ends and Means in Planning," in E. Banfield, *Here the People Rule* (New York: Plenum Press, 1985), 171–81.
42. Posen, *Sources,* 208–13.

Chapter 3. Circumstances

1. James Q. Wilson, *The Investigators* (New York: Basic Books, 1978), 180.
2. Carl Brauer, "Tenure, Turnover, and Post-Government Employment Trends of Presidential Appointees," Kennedy School of Government, Harvard University (November 1985).
3. Paul Light, *Artful Work* (New York: Random House, 1985), 36.
4. Martha Derthick, *Agency Under Stress* (Washington, D.C.: Brookings Institution, forthcoming).
5. General Accounting Office, "Social Security Administration: Stable Leadership and Better Management Needed to Improve Effectiveness," report to Congress GAO-HRD-87-39, March 1987, chap. 2.
6. John T. Tierney, *Postal Reorganization* (Boston: Auburn House, 1981), esp. chaps, 3, 4, and 5.
7. James Q. Wilson, *Varieties of Police Behavior* (Cambridge, Mass.: Harvard University Press, 1968), 30. See also Michael Banton, *The Policeman in the Community* (London: Tavistock, 1964), 168.
8. Wilson, *Varieties,* 18–19. See also Elaine Cumming, Ian Cumming, and Laura Edell, "Policeman as Philosopher, Guide and Friend," *Social Problems* 12 (1965): 276–86.
9. Vera Institute of Justice, *Felony Arrests: Their Prosecution in New York City's Courts* (New York: Vera Institute of Justice, 1977); Wilson, *Varieties of Police Behavior,* 24–25.
10. Jerome H. Skolnick, *Justice Without Trial* (New York: John Wiley & Sons, 1966), 42–48.
11. William K. Muir, *Police: Streetcorner Politicians* (Chicago: University of Chicago Press, 1977).

12. Gresham M. Sykes, *The Society of Captives* (Princeton, N.J.: Princeton University Press, 1958).

13. Ivan Belknap, *Human Problems of a State Mental Hospital* (New York: McGraw-Hill, 1956).

14. Willard Waller, *The Sociology of Teaching* (New York: John Wiley & Sons, 1932).

15. Charles Bidwell summarizes these studies in "The School as a Formal Organization," in James G. March, ed., *Handbook of Organizations* (Chicago: Rand McNally & Co., 1965), 972–1022.

16. Michael Lipsky, *Street-Level Bureaucracy* (New York: Russell Sage Foundation, 1980), esp. chap. 2.

17. Donald P. Warwick, *A Theory of Public Bureaucracy: Politics, Personality, and Organization in the State Department* (Cambridge, Mass.: Harvard University Press, 1975), 85.

18. Warwick, *Theory*, 85. See also John Franklin Campbell, *The Foreign Affairs Fudge Factory* (New York: Basic Books, 1971), esp. chaps. 1, 2, 5.

19. Warwick, *Theory*, 86.

20. U.S. Department of State, *Diplomacy for the 70s* (Washington, D.C.: U.S. Department of State, 1970), quoted in Warwick, *Theory*, 86.

21. Wilson, *Varieties*, 49.

22. John Mendeloff, *Regulating Safety: An Economic and Political Analysis of Occupational Safety and Health Policy* (Cambridge, Mass.: MIT Press, 1979), 41.

23. Cf. David P. McCaffrey, *OSHA and the Politics of Health Regulation* (New York: Plenum Press, 1982).

24. Steven Kelman, "Occupational Safety and Health Administration," in James Q. Wilson, ed., *The Politics of Regulation* (New York: Basic Books, 1980), 236–66; Kelman, *Regulating America, Regulating Sweden* (Cambridge, Mass.: MIT Press, 1981).

25. Martin van Creveld, *Command in War* (Cambridge, Mass.: Harvard University Press, 1985), chap. 7; Richard A. Gabriel and Paul L. Savage, *Crisis in Command* (New York: Hill and Wang, 1978).

26. Andrew F. Krepinevich, Jr., *The Army in Vietnam* (Baltimore, Md.: Johns Hopkins University Press, 1986), 174.

27. John Keegan, *The Face of Battle* (New York: Random House/Vintage, 1976), 173.

28. Ibid., 181–82, 241, 326.

29. Samuel A. Stouffer, *Communism, Conformity, and Civil Liberties* (Garden City, N.Y.: Doubleday, 1955).

30. Keegan, *Face of Battle*, 179–83.

31. Ibid., 189.

32. Ibid., 272–79.

33. William Darryl Henderson, *Cohesion: The Human Element in Combat* (Washington, D.C.: National Defense University Press, 1985); Gabriel and Savage, *Crisis in Command*, chap. 2.

34. Guenter Lewy, *America in Vietnam* (New York: Oxford University Press, 1978), 153–61.

35. Ibid., 159; Charles C. Moskos, Jr., "The American Combat Soldier in Vietnam," *Journal of Social Issues* 31 (1975): 32.

36. Lewy, *America in Vietnam*, 156.

37. Alvin W. Gouldner, *Patterns of Industrial Bureaucracy* (New York: Free Press, 1954), 113–16, 134–36, 146–54. Quote on p. 147.

38. James Q. Wilson, *The Investigators* (New York: Basic Books, 1978), 152.

39. F. J. Roethlisberger and William J. Dickson, *Management and the Worker* (New York: John Wiley & Sons, 1964), chap. 18 (first published in 1939).

Chapter 4. Beliefs

1. Richard Nathan, *The Plot That Failed* (New York: John Wiley & Sons, 1975), chaps. 3, 4.

2. J. Donald Kingsley, *Representative Bureaucracy* (Yellow Springs, Ohio: Antioch Press, 1944).

3. Icek Ajzen and Martin Fishbein, "Attitude-Behavior Relations: A Theoretical Analysis and Review of Empirical Research," *Psychological Bulletin* 84 (1977): 888.

4. Allan W. Wicker, "Attitudes versus Actions: The Relationship of Verbal and Overt Behavioral Responses to Attitude Objects," *Journal of Social Issues* 25 (1969): 75.

5. Jeffrey Manditch Prottas, *People-Processing* (Lexington, Mass.: D. C. Heath/Lexington Books, 1979), 24.

6. Tana Pesso, "Local Welfare Offices: Managing the Intake Process," *Public Policy* 26 (1978): 305–30, esp. 324.

7. Ibid.

8. Prottas, *People-Processing,* 38–41.

9. Donald J. Black and Albert J. Reiss, Jr., "Police Control of Juveniles," *American Sociological Review* 35 (1970): 63–77.

10. James J. Fyfe, "Geographic Correlates of Police Shootings: A Microanalysis," *Journal of Research in Crime and Delinquency* 17 (1980): 101–13; Fyfe, "Officer Race and Police Shooting," paper delivered at the annual meeting of The American Society of Criminology (November 1979).

11. Catherine H. Milton et al., *Police Use of Deadly Force* (Washington, D.C: Police Foundation, 1977).

12. Victor H. Vroom, *Work and Motivation* (New York: John Wiley & Sons, 1964); A. H. Brayfield and W. H. Crockett, "Employee Attitudes and Employee Performance," *Psychological Bulletin* 52 (1955): 396–424; L. W. Porter and R. M. Steers, "Organizational, Work, and Personal Factors in Employee Turnover and Absenteeism," *Psychological Bulletin* 80 (1973): 151–76; Wicker, "Attitudes versus Actions"; Ajzen and Fishbein, "Attitude-Behavior Relations."

13. Herbert A. Simon, "The Birth of an Organization," in Simon, ed., *Administrative Behavior,* 3d ed. (New York: Free Press, 1976), 318 (first published in *Public Administration Review* 13 [1953]: 227–36).

14. Ibid., 317–18.

15. Ibid., 322.

16. U.S. Senate, Select Committee to Study Governmental Operations with Respect to Intelligence Activities (hereinafter cited as "Church Committee Report"), *Final Report,* vol. 4, "History of the Central Intelligence Agency" (Washington, D.C.: Government Printing Office, 1976), 8–9; see also R. Harris Smith, *OSS* (Berkeley, Calif.: University of California Press, 1972), chap. 11.

17. Church Committee Report, 28.

18. Ibid., 4.

19. Ibid., 92.

20. John Ranelagh quotes Frank Wisner, an early leader of covert operations, as describing the CIA analysts as "a bunch of old washerwomen exchanging gossip while they rinse through the dirty linen." *The Agency: The Rise and Decline of the CIA* (New York: Simon & Schuster, 1986), 135. Richard Helms, who knew Wisner well, doubts he ever said such a thing. (Private communication.) Since Wisner is dead, the matter cannot be resolved. But on the general pecking order, see Robin W. Winks, *Cloak and Gown* (New York: William Morrow & Co., 1987), 383–88.

21. Ranelagh, *The Agency,* 116–21, 218–19; Church Committee Report, 92; Rhodri Jeffreys-Jones, *The CIA and American Democracy* (New Haven, Conn.: Yale University Press, 1989), 68; Thomas Troy, *Donovan and the CIA* (Frederick, Md.: University Publications of America, 1981), 8.

22. Arthur T. Hadley, *The Straw Giant* (New York: Random House, 1986), 67–73.

23. Robert A. Katzmann, *Regulatory Bureaucracy: The Federal Trade Commission and Antitrust Policy* (Cambridge, Mass.: MIT Press, 1980), chaps. 1, 2.

24. Ibid., chaps. 4, 5. A comparable analysis of the differing perspectives and roles on lawyers and economists in the FTC can be found in Kenneth W. Clarkson and Timothy J. Muris, *The Federal Trade Commission since 1970* (Cambridge: Cambridge University Press, 1981), 293–94, 298–303; and in Robert A. Rogowsky, "The Pyrrhic Victories of Section 7: A Political Economy Approach," in R. J. Mackay, J. C. Miller III, and B. Yandle, eds., *Public Choice and Regulation: A View from Inside the Federal Trade Commission* (Stanford, Calif.: Hoover Institution Press, 1987), 220–39.

25. Katzmann, *Regulatory Bureaucracy*, 40, 50.

26. Arthur Maass, "U. S. Prosecution of State and Local Officials for Political Corruption," *Publius* 17 (1987): 195–230, esp. 223–25.

27. Charles Pruitt, "People Doing What They Do Best: The Professional Engineers and NHTSA," *Public Administration Review* 39 (July-August 1979): 363–71.

28. Malcolm McConnell, A *Major Malfunction* (Garden City, N.Y.: Doubleday, 1987), 187.

29. Prottas, *People-Processing*, 39.

30. Herbert Kaufman, *The Forest Ranger* (Baltimore, Md.: Johns Hopkins University Press, 1981), 68.

31. Paul J. Culhane, *Public Lands Politics* (Baltimore, Md.: Johns Hopkins University Press, 1981), 326.

32. Ronald A. Foresta, *America's National Parks and Their Keepers* (Washington, D.C.: Resources for the Future, 1984), 16–18, 27–29.

33. Alston Chase, *Playing God in Yellowstone* (San Diego, Calif.: Harcourt Brace Jovanovich, 1987), 235, 243–44.

34. Ibid., 250–56, 382.

35. Ibid., 382.

36. Craig W. Allin, "Park Service v. Forest Service: Exploring the Differences in Wilderness Management," *Policy Studies Review* 7 (1987): 385–94.

37. *New York Times*, 22 September 1988, p. 1.

38. For a description and criticism of this planning, see Randall O'Toole, *Reforming the Forest Service* (Washington, D.C.: Island Press, 1988), chap. 11.

39. John Mendeloff, *Regulating Safety* (Cambridge, Mass.: MIT Press, 1979), 32–33; David P. McCaffrey, *OSHA and the Politics of Health Regulation* (New York: Plenum, 1982), 53–56.

40. Serge Taylor, *Making Bureaucracies Think* (Stanford, Calif.: Stanford University Press, 1984), 125.

41. Christopher K. Leman, *Managing the National Forests*, paper prepared for Resources for the Future (Washington, D.C., 1986), chap. 8.

42. Stanley Rothman and S. Robert Lichter, "How Liberal Are Bureaucrats?" *Regulation* (November-December 1983): 18.

43. Ibid.

44. Joel D. Aberbach and Bert A. Rockman, "Clashing Beliefs Within the Executive Branch: The Nixon Administration," *American Political Science Review* 70 (1976): 446–68.

45. Jeremy Rabkin, "Office for Civil Rights," in James Q. Wilson, ed., *The Politics of Regulation* (New York: Basic Books, 1980), 304–53.

46. Ibid., 333.

47. Terry Moe, "Interests, Institutions, and Positive Theory: The Politics of the NLRB," *Studies in American Political Development* 2 (1987): 236–99; and Moe, "Control and Feedback in Economic Regulation: The Case of the NLRB," *American Political Science Review* 79 (1985): 1094–116.

48. Richard Harris, *Coal Firms Under the New Social Regulation* (Durham, N.C.: Duke University Press, 1985), 37, 154–55.

49. Kenneth J. Meier, "Representative Bureaucracy: An Empirical Analysis," *American Political Science Review* 69 (1975): 526–42; K. Meier and Lloyd G. Nigro, "Representative Bureaucracy and Policy Preferences: A Study in the Attitudes of Federal Executives," *Public Administration Review* 36 (1976): 466–67.

50. Bernard Mennis, *American Foreign Policy Officials* (Columbus, Ohio: Ohio State University Press, 1971), chap. 5.

51. Charles T. Goodsell, *The Case for Bureaucracy*, 2nd ed. (Chatham, N.J.: Chatham House, 1985), 86.

52. Robert K. Merton, "Bureaucratic Structure and Personality," *Social Forces* 17 (1940): 560–68, reprinted in Merton, ed., *Reader in Bureaucracy* (New York: Free Press, 1952), 361–71.

53. W. Lloyd Warner et al., *The American Federal Executive* (New Haven, Conn.: Yale University Press, 1963), chap. 12.

54. Melvin J. Kohn, "Bureaucratic Man: A Portrait and an Interpretation," *American Sociological Review* 36 (1971): 461–74.

55. Goodsell, *Case for Bureaucracy*, 88–95.

56. Julius S. Brown, "Risk Propensity in Decision Making: A Comparison of Business and Public School Administrators," *Administrative Science Quarterly* 15 (1970): 473–81.

Chapter 5. Interests

1. Quoted in Paul K. Conkin, "Intellectual and Political Roots," in E. C. Hargrove and P. K. Conkin, eds., *TVA: Fifty Years of Grass-Roots Democracy* (Urbana, Ill.: University of Illinois Press, 1983), 28.

2. David E. Lilienthal, *TVA: Democracy on the March*, 2d ed. (New York: Harper, 1953).

3. John Ed Pearce, quoted in Dewey W. Grantham, "TVA and the Ambiguity of American Reform," in Hargrove and Conkin, eds., *TVA*, 327.

4. Rexford G. Tugwell and Edward C. Banfield, "Grass Roots Democracy—Myth or Reality?" *Public Administration Review* 10 (1950): 47–55.

5. Philip Selznick, *TVA and the Grass Roots* (Berkeley, Calif.: University of California Press, 1949).

6. Philip Selznick, *Leadership in Administration* (Evanston, Ill.: Row, Peterson, 1957), 42–45.

7. Avery Leiserson, "Administrative Management and Political Accountability," in Hargrove and Conkin, eds., *TVA*, 139; Conkin, "Intellectual and Political Roots," 30.

8. Richard Lowitt, "The TVA, 1933–45," in Hargrove and Conkin, eds., *TVA*, 41; William H. Droze, "The TVA, 1945–80: The Power Company," in Hargrove and Conkin, eds., *TVA*, 67–68.

9. William B. Wheeler and Michael J. McDonald, "The 'New Mission' and the Tellico Project, 1945–70," in Hargrove and Conkin, eds., *TVA*, 169.

10. Lynn Seeber, quoted in Droze, "The TVA," 80.

11. Marc J. Roberts and Jeremy S. Bluhm, *The Choices of Power* (Cambridge, Mass.: Harvard University Press, 1981), chap. 4.

12. Edward Mansfield, "Federal Maritime Commission," in James Q. Wilson, ed., *The Politics of Regulation* (New York: Basic Books, 1980), 49. The congressional view was expressed by the Antitrust Subcommittee of the House Judiciary Committee in its 1960 report, *The Ocean Freight Industry*, 87th Cong., 2d sess., 359.

13. Mansfield, "Federal Maritime Commission," 50.

14. Ibid., 64.

15. Quoted in ibid., 65.

16. Ibid., 65–68.

17. Paul J. Halpern, "Consumer Politics and Corporate Behavior: The Case of Automobile Safety," Ph.D. diss., Department of Government, Harvard University (1972).

18. Paul J. Quirk, "Food and Drug Administration," and Alfred Marcus, "Environmental Protection Agency," in Wilson, ed., *Politics of Regulation*, chaps. 6, 8.

19. Frank W. McCulloch and Tim Bornstein, *The National Labor Relations Board* (New York: Praeger, 1974); Seymour Scher, "Congressional Committee Members as Independent Agency Overseers," *American Political Science Review* 54 (1960): 911–20.

20. John A. Garraty, *The New Commonwealth, 1877–1890* (New York: Harper & Row, 1968); Edward A. Purcell, Jr., "Ideas and Interests: Businessmen and the Interstate Commerce Act," *Journal of American History* 54 (1967): 561–78; Robert W. Harbeson, "Railroads and Regulation, 1877–1916: Conspiracy or Public Interest?" *Journal of Economic History* 27 (1967): 230–42. These findings in my opinion demolish the argument that Congress gave to the railroads the state-supported cartel they sought, a view advanced in Gabriel Kolko, *Railroads and Regulation, 1877–1916* (Princeton, N.J.: Princeton University Press, 1965).

21. Suzanne Weaver, "Antitrust Division," in Wilson, ed., *Politics of Regulation*, 125; and Weaver, *Decision to Prosecute: Organization and Public Policy in the Antitrust Division* (Cambridge, Mass.: MIT Press, 1977). See also William Letwin, "Congress and the Sherman Antitrust Act," *University of Chicago Law Review* 23 (1955): 221–56; Hans B. Thorelli, *The Federal Antitrust Policy* (Baltimore, Md.: Johns Hopkins University Press, 1954); and Robert H. Bork, *The Antitrust Paradox* (New York: Basic Books, 1978), chap. 1.

22. Richard E. Caves, *Air Transport and Its Regulators* (Cambridge, Mass.: Harvard University Press, 1962), 433–49.
23. Quirk, "Food and Drug Administration," 207.
24. Ibid., 211–18.
25. Ibid., 217.
26. Graham K. Wilson, *The Politics of Safety and Health* (Oxford: Clarendon Press, 1985), 59–69; David P. McCaffrey, *OSHA and the Politics of Health Regulation* (New York: Plenum Press, 1982), 137–38, 160–61, 173–74.
27. John T. Scholz and Feng Heng Wei, "Regulatory Enforcement in a Federalist System," *American Political Science Review* 80 (1986): 1261.
28. McCaffrey, *OSHA*, 101–2.
29. Steven Kelman, "Occupational Safety and Health Administration," in James Q. Wilson, ed., *Politics of Regulation*, 250.
30. Weaver, "Antitrust Division," 134–40.
31. Ibid., 149. See also Robert M. Goolrick, *Public Policy Toward Corporate Growth: The ITT Merger Cases* (Port Washington, N.Y.: Kennikat Press, 1978). .
32. Kenneth W. Clarkson and Timothy J. Muris, eds., *The Federal Trade Commission Since 1970* (Cambridge: Cambridge University Press, 1981), 169–73.
33. Jeffrey M. Berry, *The Interest Group Society* (Boston: Little, Brown, 1984), 88; and Berry, *Lobbying for the People* (Princeton, N.J.: Princeton University Press, 1977).
34. Mansfield, "Federal Maritime Commission," 60–61.
35. Stephen Breyer, *Regulation and Its Reform* (Cambridge, Mass.: Harvard University Press, 1982), 320, 328.
36. Martha Derthick and Paul J. Quirk, *The Politics of Deregulation* (Washington, D.C.: The Brookings Institution, 1985), chap. 7.
37. Marcus, "Environmental Protection Agency," 267; Graham Wilson, *Politics of Safety*, 56–57.
38. Quoted in Quirk, "Food and Drug Administration," 216.
39. R. Shep Melnick provides a book-length account of the many ways in which almost every conceivable interest gets represented in environmental policy: *Regulation and the Courts* (Washington, D.C.: The Brookings Institution, 1983), 40.
40. Weaver, *Decision to Prosecute*, chap. 3; Robert A. Katzmann, *Regulatory Bureaucracy: The Federal Trade Commission* (Cambridge, Mass.: MIT Press, 1980), chap. 6.
41. Paul J. Quirk, *Industry Influence in Federal Regulatory Agencies* (Princeton, N.J.: Princeton University Press, 1981), 170. See also William D. Berry, "An Alternative to the Capture Theory of Regulation: The Case of State Public Utility Commissions," *American Journal of Political Science* 28 (1984): 524–58; and William T. Gormley, "A Test of the Revolving Door Hypothesis at the FCC," *American Journal of Political Science* 23 (1979): 665–83.
42. Quoted in Bradley Behrman, "Civil Aeronautics Board," in James Q. Wilson, ed., *Politics of Regulation*, 106.
43. Derthick and Quirk, *Deregulation*; and Derthick and Quirk, "Why the Regulators Chose to Deregulate," in R. G. Noll, ed., *Regulatory Policy and the Social Sciences* (Berkeley, Calif.: University of California Press, 1985), 214–44; Breyer, *Regulation and Its Reform*, 318–19.
44. Derthick and Quirk, *The Politics of Deregulation*, 74–85.
45. Derthick and Quirk, "Why the Regulators Chose to Deregulate," 221, 223.

Chapter 6. Culture

1. *Meeting the Espionage Challenge: A Review of United States Counterintelligence and Security Programs*, a report of the Select Committee on Intelligence, United States Senate, 99th Cong., 2d sess. (October 3, 1986), 34–35; *New York Times*, 3 April 1987, p. 1. A good journalistic account is Ronald Kessler, *Moscow Station* (New York: Charles Scribner's Sons, 1989).
2. Report from the General Accounting Office, Office of Special Investigations, to the Subcommittee on International Affairs, Committee on Foreign Affairs, U.S. House of Representatives, dated July 28, 1988.

3. Thomas J. Peters and Robert H. Waterman, Jr., *In Search of Excellence: Lessons from America's Best-Run Companies* (New York: Harper & Row, 1982).

4. For example, Yvan Allaire and Mihaela E. Firsirotu, "Theories of Organizational Culture," *Organization Studies* 5 (1984): 193–226; G. Hofstede, "Culture and Organization—A Literature Review Study," *Journal of Enterprise Management* 1 (1987): 127–35; Lynne G. Zucker, "Organizations as Institutions," *Research in the Sociology of Organizations* 2 (1983): 1–47; Edgar H. Schein, *Organizational Culture and Leadership* (San Francisco: Jossey-Bass, 1985); Linda Smircich, "Concepts of Culture and Organizational Analysis," *Administrative Science Quarterly* 28 (1983): 339–58; Vijay Sathe, *Culture and Related Corporate Realities* (Homewood, Ill.: Richard D. Irwin, 1985); William Ouchi and Alan L. Wilkins, "Organizational Culture," *Annual Review of Sociology* 11 (1985): 457–83.

5. Chester I. Barnard, *The Functions of the Executive* (Cambridge, Mass.: Harvard University Press, 1938), 279.

6. Philip Selznick, *Leadership in Administration* (Evanston, Ill.: Row, Peterson & Co., 1957), chap. 2, esp. 38, 40, 42.

7. The Hawthorne findings are summarized in F. J. Roethlisberger and William J. Dickson, *Management and the Worker* (Cambridge, Mass.: Harvard University Press, 1939). Among the critiques are Alex Carey, "The Hawthorne Studies: A Radical Critique," *American Sociological Review* 32 (1967): 403–16; Richard Herbert Franke and James D. Kaul, "The Hawthorne Experiments: First Statistical Interpretation," *American Sociological Review* 43 (1978): 623–43. Rejoinders can be found in Robert Schlaifer, "The Relay Assembly Test Room: An Alternative Statistical Interpretation," *American Sociological Review* 45 (1980): 995–1005; and Jeffrey A. Sonnenfeld, "Clarifying Critical Confusion in the Hawthorne Hysteria," *American Psychologist* 37 (1982): 1397–99.

8. For example, Richard M. Weiss and Lynn E. Miller, "The Rediscovery of Organizational Culture," Working Paper MG85-02, University of Delaware.

9. Roger Brown and Richard J. Herrnstein, *Psychology* (Boston: Little, Brown, 1975), 529.

10. Secretary of State's Advisory Panel on Overseas Security, *Report* (June 1985), esp. 18–20.

11. Donald P. Warwick, *A Theory of Public Bureaucracy* (Cambridge, Mass.: Harvard University Press, 1975), 29; Gordon Tullock, *The Politics of Bureaucracy* (Washington, D.C.: Public Affairs Press, 1965), 40–43, 168–69.

12. John Ensor Haar, *The Professional Diplomat* (Princeton, N.J.: Princeton University Press, 1969), 141–45; Andrew M. Scott, "Environmental Change and Organizational Adaptation: The Problem of the State Department," *International Studies Quarterly* 14 (1970): 85–94; and Scott, "The Department of State: Formal Organization and Informal Culture," *International Studies Quarterly* 13 (1969): 1–18.

13. Warwick, *Theory*, 30–31.

14. Chris Argyris, *Some Causes of Organizational Ineffectiveness Within the Department of State* (Washington, D.C.: Center for International Systems Research, Department of State, 1967), 37–38, cited in Warwick, *Theory*, 31.

15. Selznick, *Leadership*, 42, 62.

16. Morton H. Halperin, *Bureaucratic Politics and Foreign Policy* (Washington, D.C.: Brookings Institution, 1974), 28.

17. Jonathan B. Bendor, *Parallel Systems: Redundancy in Government* (Berkeley, Calif.: University of California Press, 1985), 254–55.

18. Jerry L. Mashaw, *Bureaucratic Justice* (New Haven, Conn.: Yale University Press, 1983), 216.

19. Robert F. Durant, *When Government Regulates Itself* (Knoxville, Tenn.: University of Tennessee Press, 1985).

20. Martha Derthick, *Policymaking for Social Security* (Washington, D.C.: Brookings Institution, 1979), 27–32.

21. Arthur L. Stinchcombe, "Social Structure and Organizations," in James G. March, ed., *Handbook of Organizations* (Chicago: Rand McNally, 1965), 142–93.

22. James Q. Wilson, *Political Organizations* (New York: Basic Books, 1973), chaps. 4, 5.

23. John R. Kimberly, "Environmental Constraints and Organizational Structure," *Administrative Science Quarterly* 20 (1975): 1–9. See also Kimberly and Robert H. Miles, eds., *The Organizational Life Cycle* (San Francisco, Calif.: Jossey-Bass, 1980).

24. Herbert Kaufman, *The Forest Ranger* (Baltimore, Md.: Johns Hopkins University Press, 1960).
25. Ibid., chap. 6.
26. Ibid., 168–69.
27. Ibid., 145.
28. Paul J. Culhane, *Public Lands Politics* (Baltimore, Md.: Johns Hopkins University Press, 1981), 232.
29. Thomas Gid Powers, *Secrecy and Power: The Life of J. Edgar Hoover* (New York: Free Press, 1987), chaps. 3, 4.
30. Sanford J. Ungar, *FBI* (Boston: Little, Brown, 1975), 59.
31. James Q. Wilson, *The Investigators* (New York: Basic Books, 1978), chap. 5.
32. Ibid., 23–39.
33. Mohammad Al-Saud, "The Field Representatives: A Case Study of Administrative Control in the U.S. Army Corps of Engineers," Ph.D. diss., Department of Government, Harvard University (1987).
34. Ibid., chap. 4.
35. Ibid., chap. 5 and 136–37, 191–216.
36. Derthick, *Policymaking,* 21.
37. A paraphrase of Eveline M. Burns, quoted in Derthick, *Policymaking,* 23.
38. Derthick, *Policymaking,* 31, and Mashaw, *Bureaucratic Justice,* 216.
39. Derthick, *Policymaking,* 30.
40. Martha Derthick, *Agency Under Stress: The Social Security Administration and American Government* (Washington, D.C.: Brookings Institution, forthcoming), chap. 2.
41. Robert M. Gates, "The CIA and Foreign Policy," *Foreign Affairs* 66 (1987): 223.
42. John Walcott, "War of the Spies," *Wall Street Journal,* 27 November 1987, pp. 1ff; George Kalaris and Leonard McCoy, "Counterintelligence," in Roy Godson, ed., *Intelligence Requirements for the 1990s* (Lexington, Mass.: D. C. Heath/Lexington Books, 1989), 127–45.
43. Robin W. Winks, *Cloak & Gown: Scholars in the Secret War, 1939–1961* (New York: William Morrow, 1987), 430–31. See also John Ranelagh, *The Agency: The Rise and Decline of the CIA* (New York: Simon & Schuster, 1986), chap. 16. For a defense of Angleton, see Edward Jay Epstein, *Deception: The Invisible War Between the KGB and the CIA* (New York: Simon & Schuster, 1989).
44. The Colby instruction was found in the U.S. embassy files in Teheran that were seized by the Khomeini radicals; it is reported in Edward Jay Epstein, "Secrets from the CIA Archive in Teheran," *Orbis* 31 (1987): 36.
45. *Washington Post,* 27 July 1987; *Foreign Report,* 20 August 1987; Jack Anderson and Dale Van Atta columns in *Washington Post,* 21 March and 23 March 1988; Walcott, "War of the Spies."
46. Bendor, *Parallel Systems,* chap. 5, esp. 186, 189, 193, 205.
47. Presidential Commission on the Space Shuttle Challenger Accident, *Report to the President* (Washington, D.C., 1986), 171. (Hereinafter, "Rogers Commission Report.")
48. Ibid., 172.
49. Quoted in Malcolm McConnell, *Challenger: A Major Malfunction* (Garden City, N.Y.: Doubleday, 1987), 187.
50. Rogers Commission Report, chaps. 5–8.
51. Washington, D.C.: Brookings Institution, 1974.
52. Arthur T. Hadley, *The Straw Giant* (New York: Random House, 1986), 35.
53. Halperin, *Bureaucratic Politics,* 41.
54. Christopher K. Leman, "Managing the National Forests: The Forest Service, a Bureaucracy that Still Works," unpub. manuscript, Resources for the Future, Washington, D.C. (1986), chap. 8.
55. Ibid.
56. Ibid., citing U.S. Forest Service, *Employee Survey, Region 6* (1984), 12, 14–15, and Forest Service, *Report on Mineral Careers in the Forest Service* (September 1981).
57. Wilson, *The Investigators,* chap. 2.
58. Marc Tipermas, "Jurisdictionalism: The Politics of Executive Reorganization," Ph.D. diss., Department of Government, Harvard University (1976), 205.
59. Ibid., 158.

Chapter 7. Constraints

1. "The Registry of Motor Vehicles: Watertown Branch," Case number C16-84-580, prepared at the John F. Kennedy School of Government, Harvard University, 1984.
2. John F. Love, *McDonald's: Behind the Arches* (New York: Bantam Books, 1986), 140ff.
3. Max Weber, *Economy and Society*, ed. Guenther Roth and Claus Wittich (New York: Bedminster Press, 1968), vol. 3, chaps. 11 and 12.
4. William A. Niskanen, Jr., *Bureaucracy and Representative Government* (Chicago: Aldine-Atherton, 1971), chaps. 2–4.
5. James S. Coleman, Thomas Hoffer, and Sally Kilgore, *High School Achievement* (New York: Basic Books, 1982).
6. John E. Chubb and Terry M. Moe, "No School Is an Island: Politics, Markets, and Education," *The Brookings Review* (Fall 1986): 21–28.
7. Steven Kelman, *Procurement and Public Management* (forthcoming).
8. John T. Tierney, *The U.S. Postal Service* (Dover, Mass.: Auburn House, 1988), 101–2.
9. National Association of Greeting Card Publishers v. USPS, 103 U.S. 2727 (1983).
10. Tierney, *U.S. Postal Service*, 94–97.
11. John T. Tierney, *Postal Reorganization: Managing the Public's Business* (Boston: Auburn House, 1981), 67.
12. Ibid., 68–73.
13. Ibid., 72.
14. 18 *U.S. Code* 1696.
15. General Accounting Office, *Progress and Challenges at the Defense Logistics Agency*. GAO report NSIAD-86-64, Washington, D.C., 1986, p. 2.
16. Wendy T. Kirby, "Expanding the Use of Commercial Products and 'Commercial-Style' Acquisition Techniques in Defense Procurement: A Proposed Legal Framework." Appendix H in President's Blue Ribbon Commission on Defense Management (the "Packard Commission"), *A Quest for Excellence: Final Report*, June 1986.
17. I discuss these matters in chap. 17.
18. Kirby, "Expanding the Use," 106–7.
19. 41 *U.S. Code* 10(a).
20. Kirby, "Expanding the Use," 82–83, 91.
21. 10 *U.S. Code* 2305(a)(4)(6).
22. Kirby, "Expanding the Use," 92.
23. General Accounting Office, *Progress and Challenges*, 34.
24. 5 *U.S. Code* 552.
25. 5 *U.S. Code* 552a.
26. 5 *U.S. Code* 552(b).
27. 42 *U.S. Code* 4332(2)(c).
28. Steven Kelman, *Making Public Policy* (New York: Basic Books, 1987), 97.
29. Cf. Daniel A. Mazmanian and Jeanne Nienaber, *Can Organizations Change?* (Washington, D.C.: The Brookings Institution, 1979).
30. Robert A. Carp and Ronald Stidham, *The Federal Courts* (Washington, D.C.: CQ Press, 1985), 42.
31. David Street, Robert Vinter, and Charles Perrow, *Organization for Treatment* (New York: Free Press, 1966).
32. James Q. Wilson, *Varieties of Police Behavior* (Cambridge, Mass.: Harvard University Press, 1968), 70–71.
33. Mark A. Emmert and Michael M. Crow, "Public, Private and Hybrid Organizations," *Administration and Society* 20 (1988): 227. This finding calls into question the claim that there are no significant differences between public and private organizations in Barry Bozeman, *All Organizations Are Public* (San Francisco, Calif.: Jossey-Bass, 1987). Some findings similar to those of Emmert and Crow are in Hal G. Rainey, "Public Agencies and Private Firms," *Administration and Society* 15 (1983): 207–42.
34. Tierney, *U.S. Postal Service*, 52–57.
35. Quoted in Graham T. Allison, Jr., "Public and Private Management: Are They Fundamentally Alike in All Unimportant Respects?" in Frederick S. Lane, ed., *Current Issues in Public Administration*, 2d ed. (New York: St. Martin's Press, 1982), 13–33. The academic literature on public-private differences is summarized in Hal G. Rainey, Robert W. Backoff,

and Charles H. Levine, "Comparing Public and Private Organizations," *Public Administration Review* 36 (1976): 233–44.

36. John Kenneth Galbraith, *The New Industrial State*, 2d ed. (New York: New American Library, 1971), chaps. 7, 16–18. A more sophisticated version of the thesis that "all organizations are public" is Bozeman, *All Organizations Are Public*. Bozeman rightly calls attention to the many governmental and political constraints on firms without, I think, refuting the view that governmental agencies have some distinctive properties. Bozeman might prefer to say that the differences between firms and agencies are matters of degree, but in my view some degrees are so great as to constitute differences in kind.

37. Galbraith, *New Industrial State*, 46.

Chapter 8. People

1. Quoted in Larry J. Wilson, "The Navy's Experiment With Pay, Performance, and Appraisal," *Defense Management Journal* (Third Quarter, 1985): 30.

2. Quoted in ibid, 32.

3. The leading works are the meta-analyses by Hunter and Schmidt. See in particular J. E. Hunter and R. F. Hunter, "Validity and Utility of Alternate Predictors of Job Performance," *Psychological Bulletin* 96 (1984): 72–98; F. L. Schmidt and J. E. Hunter, "Development of a General Solution to the Problem of Validity Generalization," *Journal of Applied Psychology* 62 (1977): 529–40; J. E. Hunter, "Cognitive Ability, Cognitive Aptitudes, Job Knowledge, and Job Performance," *Journal of Vocational Behavior* 29 (1986): 340–62; J. E. Hunter, *Test Validation for 12,000 Jobs: An Application of Synthetic Validity and Validity Generalization to the General Aptitude Test Battery*, report prepared for the U.S. Employment Service of the U.S. Department of Labor (1980). The ability of cognitive tests to predict job performance is reviewed in a special issue of the *Journal of Vocational Behavior*; see especially the summary essay by Linda Gottfredson, "Societal Consequences of the g Factor in Employment," *Journal of Vocational Behavior* 29 (1986): 379–410.

4. Angel G. Luevano et al. v. Alan Campbell et al., Civil Action No. 79-0271, "Order Granting Final Approval to the Consent Decree," United States District Court for the District of Columbia (1979), p. 6. Hereinafter cited as "Decree."

5. Decree: 16.

6. General Accounting Office, *Federal Workforce: A Framework for Studying Its Quality Over Time*, report GAO/PEMD-88-27 (Washington, D.C.: GAO, August 1988). See also Carolyn Ban and Patricia W. Ingraham, "Retaining Quality Federal Employees: Life After PACE," *Public Administration Review* 48 (1988): 708–18.

7. U.S. Merit Systems Protection Board, *Federal Personnel Policies and Practices: Perspectives from the Workplace*, report to the President and the Congress, 1987, p. 17.

8. Career Entry Group, U.S. Office of Personnel Management, "Hiring Professionals for Federal Careers: An Historical Perspective and a Plan to Meet Future Staffing Needs," paper (February 1988): 10–11.

9. Patricia A. Harris, *The Effectiveness of Grade Point Average and Level of Education in Predicting Performance in the Workplace: A Lay Summary of Findings*, report OPRD-88-1 (Washington, D.C.: Office of Personnel Management, August 1988).

10. U.S. Civil Service Commission, Bureau of Policies and Standards, *Position Classification Standard for Electronics Engineering Series GS855* (February 1971): 15, 20, 25.

11. General Accounting Office, *Testimony of the Comptroller General on the Impact of the Senior Executive Service* (Washington, D.C.: Government Printing Office, 1983): 2.

12. *Organizational Assessments of the Effects of Civil Service Reform*, Third Year Report for Fiscal Year 1982, submitted to the U.S. Office of Personnel Management by the Department of Organizational Behavior, Weatherhead School for Management, Case Western Reserve University (Contract OPM-23-80): 170–74.

13. *Organizational Assessments of the Effects of Civil Service Reform*, Third Year Report for Fiscal Year 1982, submitted to the U.S. Office of Personnel Management by the Institute for Social Research, University of Michigan (Contract OPM-22-80): 240–58.

14. U.S. Merit Systems Protection Board, *A Study of Cases Decided by the U.S. Merit Systems Protection Board in Fiscal Year 1987*, a report to the president and Congress, n.d.

15. Ibid.

16. Data supplied by the Office of Personnel Management.

17. Office of Personnel Management, "Proposed Demonstration Project: An Integrated Approach to Pay, Performance Appraisal, and Position Classification for More Effective Operation of Government Organizations," *Federal Register* 45 (April 18, 1980): 26504–44.

18. Wilson, "The Navy's Experiment."

19. Brigitte W. Schay, "Effects of Performance-Contingent Pay on Employee Attitudes," *Public Personnel Management* 17 (1988): 244, 248; Office of Personnel Management (OPM), "A Summary Assessment of the Navy Demonstration Project," Management Report 9 (unpub. report of the Research and Demonstration Staff, Office of Personnel Management, February 1986), 41; OPM, "Turnover in the Navy Demonstration Laboratories, 1980–1985," Management Report 11 (December 1988); OPM, "Effects of Performance-Based Pay on Employees in the Navy Demonstration Project," Management Report 12 (December 1988).

20. Ibid., 41–42.

21. Office of Personnel Management, "Salary Costs and Performance-Based Pay Under the Navy Personnel Management Demonstration Project: 1986 Update," Management Report 10 (unpub. report of the Research and Demonstration Staff, Personnel Systems and Oversight Group), chap. 1.

22. Susan Kellam, "Remaking the Grade," *Government Executive* (November-December 1987): 14.

23. Quoted in ibid., 18.

24. Lawrence A. Cremin, *The Genius of American Education* (New York: Vintage Books, 1965), 104.

25. Richard F. Elmore and Milbrey Wallin McLaughlin, *Steady Work: Policy, Practice, and the Reform of American Education*, R-3574-NIE/RC (Santa Monica, Calif.: Rand, 1988), 34.

26. Ibid.

27. Linda Darling-Hammond and Barnett Berry, *The Evolution of Teacher Policy*, JRE-01 (Santa Monica, Calif.: Rand, 1988), 2.

28. Ibid., 4, 11, 15.

29. Ibid., 18.

30. Ibid., 23–30.

31. Ibid., 31–36.

32. Among these reports were: A *Nation Prepared: Teachers for the 21st Century* (New York: Carnegie Forum on Education and the Economy, 1986); *Tomorrow's Teachers* (East Lansing, Mich.: The Holmes Group, 1986); and A *Survey of State School Improvement Efforts* (Denver, Colo.: Education Commission of the States, 1983).

33. Darling-Hammond and Berry, *Evolution of Teacher Policy*, 5.

34. Elmore and McLaughlin, *Steady Work*, 41.

35. Arthur E. Wise et al., *Teacher Evaluation: A Study of Effective Practices*, R-3139-NIE (Santa Monica, Calif.: Rand, 1984), vi, 22–23.

36. Ibid., 66–80.

37. Timothy B. Clark and Marjorie Wachtel, "The Quiet Crisis Goes Public," *Government Executive* (June 1988): 14ff; and U.S. Merit Systems Protection Board, *Working for the Federal Government: Job Satisfaction and Federal Employees*, report to the president and Congress (October 21, 1987).

Chapter 9. Compliance

1. The path-breaking writings include Armen A. Alchian and Harold Demsetz, "Production, Information Costs, and Economic Organization," *American Economic Review* 62 (1972): 777–95; and Stephen A. Ross, "The Economic Theory of Agency: The Principal's Problem," *American Economic Review* 63 (1973): 134–39. Good overviews of the subject include Terry M. Moe, "The New Economics of Organization," *American Journal of Political Science* 28 (1984): 739–77; and John W. Pratt and Richard J. Zeckhauser, "Principals and Agents: An Overview," in Pratt and Zeckhauser, eds., *Principals and Agents: The Structure of Business* (Boston, Mass.: Harvard Business School Press, 1985), 1–35.

2. Jonathan Bendor, "Review Article: Formal Models of Bureaucracy," *British Journal of Political Science* 18 (1988): 353–95.
3. Hugh Heclo, A *Government of Strangers: Executive Politics in Washington* (Washington, D.C.: The Brookings Institution, 1977), chap. 4.
4. Gerald F. Linderman, *Embattled Courage: The Experience of Combat in the American Civil War* (New York: Free Press, 1987), esp. chap. 3.
5. Milton D. Morris, *Immigration: The Beleaguered Bureaucracy* (Washington, D.C.: The Brookings Institution, 1985), chap. 4. See also Thomas E. Ricks, "Tough Mandate," *Wall Street Journal*, 8 July 1987, p. 1.
6. Morris, *Immigration*, 131–32.
7. John T. Tierney, *The U.S. Postal Service* (Dover, Mass.: Auburn House, 1988), 68.
8. Tana Pesso, "Local Welfare Offices: Managing the Intake Process," *Public Policy* 26 (1978): 305–30.
9. Peter M. Blau, *The Dynamics of Bureaucracy* (Chicago: University of Chicago Press, 1955), 42–43, 50–51, 78–79.
10. Tierney, *U.S. Postal Service*, 68–70.
11. James Q. Wilson, *The Investigators: Managing FBI and Narcotics Agents* (New York: Basic Books, 1978), 98.
12. Ibid., 128–29.
13. Ibid., 128–32.
14. Steven Kelman, *Regulating America, Regulating Sweden* (Cambridge, Mass.: MIT Press, 1981), 1–5, 176–83.
15. Andrew Krepinevich, Jr., *The Army in Vietnam* (Baltimore, Md.: Johns Hopkins University Press, 1986), esp. chap. 10.
16. Carl von Clausewitz, *On War*, ed. and trans. by Michael Howard and Peter Paret (Princeton, N. J.: Princeton University Press, 1976), book I, chap. 7. (First published in 1832.)
17. Blau, *Dynamics*, 101–5. Blau's observations were confirmed and updated in John T. Tierney, "The Wage and Hour Division, U.S. Department of Labor," Department of Politics, Boston College (1975).
18. Suzanne Weaver, *Decision to Prosecute* (Cambridge, Mass.: MIT Press, 1977), chap. 5.
19. Mohammad Al-Saud, "The Field Representatives: A Case Study of Administrative Control in the U.S. Army Corps of Engineers," Ph.D. diss., Department of Government, Harvard University (1987), 3.
20. Herbert Kaufman, *The Forest Ranger* (Baltimore, Md.: Johns Hopkins University Press, 1960).
21. Arthur L. Stinchcombe, "Bureaucratic and Craft Administration of Production: A Comparative Study," *Administrative Science Quarterly* 4 (1959): 170.
22. Blau, *Dynamics*, 148–53.
23. Eric A. Hanushek, "Throwing Money at Schools," *Journal of Policy Analysis and Management* 1 (1981): 19–41.
24. Michael Lipsky, *Street-Level Bureaucracy* (New York: Russell Sage Foundation, 1980), chap. 2; Charles E. Bidwell, "The School as a Formal Organization," in James G. March, ed., *Handbook of Organizations* (Chicago: Rand McNally, 1965), 978–82, 986–88; James Q. Wilson, *Varieties of Police Behavior* (Cambridge, Mass.: Harvard University Press, 1968), 70–75.
25. James Q. Wilson and George L. Kelling, "Broken Windows: The Police and Neighborhood Safety," *Atlantic Monthly* (March 1982): 29–38 (reprinted in Wilson, *Thinking About Crime*, rev. ed. [New York: Basic Books, 1983], chap. 5); Mark H. Moore and George L. Kelling, "'To Serve and Protect': Learning From Police History," *Public Interest* (Winter 1983): 49–65.
26. James Q. Wilson and George L. Kelling, "Making Neighborhoods Safe," *Atlantic Monthly* (February 1989): 46–52.
27. Anthony Downs, *Inside Bureaucracy* (Boston: Little, Brown, 1967), 88.
28. Heclo, *Government of Strangers*, 148–53.
29. James Q. Wilson, "The Politics of Regulation," in Wilson, ed., *The Politics of Regulation* (New York: Basic Books, 1980), 374–82.
30. William G. Ouchi, "Markets, Bureaucracies, and Clans," *Administrative Science Quar-*

terly 25 (1980): 129–41. Ouchi borrows the concept of clan from Emile Durkheim, *The Division of Labor in Society*, trans. G. Simpson (New York: Free Press, 1933). Similar views are offered by Chester I. Barnard, *The Functions of the Executive* (Cambridge, Mass.: Harvard University Press, 1938), 148.

Chapter 10. Turf

1. Richard A. Stubbing, *The Defense Game* (New York: Harper & Row, 1986), 272.
2. Ibid., 293.
3. Morton H. Halperin, *Bureaucratic Politics and Foreign Policy* (Washington, D.C.: The Brookings Institution, 1974), 51.
4. Stubbing, *Defense Game*, chaps. 15, 16.
5. Sanford J. Ungar, *FBI* (Boston: Little, Brown, 1976), 421–25.
6. Ibid., 392–405.
7. Halperin, *Bureaucratic Power*, 37.
8. Ibid., 43. The emergence of a separate air force is described in Perry McCoy Smith, *The Air Force Plans for Peace, 1943–1945* (Baltimore, Md.: Johns Hopkins University Press, 1970).
9. Marc Tipermas, "Jurisdictionalism: The Politics of Executive Reorganization," Ph.D. diss., Department of Government, Harvard University (1976), 35, 76–81.
10. Ibid., 39–46, 67–76.
11. Ibid., 91.
12. Gordon Tullock, *The Politics of Bureaucracy* (Washington, D.C.: Public Affairs Press, 1965), 134–36; William A. Niskanen, Jr., *Bureaucracy and Representative Government* (Chicago: Aldine-Atherton, 1971), 42.
13. Chester I. Barnard, *The Functions of the Executive* (Cambridge, Mass.: Harvard University Press, 1938), 215.
14. Philip Selznick, *Leadership in Administration* (Evanston, Ill.: Row, Peterson & Co., 1957), 121.
15. Tipermas, "Jurisdictionalism," 159.
16. John Milton Cooper, Jr., "Gifford Pinchot Creates a Forest Service," in Jameson W. Doig and Erwin C. Hargrove, eds., *Leadership and Innovation* (Baltimore, Md.: Johns Hopkins University Press, 1987), 72–73.
17. Erwin C. Hargrove, "David Lilienthal and the Tennessee Valley Authority," in Doig and Hargrove, eds., *Leadership*, 47–54.
18. Eugene Lewis, "Admiral Hyman Rickover: Technological Entrepreneurship in the U.S. Navy," in Doig and Hargrove, eds., *Leadership*, 108–11.
19. My account here follows Cecilia Stiles Cornell and Melvyn P. Leffler, "James Forrestal: The Tragic End of a Successful Entrepreneur," in Doig and Hargrove, eds., *Leadership*, chap. 12, esp. pp. 386–94.
20. Smith, *Air Force*, chap. 2, esp. p. 19.
21. Stubbing, *Defense Game*, 139.
22. Ibid., 142.
23. Wesley Frank Crave and James Lea Cate, *The Army Air Forces in World War II*, vol. 1: *Plans and Early Operations: January 1939 to August 1942* (Chicago: University of Chicago Press, 1948), 514–33.
24. Eliot A. Cohen, "Learning from Failure: American Antisubmarine Warfare in 1942," U.S. Naval War College (January 1987), 50.
25. William E. Burrows, *Deep Black: Space Espionage and National Security* (New York: Random House, 1986), 202–13.
26. Ungar, *FBI*, 107.
27. Ibid., chap. 10, esp. pp. 224–26.
28. Arthur Maass and Myron B. Fiering, "Civil Works Externalities Assessment," paper prepared for the U.S. Army Corps of Engineers (DACW31-86-M-1111), April 1987.
29. Ungar, *FBI*, 398.
30. Mohammad Al-Saud, "The Field Representatives: A Case Study of Administrative

Control in the U.S. Army Corps of Engineers," Ph.D. diss., Department of Government, Harvard University (October 1987), 142.

31. Ibid., 145–46.

32. Thomas Hilton Hammond, "Jurisdictional Preferences and the Choice of Tasks: Political Adaptation by Two State Wildlife Departments," Ph.D. diss., Department of Political Science, University of California at Berkeley (1979), esp. 324–26.

33. U.S. Senate, Committee on Armed Services, *Defense Organization: The Need for Change*. Staff report to the committee, 99th Cong., 1st sess. (October 16, 1985), 173–74. A defense of the role of the Joint Chiefs of Staff prior to the 1986 reorganization can be found in the papers gathered in *JCS Reform: Proceedings of the Conference* (Newport, R.I.: U.S. Naval War College, 1985).

34. Arthur T. Hadley, *The Straw Giant* (New York: Random House, 1986), 129.

35. James Q. Wilson and Patricia Rachal, "Can the Government Regulate Itself?" *Public Interest* (Winter 1977): 7–8.

36. Pietro S. Nivola, *The Urban Service Problem* (Lexington, Mass.: D. C. Heath/Lexington Books, 1979), 142–44.

37. James Q. Wilson and Louise Richardson, "Public Ownership vs. Energy Conservation: A Paradox of Utility Regulation," *Regulation* (September-October, 1985), 13ff.

38. Marc J. Roberts and Jeremy S. Bluhm, *The Choices of Power: Utilities Face the Environmental Challenge* (Cambridge, Mass.: Harvard University Press, 1981), chaps. 4, 5 and p. 325; and Robert F. Durant, *When Government Regulates Itself: EPA, TVA, and Pollution Control in the 1970s* (Knoxville, Tenn.: University of Tennessee Press, 1985), 28, 36–44.

39. Durant, *When Government Regulates*, 69–72, 80–88.

40. Rochelle L. Stanfield, "Government Polluters," *National Journal* (March 28, 1987): 762–66.

41. John Anthony Wanat, "Patterns of Growth and Their Correlates in Selected Federal Agencies," Ph.D. diss., Department of Political Science, University of Illinois (1972), 239–40.

Chapter 11. Strategies

1. Michael Blumenthal, "Candid Reflections of a Businessman in Washington," *Fortune* (January 29, 1979): 39.

2. U.S. Bureau of the Census, *Statistical Abstract of the United States, 1987*, 510.

3. Herbert Kaufman, *Are Government Organizations Immortal?* (Washington, D.C.: The Brookings Institution, 1976), 34.

4. Blumenthal, "Candid Reflections," 36–37.

5. Hugh Heclo, *A Government of Strangers: Executive Politics in Washington* (Washington, D.C.: Brookings Institution, 1977), 36–41.

6. Ibid., 104.

7. Ibid., 99.

8. Graham K. Wilson, *The Politics of Safety and Health: Occupational Safety and Health in the United States and Britain* (Oxford: Clarendon Press, 1985), 61–62.

9. Jameson W. Doig and Erwin C. Hargrove, *Leadership and Innovation: A Biographical Perspective on Entrepreneurs in Government* (Baltimore, Md.: Johns Hopkins University Press, 1987).

10. Jameson W. Doig and Erwin C. Hargrove, "'Leadership' and Political Analysis," in Doig and Hargrove, eds., *Leadership*, 14–17.

11. James E. Webb, *Space Age Management: The Large-Scale Approach* (New York: Columbia University Press, 1969), 73–74, quoted in W. Henry Lambright, "James Webb and the Uses of Administrative Power," in Doig and Hargrove, eds., *Leadership*, 183.

12. Lambright, "James Webb," 194–200.

13. Malcolm McConnell, *Challenger: A Major Malfunction* (Garden City, N.Y.: Doubleday & Co., 1987), chap. 3; Joseph Trento, *Prescription for Disaster* (New York: Crown, 1987); Walter A. McDougall, . . . *the Heavens and the Earth: A Political History of the Space Age* (New York: Basic Books, 1985).

14. My account follows Cecilia Stiles Cornell and Melvyn P. Leffler, "James Forrestal: The Tragic End of a Successful Entrepreneur," in Doig and Hargrove, eds., *Leadership*, chap. 12.
15. Norton E. Long, "Power and Administration," *Public Administration Review* 2 (1949): 257–64.
16. Graham Allison, *Essence of Decision* (Boston: Little, Brown, 1971), 176–78. People I call executives and operators Allison calls chiefs and Indians.
17. Blumenthal, "Candid Reflections," 37.
18. The classic account of reputation as both a reward and a resource of political executives is Richard E. Neustadt, *Presidential Power* (New York: John Wiley, 1960), chap. 4.
19. Martha Derthick, *Agency Under Stress: The Social Security Administration and American Government* (Washington, D.C.: Brookings Institution, forthcoming), chap. 5.
20. Wilson, *Politics of Safety*, 66–69.
21. Philip B. Heymann, *The Politics of Public Management* (New Haven, Conn.: Yale University Press, 1987), 15–41.
22. Quoted in Richard A. Stubbing, *The Defense Game* (New York: Harper & Row, 1986), 371.
23. Nicholas Lemann, "The Peacetime War," *Atlantic Monthly* (October 1984): 82, quoted in Stubbing, *Defense Game*, 370.
24. Stubbing, *Defense Game*, chap. 19.
25. Ibid., chap. 17.
26. George D. Greenberg, "Governing HEW: Problems of Management and Control at the Department of Health, Education and Welfare," Ph.D. diss., Department of Government, Harvard University (June 1972). See also Greenberg, "Constraints on Management & Secretarial Behavior at HEW," *Polity* 13 (1980): 57–79.
27. Quoted in Stubbing, *Defense Game*, 265.
28. Ibid., chap. 15.
29. *Washington Post*, 14 June 1970, p. A9, quoted in Greenberg, "Governing HEW," 173.
30. Greenberg, "Governing HEW," 200.
31. John Gardner, *Excellent: Can We Be Equal and Excellent Too?* (New York: Harper & Row, 1961).
32. Greenberg, "Governing HEW," 184, 195, 204–16.
33. *Wall Street Journal*, 25 October 1977; Joseph A. Califano, Jr., *Governing America* (New York: Simon & Schuster, 1981).
34. William Kristol, "Can-Do Government: Three Reagan Appointees Who Made a Difference," *Policy Review* 31 (1985): 62–66.
35. Stubbing, *Defense Game*, 291.
36. Ibid., 309.
37. Irene S. Rubin, *Shrinking the Federal Government* (New York: Longman, 1985).
38. Ibid., 196.
39. Ibid., 198.
40. Blumenthal, "Candid Reflections," 40.
41. Eugene Lewis, *Public Entrepreneurship: Toward a Theory of Bureaucratic Political Power* (Bloomington, Ind.: Indiana University Press, 1980).
42. Ibid., 230.

Chapter 12. Innovation

1. Russell F. Weigley, *History of the United States Army*, rev. ed. (Bloomington, Ind.: Indiana University Press, 1984), see, for example, 461–64.
2. Kevin Patrick Sheehan, "Preparing for an Imaginary War? Examining Peacetime Functions and Changes of Army Doctrine," Ph.D. diss., Department of Government, Harvard University (April 1988), 352–53, 371–77, 395–96.
3. Ibid., 368.

4. Quoted in Stephen Rosen, "New Ways of War: Understanding Military Innovation," *International Security* 13 (1988): 159.

5. Rosen, "New Ways of War," 158–66. See also Jeter A. Isely and Philip A. Crowl, *The U.S. Marines and Amphibious War* (Princeton, N.J.: Princeton University Press, 1951), chaps. 1, 2.

6. Ibid.

7. Graham T. Allison, *Essence of Decision* (Boston: Little, Brown, 1971), 83.

8. G. F. R. Henderson, *The Science of War* (New York: Longmans, Green & Co., 1910), 403–4; David A. Armstrong, *Bullets and Bureaucrats: The Machine Gun and the United States Army, 1861–1916* (Westport, Conn.: Greenwood Press, 1982).

9. Harvey M. Sapolsky, "Organizational Structure and Innovation," *Journal of Business* 40 (1967): 497–510.

10. James Fallows, *National Defense* (New York: Random House, 1981), chap. 3, esp. 62–63; Ralph Lapp, *Arms Beyond Doubt: The Tyranny of Weapons Technology* (New York: Cowles Book Co., 1970), 31.

11. Charles Wolf, Jr., *Markets or Governments* (Cambridge, Mass.: MIT Press, 1988), 72–73.

12. Paul Noble Stockton, "Services and Civilians: Problems in the American Way of Developing Strategic Weapons," Ph.D. diss., Department of Government, Harvard University (July 1986), chap. 1.

13. Michael W. Kirst and Gail R. Meister, "Turbulence in American Secondary Schools: What Reforms Last?" *Curriculum Inquiry* 15 (1985): 169–86.

14. Ibid., 176–78.

15. James Q. Wilson, *The Investigators: Managing FBI and Narcotics Agents* (New York: Basic Books, 1978), 121, 195.

16. Edmund Beard, *Developing the ICBM* (New York: Columbia University Press, 1976), 61–62, 72–73, 97, 105, 153, 222.

17. Harvey M. Sapolsky, *The Polaris System Development* (Cambridge, Mass.: Harvard University Press, 1972), 15–18.

18. Rosen, "New Ways of War," 152. See also Clark G. Reynolds, *The Fast Carriers: The Forging of an Air Navy* (New York: McGraw-Hill, 1968), 14–21.

19. Rosen, "New Ways of War," 157.

20. Louis Morton, *War in the Pacific: Strategy and Command: The First Two Years* (Washington, D.C.: U.S. Army Office of the Chief of Military History, 1962), chap. 6.

21. For example, Lawrence B. Mohr, "Determinants of Innovation in Organizations," *American Political Science Review* 20 (1969): 111–26; George W. Downs, Jr., *Bureaucracy, Innovation, and Public Policy* (Lexington, Mass.: D. C. Heath, 1976), 117.

22. Jerald Hage and Robert Dewar, "Elite Values Versus Organizational Structure in Predicting Innovation," *Administrative Science Quarterly* 18 (1973): 279–90. For a review of the shortcomings of theories of innovation, see George W. Downs, Jr., and Lawrence B. Mohr, "Conceptual Issues in the Study of Innovation," *Administrative Science Quarterly* 21 (1976): 700–14.

23. Creveld, *Command in War*, 270.

24. Jonathan B. Bendor, *Parallel Systems: Redundancy in Government* (Berkeley, Calif.: University of California Press, 1985), 67.

25. Creveld, *Command in War*, 105–9.

26. Quoted in ibid., 108.

27. R. O. Carlson, "Succession and Performance Among School Superintendents," *Administrative Science Quarterly* 6 (1961): 210–27.

28. Donald B. Rosenthal and Robert L. Crain, "Structure and Values in Local Political Systems: The Case of Fluoridation Decisions," in James Q. Wilson, ed., *City Politics and Public Policy* (New York: John Wiley & Sons, 1968), 217–42.

29. James Q. Wilson, *Varieties of Police Behavior* (Cambridge, Mass.: Harvard University Press, 1968), 271–77.

30. Downs, *Bureaucracy*.

31. Wilson, *The Investigators*, 128–33, 221 n.1.

32. Philip B. Heymann, *The Politics of Public Management* (New Haven, Conn.: Yale University Press, 1987), 25.

33. Jerry L. Mashaw and David L. Harfst, "Regulation and Legal Culture: The Case of Motor Vehicle Safety," *Yale Journal on Regulation* 4 (1987): 272.

Chapter 13. Congress

1. Herbert Kaufman, *The Administrative Behavior of Federal Bureau Chiefs* (Washington, D.C.: Brookings Institution, 1981), 164.
2. Ibid., 47.
3. Matthew McCubbins and Thomas Schwartz, "Congressional Oversight Overlooked: Police Patrols Versus Fire Alarms," *American Journal of Political Science* 28 (1984): 164–79.
4. Martha Derthick, *Policymaking for Social Security* (Washington, D.C.: Brookings Institution, 1979), 349–68.
5. Murray J. Horn, "The Political Economy of Public Administration: Organization, Control and Performance of the Public Sector," Ph.D. diss., Kennedy School of Government, Harvard University (1988), 199 and chap. 15.
6. Carl R. Fish, *The Civil Service and Patronage* (Cambridge, Mass.: Harvard University Press, 1920), 217–18.
7. S. M. Milkis, "The New Deal, Administrative Reform, and the Transcendence of Partisan Politics," *Administration and Society* 18 (1987): 433–72.
8. Joel D. Aberbach and Bert A. Rockman, "From Nixon's Problem to Reagan's Achievement: The Federal Executive Reexamined," paper presented at the Hofstra Conference on the Presidency of Richard Nixon (November 1987).
9. Derthick, *Policymaking,* 348–49; R. Kent Weaver, *Automatic Government: The Politics of Indexation* (Washington, D.C.: Brookings Institution, 1988).
10. Woodrow Wilson, *Congressional Government* (New York: Meridian Books, 1956), 127 (first published in 1885).
11. Terry M. Moe, "The Politics of Bureaucratic Structure," in John E. Chubb and Paul E. Peterson, eds., *Can the Government Govern?* (Washington, D.C.: Brookings Institution, 1989), 276. See also Matthew D. McCubbins, Roger G. Noll, and Barry R. Weingast, "Administrative Procedures as Instruments of Political Control," *Journal of Law, Economics, and Organization* 3 (1987): 243–77.
12. James C. Miller III, when head of the Office of Management and Budget in the Reagan administration, ordered agency heads not to be guided by these nonstatutory documents emanating from committee staffs, but he was forced to back down by congressional pressure. *Washington Post,* 12 July 1988.
13. Joel D. Aberbach, "The Congressional Committee Intelligence System: Information, Oversight, and Change," *Congress and the Presidency* 14 (1987): 51–76.
14. Arthur Maass, *Congress and the Common Good* (New York: Basic Books, 1983), 121–23. See also Robert J. Art, "Congress and the Defense Budget: Enhancing Policy Oversight," *Political Science Quarterly* 100 (1985): 227–48.
15. *National Journal* (May 14, 1986): 1282. See also David C. Morrison, "Chaos on Capitol Hill," *National Journal* (September 27, 1986): 2302–7.
16. U.S. Senate Committee on Armed Services Staff, *Report to the Senate Committee on Armed Services* (October 16, 1985), 589, as reported and updated in *U.S. Defense Acquisition: A Process in Trouble* (Washington, D.C.: Center for Strategic and International Studies, March 1987), 15.
17. Ibid., 16.
18. Jeremy Rabkin, *Judicial Compulsions: How Public Law Distorts Public Policy* (New York: Basic Books, 1989), 250–55.
19. Graham K. Wilson, *The Politics of Safety and Health* (Oxford: Oxford University Press, 1985), 46.
20. Quoted in ibid., 39.
21. Ibid., 40.
22. Rep. James Florio (D., N.J.), quoted in Bruce Yandle, "Regulatory Reform and the Rent Seekers," in R. J. Mackay, J. C. Miller III, and B. Yandle, eds., *Public Choice & Regulation: A View from Inside the Federal Trade Commission* (Stanford, Calif.: Hoover Institution, 1987), 134.

23. Graham Wilson, *Politics of Safety*, 52.
24. James Q. Wilson, "The Politics of Regulation," in Wilson, ed., *The Politics of Regulation* (New York: Basic Books, 1980), 370–71.
25. R. Douglas Arnold, *Congress and the Bureaucracy* (New Haven, Conn.: Yale University Press, 1979), esp. at 214.
26. A useful review of pork barrel politics can be found in *National Journal* (October 24, 1987): 2581ff.
27. Maass, *Congress and the Common Good*, 69.
28. Richard F. Fenno, Jr., *The Power of the Purse: Appropriations Politics in Congress* (Boston: Little, Brown, 1966), 340.
29. Jonathan Bendor, Serge Taylor, and Roland Van Galen, "Bureaucratic Expertise versus Legislative Authority: A Model of Deception and Monitoring in Budgeting," *American Political Science Review* 79 (1985): 1041–60.
30. Barry R. Weingast and Mark J. Moran, "Bureaucratic Discretion or Congressional Control? Regulatory Policymaking by the Federal Trade Commission," *Journal of Political Economy* 91 (1983): 765–800; and Randall L. Calvert, Mark J. Moran, and Barry Weingast, "Congressional Influence Over Policy Making: The Case of the FTC," in M. McCubbins and T. Sullivan, eds., *Congress: Structure and Policy* (Cambridge: Cambridge University Press, 1987). Weingast also applied this perspective to the Securities and Exchange Commission in "The Congressional-Bureaucratic System: A Principal-Agent Perspective (With Applications to the SEC)," *Public Choice* 44 (1984): 147–91.
31. Timothy J. Muris, "Regulatory Policymaking at the Federal Trade Commission: The Extent of Congressional Control," *Journal of Political Economy* 94 (1986): 884–89.
32. I am indebted to the research of Robert Katzmann for these observations.
33. Terry M. Moe, "Congressional Control of the Bureaucracy: An Assessment of the Positive Theory of 'Congressional Dominance,'" paper presented to the annual meeting of the American Political Science Association (1985).
34. Moe, "Congressional Control of the Bureaucracy," 15.
35. Steven S. Smith and Christopher J. Deering, *Committees in Congress* (Washington, D.C.: Congressional Quarterly Press, 1984), 93–95, 99–100; and Richard F. Fenno, Jr., *Congressmen in Committees* (Boston: Little, Brown, 1973), 47–51.

Chapter 14. Presidents

1. President's Committee on Administrative Management, *Report* (Washington, D.C.: U.S. Government Printing Office, 1937), 5.
2. Daniel Patrick Moynihan, *Counting Our Blessings* (Boston: Atlantic/Little, Brown, 1980), 117–18.
3. Norman J. Ornstein et al., *Vital Statistics on Congress, 1984–1985 Edition* (Washington, D.C.: American Enterprise Institute, 1984), tables 5.2 and 5.5.
4. Quoted in Moynihan, *Counting Our Blessings*, 126.
5. The effort is described in Richard P. Nathan, *The Plot That Failed: Nixon and the Administrative Presidency* (New York: John Wiley, 1975).
6. William M. Lunch, *The Nationalization of American Politics* (Berkeley, Calif.: University of California Press, 1987), 88.
7. Terry M. Moe, "The Politicized Presidency," in John E. Chubb and Paul E. Peterson, eds., *The New Direction in American Politics* (Washington, D.C.: The Brookings Institution, 1985), 260; and Chester A. Newland, "Executive Office Policy Apparatus: Enforcing the Reagan Agenda," in L. M. Salamon and M. S. Lund, eds., *The Reagan Presidency and the Governing of America* (Washington, D.C.: Urban Institute Press, 1984).
8. Peter M. Benda and Charles H. Levine, "Reagan and the Bureaucracy," in Charles O. Jones, ed., *The Reagan Legacy: Promise and Performance* (Chatham, N.J.: Chatham House, 1988), 107–8.
9. Dom Bonafede, "A White House Tilt," *National Journal* (September 26, 1981): 1735, quoted in Lunch, *Nationalization*, 89.
10. Lunch, *Nationalization*, 88.
11. Laurence H. Silberman, "Toward Presidential Control of the State Department," *Foreign Affairs* (Spring 1979): 888–89.

12. Hoover Commission, *Report on Organization of the Executive Branch of Government* (New York: McGraw-Hill, 1949), 1–30.

13. Charles A. Bowsher, "Building Effective Public Management," *Bureaucrat* 13 (Winter, 1984–85): 26; and National Academy of Public Administration, *Revitalizing Federal Management: Managers and Their Overburdened Systems* (Washington, D.C.: NAPA, 1983).

14. Quoted in Nathan, *The Plot That Failed*, 52.

15. Frederick C. Mosher, "Analytical Commentary," in F. Mosher, ed., *Governmental Reorganizations: Cases and Commentary* (Indianapolis, Ind.: Bobbs-Merrill, 1967), 514. Another good analysis of reorganization efforts is Peter Szanton, *Federal Reorganization: What Have We Learned?* (Chatham, N.J.: Chatham House, 1981).

16. Patricia Rachal, *Federal Narcotics Enforcement: Reorganization and Reform* (Boston: Auburn House, 1982), 55. See also James Q. Wilson, *The Investigators: Managing FBI and Narcotics Agents* (New York: Basic Books, 1978), 183–89.

17. Perry McCoy Smith, *The Air Force Plans for Peace, 1943–1945* (Baltimore, Md.: Johns Hopkins University Press, 1970), esp. chap. 9.

18. I am grateful to Christopher Foreman for his careful analysis of the FAA issue in an unpublished memorandum. See also Emmette S. Redford, *Congress Passes the Federal Aviation Act of 1958* (Indianapolis, Ind.: Bobbs-Merrill [for the Inter-University Case Program], 1961); and *Congressional Quarterly Weekly Report* (April 23, 1988): 1104–5.

19. Harold Seidman and Robert Gilmour, *Politics, Position, and Power*, 4th ed. (New York: Oxford University Press, 1986), 219. I attribute the quotation to Seidman alone because it appeared in earlier editions of this fine book of which Seidman was sole author.

20. Basil J. F. Mott, *Anatomy of a Coordinating Council: Implications for Planning* (Pittsburgh: University of Pittsburgh Press, 1968).

21. Ibid., 189.

22. Ibid., 107–14.

23. Roger B. Porter, *Presidential Decision Making: The Economic Policy Board* (Cambridge, Mass.: Cambridge University Press, 1980).

24. Seidman and Gilmour, *Politics, Position, and Power*, 226.

25. Herman Miles Somers, *Presidential Agency: The Office of War Mobilization and Reconversion* (Cambridge, Mass.: Harvard University Press, 1950).

26. Benda and Levine, "Reagan and the Bureaucracy," 114–20.

27. National Security Act of 1947, as amended (50 U.S. Code 401), sec. 101.

28. President's Special Review Board, *Report* (Washington, D.C., February 26, 1987).

29. Ibid., pp. IV-1–IV-6.

30. Martin Landau, "Redundancy, Rationality, and the Problem of Duplication and Overlap," *Public Administration Review* 29 (1969): 346–58. One of Landau's students has taken an important step in trying to identify empirically the uses and limits of redundancy in government: Jonathan Bendor, *Parallel Systems: Redundancy in Government* (Berkeley: University of California Press, 1985). Another student has shown how independent agencies may coordinate their activities by informal arrangements rather than formal machinery: Donald Chisholm, *Coordination Without Hierarchy: Informal Structures in Multiorganizational Systems* (Berkeley: University of California Press, 1989).

31. Richard M. Pious, *The American Presidency* (New York: Basic Books, 1979), 232.

32. These and other strategies are discussed in ibid., 232–35.

33. Douglas Yates, *Bureaucratic Democracy* (Cambridge, Mass.: Harvard University Press, 1982), 139–43.

34. Martha Derthick, *Agency Under Stress: The Social Security Administration and American Government* (Washington, D.C.: Brookings Institution, forthcoming), chap. 3.

35. Dean Acheson, "Thoughts About Thought in High Places," *New York Times Magazine*, 11 October 1959, reprinted in Committee on Government Operations, U.S. Senate, *Organizing for National Security: Selected Materials*, 86th Cong., 2d sess. (1960), 174.

Chapter 15. Courts

1. Decatur v. Paulding, 39 U.S. 497 (1840), at 515–16.

2. Citizens to Preserve Overton Park v. Volpe, 401 U.S. 402 (1971).

3. Adams v. Richardson, 480 F.2d 1159 (1973).

4. Cf. Jeremy Rabkin, *Judicial Compulsions: How Public Law Distorts Public Policy* (New York: Basic Books, 1989), chap. 5, and Rabkin, "Office for Civil Rights," in James Q. Wilson, ed., *The Politics of Regulation* (New York: Basic Books, 1980), 304–53.

5. Frothingham v. Mellon, 262 U.S. 447 (1923).

6. United States v. SCRAP, 412 U.S. 669 (1973); note the dissent of Justice White at 723.

7. At the turn of the century, a standard text on administrative law put it this way: "The rule . . . is that in all matters that involve the exercise of discretion by a public officer no process of the court will go to control the exercise of that discretion." Bruce Wyman, *Principles of the Administrative Law Governing the Relations of Public Officers* (St. Paul, Minn.: Keefe-Davidson Co., 1903), 139, as quoted in Rabkin, *Judicial Compulsions*, 121.

8. Flast v. Cohen, 392 U.S. 83 (1968).

9. United States v. Richardson, 418 U.S. 166 (1974).

10. Warth v. Seldin, 422 U.S. 490 (1975).

11. Valley Forge Christian College v. Americans United for Separation of Church and State, 454 U.S. 464 (1982).

12. R. Shep Melnick, *Regulation and the Courts* (Washington, D.C.: Brookings Institution, 1983), 8.

13. Sierra Club v. Ruckelshaus, 344 F. Supp. 253 (1972); Melnick, *Regulation*, chap. 4.

14. Richard B. Stewart, "The Reformation of American Administrative Law," *Harvard Law Review* 88 (1975): 1667.

15. Donald N. Jensen and Thomas M. Griffin, "The Legalization of State Educational Policymaking in California," *Journal of Law and Education* 13 (1984): 32.

16. Robert C. Wood, quoted in Harold Seidman and Robert Gilmour, *Politics, Position, and Power*, 4th ed. (New York: Oxford University Press, 1986), 160–61.

17. 60 *U.S. Statutes* 243. See also Graham K. Wilson, *The Politics of Safety and Health* (Oxford: Clarendon Press of the Oxford University Press, 1985), 86.

18. Ibid., 105.

19. Ibid., 106.

20. Rabkin, *Judicial Compulsions*, 26.

21. Graham Wilson, *Politics of Safety*, 108.

22. Dry Color Manufacturers Association v. Department of Labor, 486 F.2d 98 (1973); Associated Industries of New York State v. U.S. Department of Labor, 487 F.2d 342 (1973); Graham Wilson, *Politics of Safety*, 107.

23. Rochelle L. Stanfield, "Resolving Disputes," *National Journal* (November 15, 1986): 2764.

24. Alfred Marcus, "Environmental Protection Agency," in James Q. Wilson, ed., *Politics of Regulation*, 288–94; Melnick, *Regulation*, 259–60, 380.

25. Melnick, *Regulation*, 280.

26. Pennsylvania Association for Retarded Children v. Commonwealth of Pennsylvania, 334 F. Supp. 1257 (1971).

27. David L. Kirp and Donald N. Jensen, "What Does Due Process Do?" *Public Interest* 73 (Fall 1983): 87–88.

28. Robert A. Katzmann, *Institutional Disability* (Washington, D.C.: Brookings Institution, 1986), 91–93, 98–100; quotation on 92.

29. Phillip J. Cooper, *Hard Judicial Choices* (New York: Oxford University Press, 1988), chap. 7.

30. Nathan Glazer, "Should Judges Administer Social Services?" *Public Interest* 50 (1978): 78.

31. Rabkin, *Judicial Compulsions*, 63.

32. Melnick, *Regulation*, 157.

33. For example, National Resources Defense Council v. Environmental Protection Agency, 478 F.2d 875 (1st Cir. 1973).

34. Melnick, *Regulation*, 162.

35. Ibid., 156.

36. Ibid., 190–92, 351–53.

37. Train v. National Resources Defense Council, 421 U.S. 60 (1975).

38. Quoted in Melnick, *Regulation*, 346.

39. Sierra Club v. Ruckelshaus, 344 F. Supp. 253 (1972).
40. Melnick, *Regulation*, 347–48.
41. Public Citizen Health Research Group v. Auchter, 554 F. Supp. 242 (1983).
42. Rabkin, *Judicial Compulsions*, 227–28.
43. Rabkin, "Office for Civil Rights," 349–51.
44. Jerry Mashaw, *Due Process in the Administrative State* (New Haven, Conn.: Yale University Press, 1985), 26.
45. Robert A. Katzmann, "Judicial Intervention and Organization Theory: Changing Bureaucratic Behavior and Policy," *Yale Law Journal* 89 (1980): 513–37. The case was Hart v. Community School Board, 383 F. Supp. 699 (1974).
46. Cf. Donald L. Horowitz, *The Courts and Social Policy* (Washington, D.C.: The Brookings Institution, 1977), 293–98; Alexander Bickel and Harry Wellington, "Legislative Purpose and the Judicial Process: The Lincoln Mills Case," *Harvard Law Review* 71 (1957): 1–39.
47. Melnick, *Regulation*, 387–89, 392–93.
48. Ibid., 393.
49. Ruiz v. Estelle, F. Supp. 1265 (1980).
50. John J. DiIulio, Jr., "Prison Discipline and Prison Reform," *Public Interest* 89 (Fall 1987): 71–90, esp. 87–88.
51. John J. DiIulio, Jr., *Governing Prisons: A Comparative Study of Correctional Management* (New York: Free Press, 1987).

Chapter 16. National Differences

1. Steven Kelman, *Regulating America, Regulating Sweden* (Cambridge, Mass.: MIT Press, 1981), 5, 81, 221.
2. Ibid., 197, 199.
3. Ibid., 187.
4. Ibid., 180–89.
5. Ibid., 176, 182–83, 191.
6. Ibid., 197, 204.
7. Ibid., 188–90.
8. Ibid., 203.
9. Ibid., 179.
10. Graham K. Wilson, *The Politics of Safety and Health* (Oxford: Clarendon Press, 1985), 129–30.
11. David Vogel, *National Styles of Regulation* (Ithaca, N.Y.: Cornell University Press, 1986), esp. chap. 2.
12. Ronald Brickman, Sheila Jasanoff, and Thomas Ilgen, *Controlling Chemicals: The Politics of Regulation in Europe and the United States* (Ithaca, N.Y.: Cornell University Press, 1985).
13. Alfred Marcus, "Japanese Environmental Policy: Alternative to Confrontation," University of Minnesota School of Management, n.d.
14. Charles E. Lindblom attempts to prove that business dominates American politics in *Politics and Markets* (New York: Basic Books, 1977). The differences in the income distribution in Sweden and the United States are explored in Sidney Verba et al., *Elites and the Idea of Equality* (Cambridge, Mass.: Harvard University Press, 1987), chap. 6.
15. James Q. Wilson, *Political Organizations* (New York: Basic Books, 1973), chap. 5. See also Vogel, *National Styles*, 279.
16. Jeremy Rabkin, "Office for Civil Rights," in James Q. Wilson, ed., *The Politics of Regulation* (New York: Basic Books, 1980), 310–11.
17. Graham K. Wilson, *Politics of Safety*, 160–61.
18. Brickman et al., *Controlling Chemicals*, 304.
19. Graham K. Wilson, *Politics of Safety*, 159–60.
20. Maurice Walton Thomas, *The Early Factory Legislation* (Leigh-On-Sea, Essex: Thames Bank Publishing Co., 1948), as quoted in Graham K. Wilson, *Politics of Safety*, 156–57.
21. Edward Shils, *The Torment of Secrecy* (Glencoe, Ill.: Free Press, 1956).

22. Stephen Richardson, "Organizational Contrasts in British and American Ships," *Administrative Science Quarterly* 1 (1956): 206.

23. Ronald Dore, *British Factory, Japanese Factory* (Berkeley: University of California Press, 1973); Koya Azumi and Charles McMillan, "Management Strategy and Organization Structure," in D. J. Hickson and C. J. McMillan, eds., *Organization and Nation: The Aston Programme* (Westmead: Gower, 1981), 155–72; Lewis Austin, *Saints and Samurai: The Political Culture of American and Japanese Elites* (New Haven, Conn.: Yale University Press, 1975); Edwin Dowdy, *Japanese Bureaucracy* (Melbourne: Cheshire Publishing Co., 1973); Rodney Clark, *The Japanese Company* (New Haven, Conn.: Yale University Press, 1979); Michael Y. Yoshino, *Japan's Managerial System* (Cambridge, Mass.: MIT Press, 1968); James R. Lincoln, Mitsuyo Hanada, and Kerry McBride, "Organizational Structures in Japanese and U.S. Manufacturing," *Administrative Science Quarterly* 31 (1986): 338–64.

24. Michel Crozier, *The Bureaucratic Phenomenon* (Chicago: University of Chicago Press, 1964), 31, 40–46, 50–55, 139–42, 214–16.

25. Kelman, *Regulating America*, 118–48.

26. Thomas J. Anton, "Policy-Making and Political Culture in Sweden," *Scandinavian Political Studies* 4 (1969): 88–100; M. Donald Hancock, *Sweden: The Politics of Post-Industrial Change* (Hinsdale, Ill.: Dryden Press, 1972); Sten Johansson, "Liberal-Democratic Theory and Political Processes," in Richard Scase, ed., *Readings in Swedish Class Structure* (New York: Pergamon Press, 1976).

27. Steven L. Elkin, *Politics and Land Use Planning: The London Experience* (Cambridge: Cambridge University Press, 1974), 1–2, 165–168.

28. Crozier, *Bureaucratic Phenomenon*, chap. 8.

29. Alexis de Tocqueville, *The Old Regime and the French Revolution* (Garden City, N.Y.: Doubleday/Anchor Books, 1955). (First published in 1856.)

30. Ibid., part II, 41–51.

31. Ibid., part II, 81.

32. *Federalist*, No. 48.

33. *Federalist*, No. 51.

34. Yoshino, *Japan's Managerial System*, 205.

35. Gregory W. Noble, "The Cultural Context of Bureaucracy in Japan and the United States," Harvard University Department of Government (May 1982), 18.

36. David H. Bayley, *Forces of Order: Police Behavior in Japan and the United States* (Berkeley, Calif.: University of California Press, 1976), 36.

37. Thomas Rohlen, *For Harmony and Strength* (Berkeley, Calif.: University of California Press, 1974), chap. 7.

38. Noble, "Cultural Context of Bureaucracy," 20–21.

39. Austin, *Saints and Samurai*, 23–40.

40. Chalmers Johnson, "Who Governs? An Essay on Japanese International Economic Policy," *Journal of Japanese Studies* 2 (1975): 10.

41. Bernard S. Silberman, "Bureaucratic Development and Bureaucratization: The Case of Japan," *Social Science History* 2 (1978): 385–98.

42. Ezra G. Vogel, *Japan as Number One* (Cambridge, Mass.: Harvard University Press, 1979); W. Clifford, *Crime Control in Japan* (Lexington, Mass.: D. C. Heath/Lexington Books, 1976); David H. Bayley, "Learning About Crime: The Japanese Experience," *Public Interest* 44 (1976): 55–68.

43. John W. Sloan, *Public Policy in Latin America: A Comparative Survey* (Pittsburgh, Penn.: University of Pittsburgh Press, 1984), 128–29.

44. Howard J. Wiarda and Harvey F. Kline, *Latin American Politics and Development* (Boulder, Colo.: Westview Press, 1985), 81.

45. Edward J. Williams and Freeman J. Wright, *Latin American Politics* (Palo Alto, Calif.: Mayfield Publishing Co., 1975), 430–31.

46. Wiarda and Kline, *Latin American Development*, 83–85; Williams and Wright, *Latin American Politics*, 425.

47. Sloan, *Public Policy*, 141.

48. Ibid., and Williams and Wright, *Latin American Politics*, 439–41.

49. Sloan, *Public Policy*, 142.

50. Peter D. Bell, quoted in Williams and Wright, *Latin American Politics*, 439.

51. Jerry Weaver, quoted in Sloan, *Public Policy,* 142–43.
52. Wiarda and Kline, *Latin American Development,* 86–87.
53. I adapt this definition from Stephen Skowronek, *Building a New American State* (Cambridge: Cambridge University Press, 1982), 20.
54. Stephen Krasner, "United States Commercial and Monetary Policy," in Peter Katzenstein, ed., *Between Power and Plenty* (Madison, Wisc.: University of Wisconsin Press, 1978), 57; Peter Katzenstein, *Small States in World Markets* (Ithaca, N.Y.: Cornell University Press, 1985); Phillipe Schmitter and Gerhard Lehmbruch, eds., *Trends Toward Corporatist Intermediation* (Beverly Hills, Calif.: Sage Publications, 1979); David Vogel, *National Styles,* 265.

Chapter 17. Problems

1. *New York Times,* 21 November 1986, p. B1
2. James Q. Wilson, "The Bureaucracy Problem," *Public Interest* 6 (Winter 1967): 3–9.
3. *New York Times,* 21 November 1986, p. B1.
4. Herbert Kaufman, *Red Tape* (Washington, D.C.: The Brookings Institution, 1977), 29.
5. President's Private Sector Survey on Cost Control, *War on Waste* (New York: Macmillan, 1984). Known as the Grace Commission, after its chairman, J. Peter Grace.
6. General Accounting Office and Congressional Budget Office, *Analysis of the Grace Commission's Major Proposals for Cost Control* (Washington, D.C.: Government Printing Office, 1984).
7. Ibid, 9.
8. President's Blue Ribbon Commission on Defense Management, *A Quest for Excellence: The Final Report* (June 1986), 46–47. Known as the Packard Commission after its chairman, David Packard.
9. J. Ronald Fox (with James L. Field), *The Defense Management Challenge: Weapons Acquisition* (Boston: Harvard Business School Press, 1988), 161–63.
10. General Accounting Office, *Can the United States Major Weapon Systems Acquisition Process Keep Pace with the Conventional Arms Threat Posed by the USSR?* Report GAO/PSAD/GP (May 27, 1980), 56–57, as quoted in Fox, *Defense Management,* 162.
11. Ibid., 162. The book by Fox is only the latest in a series of at least twelve major studies of weapons acquisitions procedures beginning in 1962. The analysis and conclusions of each are broadly similar. For a list of these studies, see Fox, *Defense Management,* 41.
12. Ibid., 164–68, 271–97.
13. Ibid., 45.
14. Ibid., 201.
15. Ibid., 216–20.
16. General Accounting Office, *DOD's Defense Acquisition Improvement Program,* Report GAO/NSIAD-86-184 (July 1986), 11, as quoted in Fox, *Defense Management,* 180.
17. Fox, *Defense Management,* 28–29.
18. Ibid., 251.
19. Quoted in ibid., 257.
20. Ibid., 259.
21. President's Blue Ribbon Commission on Defense Management, *A Quest for Excellence: Appendix* (June 1986), 168, 174.
22. Fox, *Defense Management,* 21.
23. Martin Marietta Corporation, "Report to the Packard Commission," as reported in Center for Strategic and International Studies, *U.S. Defense Acquisition: A Process in Trouble* (Washington, D.C.: Georgetown University, 1987), 20.
24. James L. Kurth, "Aerospace Production Lines and American Defense Spending," in Steven Rosen, ed., *Testing the Theory of the Military-Industrial Complex* (Lexington, Mass.: D. C. Heath/Lexington Books, 1973), 135–56.
25. Michael Rich and Edmund Dews, *Improving the Military Acquisition Process,* Report R-3373-AF/RC (Santa Monica, Calif.: Rand, 1986), 4–17.
26. Ibid., 11, 51.
27. Kaufman, *Red Tape,* 30.

28. James Q. Wilson, *The Investigators: Managing FBI and Narcotics Agents* (New York: Basic Books, 1978), 23–31.
29. John J. DiIulio, Jr., *Governing Prisons* (New York: Free Press, 1987), 104–9.
30. Ibid., 118–27; quote on 120.
31. Michael Lipsky, *Street-Level Bureaucracy* (New York: Russell Sage Foundation, 1980), 201.
32. James M. Landis, *The Administrative Process* (New Haven, Conn.: Yale University Press, 1938). See also the splendid analysis of Landis in Thomas K. McCraw, *Prophets of Regulation* (Cambridge, Mass.: Harvard University Press, 1984), chaps. 5 and 6.
33. Michel Crozier, *The Bureaucratic Phenomenon* (Chicago: University of Chicago Press, 1964), 156–59, 171–74.
34. Federal Communications Act, 15 *U.S. Code* 309.
35. Quoted in James Q. Wilson, "The Dead Hand of Regulation," *Public Interest* 25 (Fall 1971): 50.

Chapter 18. Rules

1. May Hipshman, *Public Housing at the Crossroads: The Boston Housing Authority* (Boston: Citizens Housing and Planning Association, 1967), as quoted in Jon Pynoos, *Breaking the Rules: Bureaucracy and Reform in Public Housing* (New York: Plenum, 1986), 15.
2. Quoted in Pynoos, *Breaking the Rules*, 28.
3. Perez v. BHA, 368 Mass. 333, 331 NE 2d 801 (1975). HUD report cited in Pynoos, *Breaking the Rules*, 161.
4. Pynoos, *Breaking the Rules*.
5. Jeffrey Manditch Prottas, *People-Processing* (Lexington, Mass.: D. C. Heath/Lexington Books, 1979), chap. 2.
6. Pynoos, *Breaking the Rules*, chaps. 3, 4, and 6, esp. 39–43, 52–54, 60, 114, 131; Prottas, *People-Processing*, chap. 2.
7. Max Weber, *Economy and Society*, vol. 3, ed. Guenther Roth and Claus Wittich (New York: Bedminster Press, 1968), 958, 973–75, 979.
8. Theodore J. Lowi, *The End of Liberalism* (New York: Norton, 1969), 85–93. Lowi's views are criticized in David Lewis Schaefer, "Theodore J. Lowi and the Administrative State," *Administration and Society* 19 (1988): 371–98. There is a response by Lowi in the same issue.
9. Lowi, *End of Liberalism*, 297–303.
10. Lawrence Friedman, "Public Housing and the Poor," *California Law Review* (May 1966): 687, as paraphrased in Pynoos, *Breaking the Rules*, 3.
11. Aristotle, *Politics*, trans. Ernest Barker (Oxford: Clarendon Press, 1952), 146. Of course Aristotle knew that laws could not "cover the whole of the ground" because "rules must be expressed in general terms, but actions are concerned with particulars." Ibid., 148, 73.
12. Sir Edward Coke, *The Reports of Sir Edward Coke*, vol. 4 (London: Butterworth, 1826), part 8, 355–83.
13. John Locke, *Second Treatise of Civil Government*, ed. Thomas I. Cook (New York: Hafner, 1956), 132.
14. Jerry L. Mashaw, *Bureaucratic Justice* (New Haven, Conn.: Yale University Press, 1983), 220–22; see also 17–19, 41–42, 65–66.
15. Joel F. Handler and Ellen Jane Hollingsworth, *The "Deserving Poor": A Study of Welfare Administration* (Chicago: Markham, 1971), 209–10; and Joel F. Handler, *Protecting the Social Service Client* (New York: Academic Press, 1979), 121–23.
16. Handler and Ellingsworth, *Deserving Poor*, 81, 85.
17. James Q. Wilson, *Varieties of Police Behavior* (Cambridge, Mass.: Harvard University Press, 1968), 21–22.
18. Richard A. Weatherly, *Reforming Special Education* (Cambridge, Mass.: MIT Press, 1979), 1–2.
19. For example: ibid., 10, 60, 125; William H. Clune and Mark H. Van Pelt, "A Political Method of Evaluating the Education for All Handicapped Children Act of 1975 and the

Several Gaps of Gap Analysis," *Law and Contemporary Problems* 48 (Winter 1985): 7–62; John C. Pittenger and Peter Kuriloff, "Educating the Handicapped: Reforming a Radical Law," *Public Interest* 66 (Winter 1982): 72–96.

20. Clune and Van Pelt, "A Political Method." See also Arthur E. Wise, *Legislated Learning* (Berkeley: University of California Press, 1979).

21. Mashaw, *Bureaucratic Justice*, 122; "NLRB Rulemaking: Political Reality versus Procedural Fairness," *Yale Law Journal* 89 (1980): 982; NLRB v. Wyman-Gordon Co., 394 U.S. 759 (1969).

22. Public Law 85-929.

23. Congressional Quarterly, Inc., *Congress and the Nation*, vol. 5 (Washington, D.C.: Congressional Quarterly Press, 1981), 612.

24. Public Law 95-203; Public Law 96-273.

25. Richard M. Cooper, "Stretching Delaney Till It Breaks," *Regulation* (November-December 1985): 13. See also Richard A. Merrill, "FDA's Implementation of the Delaney Clause: Repudiation of Congressional Choice or Reasoned Adaptation to Scientific Progress?" *Yale Journal on Regulation* 5 (1988): 1–88.

26. Harvey M. Sapolsky, *Consuming Fears: The Politics of Product Risks* (New York: Basic Books, 1986), 191. The HHS secretary was Margaret Heckler as quoted in *New York Times*, 27 July 1983.

27. R. Shep Melnick, "Pollution Deadlines and the Coalition for Failure," *Public Interest* 75 (Spring 1984): 123–24.

28. Eugene Bardach and Robert A. Kagan, *Going by the Book: The Problem of Regulatory Unreasonableness* (Philadelphia: Temple University Press, 1982), 99.

29. Bardach and Kagan, *Going by the Book*, 100.

30. John Mendeloff, "Costs and Consequences: A Political and Economic Analysis of the Federal Occupational Safety and Health Program," Ph.D. diss., University of California at Berkeley (1977), as cited in Bardach and Kagan, *Going by the Book*, 100–1.

31. Bardach and Kagan, *Going by the Book*, 96.

32. Ibid., 89–91, 103.

33. Ibid., 109–16.

34. Alvin W. Gouldner, *Patterns of Industrial Bureaucracy* (Glencoe, Ill.: The Free Press, 1954), 174–76.

35. Bardach and Kagan, *Going by the Book*, 107–8.

36. Kathleen Kemp, "Social Responsibility and Coercive Sanctions in Economic Regulation," paper presented at the Symposium on Regulatory Policy, Houston, Texas (November 1979), as cited in Bardach and Kagan, *Going by the Book*, 129.

37. William K. Muir, *Police: Street-Corner Politicians* (Chicago: University of Chicago Press, 1977), esp. chap. 4 and 208–13.

Chapter 19. Markets

1. Roger S. Ahlbrandt, Jr., *Municipal Fire Protection Services: A Comparison of Alternative Organizational Forms* (Beverly Hills, Calif.: Sage, 1973).

2. Randall O'Toole, *Reforming the Forest Service* (Washington, D.C.: Island Press, 1988).

3. E. S. Savas, *Privatization: The Key to Better Government* (Chatham, N.J.: Chatham House, 1987), 58.

4. For example: Arman Alchian and Harold Demsetz, "Production, Information Costs, and Economic Organization," *American Economic Review* 62 (1972): 777–95; and Louis De Alessi, "The Economics of Property Rights: A Review of the Evidence," *Research in Law and Economics* 2 (1980): 1–46.

5. Thomas E. Borcherding, Werner W. Pommerhene, and Friedrich Schneider, *Comparing the Efficiency of Private and Public Production: The Evidence from Five Countries* (Zurich: Institute for Empirical Research in Economics of the University of Zurich, 1982). The list of these studies is reproduced in the appendix to Charles Wolf, Jr., *Markets or Governments: Choosing Between Imperfect Alternatives* (Cambridge, Mass.: MIT Press, 1988), 192–99. See also Anthony E. Boardman and Aidan R. Vining, "Ownership and Performance in Com-

petitive Environments: A Comparison of Private, Mixed, and State-Owned Enterprises," *Journal of Law and Economics* 32 (1989): 1–33.

6. Savas, *Privatization*.

7. My count is based on combining the studies listed by Borcherding et al., with those cited in Savas, *Privatization*, at pages 126–27, and eliminating duplications.

8. W. Mark Crain and Asghar Zardkoohi, "A Test of the Property-Rights Theory of the Firm: Water Utilities in the United States," *Journal of Law and Economics* 21 (1978): 395–408.

9. Savas, *Privatization*, 131–32.

10. Comptroller General, *The Navy Overhaul Policy* (Washington, D.C.: General Accounting Office, 1978), as reported in James J. Bennett and Thomas J. DiLorenzo, "Public Employee Unions and the Privatization of 'Public' Services," *Journal of Labor Research* 4 (1983): 37; and James J. Bennett and Manuel Johnson, "Tax Limitation Without Sacrifice: Private Sector Production of Public Services," *Public Finance Quarterly* 8 (1980): 363–96.

11. Richard Muth, *Public Housing: An Economic Evaluation* (Washington, D.C.: American Enterprise Institute, 1973).

12. Robert A. McGuire and T. Norman Van Cott, "Public versus Private Economic Activity: A New Look at School Bus Transportation," *Public Choice* 43 (1984): 25–43; and Randy L. Ross, *Government and the Private Sector: Who Should Do What?* (New York: Crane Russak & Co., 1988), 36–63.

13. Bennett and DiLorenzo, "Public Employee Unions."

14. R. I. Schultz, J. R. Greenley, and R. W. Peterson, "Differences in the Direct Costs of Public and Private Acute Inpatient Psychiatric Services," *Inquiry* 21 (1984): 380–93.

15. Ross, *Government*, 76–77.

16. Cited in Savas, *Privatization*, 209. See also Michael Krashinsky, "The Cost of Day Care in Public Programs," *National Tax Journal* 31 (1978): 363–72.

17. David G. Davies, "The Efficiency of Public versus Private Firms: The Case of Australia's Two Airlines," *Journal of Law and Economics* 14 (1971): 149–65; and Davies, "Property Rights and Economic Efficiency: The Australian Airlines Revisited," *Journal of Law and Economics* 20 (1977): 223–26.

18. Ole P. Kristensen, "Public versus Private Provision of Governmental Services: The Case of Danish Fire Protection Services," *Urban Studies* 20 (1983): 1–9.

19. Lawrence S. Lewin, Robert A. Derzon, and Rhea Margulies, "Investor-Owneds and Nonprofits Differ in Economic Performance," *Hospital* 55 (1981): 52–58; Robert V. Pattison and Hallie M. Katz, "Investor-Owned and Not-for-Profit Hospitals: A Comparison Based on California Data," *New England Journal of Medicine* 309 (1983): 347–53; National Academy of Sciences, *For-Profit Enterprise in Health Care* (Washington, D.C.: National Academy of Sciences, 1986). See also Savas, *Privatization*, 190–93.

20. George W. Wilson and Joseph M. Jadlow, "Competition, Profit Incentives, and Technical Efficiency in the Provision of Nuclear Medicine Services," *Bell Journal of Economics* 13 (1982): 472–82.

21. Sam Peltzman, "Pricing in Public and Private Enterprises: Electric Utilities in the United States," *Journal of Law and Economics* 14 (1971): 109–47; Robert A. Meyer, "Publicly Owned versus Privately Owned Utilities: A Policy Choice," *Review of Economics and Statistics* 57 (1975): 391–99; Louis De Alessi, "An Economic Analysis of Government Ownership and Regulation: Theory and the Evidence from the Electric Power Industry," *Public Choice* 19 (1974): 1–42; Robert M. Spann, "Public versus Private Provision of Governmental Services," in Thomas E. Borcherding, ed., *Budgets and Bureaucrats* (Durham, N.C.: Duke University Press, 1977), 77–82; Ross, *Government*, 24–36.

22. James Q. Wilson and Louise Richardson, "Public Ownership vs. Energy Conservation: The Paradox of Utility Regulation," *Regulation* (September-October 1985): 13ff.

23. E. S. Savas, "Municipal Monopolies versus Competition in Delivering Urban Services," in Willis D. Hawley and David Rogers, eds., *Improving the Quality of Urban Management* (Beverly Hills, Calif.: Sage, 1974), 476.

24. Barbara J. Stevens, ed., *Delivering Municipal Services Efficiently: A Comparison of Municipal and Private Service Delivery*. A technical report prepared by Ecodata, Inc., for the U.S. Department of Housing and Urban Development, Office of Policy Development and Research (June 1984), 545–50.

25. Roger F. Teal, "Contracting for Transit Service," in John C. Weicher, ed., *Private Innovations in Public Transit* (Washington, D.C.: American Enterprise Institute, 1988), 50.

26. J. Ronald Fox, *The Defense Management Challenge: Weapons Acquisition* (Boston, Mass.: Harvard Business School Press, 1988), 300; Michael Rich and Edmund Dews, *Improving the Military Acquisition Process*, report R-3373-AF/RC (Santa Monica, Calif.: Rand, 1986), esp. 49–50.

27. John J. Kirlin, John C. Ries, and Sidney Sonenblum, "Alternative to City Departments," in E. S. Savas, ed., *Alternatives for Delivering Public Services* (Boulder, Colo.: Westview Press, 1977), 137.

28. Stephen L. Mehay and Rodolfo Gonzalez, "Economic Incentives Under Contract Supply of Local Government Services," *Public Choice* 46 (1985): 79–86.

29. Stephen Mehay, "Governmental Structure and Performance: The Effects of the Lakewood Plan on Property Values," *Public Finance Quarterly* 6 (1978): 311–25.

30. Gary S. Becker, *The Economics of Discrimination* (Chicago: University of Chicago Press, 1957).

31. Wolf, *Markets*, 81.

32. *Statistical Abstract of the United States, 1987*, table 183.

33. Gary Bridge, "Citizen Choice in Public Services: Voucher Systems," in Savas, *Alternatives*, 61.

34. Savas, *Privatization*, 200.

35. Bernard J. Frieden, "Housing Allowances: An Experiment That Worked," *Public Interest* (Spring 1980): 17.

36. The results were studied by many people; among their reports are: Ira S. Lowry, *Experimenting with Housing Allowances*, report R-2880-HUD (Washington, D.C.: Department of Housing and Urban Development, April 1982); Raymond J. Struyck and Mark Bendick, Jr., eds., *Housing Vouchers for the Poor* (Washington, D.C.: Urban Institute, 1981). Here I rely on the excellent summary in Frieden, "Housing Allowances."

37. Quoted in Frieden, "Housing Allowances," 33.

38. Frieden, "Housing Allowances," 34–35.

39. Oliver O. Williamson, *The Economic Institutions of Capitalism* (New York: Free Press, 1985); and Williamson, *Markets and Hierarchies* (New York: Free Press, 1975).

40. Williamson, *Economic Institutions*, 19.

41. Harry P. Hatry, *A Review of Private Approaches for Delivery of Public Services* (Washington, D.C.: Urban Institute, 1983), 21.

42. Edward J. Clynch and Carol A. Gaudin, "Sex in the Shipyards: An Assessment of Affirmative Action Policy," paper presented to the annual meeting of the American Political Science Association, April 1979.

43. Wilson and Richardson, "Public Ownership."

44. James Q. Wilson and Patricia Rachal, "Can the Government Regulate Itself?" *Public Interest* (Winter 1977): 3–14.

45. Savas, *Privatization*, 185–88; Charles H. Logan, "Proprietary Prisons," in Lynne Goodstein and Doris L. MacKenzie, eds., *The American Prison* (New York: Plenum, in press); John J. DiIulio, "What's Wrong With Private Prisons," *Public Interest* 92 (1988): 66–83.

46. Pierce v. Society of Sisters, 268 U.S. 510 (1925).

47. Chester E. Finn, Jr., "Decentralize, Deregulate, Empower," *Policy Review* (1986): 58.

48. John McClaughry, "Who Says Vouchers Wouldn't Work," *Reason* (January 1984): 24–32, as cited in Chester E. Finn, Jr., "Education Choice: Theory, Practice, and Research," testimony before the Subcommittee on Intergovernmental Relations, Committee on Governmental Affairs, U.S. Senate (October 22, 1985), 2–3.

49. Finn, "Education Choice," 3.

50. Ibid., 6–7.

51. Ibid., 17–27; Bridge, "Citizen Choice," 83–87.

52. Bridge, "Citizen Choice," 84–85; Edward M. Gramlich and Patricia P. Koshel, *Educational Performance Contracting* (Washington, D.C.: Brookings Institution, 1975).

53. James S. Coleman, Thomas Hoffer, and Sally Kilgore, *High School Achievement* (New York: Basic Books, 1982), 32–37, 182–83; see also Finn, "Educational Choice," 22.

54. Gallup poll, 1985, as reported in Finn, "Education Choice," 8 and table 1.

55. Bridge, "Citizen Choice," 87–88. For some angry statements by leaders of public employee unions see Bennett and DiLorenzo, "Public Employee Unions," 35–36.

Chapter 20. Bureaucracy and the Public Interest

1. Arthur T. Hadley, *The Straw Giant* (New York: Random House, 1986), 53–57, 249–52.
2. CSIS, *U.S. Defense Acquisition: A Process in Trouble* (Washington, D.C.: Center for Strategic and International Studies, March 1987), 13–16.
3. Herbert Kaufman, *The Administrative Behavior of Federal Bureau Chiefs* (Washington, D.C.: The Brookings Institution, 1981), 192.
4. Martha Derthick, *Agency Under Stress: The Social Security Administration and American Government* (Washington, D.C.: Brookings Institution, forthcoming).
5. Ibid., chap. 3.
6. Charles Wolf, Jr., *Markets or Governments: Choosing Between Imperfect Alternatives* (Cambridge, Mass.: MIT Press, 1988).
7. James Colvard, "Procurement: What Price Mistrust?" *Government Executive* (March 1985): 21.
8. NAPA, *Revitalizing Federal Management: Managers and Their Overburdened Systems* (Washington, D.C.: National Academy of Public Administration, November 1983), vii, viii, 8.
9. Steven Emerson, *Secret Warriors* (New York: G. P. Putnam's Sons, 1988).
10. John E. Chubb and Terry M. Moe, "Politics, Markets, and the Organization of Schools," *American Political Science Review* 82 (1988): 1065–87.
11. Chester E. Finn, Jr., "Decentralize, Deregulate, Empower," *Policy Review* (Summer 1986): 60; Edward A. Wynne, *A Year in the Life of a School* (forthcoming).
12. William E. Turcotte, "Control Systems, Performance, and Satisfaction in Two State Agencies," *Administrative Science Quarterly* 19 (1974): 60–73.
13. Richard P. Nathan, *Social Science in Government: Uses and Misuses* (New York: Basic Books, 1988), chap. 3.
14. These projects were all done by the Police Foundation and are described in James Q. Wilson, *Thinking About Crime*, rev. ed. (New York: Basic Books, 1983).
15. See Joseph A. Pechman and P. Michael Timpane, eds., *Work Incentives and Income Guarantees* (Washington, D.C.: Brookings Institution, 1975); and R. Thayne Robson, ed., *Employment and Training R&D* (Kalamazoo, Mich.: Upjohn Institute for Employment Research, 1984).
16. Nathan, *Social Science*, chap. 5; and Manpower Demonstration Research Corporation, *Summary and Findings of the National Supported Work Demonstration* (Cambridge, Mass.: Ballinger, 1980).
17. See studies cited in chap. 19.
18. See references to China Lake research cited in chap. 8.
19. Clarence E. Ridley and Herbert A. Simon, *Measuring Municipal Activities* (Chicago: International City Managers' Association, 1938).

NAME INDEX

SUBJECT INDEX